The Best American
Sports Writing
2018

GUEST EDITORS OF
THE BEST AMERICAN SPORTS WRITING

1991 DAVID HALBERSTAM
1992 THOMAS MCGUANE
1993 FRANK DEFORD
1994 TOM BOSWELL
1995 DAN JENKINS
1996 JOHN FEINSTEIN
1997 GEORGE PLIMPTON
1998 BILL LITTLEFIELD
1999 RICHARD FORD
2000 DICK SCHAAP
2001 BUD COLLINS
2002 RICK REILLY
2003 BUZZ BISSINGER
2004 RICHARD BEN CRAMER
2005 MIKE LUPICA
2006 MICHAEL LEWIS
2007 DAVID MARANISS
2008 WILLIAM NACK
2009 LEIGH MONTVILLE
2010 PETER GAMMONS
2011 JANE LEAVY
2012 MICHAEL WILBON
2013 J. R. MOEHRINGER
2014 CHRISTOPHER MCDOUGALL
2015 WRIGHT THOMPSON
2016 RICK TELANDER
2017 HOWARD BRYANT
2018 JEFF PEARLMAN

The Best AMERICAN SPORTS WRITING™ 2018

Edited and with an Introduction
by Jeff Pearlman

Glenn Stout, *Series Editor*

A Mariner Original

HOUGHTON MIFFLIN HARCOURT

BOSTON • NEW YORK   2018

hmhco.com

ISBN 978-1-328-84628-0 (print)   ISBN 978-1-328-84629-7 (ebook)
ISSN 1056-8034 (print)   ISSN 2573-4822 (ebook)

Printed in the United States of America
DOC 10 9 8 7 6 5 4 3 2 1

Contents

Contents

Foreword

EVERY YEAR THERE are actually multiple editions of this book. The first edition of this book includes those stories selected by the guest editor and reprinted in full. This edition contains a total of 25 stories, a combination of selections chosen from among 80 stories that were put forward by me, as well as the guest editor's own choices.

But there are also other editions. In the back of every volume is "Notable Sports Writing"—a list of another 100 or so stories and writers from the previous year. I hope that, on occasion, readers of the first 25 stories make the time to go to the back of the book and continue their reading from among these selections.

When I first started compiling the annual list at the beginning of this series in 1991, it was primarily a list of those stories that "almost" made the front of the book—the stories I'd put forward that were not selected by the guest editor, as well as a selection of those that caused me pain to leave out. To a degree, it still is. But over time my criteria for the back of the book has evolved. I don't always see the value in giving a ribbon to a writer who might already be established at a well-recognized outlet (although, as my inbox well knows, no group does more scorekeeping—or score settling—than sportswriters). Besides, the definitions of both the "best" and the "notable"—and the differences between them—are notoriously fluid. Over the years I've become increasingly uncomfortable with the perception that the editors of this book are arbiters of anything more than what interests either of us at a given moment.

This is a tough time to be in this business, and while paying work is at a premium, quality work is not. I believe there could be three or four editions of this book every year and there wouldn't be a dime's worth of difference in quality between them. Despite the troubles of our industry, the writers will not be denied. In the last decade, after the 2008 recession hit, an entire generation of young writers just gaining traction, many of them women and minorities, were wiped out when the newspaper industry began its death spiral, leaving thousands of stories untold. Today magazines both well known and not so well known have cut back on their publishing schedules and their page counts, and after a brief flourishing, digital media seem to be following the same path, shedding jobs almost as quickly as they are created, pivoting from word to video to . . . I don't know, what's left—semaphore? Most have cut back on storytelling or treat it as a marketing indulgence, a bait-and-switch tactic to trick "consumers" into watching (yet another) video rather than treating storytelling for what it is and always has been—a genuine human need. One particularly cynical digital editor actually once told me the "best" stories were those that readers clicked on . . . and then stopped reading quickly so they would visit other destinations on the website as soon as possible.

I reject that. Utterly. I believe the only way we really come to know and understand one another is through stories. Writers are relentless, and they understand that. In the beginning, after all, was the word.

As a result, I now view the "Notable Sports Writing" list differently, as a kind of curated archive unto itself, evidence of storytelling's vitality. I still tend to include stories that I believe in another year might have made their way to the front—that's always some kind of factor. In most years the "Notable" list probably includes at least 30 or so stories that I put forward that were not selected. There are probably a few more of those this year, as guest editor Jeff Pearlman exercised his prerogative and selected 15 of the 25 stories in this anthology from outside the group I sent him. This is the nature of the collection. I mean, ask 100 basketball fans to name the "best" 25 basketball players and you'll get 100 different lists that probably include hundreds of players, each list created according to one kind of player—pro, college, men, women, American, foreign, active versus retired, living versus dead—and one measure of "best"—team success, season versus career, or ranked by position, scoring average, or some other standard for defense, rebounding, jump shooting, ball handling, passing, etc. —over some other.

A number of annual "best" lists are put together in this field, ranging from those accumulated by sources such as *Longreads, Longform,* and *The Sunday Long Read* to lists curated by individuals and outlets to the annual industry awards sponsored by organizations like the American Society of Magazine Editors, the Canadian Society of Magazine Editors, the Associated Press Sports Editors, the City and Regional Magazine Association, and others. Together, these sources alone cite several hundred sports stories a year as among the "best" in one way or another. I look at all these lists, primarily to make sure I don't miss anything, read virtually all of them (as well as thousands of others on my own and through submissions), and rarely find much consensus: each audience has its own definition of "best," and only a scant few individual stories each year are cited by more than one or two of these lists. At best, like this volume, they're a rough guide, nothing more. At the same time, many equally fine stories slide through the cracks, whether excluded by gatekeepers or simply overlooked and never even considered for recognition. The end result is that the "best" sports writing each year actually includes hundreds of stories of all kinds.

One of the reasons the publisher of the Best American series chooses a guest editor for each volume every year—beyond the obvious marketing advantage—is to ensure that the texture of the books in the series varies from year to year. And it does. The publisher's only charge is to select stories published in the United States or Canada during the calendar year based on their "literary merit," however each guest editor chooses to define that. Although I put forward stories blindly—not identified by source or author—guest editors' selections reveal their own preferences, some more overtly than others. One guest editor excluded all but narratives; others had a distinct preference for reported or investigative work. Others preferred more stories from newspapers, others favored those from magazines or websites, and some eschewed all forms of first-person writing. Some were comfortable selecting more political and socially conscious stories, and others preferred the more orthodox. Some hated football and loved soccer, while

others valued adventure sports more than team competitions. One
guest editor demanded more "sportswriting," and another chose
stories according to a more literary definition. Moreover, each editor is free to determine what qualifies as a "sport" and what does
not.

Under the only criterion for selecting stories that I've ever
been able to come up with—after reading them once, I want to
read them again—I do my best to put forward as representative
a sample as possible. Any selection of 75 or 80 stories will always
be lacking in some perspectives. This explains why the variety and
scope of sports writing are usually on better display in the more
expansive "Notable" list than on the narrower contents page.

Writers occasionally let me know that inclusion in the back of
the book provided a career boost, helping them find a job or get
their work into better-paying, more prestigious, or more visible
outlets. In recent years, I became even more interested in using
this portion of the book to provide some recognition for the writers and outlets that produce interesting and ambitious work but
are either still under the radar or otherwise marginalized. Every
year the "Notables" list includes stories that might have been selected for the front of the book in another year with a different
editor. In a business that is too often harsh and unfair, I feel a
responsibility to let these writers know that their work isn't disappearing into the void, that someone is paying attention.

Digital access makes it easy enough to look up many of these
stories if you choose, and I encourage you to do so.

Looking back through the last pages of earlier editions of this
book, I find many names working their way up, often appearing
first for work they did at small papers or obscure magazines (or,
more recently, dot-coms of unknown origin) and then, over time,
having their work cited at larger outlets before finally appearing in
the front of this book (and beyond). Of the writers in this volume,
I recall that Howard Bryant, Wright Thompson, Reid Forgrave,
and Mike Sielski—at least—appeared in the back of the book first,
writing for less visible outlets than those where their work now appears. Following writers from edition to edition is like tracking a
ballplayer's career on the back of a baseball card. I first read and
made note of some writers on today's best-seller lists when they
were writing for publications that no longer exist, and I am certain

there are writers in the back of this 2018 edition who will be as readily recognized in 25 years as John Branch, Chris Ballard, and Sally Jenkins are now.

These discoveries make the labor of this book worthwhile. I sometimes feel like a scout checking out the scramble on the distant courts at the far reaches of the playground, trying to spot that special shooting touch or the kid with the extra hops. Nothing excites me more than finding either a writer or just good writing in a place where I know very few others are looking. That's one of the reasons I encourage everyone—readers and writers both (not just their editors)—to send me work they feel might belong in this collection, since neither I nor anyone else can make it to every game on every playground.

An example this year would be something called the Awesome Sports Project, a small website created by Bea Chang. A former Haverford College point guard and now a basketball coach and emerging writer, Chang was frustrated by the few existing platforms for sports writing focused on women's sports. So she and her friends created one, an online literary journal "committed to inspiring girls' and women's voices in sports." Since its inception three years ago, Chang and her all-volunteer group of editors have published nearly 100 stories by writers of all ages and genders and created an annual internship program for four high school students from around the United States to assist with the editorial process and be mentored in their own work. For the first few years, Chang absorbed the cost of the program herself; last year a modest GoFundMe proposal helped defray costs. In addition to the website, they have a Facebook page and a Twitter account, neither of which has more than a few hundred followers. The Awesome Sports Project is about as grassroots as it comes.

I knew nothing about the Awesome Sports Project until a manila envelope arrived in my mailbox one day from a writer I'd never heard of, featuring work from a website I'd never seen. But when I read the stories she submitted from the website—one by Chang, another that won their annual contest, and a third story by another contributor—I had one of those moments that make me smile: here was work that I otherwise never would have encountered, telling stories that otherwise might have gone untold.

Chang's own submission was a personal essay about the challenge of being a woman coach in a sport that, even for a women's team, is dominated by men—other coaches, referees, and fathers. That's a subject I've rarely seen treated more eloquently than in her essay. It ends, "I pray that one day, when the girls ask me how it was possible that the foul count was 28–7 after we lost by four points, I would not have to glance at the parents—mothers, mostly—and try to swallow what we are all terrified to say in front of them: because the other coach was a man and I am a woman."

And now I know, and so do you, about this small but ambitious website creating a place for writing that, without it, might be homeless or even go unwritten, writing that may now be noticed and help launch careers. The Awesome Sports Project reminds me in some ways of Vela, the website created in 2011 by Sarah Menkedick and several other women. Frustrated by more mainstream outlets, as contributor Eva Holland recently told me, "the idea was to write exactly the kinds of stories we wanted to write, put them out there into the world, and say to editors, 'Hey, we can do this, assign us these kinds of things.'" In creating their own space—each writer editing the work of the others—they not only made their case but alerted me to a place where I first discovered outstanding writers (among their occasional sports pieces) in the same way I did recently with the Awesome Sports Project. Now, some years later, not only have many of these writers established careers, but Vela has evolved into a well-known outlet in its own right, one to which many other writers now aspire, without losing its ambitious fire and focus.

This is the kind of discovery that awaits, the kind that I believe has caused readers to return to this book for 28 years and counting. So, as you read through the pages, I suggest that when you reach the end of the final story, you do exactly what so many writers who appear in the "Notable" list have done themselves: keep going, and see what you might discover when you really look.

Each year I read hundreds of sports and general interest newspapers and magazines in search of work that might merit consideration in *The Best American Sports Writing,* looking for writing wherever significant sports writing might be found. I also make periodic open requests through Twitter and Facebook and contact editors and writers from many outlets and request submissions.

And because this book really belongs to the reader, I also encourage submissions from anyone who cares about good writing—including readers. The process is open to all. For the 28th time, not only is it okay to submit your own work, it is actually encouraged. To be considered, work must be seen.

All submissions to the upcoming edition need only adhere to the publisher's criteria for eligibility, which also appear here each year, on my own website (www.glennstout.net), and on the Facebook page for *The Best American Sports Writing*. Each story:

- Must be column-length or longer
- Must have been published in 2018
- Must not be a reprint or book excerpt
- Must have been published in the United States or Canada
- Must be postmarked by February 1, 2019

All submissions from either print or online publications must be made in hard copy—do not simply submit a link or bibliographic citation—and should include the name of the author, the date of publication, and the publication name and address. Photocopies, tear sheets, or clean copies are fine. Newspaper submissions should be either a hard copy of the article as originally published or a copy of it—not a printout of the web version.

Individuals and publications should use common sense when submitting multiple stories. The volume of material I receive makes it impossible to return or acknowledge submissions, and it is inappropriate for me to comment on or critique any submission. Magazines that want to be absolutely certain their contributions are considered are advised to provide a complimentary subscription to the address that follows. Those that already do so should extend the subscription for another year.

All submissions must be made by U.S. Mail—midwinter weather conditions often prevent me from easily receiving UPS or FedEx submissions. Electronic submissions by any means—email, Twitter, URLs, PDFs, online documents—are not acceptable. Please send some form of hard copy only. The February 1, 2019, postmark deadline is real; work received after that date cannot be considered.

Please submit either an original or clear paper copy of each story, including publication name, author, and date the story appeared, to:

Glenn Stout
PO Box 549
Alburgh, VT 05440

If you have questions or comments, contact me at basweditor@ yahoo.com. Previous editions of this book can be ordered through most bookstores or online book dealers. An index of stories that have appeared in this series can be found at glennstout.net. All my submissions to the guest editor were made blindly, not identified by source or author. For updated information, readers and writers are encouraged to join The Best American Sports Writing group on Facebook or to follow me on Twitter @GlennStout.

Thanks to guest editor Jeff Pearlman, to all those at Houghton Mifflin Harcourt who help with the production of this series, and to Siobhan and Saorla for sharing space with this annual onslaught of paper. But most of all, thanks to all those writers who aspire to these pages and continue to put their faith in words.

GLENN STOUT
Alburgh, Vermont

Introduction

MY ALL-TIME FAVORITE lede wasn't written by Leigh Montville
or Steve Rushin. It wasn't written by Ralph Wiley or Sally Jenkins.
It wasn't written by Mike Freeman, Frank Deford, Howard Bryant,
Susan Slusser, William Nack, or Claire Smith.

Nope. My all-time favorite lede was written by Greg Orlando.

And, unless you attended the University of Delaware in the early
to mid-1990s, you almost certainly have no idea who he is.

Back some 24 years ago, Greg and I were editors on the staff of
The Review, the UD student newspaper. A short kid with glasses and
a bad haircut, Greg always seemed to wear the same outfit—Chuck
Taylors, loose-fitting jeans, and the yellow-and-black squiggly-line
T-shirt made famous by Charlie Brown.

Along with his duds, what separated Greg from the rest of us
was vision. At a time when we were all young and hungry and dedicated to "doing journalism" (whatever the hell that meant), Greg
just wanted to write about really odd, really quirky stuff. He didn't
think twice about inverted pyramids or nut graphs or whether a
subject's name should come before or after his job title.

Nope. Greg couldn't care less.

That's why, on February 8, 1994, our paper published Greg's review of *Face the Music,* the latest release from that immortal gaggle
of crooners, New Kids on the Block.

Was Greg a big Danny Wood fan? Hardly. Did he know all the
words to "Step by Step"? Certainly not. In hindsight, I'm quite certain he simply saw the New Kids as a meaty softball floating toward
the plate at 5 miles per hour.

So he drew back his Louisville Slugger, pumped his elbow, called upon his (deep) understanding of Norse mythology, and swung away . . .

> Somewhere in Asgard, Loki is screaming.
>
> He has a right to, one supposes. The Aesir have bound him to a cavern, trapped forever like a fly in amber. From a hole in the ceiling, a steady stream of acid is dripping down, poised to strike the chaos bringer on his evil forehead.
>
> His lovely wife Sigin is the only thing standing between the God of Mischief and mortal agony. She has a cup, you see, and catches the acid before it can hit.
>
> Alas, the cup runneth over from time to time. When his wife goes to empty the container . . .
>
> Somewhere in Delaware, I am screaming and there is nary a cup for miles.
>
> The New Kids on The Block are back. Back after a three-year hiatus. Back to Face the Music.
>
> A most heinous day of reckoning it is.

I still remember the puzzled looks in our newsroom, the "What is he talking about?" glares from staffers who thought Greg's take needed to be simpler, plainer, more conventional. A year later, as a cub reporter at *The Tennessean* in Nashville, I was trying to convince my editor to hire Greg for an internship. I showed her the New Kids lede, convinced she would love it.

Um, no.

"That's terrible," she said. "First, I have no idea what he's talking about. And second, you can't challenge the reader like that. It's begging people to put down the paper and walk away."

As I read through the dozens upon dozens of articles submitted for consideration for this book, I kept thinking back to the University of Delaware and to Greg Orlando and to "*Somewhere in Asgard, Loki is screaming.*" All these years later, the reason I so passionately love that piece (and the reason I still share it with my journalism students at Chapman University) is the very reason it turned so many off. Namely, it makes the reader work. And think. And perhaps (gasp!) reread the lede once or twice or three times. There's a payoff that doesn't come with 99 percent of the world's articles: a lightbulb, ah-ha moment when you fully understand that Greg is linking a legitimate piece of Norse lore (Sigin is actually Loki's wife; she did hold a cup above her husband and used it to catch acid) with—of all things—the wretched experience of hearing Jordan Knight sing.

I'll say it again: Greg Orlando had a vision the rest of us on the *Review* staff lacked.

Now, as I sit here overseeing yet another year of entertaining, engrossing, *important* sports journalism, I can't help but think the majority of scribes whose work is included on the following pages would appreciate Greg Orlando too. I've only met—face to face —seven of the 25 selected writers, yet all exercise at least some element of the spirit and derring-do encapsulated in "New Kids, New Album, but the Song Remains the (Stinky) Same." Or, put differently, they take shots in their work. They approach things with funk and pizzazz. They play with words, dance with imagery, ponder the easiest passageway into a narrative, and say (consciously or subconsciously), "Nah." Far too many of us have been told (by editors, by journalism professors, by readers) that there's a clear, definitive methodology to storytelling, and one should resist all urges to deviate from the norm. *Never begin a passage with "But." Don't use. Fragments. If they. Don't make grammatical. Sense. Stay away —even if it's correct—from long dashes. Avoid obscure word choices, for they might upset a gobemouche with an abomasum.*

Hell, the majority of the first two and a half years of my career was spent fighting back against the corporate Gannett directive that one must—quickly and literally—tell a person what the piece he's reading is about. [STANDARD PARAGRAPH THREE: *In case it's not clear, Johnny Wilson is the Nashville Sounds' second baseman. He's batting .322 and having a terrific season.*] That wasn't merely a fringe concept inside the *Tennessean* offices. No, it was dogma. Readers, the thinking went, were too stupid, too lazy, too distracted to hang out. So hook them on the fly. Tell them exactly what to expect. Don't give them any reason to feel challenged, or uncomfortable, or ill at ease.

Nearly 25 years later, the concept still infuriates me and is, I believe, a culprit in the ongoing death of the American newspaper.

In his gut-wrenching piece on Monty Williams, whose wife died in a tragic automobile accident, *Sports Illustrated*'s Chris Ballard begins with us witnessing the veteran NBA coach meticulously wiping up the vomit produced by his two flu-stricken sons. It is simultaneously grotesque and beautiful. Writes Chris: "They threw up on the carpet, in the bed, on the bathroom floor. Everywhere but in the toilet and the trash can." Jane Bernstein's essay "Still Running" could have read perfectly fine and dandy as a boilerplate article on her fitness journey. Instead, she brings forth choppy little vignettes that create one of the most memorable pieces of 2017. Nine of ten editors I've worked with would have told Jane that her technique was wrongheaded and contrived and over the top. *The Sun* saw her work for what it is—inventive, spunky, and brilliant.

Of all the stories included in this anthology, the one that most meets the Greg Orlando sniff test comes from Tyler Tynes, a 24-year-old *SB Nation* staff writer who identifies himself on Twitter as "Another black boy from the forgotten blocks of Norf Philly." Tyler's essay, "There Is No Escape from Politics," runs 4,198 words. It begins with him sitting in the White House basement as the Pittsburgh Penguins meet Donald Trump, and it ends with two sentences and a single paragraph: "Nigga, maybe you right. Maybe one day we actually will." In between, the article jumps from Colin Kaepernick kneeling to a 39-round boxing match in 1810, to Johnny Bright, the Drake University halfback and 1951 Heisman Trophy candidate, to Jim Crow–enforced seating at a 1961 NFL game, to Kendrick Lamar. It is a hot mess of roundabout touch and beauty—a culturally significant shrapnel explosive that leaves little of 2018 America unscathed. There is nothing easy about Tyler's piece. The words demand a reader's full concentration.

It is a punch to the ribs.

It's a blow worth taking.

In case you haven't noticed, we live in disconcerting journalistic times.

While I write this introduction, our 45th president is almost certainly plotting his next assault on the media. As sure as gelato melts and Justin Upton swings through sliders, Donald Trump is reading (or being told about by Sean Hannity) an unflattering piece in the *Washington Post* or *New York Times* and bringing forth his cherished #FakeNews hashtag. It matters not whether the news is, in fact, "fake." If the commander in chief feels threatened, he will—à la a rabid raccoon inside a garbage pail—lash out and attack. His trained lemmings instinctively follow Grand Master's lead, overflowing the social media feed of the alleged media member/culprit with a rancid vileness unworthy of the lowest snake. (Don't believe me? Ask my friend Jemele.)

Hence, I won't try and sugarcoat this one: it's a hard time to be a member of the fourth estate. Without fail, we're repeatedly told how dishonest we are, how corrupt we are, how slanted we are. It matters not whether you cover the Pentagon or Broadway or local weather or the Bucknell women's softball team—you're all but certain to endure an irrational, Trump-inspired backlash that didn't exist pre-2016.

In my one-day-per-week gig as an adjunct journalism professor, I'm asked fairly often whether the field is even worth pursuing any longer. The glory, after all, is minimal. The hours can be long and relentless. Print is three steps from the grave, and too many websites continue to pay approximately six cents per word—*if they pay at all.* Throw in the nonstop criticism, and it's hard to blame young aspiring writers for turning toward the dark side that is public relations. (I kid—*sort of.*)

To this, I say: snotcicles.

Yes, *snotcicles.*

The year was 2003, and—battered by life as a Major League Baseball beat guy—I had just left *Sports Illustrated* to take a position in the features department at *Newsday.* The new job was, in a word, preposterous. Actually, I'll go two words—preposterously sweet. My task was to roam the streets of New York City and profile the weird, the eclectic, the eye-catching, the batshit insane. So day after day I would walk up and down, left and right, nibbling on pretzels and hot dogs, finding the homeless flutist in front of Ground Zero; sitting across from the Naked Cowboy inside the Times Square Howard Johnson; shadowing an upstart hip-hop group as its members tried pushing CDs to passers-by.

One day, during a particularly brutal winter stretch, I was summoned into the Long Island–based office (a place any journalist worth his weight avoids like Dengue fever) for a rare meeting with the higher-ups. The gig had to be up, right? I mean, who pays a reporter six figures to try every variety at the Nuts 4 Nuts cart?

Instead, I was greeted by Barbara Schuler, my editor, who wore a sinister look across her face.

"Jeff," she said, "we have an assignment for you."

"A good assignment?" I replied.

"Well . . ."

Within an hour, Barbara and I were hunched over a map of North America, trying to determine the coldest spot on the continent. "We want to show readers what it's like to live in this sort of climate all the time," she said.

Glub.

The two of us settled upon Yellowknife, the capital of Canada's Northwest Territories and a place I knew not existed. Three days later I was on a plane, then another plane, then another plane. This was *not* why I had left *Sports Illustrated*, and when I finally touched down in the depths of hell—eh, Canada—the temperature was –40 degrees.

(Take a sharp knife. Cut off your nose and lips. *That's* what it feels like.)

It was not a fun trip. The town was pewter drab, the weather was awful, the wind sliced through my body. But then, on my final day, I drove out to Great Slave Lake, where a man named Anthony Foliot parked his camper and devoted himself to building majestic life-sized castles of snow and ice. He went by the moniker "Snowking" and featured a child's smile hidden behind a brown bushy beard. It was truly one of the most magical sights I'd ever witnessed—using his own hands and imagination, Foliot created a café, an auditorium, a slide. All from ice and snow.

We spoke at length, and toward the end I asked about the icicles affixed to his facial hair. There were, oh, a half-dozen of them —jagged objects protruding at myriad angles. Snowking took hold of a yellow-ish white one dangling beneath a nostril.

"It's not an icicle," he said. "It's a snotcicle!"

With that, he laughed and laughed and laughed.

It wasn't actually all that funny. Giggle-worthy, maybe. But as I stood there, toes numb, cheeks peeling, staring at this hairy extraterrestrial and his snotcicles, I thought how beautifully weird my life had become.

No, writing isn't easy. It beats you down and chews you up and leaves you open to an endless stream of criticism. You write something, hate it, start all over again, hate it even more. You lose sleep, gain weight, pull out your hair, curse at the television, wish you'd majored in accounting. Hell, I often find myself in the corner of some random coffee shop, talking aloud to Phantom Jeff (and my laptop) as other patrons stare bewilderingly.

But when I'm down—when *you're* down—think of all the places you've been and all the places you'll go. Think of the impact of the written word, and (genuinely) the power of the pen.

Think of snotcicles.

JEFF PEARLMAN

TOM JUNOD

The Greatest, at Rest

FROM ESPN: THE MAGAZINE

A WEEK BEFORE HER husband dies, Lonnie Ali changes the plans for his funeral. The funeral she had envisioned is too big, she thinks. It is too complicated. At her annual meeting with the man who has been doing most of the planning, she says, "Sit down. I have to talk to you about something."

She is making changes because she believes she has time to make them. Her husband is not even sick. And besides . . . he's *Muhammad Ali*. She began working on the plan a decade earlier in response to counsel, and she's come to regard it as part of his routine upkeep, not so different from helping him with his meds. There are just some things you have to do, she says. She is not planning his funeral because she thinks he is going to die but because she has known him since she was a small child—and a part of her thinks he is going to live forever.

Her meeting with the man planning her husband's funeral, Bob Gunnell, takes place right before Memorial Day weekend in 2016. When he goes back to the office on Tuesday, May 31, he tells members of his staff that they're going to have to scrap a good part of the plan they've so painstakingly crafted. Then, after work, he gets a call from Lonnie. "Bob," she says, "I just want to make you aware that Muhammad has got a little cold. It's nothing to worry about, but as a precaution I'm going to take him to the hospital to get checked out."

The sound Muhammad Ali hears as he dies is the sound that babies hear right after they're born. It is just after 8:30 p.m. MT on

June 3, 2016, a Friday. He is in Room 263, in the intensive care unit of the HonorHealth Scottsdale Osborn Medical Center, near his home in Paradise Valley, Arizona. He has been disconnected from the ventilator that has been keeping him strenuously alive, and the imam at his bedside has begun the call to prayer, as if ushering a newborn into the world.

The imam, whose name is Zaid Shakir, does not know why he has sung the familiar keening song; it is traditional to sing to those who are close to their first breath but not to those close to their last. But he has flown into Arizona from California, and he reached Ali's room not long before what he calls "the paraphernalia of life support" was removed. Lonnie Ali is there. Ali's nine children are there, along with many of his grandchildren, and after reciting supplications and reading from the Quran with them, Shakir suddenly finds himself in the grip of spontaneous necessity. He has been watching the pulse in Ali's neck, watching it surge with life after he started breathing on his own and then watching it slowly ebb, and now he leans over and with his mouth close to Ali's right ear, he sings, "There is no God but Allah, and Muhammad is his messenger."

Shakir is tall and thin, nearly spindly, with a crooked smile and a beautiful voice, a voice that even when he's speaking carries a hint of a jazz, a way of hanging behind the beat before finding all the right notes. He does not whisper to Ali. He does not sing softly. He sings out loud, so that everyone can hear, so that the words will fill Ali's consciousness. Then he places in Ali's right hand a string of prayer beads offered by one of his grandsons and closes Ali's fingers around it. He begins talking to Ali, entreating him, exhorting him, telling him, "Muhammad Ali, this is what it means, God is one; say it, repeat it, you've inspired so many, paradise is waiting—"

When Shakir begins the call, Ali is alive. When he finishes, a doctor comes in, presses his stethoscope against Ali's chest and gently closes Ali's eyes. He lived for approximately 35 minutes after the disconnection of the ventilator, but now, at 9:10, Muhammad Ali, 74 years old, the three-time heavyweight champion of the world from Louisville, Kentucky, is pronounced dead, of septic shock.

*

Lonnie asks Imam Shakir to stay with her husband while the family files out of Room 263 and enters a new and diminished world —the world without Muhammad Ali in it. He does for a while, but the room begins to give way to professionals. There are nurses and hospital staff. There are two funeral directors who were literally hidden in another room when Ali was dying and now emerge from the shadows. And there are three men who wear hastily packed suits and faces of seen-it-all vigilance but who have never seen what they're seeing now. Their names are Todd Kessinger, Brian Roggenkamp and Jon Lesher. They're off-duty homicide detectives from the Louisville Metro Police Department, and they flew to Phoenix the day before on a private jet to provide security for the Ali family. They're no strangers to death, horrible and unnatural. They've been around bodies in every possible condition. But the body in the bed is the body of Muhammad Ali. He is covered, at first; then, after the nurses have removed the tubes and disconnected the monitors that sustained him, uncovered. It is their job to secure the room against intrusion, and Ali against exploitation—they've heard rumors that a tabloid television show is offering a $200,000 bounty for the first photos of The Greatest on his deathbed. But now they wonder how easily a photograph of the gaunt and balding man on the bed could be recognized. They feel tremendously solicitous toward him yet also somehow ennobled, as if they have come into the presence of a force larger and stronger than themselves. It is not fame, exactly; it is history, and Lesher keeps thinking that no matter what happens to him in the course of his life, no one will ever be able to take this moment away from him. So many people had encounters with Ali when he was alive: chance meetings that became, by the force of Ali's personality, indelibly personal, the stuff of stories told and retold. Lesher never did; neither did Kessinger or Roggenkamp. They encounter Ali dead, yet even with his life fled, his power persists, as if it's part of the atmosphere around his body. They are in the room with Muhammad Ali for 45 minutes. They have responsibility for Muhammad Ali for 45 minutes, until Roggenkamp departs to drive Lonnie Ali home. But there is a problem as they go to leave; Ali was not admitted as Muhammad Ali. He was admitted under an alias, confusing one of the funeral home directors. Finally, Kessinger says, "Look, it's Muhammad *Ali*. Let's just go."

*

When Lonnie goes home, she goes to a home absent of Ali. It is the singular advantage of living with an immobilized man—he is always there. Now he is not. She was his caregiver even before she was his wife, and she has been his wife for 30 years. People mistakenly assume that she has prepared for this eventuality, this night; that she prepared to be his widow as soon as she married him. She did not. She is in shock. When she was—when they were—younger, she saw him snatch flies from the air. She saw him bleed from a cut one day and wake up the next morning with the cut nearly erased. She believed his blood was different from the blood of other humans. Even much later, when her husband was in exile from his body because of Parkinson's disease, he was not in exile from himself—he was able to speak most mornings, and when he was finally silenced, he communicated through his touch and through the look in his eyes. He paid attention; he nodded; he squeezed her hand. And so now she does not feel as though she's lost an old man with a terminal illness.

She feels as though she's lost a child.

Jeff Gardner wears a suit and tie for the embalming. It's a Saturday morning, and there is very little traffic, human or automotive, stirring the desert calm of Mesa, Arizona. It doesn't matter that no one is likely to see him. Over the past 30 years, Gardner has embalmed, by his estimate, some 5,000 bodies, and he has worn a suit and tie for all of them that have not presented a risk of infection. He is a stout man, fastidious, with a contemplative manner, a bass note in his voice, and a taste for somber suits and splendid shoes. He wears the clothes he wears as a matter of reverence—because, as he sometimes says, you never know when you'll go from looking at the body to meeting the family.

Gardner is Catholic; he is about to embalm a Muslim at the Bunker Family Funeral Home, which is owned by a family of Mormons; but his trade has a way of erasing distinctions. The day before, he flew in from Louisville, the only passenger on a private jet, carrying the case of embalming fluid that would allow Ali's body to be preserved in a way not forbidden to Muslims. Gardner had learned about this necessity about eight years earlier, when he and Woody Porter, his associate at the A. D. Porter and Sons Funeral Home, were summoned to meet with the Alis at their house in Louisville. It was the meeting that set Muhammad Ali on the course of which today represents the first fulfillment—the planning of his own death and burial. Ali was in attendance; so was Lonnie; so were their lawyers and their accountant; and so were Zaid Shakir and Timothy Gianotti, an Islamic studies professor called in to advise the Alis. Ali was well into what Gianotti calls his "purification," his humbling at the hands of Allah. But at the time, he still had his good days. And even at his sickest—even at his last—he never stopped knowing exactly who he was. He was, in Shakir's description, "a praying man" who understood he belonged to Allah. But he also knew he was Muhammad Ali, and so belonged to the world.

It is desirable for a Muslim to be buried within a day of dying rather than be embalmed. It is desirable for a Muslim to go straight into the ground rather than be casketed, so that the ground can have him. But Muhammad Ali wanted to be laid out in Yankee Stadium. He wanted an open casket, so the world could see he was still so pretty! He had dreams about them—the crowds. So he sought compromise. According to Shakir and Gianotti, embalming is not strictly forbidden; an embalming solution containing alcohol or formaldehyde is. Not only are those elements poison, but they are the manifestation of a desire to attain immortality of the body rather than the soul. The body should rot, at the bottom of a hole in the ground, while the soul goes on to paradise.

Gardner invested in a case of "green" embalming fluid that contained no substance offensive to God. For the next eight years, he wore a dedicated pager as dutifully as he wore his jackets, his ties, and his alligator shoes . . . and now that he has gotten the call, he is ready to embalm Muhammad Ali, who came from the hospital last night and this morning is laid out in the basement of the Bunker Funeral Home. It is the most extraordinary circumstance of Gardner's earthly existence, but the job he has to do is anything but extraordinary; he has done it thousands of times. He embalmed his mother; he embalmed his father; now his touch falls upon a man who has touched so many, and whose message went around the world. It is an honor and privilege for Jeff Gardner to have been chosen to serve Muhammad Ali. Yet he has no choice but to start the way he always has, the way he was taught: He thinks. He breathes. He goes to work.

*

After Ahmad Ewais eats breakfast with his family, he drives to the Bunker Funeral Home. He is calm. He wears what he usually wears, a polo shirt and khakis. He is a tall man in his midforties, with close-cropped hair and a salt-and-pepper beard, and it is impossible to meet him without looking at his hands. They are large and very clean. They are never balled in fists; he holds them as if he were holding a large bowl, and they shape themselves into imploring gestures when Ewais, as is his habit, turns his eyes toward heaven. He is a devout man who has turned his simplest movements into prayers. His fingernails are the color of pearls.

When Ewais gets to the funeral home, Jeff Gardner is waiting for him. Gardner has finished his work, but he wants to make sure Ewais has the linen wrappings he brought with him on the private jet from Louisville—the linen Ali bought for himself years ago. Ewais has brought linen of his own, some of it cut into long strips he uses for tying. He has brought two plastic pitchers, one of them red and the other purple. He has brought a bottle of liquid Dial soap. He has brought towels he bought at Costco. He has brought a mask and gloves and cotton, in case he needs them. He has brought sticks of incense. From Saudi Arabia he has brought water said to be from the spring that bubbled up under the son of Abraham, and a bagful of lotus leaves. He has brought several kinds of perfume. He has brought camphor, which he ground himself in a coffee mill. He has also brought a friend from his mosque in Tempe, who will assist him, along with Zaid Shakir and Timothy Gianotti when they arrive. At approximately 10 o'clock, they do, and Gardner leads them into the room where Ali lies under a sheet. He watches for a while, until Ewais starts washing the body.

Ahmad Ewais is a body washer. He has washed nearly 1,000. It is his vocation, and it has seeped into him, all the way to his fingertips. He believes it is a mercy, and therefore an obligation. He believes that for every body he washes, 40 of his sins are forgiven. He believes that Allah commands the faithful to help the helpless, and he knows from experience that there is nothing in creation as helpless as a dead body, even when the body belongs to Muhammad Ali.

Ewais lights a stick of incense. With soap and water, he washes Ali's hands and arms up to the elbow, as if Ali were alive, preparing for prayer. Then he cleans Ali's privates, sliding his hands under a towel. At no time is Ali uncovered or exposed; the towel extends from his belly to his knees, and Ewais lifts it with his left hand and washes with his right, pouring water from the plastic pitchers. It is quiet in the room, Shakir and Gianotti helping turn the body when Ewais asks them to, and the quiet is sacramental. They are transfixed, watching Ewais—how much care he takes, how unhurried are his movements and how certain his hands—and Shakir thinks to himself that Muhammad Ali is being washed by the Muhammad Ali of body washers. But Ewais is transfixed by Ali himself. It is not that the great champion is more than a man; it is that he is precisely a man, and so has wound up here, on the table with him.

He washes him three times, as tradition prescribes, the first time with soap; the second time with the ground lotus leaves, which foam like soap when he adds water; and the third time with camphor and perfume. He covers him with three sheets, stretching from his shoulders to his knees, from his waist to his feet, and then from head to toe. But he also talks to him, and prays for him, thinking the thoughts instead of speaking the words. "Here you are, Muhammad Ali, no matter what you do in life, this is the final destination! You were The Greatest—may God make you The Purest!" As a Muslim, he believes that when humans die, their souls leave their bodies but linger, unable to respond but hearing and seeing and feeling, until their bodies are put to rest. Ewais is working to bring Ali's soul back to God. It takes him 45 minutes, maybe an hour, to finish, to reach the point where he is tying Ali's wrappings up with the long strips of linen. He is about to apply perfume to Ali's face when he calls Shakir and Gianotti over to look. Ali is wearing a linen turban; his face is all that shows, and Shakir and Gianotti are both struck by how regal he looks, like an African king. But there is something else: he gleams. All through the course of his life, people asked if they could touch his face, because it was so smooth and so unmarked and so shiny. Now some of that luster has been restored, and the man who washes him says to his assistants, "Look—his face is as bright as the moon."

Late that night, Timothy Gianotti goes for a walk to contemplate what he has seen. He remembers when he first met Ali, years before—how shorn he was of all that made him great, yet how great he still was. He lacked physical power, yet it was as though Gianotti had encountered a purified soul sitting in a chair. Now he has seen Ali in death, laid out on a table. Here was a man who never

declined God's call. Called upon to fight, he poured his genius
into fighting, and once or twice fought nearly to the death. Called
upon to make peace, he made peace at the cost of his athletic
prime. Called upon by crowds of people all over the world, he gave
himself to them, and moved among them. Called upon to endure
the mortification of his body, he surrendered without sacrificing
his spirit. He never complained, never lost his faith, and this morning, there it was, returned to him: the shine on his face.

Gianotti has lost track of time and place, and goes outside to
regain his sense of purchase under the desert sky. It is Saturday
night, June 4. In the morning, he will get on the plane that is
taking Ali back to Louisville. But right now he is walking around
the Arizona resort where he is staying. This is reality enough. A
woman approaches. She is African American. He has never seen
her before, but she knows him. She says, "You're here for Muhammad Ali."

"Yes, I am."

"You know," she says, "he belonged to *us*."

There is nobody watching. There is nobody cheering. There are
no crowds. It is early on Sunday morning, and three vehicles are
making their way to the airport. One is a white hearse containing
a travel casket draped with a funeral cloth provided by Zaid Shakir,
black and stitched in gold with Islamic verses. The two others are
a police car and a black SUV. The vehicle at the front of the procession carries a detail from the local police; the one in the rear
carries the three homicide detectives from Louisville. It is so quiet
that the men who make up this cortege of strangers share a sense
of disbelief—surely they will be discovered, set upon. They are
not. They make it to the airport, where a chartered jet is waiting.
They drive right on the tarmac, right up to the cargo hold. A few
of Ali's friends are on hand to help the undertakers, the police,
and the flight crew load the sheathed casket on the plane; they put
their hands on it, on him, then go up the stairs to join the living.
The police car, the SUV, and the hearse begin to leave; the plane
prepares for takeoff. But as it does, the driver of the hearse sees
a squabble of television trucks speeding onto the tarmac. They
come to a stop at the same time their quarry lifts into the sky.

The plane is a 737 leased from the San Francisco Giants. It is
the large plane the man in the hold wanted it to be. There are

not quite 30 passengers. Although they are scattered around the ·cabin, they all have something in common. It is no accident that they are together; it is no surprise that they are here. To the extent that they know one another, they know one another because for years they were bound to the same secret: long before Muhammad Ali died, they were chosen to lay him to rest.

Lonnie sits in the front of the plane with his children and grand-children, many of them wearing shirts proclaiming her husband THE GREATEST OF ALL TIME. Some of the family is not on the charter, and when Lonnie tried to make plane and hotel reservations for them while she was still in Arizona, she received the first inkling that the size and scope of the funeral might exceed her expectations: "What is going on in Louisville?" the travel agent said. "Why is it so difficult to find flights into Louisville?"

"Well, my husband died," Lonnie said.

"I'm sorry to hear that," the travel agent said, as though Lonnie had spoken a non sequitur. "Yeah, but what is going on there?"

Lonnie never informed the agent that her husband happened to be Muhammad Ali. But that's Lonnie. Though her face is gaunt with strain and she walks with a slight limp, she still has the freckles and talent for rolling her eyes that identify her for what she was, is, and always will be: Yolanda Williams, the girl from the neighborhood. She was 6 years old when she met Cassius Clay; he was 21, and about to become the heavyweight champion of the world. She lived across the street from his parents; his mother and her mother were friends. She is living proof of how important Louisville remained to him, because one of the many things she wound up doing for him was keeping Louisville in his life. When Lonnie calls herself a "Louisville girl," she means that she is at once a Southern girl and a Catholic-school girl, not to mention a girl Ali recognized early on for having good sense. She refers to herself as "ol' Lonnie"; she insists she and Ali were nothing more and nothing less than normal people, despite her husband being the most famous man in the world. Her father had polio, so even Ali's Parkinson's disease seemed normal to her. From personal experience, she knew he belonged to anyone who asked for his autograph, but it was hard to fathom he belonged to *everyone*. And when he spoke of holding his memorial service in an arena or a stadium, she'd say, "Yeah, right, Muhammad." This is not to say

she isn't consumed by a sense of mission as she sits on the plane.
She is, but it's the mission of a Louisville girl who wants to take
Muhammad Ali home.

In the Quran, it is written that all is written—"nothing will happen
to us except what Allah has decreed for us." And so it is with Ali, in
the most literal sense. There is a book, called The Book, that is the
chronicle of his death, foretold. It is a compilation of sorts, drawing upon the expertise of lawyers, cops, clerics, masters of the mor-
tuary arts. It was written by Bob Gunnell. Eight years ago, when the
Alis were looking for someone to plan Muhammad's funeral, they
chose Gunnell, a Louisville public relations man who would later
start his own firm, BoxcarPR, and who had no experience in event
planning. They were comfortable with the Louisville guy, though
in fact Gunnell began as a country boy from Eminence, Kentucky.
He found out what kind of stage he was about to occupy when he
was watching Michael Jackson's funeral in 2009. Lonnie called and
said, "Bob, I don't want the funeral to be like this. We want it to be
in the Muslim tradition. It needs to be carried out to Muhammad's
wishes, to the T."

Gunnell and his associate at Boxcar, Danielle Rudy Davis, completed three drafts of The Book before submitting it for approval,
and when they did, Ali reviewed and initialed each page. There
were 169 of them. In addition, there was a sheaf of nondisclosure
agreements, several of which have been signed by passengers on
the flight from Phoenix to Louisville. Jeff Gardner, in his suit and
tie; Todd Kessinger and his crew, in their dress blues; Zaid Shakir
and Timothy Gianotti; Gunnell himself: they were all bound to
secrecy, and The Book is called The Book because under no circumstance is there to exist—and be available to prying eyes—a
document titled "The Funeral of Muhammad Ali."

And yet who knows what God's own book looks like, how many
second thoughts and scratch-outs complicate its pages? The Book
might be stored in Boxcar's safe, but it is always and forever subject to revision. Five days before Ali was admitted to Scottsdale Osborn, Gunnell had the meeting with Lonnie, and he had to halve
his estimate of the crowd. Yesterday, not long after Ali's body was
purified by Ahmad Ewais, Gunnell met Lonnie in the shoe section
of Nordstrom, and they came to what seemed a final plan for the
week to come. And yet . . . who knows what awaits them in Louis-

ville? The Book, in its present iteration, is based on an estimated 5,000 to 6,000 people attending Ali's memorial. But Gunnell, here on the plane, in one of the suits he bought at Nordstrom, can't help but be haunted by a conversation he'd had with Matt Lauer the day Ali died. Lauer had been the first newsman to know that death was imminent, and in one of their conversations, Gunnell had asked how big he thought the funeral was going to be. Lauer's answer: "Think Nelson Mandela."

"We have to have an emergency meeting," Shakir says to Gunnell. They are still in the air. It's a three-hour flight, and there is still time before they touch ground. Yet there is a sense of urgency. It is Sunday; when the plane lands, the death of Muhammad Ali, still a private event, becomes a public one. Gunnell has already directed the Boxcar staff to clear hotels and event halls all over Louisville, and Boxcar and Lonnie have been overwhelmed by the inquiries they've received from celebrities and world leaders. One of them has been from Turkish President Recep Tayyip Erdogan, who wants to join the ranks of eulogists at Ali's public memorial service.

Ali selected his eulogists long ago, and Erdogan was not among them. But when Lonnie suggests maybe he should be able to pray or read from the Quran at the Islamic prayer service known as the *jenazah*, Gunnell reminds her the jenazah, at least as envisioned in The Book, is supposed to be a small and private affair, open only to family and friends. So the question is not how big the funeral is going to be, nor how many famous people can be accommodated, but to whom does Muhammad Ali belong?

He had that kind of soul, the kind people claim for themselves, so burying him requires sorting through any number of constituencies. He was a husband and a father. He was a citizen of Louisville; he was a citizen of the world. He was a proud black man who held the truth of his own beauty self-evident; he was offered—especially in his later years when he had been made safe by silence—as the embodiment of postracial possibility. He became a global figure not when he became heavyweight champion of the world but when he changed his name from Cassius Clay to Muhammad Ali, exchanging the name of a proud young man for a name that made his people proud. He was a Muslim, devout and conservative, and he was a celebrity who tended to speak of himself in superlatives. He never stopped calling himself The Greatest and he never stopped saying God is great, and he somehow reconciled those assertions.

It is easy to say that Ali belongs to everyone. It might even be true. But on the plane, Shakir sits with Lonnie Ali and Bob Gunnell and says that he belongs to the people who need him, and the people who need him are Muslims and African Americans. He belongs to Allah, yes, but he belongs to Allah because he belongs to the people. If you deny the people the chance to pray for him — well, it will do damage not only to them but to him. He is not just here to be celebrated; he is crossing over, and so he is here to be ferried, by many hands. Allah needs his soul; therefore the people need his body, to pray for his soul's release.

The plane flies into Louisville, and when it lands, and the passengers begin their restless stirring, Lonnie stands up. She is a soft-spoken woman but also a plainspoken one, and now she makes an announcement that sounds like a statement of general principle: "You can all sit down. Ali goes first."

It is a windy day in Louisville, and the wind keeps peeling the black and gold funeral cloth off the casket as it is unloaded from the cargo hold of the plane and loaded in the back of a black hearse. The mayor, Greg Fischer, is waiting in Louisville, along with a crescent-shaped formation of eight black SUVs, containing a full security contingent run by Kelly Jones, the head of special ops for the Louisville Metro Police. There are helicopters in Louisville, taking soundless footage, and there are jangled nerves in Louisville, and on the way to the funeral home, Jones sees people in cars pulling out their phones and taking photographs, so he orders the procession to start running lights.

Woody Porter is waiting for Lonnie at the second of the A. D. Porter Funeral Home locations, away from downtown. Porter is the scion of four generations of African American funeral directors. He is bald-headed and dapper, and though he is hobbled by diabetes and knows how to lower his voice in reverence when called upon to do so, he is a beaming presence with a wheezy laugh — an ebullient undertaker. He buried both of Muhammad's parents and Lonnie's mother, and when Ali used the visitation of Cassius Marcellus Clay Sr. as an opportunity to hand out Islamic literature at the head of the casket, Porter knew Ali well enough to say, "Ali, sit down. You don't have to stand during your father's visitation." Lonnie trusts him because he is family and can make her laugh.

Eight years earlier, he went with Jeff Gardner to Ali's Louisville home for a preliminary meeting about Ali's funeral. When Zaid Shakir and Timothy Gianotti explained to him that Ali, as an observant Muslim, should be buried in as plain a casket as possible, Porter turned to Ali and said, "Ali, what do you want—metal or wood?" Ali answered, "Wood." Porter stayed on Lonnie for a long time to go ahead and buy the casket, and when she did, it stayed at A. D. Porter for nearly four years. Now, as he waits for Lonnie, the casket waits for Ali.

The casket is not overly embellished, in accordance with the Alis' wishes. But neither is it a pine box; neither is it anything less than what Porter calls "one beautiful piece of furniture." He had to order a custom casket, given Ali's size—or, in Porter's words, his length. It is made of African mahogany, each plank 4 to 6 inches thick, so that the entire wooden box weighs 700 pounds, empty.

After Ali arrives at A. D. Porter Southeast, Porter helps move his body from the shipping casket to the casket he has prepared for him. So do Jeff Gardner, Zaid Shakir, Timothy Gianotti, and Ali's youngest son, Asaad. Porter sees Ali's face and thinks, *He looks good. Ali looks* good! When Lonnie and Asaad are about to have their own private visitation with him, Lonnie's first quiet time with her husband since his death, Porter asks her whether she wants to see him. Gardner opens the casket for her, and she beholds her husband's face. He was always so careful about his face, and now, yes, it shines. But she can't bring herself to call it beautiful, because it is shadowed by the fact that she will never see it again.

When Todd Kessinger returns to work on Monday, he checks to see what has happened in his absence. As the detective in charge of the homicide department, he has been busy because Louisville has been bloody; indeed, the city in 2016 is in the middle of a record run of murders. But the last killing had occurred on June 2, when a 21-year-old named Maulik Patel was shot on his way home from a gas station. There has not been another since Ali died, and Kessinger begins to count the days of grace.

At 9:04, the sun sets and Ramadan begins.

*

The champ had a persistent dream—he is running on Broadway in downtown Louisville, and all of the city has turned out for him, chanting a name meant to be chanted, "Ali! Ali! Ali!" until at last the chant gives him wings, and he takes a step into the air and begins to fly. But Broadway, in downtown Louisville, does not end in sky; it ends in Cave Hill Cemetery, where he will be buried.

Cave Hill is an elaborate historical cemetery, a rolling and well-tended garden the first graves of which were dug in 1848 and out of which grow the granite monuments of the families who made their names during Louisville's industrial heyday. It is white, in terms of the impression left by its pale stone flora, and also white in terms of its venerable clientele—as white, indeed, as the suit coat of one of its most famous inhabitants, Colonel Sanders. It is home to 6,100 Union soldiers and 228 Confederate ones, all interred under the flags of their respective nations. It is heartbreakingly beautiful and beautifully heartbreaking, a dream not of eternal life but rather of eternal status, and eight years before Ali's death, Lonnie visited with Woody Porter and bought a 12-grave lot in Section U, on a hill positioned between the maintenance shed and the pond set aside for the scattering of ashen remains. While it might be tempting to ascribe symbolic significance to the Alis' deciding to settle forever among those whose homes their ancestors could only have visited by way of the back door, Lonnie, forever of Louisville, keeps it simple: "It was either Cave Hill or Mecca."

Now, on Tuesday, Lonnie returns with a contingent of advisers, not only Woody Porter but also Bob Gunnell, Jeff Gardner, Zaid Shakir, and Timothy Gianotti. A funeral tent stands upon the real estate the Alis have already purchased, but Lonnie has come to entertain an offer: would she like to move? She meets with Gwen Mooney, a friendly and forthcoming woman who gives off the impression that she is continually pinching herself out of disbelief that she runs a place as charming as Cave Hill. Mooney says she is simply making sure there is no room for regret, but at the same time she frets that the lot Lonnie has selected is not the most desirable one available—and so she offers her a lot near Cave Hill's Broadway gate, off one of the circular avenues that have traditionally provided the cemetery's most prestigious addresses. Shaded with old trees, it is, Mooney says, sacred ground, a place untouched by backhoe or spade—until now. No burials have occurred here;

no burials have been allowed here, but for Ali, Cave Hill is willing
not only to make an exception but to make an exception that will
cost no more than Section U.

Lonnie says no—no, no, as briskly as that. It is not simply that
she prefers the seclusion of the lot she has already purchased, or
that Zaid Shakir is on hand to tell her that the prescribed orienta-
tion of Ali's body, with his feet to the north and his head to the
south, is more easily attained on the little hill by the scattering
pond. It is that Ali needs to go where Ali died believing he was
going to go. Her plans are his plans; years ago, he came here with
Lonnie, staying in the car as she showed him the lot, and the lot is
where she will come for peace, if peace ever comes.

They go from Cave Hill to the Kentucky Fairgrounds, where the
jenazah is to be held Thursday—the jenazah, the prayer service
now with a life of its own, having gone from something unplanned
to something aswirl with unreconciled energies. The body will be
there. In a closed coffin, under the black and gold cloth . . . but the
body will be there, it has to be there, in a room among the faithful,
all of whom will have unrestricted access. At the fairgrounds, there
is an arena called Freedom Hall, where the Louisville Cardinals
used to play basketball and where Cassius Clay had his first professional fight. It is the venue Lonnie's security consultants have
suggested, because they can control the access points. But for Zaid
Shakir it is still not big enough for Ali—and so fairgrounds officials show him the commercial exhibition hall next door. It is vast
and it is the color of linen, with high ceilings held up by graceful
columns, and as soon as Shakir sees it he thinks:

This looks like a mosque.

They don't sleep. Nobody does—Bob Gunnell and his staff have
set up a "war room" in the Marriott in downtown Louisville, where
the people never stop calling and the phones never stop ringing
and the adrenaline never stops surging. They don't sleep because
they can't sleep, and no matter when Gunnell finally collapses into
his hotel-room bed, he starts his day by checking in with Lonnie
at sunrise.

On most days, they face the dawn before Louisville does. On
Wednesday, however, Gunnell texts Lonnie at 6 a.m. with news
of something that started happening in the smallest hours of the
morning. They'd gone to sleep expecting the KFC Yum Center,

the big downtown arena, to start distributing tickets at 10 for the
Friday memorial service. The tickets are free, but anybody who
wants them has to get in line and pick them up in person. Now
Gunnell wakes up to the news that there is a line at the Yum Center—a line that started forming at 4 in the morning; a line that
extends over the Clark Memorial Bridge on Second Avenue, all
the way to Indiana; a line that is forcing Mayor Fischer to open the
Yum Center's ticket windows immediately. Gunnell sends Lonnie
a text, and she answers: *Did I read this right?* He calls her back. *Yes,*
he says. *All the way to Indiana.*

The windows open, and in about 45 minutes 15,000 tickets are
gone. And Lonnie has to smile because it has such an Ali-esque
ring to it. *Even when I died, the people lined up all the way to Indiana.*
She is not happy; happy is not the word for what she is feeling,
and won't be for a long time. But something is going on, a fulfillment of what she thought was fantasy. Muhammad had told her
the truth. The man who dreamed of crowds knew they were coming for him, and now here they came.

A plane comes out of the sky. It is early Wednesday morning, 2:30
or thereabouts, but a motorcade occupies the ramp, waiting for
the plane to land. It is a large motorcade, indeed a presidential
one, comprising about 50 cars, engines running, lights throwing
spinning shadows. When the plane lands, a trim figure in a suit
descends the air stairs, then steps onto a red carpet that's been
rolled out for him. He is not a large man, but he has a certain
coiled swagger, as though a red carpet stretches before him no
matter where he goes. He also has his own armed security force,
men with a coiled swagger all their own.

Barack Obama will not be attending Ali's funeral because, now
in the last year of his presidency, he is going to his older daughter's high school graduation. But Recep Tayyip Erdogan, president
of Turkey, has come to Louisville bearing gifts. He has brought
a piece of fabric said to be from the Kaaba, the cubelike shrine
at the center of Mecca, and therefore at the very heart of Islam.
He wants to drape it over Ali's casket at Thursday's jenazah. He is
not so different from the multitudes who have made pilgrimages
to Ali's funeral. He wants to bring something of himself to Ali;
he wants to establish his connection to Ali; he wants to celebrate
Ali, and therefore celebrate himself and his people. On the other

hand, he is Recep Tayyip Erdogan, a powerful man for whom the funeral represents not just an occasion but an opportunity. He is, his representatives insist, the leader of the Islamic world. And he wants a platform at the jenazah commensurate with his exalted position.

Seven years earlier, Lonnie Ali saw the funeral of Michael Jackson and knew she didn't want her husband's funeral to be like that —a funeral in which the mourners seemed to have an individual stake. She envisioned something very different, a funeral in the spirit of Muhammad Ali and for the spirit of Muhammad Ali, in which believers gather only to pray the fallen hero to paradise. In that way, the funeral would be similar in spirit to the hajj, the pilgrimage to Mecca required of all observant Muslims. There would be no distinctions made between rich and poor or black and white, nor would there be special accommodations made for the exercise of political power, since all are equal in the eyes of God.

And so it is that by the time the sun rises on Thursday, the atmosphere of the north wing of the exhibition hall at the Kentucky Exposition Center is already charged with a mixture of devotion and conflict. The security teams assigned to the jenazah from the U.S. Secret Service and the Louisville Metro Police don't like the hall, for precisely the same reasons that Zaid Shakir and Timothy Gianotti do—because it is vast, and flat, with no "advantage points" should the presence of Muhammad Ali's body inspire a free-for-all. The believers begin arriving when the officers do, forming a line at 6 in the morning, and by the time Zaid Shakir begins the jenazah six hours later, standing next to the casket in which lies the body of Muhammad Ali, there are thousands on hand to join him in prayer. They are black and they are white; they are Muslim and they are non-Muslim; they are members of Ali's family and they are members of the family of the famous; and they have made the Kentucky Exposition Center into an impromptu temple when the president of Turkey arrives with his security team.

Erdogan has indeed come with his gift, the piece of cloth from the sacred Kaaba. But the gift has been refused because it came with conditions, and the men around him are determined to see those conditions met. They form a phalanx around their president, and they begin elbowing and muscling their way to the body of Muhammad Ali. They are invited to sit in the VIP section, with the American politicians and sports figures, but no, they seek a po-

sition not only of prominence but of proximity so they can grace
Ali's casket with the cloth from the Kaaba. The standing room–
only crowd responds to the jostling as crowds do, with an electric
sense of unease; the Louisville police officer who has been standing alone in front of the casket is joined by seven of his colleagues,
who form a line of their own. The two phalanxes meet; there is
talk of the body being evacuated; and then Timothy Gianotti steps
forward, to remind Erdogan's men of the spirit of the hajj. It is a
moment of uncertainty that turns out to be a moment of truth, for
Erdogan withdraws. He leaves the hall; he leaves Louisville; and
the plane on which he came returns to the sky.

That night, visitors come to Porter's, one after another. Ali is in a
closed casket set in a private room, and they each receive a prescribed amount of time to visit with him. Louis Farrakhan goes
first, with representatives from the Nation of Islam; they get half
an hour. Next come the children, for an hour. Then comes Rah-
man Ali, in the grip of the same disease that shackled his brother.
When he was a young man, he had a sharply chiseled face; now it
is wide, almost burgeoning, like Muhammad's. He has an hour at
Porter's, but he is a man inclined to show up and to leave unexpectedly, and he doesn't take all of the allotted time. Ali is alone
as the funeral home clears out; then four men open the casket
and take a last look. It is not out of love, or the impulse that takes
over in mythology, when mortals make the mistake of sneaking
one final glimpse at the gods. It is a matter of duty. They have to
turn his body so that when he's in the ground at Cave Hill, feet to
the north and head to the south, he's lying on his right side, with
his face facing east. Woody Porter, Jeff Gardner, Zaid Shakir, and
Timothy Gianotti: they all have a hand in it; they all turn him and
rig the casket so he stays turned. And they see him. He had an
unusual face for a man universally considered handsome—it was
round and soft, lacking in sharp edges and more notable for its
skin than its bones. He rarely called himself handsome; he called
himself pretty, and he was right. "I'm a bad man," he said, yet he
never gave up the face of a beloved child until his face gave up on
him. It is the pampered softness that left him, and as he lies in his
casket, it's been replaced by a turbaned hauteur and that ineradi-
cable shine. When the four men finish their work, they become

the last men on earth to see his face; and when they close the lid, they know that no human being will see Muhammad Ali again.

There is a prayer service Friday morning, led by Zaid Shakir, and then the pallbearers take the casket to the shiny black hearse. There are 10 of them, because of the mass of what they're carrying, and they all have one thing in common: they've been chosen. Some are relatives, mostly from the Clay side; some are famous, Mike Tyson and Lennox Lewis and Will Smith; and one has been chosen to be a pallbearer because Ali chose him to be his friend. John Ramsey was just a fan when he met Ali; a worshipful young man in his twenties goaded by friends to approach Ali at a party. He went with his Howard Cosell impression, to which Ali responded: "Howard Cosell gets paid for that. What's your excuse?" Later, he looked at Ramsey and said: "I like you. Write down your number. I'll come see you some time." Two weeks later, Ramsey's mother told him to get the door, and it was Ali. They'd been friends ever since, and Ramsey, who has a sports talk show on Louisville radio and has never quite been able to extinguish the light of worship in his face, has always wondered why. He traveled with Ali; he gave Ali his meds and buttoned his shirts; and seeing how Ali acted with other people—and the people to whom he gave his attention—has led him to one conclusion: Ali chose Ramsey to be his friend because Ali saw that Ramsey needed to be his friend. Ali responded to the need in people and people responded to the need in Ali, and what Ramsey can't help thinking as he meets Mike Tyson in the morning, and sits in a car in the funeral procession in the unlikely company of Lennox Lewis and Will Smith, is that they must have needed him too.

There are 17 vehicles in the procession. The hearse is three vehicles from the lead; Lonnie's SUV is three from the hearse, behind the imams and the pallbearers. She is in the first family car, with Asaad, her sister Marilyn, and her nephew. And so others in the procession see them before she does: the people. It is not merely a crowd lined up along Bardstown Road; it is her husband's dream of crowds. Not dozens, not hundreds, but thousands upon thousands, giving voice to billions, in an incessant cheer that echoes over the miles. Ali! Ali! Ali!

At first Yolanda Williams thinks it will go away—that they will go away—when they get past the exit of A. D. Porter, and then again when they leave Bardstown Road and get on the highway. But the chant keeps getting louder, the crowd keeps growing thicker, until Lonnie Ali at last surrenders, to them, to him, and to their need for one another.

The route to Cave Hill is 23 miles long, and the procession takes two hours to complete it. They go on the highway, they stop in front of the Muhammad Ali Center, they loop through downtown Louisville on Muhammad Ali Boulevard, and then they head west, to the home where he grew up. He never stopped visiting the old street. He used to ask Ramsey to drive there, and when he saw men hanging around on the corner, he'd roll down his window and say, "I'll still whip all you n—s." They'd stop and do a double take, then cry, "Ali!" They are all here now, all the men from the neighborhood, all the women and the children, all the babies, all of black Louisville celebrating his return and laying their final claim on him. Lonnie had asked Kelly Jones and security consultant Jim Cain whether the procession could stop in front of his old house, painted pink; they said yes, for 15 seconds, fearing that they would be overwhelmed. But now they have to stop. They have no choice. When they make the left onto Grand Avenue, they are enveloped not by a crowd but by a populace, not by people but by a people, and they feel the tug of humanity itself, this warring entity made up of hands, tears, laughter, dancing, music, signs, babies, wheelchairs, voices raised in a two-syllable chant, an articulated roar: AH-LEEEEEE. Lonnie rolls down her window. Even Will Smith rolls down his window, saying, "Muhammad wouldn't want us to be in a bubble!" More hands, outstretched, imploring; and now kisses.

And then tears. They all cry, even the hard ones, especially the hard ones, Bob Gunnell, Mike Tyson, and, yes, Lonnie, crying for him, crying for them, crying for the crowd touching their cars and piling roses on Ali's hearse, but also crying for themselves, the certain knowledge that for as long as they live they will never live through something like this again, nor feel quite so alive. The procession starts moving again, the police officer who stood alone in front of Ali's casket at the jenazah now at the front, in a "piercing" car that parts the waters and allows Ali passage home, down Broadway, where this man who dreamed of crowds also dreamed of flight.

*

Maggie Cassaro's mother died unexpectedly the previous September. Grief-stricken, the artist wanted to do something special
for her, so she collected roses and scattered their petals over the
entrance of her house. The sidewalk, the path to the porch, the
porch itself: all graced by a gust of roses. When Ali died, Cassaro
called Cave Hill to ask permission to dress its venerable gates. The
office told her to call Boxcar. She did, and the Boxcar folks called
Lonnie. They'd heard dozens of similar offers and requests from
people wanting to participate in some way in Ali's funeral. Maggie Cassaro's was the only one Lonnie accepted, the only one that
made her cry.

An average rose has 44 petals. With the help of the old-line Louisville florist Nanz & Kraft, Cassaro bagged some 88,000 of them.
Now, as the procession makes its way toward Cave Hill, Cassaro is
one of the multitudes at the gates, tending to a drift of red and
pink snowflakes on a 90-degree day in June. There are roses everywhere in Louisville, roses in the streets, roses on Ali's hearse, roses
still in people's hands. But Cave Hill was swept by bomb-sniffing
dogs at 6 in the morning. All of its employees are employed on this
day, many of them posted at the perimeter to make sure nobody
gets over the cemetery walls. It is shut down and sealed tight, and
as Ali enters a place he will never leave, the petals piled at the gate
linger like Louisville's last kiss.

They dug the hole the day before. It is usually a job for four, but
this time it was a job for all of the men in Cave Hill's excavation
crew so all eight could one day tell their children they dug Muhammad Ali's grave. They cut the hole with a sod knife and dug it
out with a backhoe, one man after another working the controls.
They gave way to a two-man team from a local manufacturer of
funeral vaults, who brought Ali's vault to the cemetery on the back
of a flatbed truck, then lowered it into the ground with a winch. It
was—is—a basic vault, black with silver highlights, set in a hole 63
inches deep and 36 inches wide, from which has been displaced a
hillock of earth and to which a hillock of earth is waiting patiently
to return.

It is easy to get lost at Cave Hill Cemetery, with its 16 miles of
coiled roads, so as soon as the gates are closed, Gwen Mooney
goes to the head of the funeral procession. She knows the way to

Section U. Not only has the procession been returned to a world of quiet and privacy, but the mourners have been introduced to their own fatigue. In their black sunglasses and black clothes, they emerge from their cars into the sun and listen to Zaid Shakir say prayers at the graveside. Up on the hill, the excavation crew and the two men from the vault manufacturer stand ready to go to work, close enough to see but too far away to listen, until they are summoned to the burial. At many funerals, the family leaves before the casket is lowered into the ground, the vault sealed, and the hole filled back up with dirt. At Ali's funeral, however, the family is determined to see the whole thing through because of what it owes Allah and because of what it owes Muhammad Ali. The family members cannot bear to leave him to unseen mercies, so they witness the Cave Hill crew lower him into the grave, then a man named Ricky Barnett use a small crane to seal the vault with a 1,000-pound concrete lid swinging from short chains. The lid makes the vault airtight and virtually waterproof, transforming it into an underground tomb that exists in contradiction of God's will. But God is merciful, as long as his mercy is not flaunted, and now Zaid Shakir picks up a handful of dirt and tosses it onto the casket of Muhammad Ali. It makes a thumping, rattling sound.

"From this earth we have created you," Shakir says.

The second handful:

"To this earth we return you."

And then the third:

"From this earth we will resurrect you."

As Muhammad Ali died, Shakir told him what to say to God. He does the same now that Ali's body has been laid to rest and his soul has been released to face the questioning of angels. He addresses him directly: "Muhammad Ali, say Allah is Lord . . ." But now there is work to be done, and he is not alone. He watches Mike Tyson take off his suit jacket and grab one of three gleaming new stainless steel shovels that Cave Hill has provided for the occasion. Tyson digs, hard, and then turns one shovelful of dirt into the grave, and then another. His contribution is not ceremonial; he does not hand over the shovel; he begins to sweat, and then Shakir hears that sound, the unmistakable *uuungh* of Mike Tyson getting to work. He thinks, *I have to keep up with Mike Tyson . . .* but that's what they all think as they grab shovels and sweat through their clothes in the heat and keep working until the vault is cov-

ered and all that is to be seen of Muhammad Ali is a layer of Louisville earth, even though they still smell roses.

Then they go. Fifteen thousand ticket holders are waiting for
them at the Yum Center, along with Bill Clinton and the other eulogists; the famous friends; the honored guests; the convocation of
all-timers hanging out in the University of Louisville locker room
pressed into service as a green room. Kareem and Beckham, Jim
Brown, George Foreman and Sugar Ray Leonard . . . But as the
mourners leave the mortal remains of Muhammad Ali to the backhoe and the shovels, three men in suits and ties stay behind until
the work is done. Todd Kessinger, Brian Roggenkamp, and Jon
Lesher. A week ago, they were the only ones left in the hospital
room after Muhammad Ali died. Now they're the only ones left at
his grave. It has been an easy week for them in many ways; no one
has been killed since June 2. But the next morning, Kessinger will
go back to work and find that he has to investigate the murder of
a woman named Jacoya Mangrum, killed at 4 in the morning on
June 11, 2016, in a world without Ali.

It is tempting, when paying a visit, to believe that Ali has been set
free—to believe that he exists in the beauty of the setting, in the
sun in the sky and the wind in the magnolia tree that overhangs
his grave, instead of in the ground. But he has been there a year
now. He is at the bottom of a hole dug by eight men sharing a
backhoe. He is in a vault, black with silver highlights, manufac-
tured less than two miles away and then sealed, in front of his
family, by a man who lowered a 1,000-pound lid with a crane. He
is in a casket made of African mahogany, with each plank 4 to 6
inches thick, so that the casket weighs 700 pounds, empty. Still
very clean, he is perfumed and wrapped in three pieces of linen
tied together with linen strips. Only his face shows, but it is facing
east, toward Mecca, because before his casket was closed for the
last time, four men—two of them Muslim and two of them Chris-
tian—turned him on his right side. The vault is airtight, and in his
veins there are traces of the fluid used to embalm him, not desirable by Islamic standards but also not forbidden. Time conquers
everything, and the elements will eventually have their way with his
body, and him, as Allah intended.

And because Muhammad Ali is still there, so is the woman born
Yolanda Williams, known to all as Lonnie. She visits, knowing she

was right all along: it's not only a beautiful site, it's the right site for Muhammad. It is secluded and it is peaceful, but above all it is welcoming, with two benches made from the same black African granite out of which his stone was cut. She sits on them, hoping to get the chance to speak to him. So many people think she took care of him. What they don't know—what they can never understand—is that he took care of her. He was always with her; he has always been with her. She met him when she was a child, so when she says that losing him was like losing a child, she says, in nearly the same breath, that losing him was like losing a father. A father, a husband, a child: a totality. He *raised* me, she says. And so one afternoon, as she approaches with trembling the anniversary of his death, she goes to see Muhammad again. It's Derby weekend in Louisville, so Maggie Cassaro gets to the grave before Lonnie does, dressing the lot in a flutter of rose petals in the shape of a horse collar. It overwhelms Lonnie, but then so much does since she lost her husband. She insists that people don't know her, "ol' Lonnie." But she is the beneficiary of one kindness after another. She and Muhammad were optimists, she says. He not only never complained about his condition, he never complained about anything. And he never talked about death; he talked only—and incessantly—of the afterlife. She is an optimist still, for all her tears. She still cries easily. But she doesn't cry often at the grave because she doesn't get a chance to. She goes there to have time alone with Muhammad, but then he is never alone. He was a warrior and a will-o'-the-wisp; a praying man and a trickster; a magician who always had mischief on his mind, and he is making mischief still. Time alone with Muhammad Ali? Lonnie doesn't get five minutes. She doesn't get two minutes. She doesn't get a minute, before someone comes and visits his grave. She's supposed to have the last word. But the last word is written now for all to see, atop the shiny black stone quarried from Africa, and she can't complain if she has to share it:

ALI.

HOWARD BRYANT

Serena, Venus, and the Williams Movement

FROM ESPN: THE MAGAZINE

YOU WATCH THE protests, hear them outside your window and see them on TV, millions of women marching across the globe on January 21. You talk with a man you've known since 11th grade — white, respectable, of unremarkable wealth or accomplishment yet carrying a learned smugness, completely secure in the legitimacy of his status — who you discover is offended more by the vulgarity of the protest signs than the vulgarity that created them. Fortified by the protections and perks of maleness in perpetuity, he speaks of the women as a minor inconvenience, a moth on his tweed. "It was a moment, not a movement," he tells you. "It changed nothing."

After a lifetime of diminishment, these words should carry no value, yet they remain inside you, eating at you. During this same conversation, he tells you of his "loss of respect" for civil rights icon John Lewis, and you know then that this person you've known for decades is not only talking about the women marching. He's talking about you too.

You watch the Australian Open championship between Venus and Serena Williams with this tumult in mind, and when Serena becomes a champion again, *It was a moment, not a movement* rises up like bile, and you wonder whether their presence will *not* feel like defiance. But you know better. It will not.

You see them hug, see the teary fans. The humanity of it all. You want to trust that this breathtaking show of respect for these two champions is part of the natural ritual of sports—swords falling as the twilight nears, a ceremonial and final, unifying act—but you cannot shake the slights.

If you have eyes and a heart, you see just how difficult these matches really are. You see Serena turn her back to Venus after a point to cloak her emotion. She will scream "*Come on!*" directly toward Victoria Azarenka, but she will not embarrass her sister. You see Venus, and when she says to the audience, "Serena Williams, that's my little sister, guys," she receives compliments for being gracious and elegant, but she is both elegant and protective. Even in their finals, it was never one against the other but two against everyone.

Watching weak shots get pummeled, you realize that the legacy of Venus and Serena cannot be found in a trophy case but in all of the athletic big hitters—the Maria Sharapovas and Garbine Muguruzas—who now define the women's game. The Williams sisters became the measure, and if you couldn't hit with them, you couldn't play. In turn, they forever diminished the championship hopes of the waifish and the crafty, the Agnieszka Radwanskas and Carla Suarez Navarros, and thanks to the sisters, there will be youngsters weeded out of the game earlier because they just don't hit the ball hard enough. You see a sport revolutionized. You see legacy in action.

You watch the patriarchy step on the Williamses, even when it wants to blow them kisses. Serena thanks the crowd, the tournament, her blood—but not her new fiancé, Reddit cofounder Alexis Ohanian, an omission that was mentioned often by broadcasters. In your mind, you flip through years of victory speeches, trying to remember a moment when Roger Federer or Rafael Nadal or Andy Murray was chastised for not mentioning his spouse or girlfriend by name. You can find none.

As an all-Williams final became inevitable, you hear only the legend Chris Evert giving credit to Richard Williams, head of the family that didn't belong until the championship trophies piled so high even the critics finally had to surrender. You remember talking with him at Wimbledon 2012. He spoke about his daughters, about the family not being wanted by the blue bloods of tennis, and you knew by the way his eyes fixed on you—older black man to younger one in the United Kingdom—that he was really talking about America, how if you are not white, you don't get to be smug because you're not protected by perks in perpetuity, how you never have the luxury of determining what is a movement and what is a moment because you are always the target.

"There was only one way: win," Richard Williams said, and when the sisters are standing on the podium in Melbourne, you see their excellence triumph, their blood vindicated. "Win and make them deal with us. Win and they have to give you a seat at the table, even if they don't want you there."

REID FORGRAVE

The Concussion Diaries: One High School Football Player's Secret Struggle with CTE

FROM GQ

ZAC EASTER KNEW what was happening to him. He knew why. And he knew that it was only going to get worse. So he decided to write it all down—to let the world know what football had done to him, what he'd done to his body and his brain for the game he loved. And then he shot himself.

My Last Wishes

It's taken me about 5 months to write all of this. Sorry for the bad grammar in a lot of spots.

I WANT MY BRAIN DONATED TO THE BRAIN BANK!! I WANT MY BRAIN DONATED TO THE SPORTS LEGACY INSTITUE A.K.A THE CONCUSSION FOUNDATION. If you go to the concussion foundation website you can see where there is a spot for donatation. I want my brain donated because I don't know what happened to me and I know the concussions had something to do with it.

Please please please give me the cheapest burial possible. I don't want anything fancy and I want to be cremated. Once cremated, I want my ashes spread in the timber on the side hill where I shot my 10 point buck. That is where I was happiest and that I where I want to lay. Feel free to spread my ashes around the timber if you'd like, but just remember on the side hill is where I would like most of my remains. I am truly sorry if I put you in a financial burden. I just cant live with this pain any more.

I don't want anything expensive at my funeral or what ever it is. Please please please I beg you to choose the cheapest route and not even buy me a burial plot at a cemetary. . . I also do not want a military funeral. If there are color guardsmen or anyone else at my funerial or whatever you have I will haunt you forever.

I want levi to keep playing clash of clans on my account. I am close to max have spent a lot of time playing that game. Though you think its stupid, I ask you keep playing it for me when you can and let my fellow clan mates know what happened. My phones passcode is 111111, so that's six 1's. . .

Levi gets my car, it will need a oil change and breaks/tires done her shortly. Please take care of old red. It will need cleaned out as well because I am a slob.

Thank you for being the best family in the world. I will watch over you all and please take my last wishes into consideration. Do not do something I do no want. Just remember, I don't want a military funeral like grandpas. It is my last wishes and last rights.

I am with the lord now.

—Look, Im sorry every one for the choice I made. Its wrong and we all know it.

November 13, 2015

Zac Easter texted his girlfriend shortly before 10 a.m.

"Can you call me when you get out of class? I'm in hot water right now and idk what to do"

He typed as he drove, weaving Old Red, his cherry red 2008 Mazda3, down the wide suburban boulevards of West Des Moines. He'd already been awake for hours, since well before sunrise. At 5:40 a.m., he texted Ali an apology: "Sorry about last night." Then he started drinking. By now he was shitfaced and driving around the suburbs. She called as soon as she got out of class, and he was slurring his words. Ali was scared. She wanted him off the road. She talked him down and into a gas-station parking lot, and then he hung up.

"Do not leave," she texted back at 11:27 a.m.

Ali Epperson was nearly 700 miles away, at her contract-law class at the Case Western Reserve University School of Law in Cleveland. In football terms, Zac had outkicked his coverage: Ali was an ex-cheerleader but no vacant princess. She had a diamond stud in her left nostril and a knifing wit. They were a pair of scrappers whose jagged edges fit. Zac loved Trump; he kept a copy of *Trump: The Art of the Deal* in his bedroom. Ali was a budding progressive: a first-year student at a good law school who'd interned at Senator Tom Harkin's D.C. office. They were just friends in high school; she used to cut fourth-period music class to hang with Zac. After they graduated, they became more than friends.

Sometimes he called her Winslow, her middle name, and only Winslow knew the full extent of Zac's struggles in the five and a half years since high school: the brain tremors that felt like thunderclaps inside his skull, the sudden memory lapses in which he'd forget where he was driving or why he was walking around the hardware store, the doctors who told him his mind might be torn to pieces from all the concussions from football. She knew about the drugs and the drinking he was doing to cope. She knew about the mood swings, huge and pulverizing, the slow leaching of his hope.

"I'm not leaving," he texted back.

"Promise?"

He pulled into a Jimmy John's and ate something to sober up, sending Ali Snapchats every so often to prove he wasn't driving. Then, a couple of hours later, he texted her again:

I'm home now. Don't worry about it

> Zac. You promised you weren't gonna drive.

Ok sorry Alison. For everything. Idk
what's happening to me, but I'm sorry
I brought you into it.

> Don't be sorry you brought me into it.
> I told you I'd always be there for you.
> I just want you to get better.

Idk if there is better for ppl like me.
Like I said before. If anything happens
to be just by a chance of luck. Tell my
family everything

Zac Easter went inside his parents' house, past the five mounted deer heads on the living room wall, past the Muhammad Ali poster at the top of the stairs ("Impossible Is Nothing"), and into his room: Green Bay Packers gear, bodybuilding supplements, military books bursting from the shelves, a T-shirt he got from his high school football coach with the words BIG HAMMER.

His laptop was open to a 39-page document titled "Concussions: My Silent Struggle." "MY LAST WISHES," it began. He'd created the document five months ago, and the final revision was made today.

Zac Easter grabbed some ammunition, packed up the .40-caliber pistol he'd given his dad as a Father's Day gift, and drove a few miles down the road to Lake Ahquabi State Park. It was a place where he'd gone swimming throughout his childhood; he and Ali liked to go there and lie on the beach and look at the clouds. "Ahquabi" is from an ancient Algonquian language. It means "resting place."

Around sunset, Zac took a picture of the lake, then he posted a status update on Facebook:

Dear friends and family,
    If your reading this than God bless the times we've had together. Please forgive me. I'm taking the selfish road out. Only God understands what I've been through. No good times will be forgotten and I will always watch over you. Please if anything remember me by the person I am not by my actions. I will always watch over you! Please, please, don't take the easy way out like me. Fist pumps for Jesus and fist pumps for me. Party on wayne!!;)

Growing up, his nickname was Hoad. On Saturday mornings, the three Easter boys—Myles Jr. was the eldest, then Zac, then Levi—would crowd around the TV to watch *Garfield and Friends*. Odie was the mutt—impossibly energetic, tongue wagging, ears flopping. Friends with everyone. That was Zac. "Zac never stopped running. Everything he did was at full charge," says his mother, Brenda. Over time the name evolved, the way nicknames do—Odie morphing into Hodie, Hodie shrinking to Hoad.

He was a sweet, curious kid, and seemingly programmed to destroy. He went through four of those unbreakable steel Tonka dump trucks—broke the first three and disassembled the fourth, trying to figure out how it worked. He was seven. One winter, the family couldn't figure out why the lightbulbs on the Christmas tree kept bursting. Faulty wiring? It turned out Zac was taking swings at the bulbs with a baseball bat. As he got older, the blast radius got bigger. He was Tom Sawyer reborn: unleashed, unbound Midwestern middle-class American *boy*. The Easter family's acreage was off a dirt road, surrounded by cornfields, just east of where *The Bridges of Madison County* was filmed, and Zac and his brothers would go on hikes to the creek, bringing along an artillery of Black Cat fireworks to blow up minnows and bullfrogs. As a teenager he graduated to the family's Honda Recon ATV, his first taste of real adrenaline and real recklessness. He'd fly through the woods, build jumps, and hurdle over them. "GODDAMMIT!" his dad, Myles Sr., would yell from the porch as he shot by.

Zac was fearless, certain of his invincibility, confident he could push his limits to the very edge yet always stay in control. He was perfect for the one thing that mattered most in the Easter family: football.

When Myles Easter Sr. talks about his own football career, there's a joyful worship of the sport's violent side: "I just wanted to knock the fuck out of somebody." He was a safety at Drake University, a small school in Des Moines. He and Brenda got together in 1982, soon after his football career ended, and they married two years later, which meant she was now married to football too. Before Zac was born, Myles took a job as defensive coordinator at Simpson College, a Division III school in Indianola, Iowa, a town of 11,000 known for an annual hot-air-balloon festival. He never made his boys play football—it was more like it was just assumed. "I loved football," he says. "I was getting to the point where I loved it more than the kids did back in high school." Not that the boys didn't love it too. They'd come to practice every day and hang off to the side with the kickers. On Saturday afternoons in the fall, they'd sneak up to the overhead track at Simpson College's century-old gym and listen to their dad's halftime pep talks.

The Easters were a Minnesota Vikings family, but early on Zac defected and chose the Green Bay Packers. Zac loved Brett Favre—he had the same swagger. Zac's elder brother, Myles Jr., was taller, faster, talented enough to earn a college football scholarship and a spot in his high school's sports hall of fame. Zac was shorter and slower, but he was the toughest son of a bitch on the field. "He was out there to fuck people up," says Myles Jr. "He was there to do some damage." He had a lot to live up to, and he wasn't born with what he needed, so in high school he secretly began taking prohormones, a steroid-like supplement banned in many sports.

It worked. "Zac was a thumper," his father says, standing in the family kitchen. "Of all the boys, he was the one who wouldn't show pain, who'd be fearless . . . He'd throw his head into anything. He was the kind of guy I like on defense."

Myles Sr. pauses, takes a heavy breath, and shrugs. On the mantel behind him is a picture of Zac sitting in the back of a pickup, cradling the ten-point buck. When he speaks again, his voice is a stew of pride and guilt: "He was my type of guy."

From "Concussions: My Silent Struggle"

I started playing youth football a year early in 3rd grade because my older brother was on the team and my dad was the coach. I started off playing the two positions that I played throughout my career, linebacker and full back. I remember being one of the hardest hitting linebackers ever since I started. You could even go back and ask some of the old players on the 49ers if you don't believe me because I'm sure they only remember me leading with my head. I even remember Austin Shrek's dad offering to buy him a PS2 if Austin would learn to hit as hard as me on game days . . .

I learned around this age that if I used my head as a weapon and literally put my head down on every play up until the last play I ever played. I was always shorter than a lot of other players and learned to put my head down so I could have the edge and win every battle. Not only that, but I liked the attention I got from the coaches and other players. I can look back and remember getting headaches during practice. Of course by now, I had gained the reputation from my coaches and classmates about being a tough nosed kid and a hard hitter so I took this social identity with pride and never wanted to tell anyone about the headaches I got from practices and games. In 6th grade, I really became a road grater as a fullback and running back. I was short and chubby, but I would try to run over the linebacker's every time I got the ball. I'm sure my parents still have the game tapes to prove it . . .

I won't lie I look back now and always felt like I had something to prove to my dad and trying to fill my older brothers football shoes . . . I was tired of teachers and even Principal Monroe comparing me to my brother and asking me why I wasn't as good of a student as my older brother. I guess I got to the point then where I just didn't care and realized the only way to fill adequate to fill the Easter family shoes was to play football . . . There was also the "Easter Mentality" stereo type that I had to live up to. This "Easter Mentality" is the name that all the other coaches and kids in sports called us because the Easter family was such a tough nosed football family and the reputation was that football was our lives and we would play through any pain. My dad was an intimidating hard ass football coach and the Easter mentality meant that we were supposed to always be tough as nails, show no weakness, and never get taken out of game for being hurt . . . [*From another journal around the same time*] I've never really felt good enough for him. I know the remarks he will say. Im sure he loves me but he's always had a hard time showing it. I feel like all my concussions were for him in the first place because I just wanted to impress him and feel tough. I regret all that now and wish I never even played sports.

Zac's football career ended in October of his senior year. The team at Indianola High School was a perfect fit for Zac: they were always smaller, always scrappier, and always played like the chips were stacked against them. Indianola had the lowest enrollment in a conference filled with schools from Des Moines's suburbs, but they took pride in not playing like it. When their head coach, Eric Kluver, had arrived years before, he quickly realized there was a gem in his own backyard: Myles Easter Sr., a veteran college coach who had three sons coming up in the Indianola youth football system and was eager to help. Myles was tough. So were his players. Kluver hired him.

At first Kluver tried to innovate with a speedy spread offense, but he quickly realized that wouldn't fly here; he simply couldn't get the type of athletes to make it work. So instead he went old-school: a smashmouth I-formation offense. Pound the ball and wear out bigger, faster, stronger—but softer—teams. It was catnip to Iowa country boys like Myles Easter Sr. Soon, things began to change for Indianola. Local fans would come to games just to watch the special teams tee off on opponents during kick returns. Kluver handed out a BIG HAMMER T-shirt for the most crushing hit in that week's game; Zac earned one his junior year and another his senior year. The Easter Mentality had become the Indianola football mentality.

By his senior year, Zac had become an anchor of the team's defense. On this chilly Friday night, the seventh game of the 2009 season, Zac was taking the field for the first time in a month. A concussion had knocked him out in the season's fourth game, but Zac was determined to be back for the game against league rival Ankeny High School. Ankeny was much bigger than Zac's school, one of the largest in the state, more affluent, and most obnoxiously, they were good. "We just thought they were kind of rich pricks," says Nick Haworth, Zac's best friend since preschool and an offensive lineman on the team.

Zac was fired up. Indianola's athletic trainer, Sue Wilson, was not. She'd been hired in 2005, and her focus was concussions; this was the same year that Bennet Omalu, a neuropathologist in Pittsburgh who studied the brain of deceased Pittsburgh Steelers star Mike Webster, had published his groundbreaking paper "Chronic Traumatic Encephalopathy in a National Football League Player." Even now, in 2009, she was a mostly unwelcome presence on the sidelines. Parents yelled at her when she took away their sons' helmets in the middle of a game; they wanted them to play. So did the coaches.

On this Friday night, Wilson was already focused on Zac. He'd always played through pain. He'd already suffered two concussions in as many months: one in August, before games started, during a tackling drill at a full-contact football camp, and then another during a game in early September—the one that sidelined him for a month. By now, Myles Sr. had grown concerned enough about the repeated head injuries that he'd ordered a special Xenith helmet. The helmet was supposed to reduce the risk of concussion, but it kept falling off Zac's head during games. He was also wearing a cowboy collar to protect his neck. He was armored up, like a soldier heading into battle.

Prior to the game, Zac had passed Wilson's concussion protocol, but if she'd known what was really going on inside his brain, there's no way she would have let him near the field. After the concussion during the game in September, a teammate told Zac that he was looking at him cross-eyed. Later that night, he would write in his journal, "I saw a doctor and lied about all my concussion symptoms."

Of course he lied. It was his senior year. He wanted to play.

From "Concussions: My Silent Struggle"

The truth was I had severe headaches every day and constantly felt sick or dizzy, but the tough guy in me told them I was still totally fine. I remember leaving some of my classes because I would be feeling sick and sitting there soaking myself in sweat. Around this time is when I started feeling depressed. I felt ashamed that I was hurt and had to sit out . . .

I finally got to play in the next game against Ankeny . . . Even my friends noticed that week that I wasn't as willing to hit as hard and I would actually shy away from contact. During the Ankeny game I remember the first play of the game is when I got my bell seriously rung . . . I went head to head with the running back at full speed on the first play during a quarter back rollout to try and run him over. I could of ripped through the running back and made a sack, instead I wanted to punish this running back on the first play and get inside his head. Instead he got inside of mine, I never pulled myself out of the game though and Chia told me that during halftime he remembered me trying to take a knee in the locker room and I fell over because I was so disorientated and I couldn't get back up without a friend helping. Ofcourse I told him I was fine and showed no weakness.

It wasn't long during the 3rd quarter when my helmet came off during a play and I guess I hit a guy without a helmet on, head to head. The next play I shit canned a pulling guard and that's about all I remember. From what I was told I could barely get up and wasn't able to walk off the field on my own.

It happened away from the ball, so the collision that ended Zac Easter's football career can't be seen on the game tape. But on a third-quarter drive, you can tell that No. 44 is suddenly missing from Indianola's defense. And later in the game, at the bottom of the screen, Zac can be seen on the sidelines, arguing heatedly with someone: Wilson, the trainer. She is clutching his helmet. He wants to go back in. No way, she says.

What happened in the moments just after Zac's final play remains burned into Wilson's memory: two teammates pulled a player off the ground and dragged him toward her. She couldn't tell who it was until she saw the jersey number, 44, and her heart dropped into her stomach. Zac's feet were barely under him.

"Sue, he's not right," one teammate told her.

"I looked at him, and he looked at me, and he just didn't say a word," Wilson says now. "I took his helmet. And he just put his head down. He started crying on the bench. I walked away to give him his space. I came back and asked him if there's anything I could do. He just said, 'No. I just don't feel good.' I said, 'Are you going to get sick?' He said, 'I don't know.'"

She kept an eye on him the rest of the game. He could still speak. He could still stick his tongue out. He wasn't vomiting. His head was pounding, but he didn't seem to be in need of urgent medical attention. In the locker room after the game, Haworth says, Zac's blue eyes had drifted into a haze—"a thousand-yard stare."

Wilson ordered Zac to rest for the next week. No football, no exercise, nothing. But Zac ignored her. By this point, he'd figured out that exercise was the only way to ease the pounding in his brain, so he'd run on a treadmill—sometimes an hour, sometimes two. He knew his football career was over. No one had told him yet, but he knew it. Still, he needed to stay in shape for wrestling season.

About a month later, though, he was still exhibiting symptoms. When he saw Wilson to get cleared for wrestling, she wouldn't sign off.

"I'll never forget the look in Zac's eyes when I told him he wasn't going to wrestle his senior year," she says now. "I think his exact words were 'Fuck you.'"

From "Concussions: My Silent Struggle"

Something changed in me after that last concussion against Ankeny. My depression kicked into full gear and I started having symptoms of anxiety. My emotions have never been the same after the last football concussion either . . . I love my family to death, but I felt like I was snapping on them for no reason some days and I could see that somethings I said were hurting them. It just seemed like anything and everything would want to set me off . . . [At college] I kept going out on the weekends and drinking my ass off though and using any drug I could find . . . I started drinking and getting so shitfaced I often started pissing the bed and started to have my drinking problem come back. Some nights I would tell my friends and roommate I'm busy and sit in my room and drink alone. Before my senior year [of college] started I also got a prescription of Adderall because I thought I had adhd. All I did was start abusing the Adderall right away. When I picked up my first prescription

I went home and snorted several lines . . . It seemed the only I could get myself to seem smart and outgoing was to be high on amphetamines from the Adderall.

I feel like I've started to become delusional or I've been kind of hearing and seeing things. A few times I've gone down stairs and have asked the guys what they wanted because I sware I heard someone calling my name. A lot of this freaked me out because I'm not sure if I was going schitzo or not. I've felt like some days I've just been out of it. Over the years I've been starting to forget peoples names and just forget daily things. My roommates even joked about an alzhiemers commercial about an old lady losing her shit because I've felt like I've lost mine slowly.

My impulse control problems have been killing me a lot lately to. I can't seem to get a grip with my money spending habits. I used to be a tight ass and all about money, but now I just find myself spending all my money and money that I don't even have. I think I've spent about 10k in the past three months and nothing to show for it. I cant seem to stop binge eating unless im on Adderall. I don't know if I have that brain decise that people talk about or if I really am crazy.

On the night of his 24th birthday, Zac Easter and his cousin met at the Sports Page Grill in Indianola, ordered Coors Lights, and waited for Zac's parents to arrive. Zac was nervous. His cousin could hear it in his voice. By this point, June 2015, not quite six years since his final football game, he'd become convinced that his five diagnosed concussions (plus countless more that weren't) across a decade of using his head as a weapon had triggered his downward spiral.

"I've noticed I'm relying on drugs to try and be who I want to be," he wrote in his journal around this time. "I need to stop, but at the same time I'm like Fuck it. I won't lie, I feel kind of scared and depressed bout my future. I found some info online about CTE and got scared. I'm not looking at that stuff again."

Meanwhile, Zac's parents believed their son was on top of the world. He'd just graduated from college with honors. He was a star in the Iowa National Guard—he won a Soldier of the Year award for his unit and was short-listed for Army Ranger school. He turned it down because the war in Afghanistan had become so dangerous. Inspired by *The Wolf of Wall Street*, he'd made a get-rich-soon pact with his elder brother, Myles Jr. They'd pound their fists on their chests, like Matthew McConaughey in the film. He'd grown closer with Ali, their on-again-off-again relationship inching toward something real and special. A full life awaited him.

But what his parents saw—the degree, the girlfriend, the job, the stability—was a mirage. Yes, he had just graduated from college, but he'd also just told his first employer, an annuity-and-insurance marketing company, that he needed time away from work. When he was making sales calls, he would forget what he was talking about midsentence. It got so bad that he even wrote himself a two-page script to get through a call.

When his parents arrived for his birthday dinner, Zac took an anxious swig from his Coors Light, gathered himself, then told them he needed to talk. "Something's been going on with my head," he began.

From there, he laid it all out: He was quitting his job because he needed to focus on his health. He was often tired and dizzy and nauseated. During college he used to set his alarm for 3:30 a.m. to work out and run for hours; now he would go for a jog, feel sick, and only make it 1.4 miles in 20 minutes. He got headaches all the time. Sometimes while driving, he'd go into these trances; he'd snap out of it when he drove his car into a curb. Panic attacks came without warning. He had started writing down a long list of questions for his doctor; one of them was "Do you think I'm showing signs of CTE or dementia?"

In fact, he already knew the answer to that one. He had just visited a doctor who specialized in concussions and who told him that, yes, he very well might have CTE. He had started seeing a speech pathologist to help him manage his cognitive struggles and improve his memory, attention span, language-processing abilities, and problem-solving skills.

His parents were stunned. They knew some things were off. Sometimes on the phone it sounded like Zac was talking with marbles in his mouth. And they'd noticed that his bank account was suddenly hemorrhaging money. But mostly they just assumed their son was a young man grappling with adulthood and independence.

But now he was telling them that he might have a mysterious brain disease that afflicted NFL players, haunting them for decades after their careers had ended. One psychologist even told Zac that he would—not could, *would*—end up penniless, homeless, and in a mental institution. Zac had walked out of that guy's office terrified.

Myles Easter Sr. had seen the news reports of ex-NFL stars whose lives unraveled post-retirement and ended in suicide. Mike Webster, Andre Waters, Dave Duerson, Junior Seau—the Sunday gladiators who once were the apotheosis of all that he worshiped about the game of football. But Myles never really believed the disease existed. To be honest, even the mention of it kind of disgusted him. CTE was an excuse, he had always thought: a bunch of millionaire athletes who had it made, blew through all their money, fell out of the limelight, got depressed, then killed themselves. But now, hearing his own son—still just a kid, no jaded pro, someone who had never played a day of football above the high school level —say that he might have CTE?

"It just caught me so off guard," Myles Sr. says. "I was honestly dumbfounded."

The dinner table went quiet. Then Brenda, Zac's mom, broke the silence.

"Well," she said, "let's fix it."

Zac Easter's Journal

June 2015

Even with two 30 mg Adderall in me about another 10 mgs I poored out and snorted, I still got lost all around Menards and the dollar store . . . IDK what it was but I felt like I kept walking all around the store and passed what I was looking for several times. I straight up felt confused on what I was looking and kept forgetting even right after I looked at my list . . . I only went for like 3 things to. I guess [my speech pathologist] is right, I only have about a 3 minute memory after that I'm fucked. I even took three wrong turns on the way home. Shit happens I guess.

July 2015

I wish I could put a finger on what is wrong with me. Its either from the concussions or Im just bat shit crazy. Im tired of feeling emotionless or too many emotions. Im trying to find a new hobby but nothing really quite makes me want to do it. Tomorrow I meet w/ Spooner [the concussion specialist] about everything to me, theres just NO way those concussions didn't change me. I think I might just donate my brain and let them figure it out.

August 2015

I still havent been working or looking for work. I got put on Zoloft and my new psychiatrist seems to know his meds. I'm still fighting the side effects. Sleep has been dismal and I've still been going to speech therapy and PT. It sounds like they really arent on my side anymore and they want me to be focusing on my mood disorder. I cant really blame them. I have been fucked up with depression the past few weeks. I've been going out more but using more drugs. Smoked pot a few times, rolled on Molly and now I got some coke. All that plus Adderall fuck it! Its the only way I feel normal

September 2015

Im scared if I can't get help or feel better I may want to just end it all. As in suicide. Im just so tired of feeling so shitty and anxious. I had a job interview, two of them and its hard for me to not have panic attacks. It seems like I still cant get over my anxiety. IDK lifes just a bitch. Im try to forget about that fact that Im mentally ill and that I might have a traumatic brain disorder. I plan on going home tonight so hopefully I'll be able to talk to my rents a little more. I might even move home next month if I cant get some income coming in . . .

I just got my Adderall script and started snorting it right away! Im going to try and leave it home when I go home so I don't use it all. Physically my heart rate is still always nuts whether I'm Adderall or not. I'm trying to work out but its just getting harder each day.

Friday, November 13, 2015. 1:34 p.m.

Text exchange between Zac and Ali.

I'm sorry you fell in love with a guy with a ducked up brain.

You can't choose who you fall in love with. You just fall in love.

True. Sorry you chose me
when I'm scitzo lol

Like I said before. If anything happens to be just
by a chance of luck. Tell my family everything

You're gonna be ok. And of course I'll tell
them but nothing is gonna happen

Friday, November 13, 2015. 5:30 p.m.

Zac Easter stood on the dock leading out onto Lake Ahquabi, pistol in hand, ignoring the calls that had started pouring into his cell phone a few minutes after his Facebook post. Instead, he opened Snapchat and posted a photo of the lake: "God bless America," he typed.

The third time Ali called, he picked up. She heard terror in his voice. "I can't do this," he told her. "It's never going to get better."

A friend recognized the lake from the Snapchat photo. Deputies from the county sheriff's department rushed to the state park while Ali tried to keep Zac on the phone. "Listen to the sound of my voice," she told him.

"I'm losing my mind," he replied. "This is it for me."

Then a pause, a shift in tone: "Ali, did you send these cops here?"

His phone died. Ali sent him a frantic text at 6:12 p.m.: "Baby its my Winslow jist talk to me. I need to know you're okay."

Out on the dock, Zac pointed the gun at the sky and fired: a warning shot to tell the police to keep away.

Zac's father, alerted by friends, sped his pickup truck into the park, down the hill toward the lake. The first sheriff's deputy he saw recognized him. More squad cars raced into the parking lot. Another deputy—a former all-conference linebacker for Easter Sr. a few years back—pointed an assault rifle at his son. Lasers from police rifles danced on Zac's body. It was past dark and getting cold. Myles Sr. peered inside Zac's car. He saw an empty six-pack of Coors Light, an empty bottle of Captain Morgan, and a pill bottle.

Floodlights illuminated Zac. The sun had set on the far side of the lake, dropping a black curtain on the water behind him. He stood up from a picnic table and walked wordlessly down the pier toward a wooden fishing hut at its edge. A few more steps and he'd be inside, alone on the water, out of sight.

"Put your gun down!" the deputies shouted.

"Nope!" Zac yelled with an anguished laugh. "Not gonna do that!"

His father realized with a flash: *Zac wants the police to shoot him. I can't let this happen.* He sprinted down the wooden pier. "Zac!" he shouted.

If he shoots me, he thought, *he shoots me.*

"Dad, stop!"

"Nope, I'm coming. Put your gun down."

Zac laid the gun down, then disappeared inside the hut.

Seconds later his father reached the door. Inside, he saw a sad, sick look on his son's face. His vibrant boy was gone. Zac looked worn-out. Beaten.

"Dad, I'm in trouble," Zac said quietly.

Myles Easter Sr. spoke gently to his son. "I don't know what's going on, but we'll get this figured out. But we gotta get through this part right now. We're in deep shit. We can't make it any worse."

Back on land, the deputies surrounded Zac and eased his wrists into handcuffs. They put him in the back of an ambulance, drove him to Des Moines, and checked him into Iowa Lutheran Hospital.

Seven hundred miles away in Cleveland, Ali was still in limbo, panicked, convinced Zac had hurt himself. Before he hung up the phone, his voice had gone flat. For 62 minutes, she had no idea if he was dead or alive.

Finally, a text popped up on her phone. Zac's elder brother: "They got him."

December 5, 2015

They took all the guns out of the house. They took all the alcohol out of the house. They were constantly on edge. Myles Sr. and Brenda encouraged Zac to go to his therapy appointments, and he would—but then he'd sit in the parking lot and have a panic attack and never leave his car. He went to Alcoholics Anonymous meetings, but then he'd wake up in the middle of the night after a bad dream and start drinking from a whiskey bottle he'd hidden in his room.

Something had shifted inside of him. No longer did he worry that he might be going crazy; now he was *certain* of it. Fatalism swept over him. He told his mother he'd made a bucket list: Things to Do Before CTE Takes Away My Mind. Travel overseas. Camp in the timber in winter. Hike across the country, or at least through Colorado. Go rattlesnake hunting on the family's land.

On the sixth anniversary of the day Zac bagged his ten-point buck, Myles Sr. decided to take his son hunting. Perhaps they could recapture some of the tranquillity of those days. They got up before sunrise, ate bacon and eggs, and got in the truck.

It's a 40-minute drive from their house to the family's timber, a good time to talk. They sipped coffee. Myles told his son that he was proud of him, that Zac was smart and talented and successful. He said they would fight through this as a family. "I'm sorry about the concussions from football," he told his son. "I didn't understand it earlier." Zac didn't want his dad feeling guilty. He told him that he loved football. He told him he even missed football.

They got out of the truck. Zac watched his dad pull the shotguns out from behind the seat, where he'd stashed them away. Myles Jr. met them and they hiked into the woods. From the tree stand Myles Sr. was heartened by the sight of his boys together, walking down the hill, laughing. Today, at least, Zac seemed like his old self. "I thought maybe we were getting better," Myles Sr. says.

They hunted till after sunset. On the ride back home, Myles Sr. picked up a six-pack of Coors Light tallboys for them to split. Zac's mom wouldn't have liked this—alcohol, she knew, only made his problems worse—but hell, Myles just wanted things to go back to the way they used to be with his son. As they rumbled home on the gravel country roads, Zac turned to his father. "This was one of the best days I've had," he said.

They fell asleep next to each other in the living room, watching Iowa play Michigan State in the Big Ten championship game. It was a tough, ugly defensive battle, the exact kind of football game they loved.

December 7, 2015

Brenda Easter came home to find Zac's car gone from the driveway. She called Ali, catching her in the middle of an exam, and Ali texted Zac.

Where are you babe?

I'm ok and I'm in Oklahoma ;)

He told her he'd been feeling cooped up at his parents' house, thinking about losing his mind, and he needed to get away. So a few hours earlier he'd gotten in the car and just started driving. He was headed for Oklahoma, then turned around and started making his way back; after a wrong turn he wound up in Kansas City and got a hotel room for the night. He joked to Ali that he was going to hit a strip club, but all he did was sit in his hotel room and order pizza. The next morning, he made the three-hour drive back home.

Friday, December 18, 2015. 8 p.m.

Myles Sr. was in the upstairs bathroom, covered in blood. He'd taken their two dogs hunting in the woods behind the house, and Tito, the fat white rat terrier, had killed a possum. Tito was squirming in the tub when Zac walked in. He'd just gotten a haircut for family pictures the next day.

"Boy, you sure look good," his dad said, grinning.

"You're in deep shit if Mom sees that," Zac said, looking at the blood-soaked dog. Myles asked him for a hand, so Zac held the dog in place while he finished washing off the blood. Then Zac disappeared into his bedroom. Ali was home for winter break and she'd invited him out with friends that night, but Zac declined. He was feeling down and didn't want to be around people. Myles turned the dog loose, then went downstairs and fell asleep on the couch.

Five weeks had passed since Zac's suicide attempt. Next week —the day after Christmas—Zac was heading to California for a facility that treated both alcohol addiction and mental illness. But Zac wasn't sure he wanted to go. He didn't see the point.

Saturday, December 19, 2015. 12:24 a.m.

Ali was still out with her friends at a bar in downtown Des Moines when a text arrived from Zac.

"Thank you for everything," he wrote. "You've helped me through so much and never ever blame yourself for anything. I love you and will always be over your shoulder looking after you no matter what. Always keep having fun. Always remember me. Always keep striving for greatness or shall I say first female president. Never quit fighting for what you believe for ;) I love you Winslow"

Ali wrote back immediately: "I love you, too babe but that sounds so past tense and is making me worried. I don't want you to talk that way . . . Are you okay. Please be honest. I can call you"

No reply. She called him, but he didn't answer. Called again. No answer.

"Seriously zac," she texted. "I'm worried now. I know you're having an off day but it will be okay—I know you have the fight in you, Please talk to me"

No reply.

"Zac. Please talk to me"

Back at the house, Myles Sr.'s ringing phone woke him up. It was his eldest son, asking if Zac was upstairs. Myles Sr. went up to Zac's room, but it was empty. He noticed a frayed piece of notebook paper on Zac's bed and went back downstairs to get his glasses.

Ali texted Zac again: "Baby. It's winslow. Please think of me please talk to me. I believe in you. I know you're upset but please talk to me"

No reply.

"I need you to text me back"

Myles Easter put on his glasses and read what his son had scrawled on the sheet of paper.

"Please!" it began. "Look on my computer and print off my story and last wishes to everyone. PLEASE FULLFILL MY last wishes! My comp pass zacman (all lowercase)"

The 20-gauge shotgun that Myles had given Zac for his 12th birthday was missing from the backseat of his truck. One hollow-point 20-gauge Winchester slug was missing from Myles's ammunition cache in the basement. Brenda's keys weren't in the kitchen, and her car wasn't in the driveway.

By the time Myles got to Lake Ahquabi, a patrol car was already there. "I'm sorry," the deputy told him. His son's body was in the parking lot, the 20-gauge slug torn through his chest.

Four Days Later

Eric Kluver stood over his former player's casket at the cavernous Catholic church in Indianola. Kluver loved all his players, but this wasn't just one of his players. This was Zac Easter. His top assistant's son. Every summer, Kluver picks hardworking students in need of extra cash to help him with his landscaping business. Two summers in a row, Kluver picked Zac. It wasn't even that long ago. Now Zac was in a casket.

Is this my fault? Kluver kept wondering. He and his staff had always taught Zac proper tackling technique, of course . . . but they never discouraged his aggression. If anything, they'd encouraged it. Zac was the model—the type of hard-nosed player every football coach dreams of. And yet Kluver knew that football had played a role in Zac's destruction. Football, and football culture.

When Kluver played high school football, one of his best friends suffered a brain injury after a big hit. He wound up in a wheelchair and later died. During a practice in 2008, when Kluver was already well into his career at Indianola, a sophomore line-backer named Joey Goodale absorbed what seemed like a normal hit on a kick return and smacked the back of his head on the turf. A few minutes later, he collapsed. He was unconscious, his body rigid. Zac Easter was there on the field that day, watching his childhood pal get loaded into an ambulance. Goodale was in a coma for three weeks. He spent months in a rehab facility. He never really recovered. He's 23 now, lives with his parents, works at UPS and unloads trucks at a local grocery store, and has struggled with addiction.

Kluver could always set those two memories aside and keep going. Those were accidents. But with Zac, this was no accident. This was football. "To see him lying in that casket," he says now, "you would think that would be enough to make you say that enough is enough."

And yet. Months later, Kluver would lead his team onto the field for their first game of the 2016 season. After the game, he would retreat to his windowless office in the bowels of Indianola High School, the redbrick walls covered with posters of all the teams he's coached, the three Easter boys and their father pictured in nearly all of them. In the hallways of the school, he'll still see an occasional BIG HAMMER T-shirt. He stopped giving them out a few years ago, when it started to feel wrong.

Kluver still believes in football. He believes there is more good that comes from the sport than bad. He believes life is full of risks, and that we should not pad our children with bubble wrap. But his faith is rattled. When he hears of what Zac wrote in his journal —that he wished he'd never played football—Kluver squeezes his eyes shut and puts a hand to his forehead.

"I've seen both ends of the spectrum," he says. "All the great times and the big wins, but I've also been attending funerals. There's definitely been times where I've said, 'Is this worth it?'"

Two Weeks Later

In the kitchen, Brenda Easter's aunts sit at the table writing thank-you letters to people who attended Zac's funeral. In the living room, under Zac's mounted ten-point buck, his father, his mother, his elder brother, and Ali sit in a semicircle. There aren't many tears now; they are trying to move from mourning into doing something. Start a foundation in his honor, speak to football players about the risk of concussions, push the NFL to take the risks more seriously.

But in the living room, the television is on mute, tuned to

Vikings-Packers. January football. Huge game. Hated rivals, the NFC North title on the line. The men in the house, including this reporter, peek at their phones checking fantasy-football scores.

Brenda and Myles Sr. and Myles Jr. are talking about how Zac's suicide must not be in vain, about how they must use his name to push for awareness and research into concussions and CTE. They plan to send Zac's brain tissue to Omalu, the pioneering neurologist and inspiration for the Will Smith movie *Concussion* (which itself was based on an article in *GQ*). They've found the diaries, and they've read as much as they could bear. They're going to do what Zac asked. He left instructions.

Four Months Later

"Here's what I do, and this is terrible," Myles Easter Sr. says, standing in his kitchen, his voice low so his wife in the next room can't hear. "I'll drink like 18 beers maybe on a Tuesday night. I make sure I don't drive. I'll drink a fifth of vodka or something."

It's a breezy spring afternoon. Myles is wearing a chain around his neck with a metal pendant—a reproduction of Zac's thumbprint. Zac's ashes are in an urn on the mantel. In a few weeks, the Easters will get the medical report back from Omalu's lab, confirming what Zac already knew: CTE. The official diagnosis brings with it a peculiar kind of relief.

But now what?

Zac left instructions: Print his story off his laptop, post it to Facebook, use the pain of his life and too-early death to warn the world about CTE. Get people like us—football fans, football players, football lifers—to face the truth about people like him.

And now we have. Those were his instructions, so that's what his family did. So now what?

We could ban football. (But we love football.) We could allow people to play football only once they turn 18, which is what Omalu has proposed. (And what happens when 18-year-old athletic phenoms—freight trains who have never learned to tackle properly—are suddenly turned loose on one another? Is that *better?*) We could take away tackling. (Sorry, no one's watching the National Flag Football League.) We could build a safer helmet. (Which will only encourage players to use their heads as weapons.) We could have a consistent concussion protocol through all levels of football. (We already do in the NFL. Ask Cam Newton how well it's working.)

Every solution ends up not solving enough of the problem.

And for most of us, this is perfectly okay. The paradox of CTE's discovery is that it's given most of us a sneaky ethical out, hasn't it? No professional football player can claim now to be unaware of the risks. It's a free country. We're all adults here.

Unless we're not adults. Unless we're kids, like Zac was. Can we really let kids keep doing this? If so, how? Now what?

After Zac's suicide, Brenda wanted the entire family to get counseling, but Myles Sr. declined. "Fuck, I don't need no counseling," he said. He doesn't cry for his son. He wants to do something for his son, so he can be able to say, "Zac died for *this*." But in the meantime, he drinks a few beers. He takes the dogs on walks. And then after his wife goes to sleep, he stands alone in the kitchen, and he drinks some more.

"That's how I deal with it."

To my family,

I just want everyone in my family to know that I love them dearly and to not dwell on my death. I have been thinking about this for years now and there is truly nothing anyone could have done to prevent this.

I ask that you do not feel guilty or blame each other! Do not blame football or specifically anything that had to do with me. Just know that I enjoyed playing through it and after fighting through it all, I still consider myself to be one of the toughest people I know. IT IS NOT YOUR FAULT. I love all of you and hold no grudges. If only you all knew how guilty and ashamed I feel for taking the easy way out.

Mom and Dad. I love you both dearly and I am truly sorry that one of your sons has passed before his time. I loved both of you dearly and there is nothing you could of done parenting wise to prevent this. I know that both of you will mourn naturally over the loss of your son, but just know that I am in a place where I am free of the pain.

CHRIS BALLARD

"You Can't Give In": Monty Williams on Life After Tragedy

FROM SI.COM

THE LOW POINT came last March. Or maybe it was April. Monty Williams isn't sure. Time blurs.

For two weeks Micah and Elijah passed the stomach flu back and forth, as five- and eight-year-olds do. They threw up on the carpet, in the bed, on the bathroom floor. Everywhere but in the toilet and the trash can. Finally one night, well after midnight, they combined for a particularly messy episode. As his three teenage daughters slept in nearby rooms, Monty—who'd spent a lifetime in basketball, first as a player and then as a coach, most recently as an assistant for the Thunder—stumbled out of bed and herded the boys into the shower, then into clean pajamas and back to sleep. Next he cleaned the rug, scrubbed the tile floor, and disinfected the toilet. He longed to go back to bed but knew Ingrid never would have left the sheets to sit overnight in the laundry room, clumped with all that sickness. Which meant he couldn't either. He'd promised the kids nothing in their day-to-day lives would change. If anyone's life was going to change, he'd said, it would be his.

So at 2:30 a.m., Monty trudged downstairs and out the back door into the cold Oklahoma night, where he hung the sheets over the fence. As he hosed them down he shivered and stared up at the sky, feeling lost. He was supposed to be sleeping next to his wife, or watching film, or on the road with his team.

Instead he was here, alone and overwhelmed. *How in the world is this my life?* he wondered.

The morning of February 9, 2016, began like so many others. Monty awoke at 7, still groggy from the previous night's flight back from Phoenix, where the Thunder had beaten the Suns. Ingrid was already downstairs, conquering the morning. They'd been together 26 years, through five kids and eight cities, and he remained in awe of her. While many NBA wives contracted out the more mundane duties of parenting, Ingrid would not consider hiring a cook, a cleaner, or a nanny. On game nights she bundled up the kids and brought them to the arena, but only after their homework was done. Then, at the end of the first quarter—sharp—they'd file out, because Dad may be an NBA coach, but nothing overrules bedtime.

On this morning Ingrid was out the door by 7:15, trailing five clean, neatly attired Williams children between the ages of five and 18, all of whom unfailingly addressed adults as Sir and Ma'am. She spent the rest of the day driving from this day care to that high school to this basketball practice to that doctor's appointment, in addition to making her regular stops at the church and the center for inner-city kids, where she volunteered.

So when Monty didn't hear from her that evening, as she returned from Faith's basketball game, it didn't strike him as strange. He was preoccupied anyway, at home preparing for the next Thunder opponent as Lael, his eldest, watched TV on the couch with Elijah.

Then, around 8:30, Lael's cell phone rang. It was Faith, calling her sister. Monty saw Lael's face fall.

This is what the police know: a little after 8 p.m., Ingrid was driving north on a four-lane road in downtown Oklahoma City in the family's SUV with Faith, then 15; Janna, 13; and Micah.

A sedan driven by a 52-year-old woman named Susannah Donaldson approached from the opposite direction. During the preceding hours, toxicology reports would show, Donaldson had taken a substantial amount of methamphetamine. Police also believe she may have been cradling a dog on her lap. By the time she approached the 1400 block of South Western Avenue, she was in the left lane, going more than twice the posted limit of 40. She swerved to avoid the car in front of her, sending her vehicle across the center line. Impact with Ingrid's SUV was head-on. Donaldson and the dog died at the scene. The Williams family was rushed to a hospital.

In the days that followed, local TV reporters stood by the road, grim-faced, noting the dark burn marks staining the asphalt, the spray of glass, debris lying on the side of the road. The newscasts showed photos of Ingrid and Monty together, her face frozen in that familiar smile, and her at a Thunder game. Interviews rolled with NBA coaches and players. They are difficult to watch, warned a reporter.

Monty clung to the fact that the children all survived, and without life-threatening injuries. For a while it seemed Ingrid might too, but the following afternoon she slipped away, at the age of 44.

Friends and family descended. Ingrid's parents drove through the night from their home in San Antonio. Clippers coach Doc Rivers, who'd played with and later coached Monty, canceled his vacation to fly in. Monty's pastors from Portland and New Orleans arrived. Gregg Popovich, his longtime mentor, reached out immediately. Charlie Ward, Billy Donovan, Sam Presti, Avery Johnson, Tim Duncan: they visited, called, texted. Anthony Davis and Ryan Anderson, players he was close to on the Pelicans, in town to play the Thunder, came to the house to sit with him. So many people sent flowers that Ayana Lawson, the Thunder's director of player services and appearances, finally contacted local florists and requested they send the gifts to one of Ingrid's charitable causes. Even so, Shaquille O'Neal managed to have a white orchid the size of a small tree delivered.

Monty couldn't process all of it. He knew people meant well, but he just wanted everyone to leave. Either that or to flee himself. Frustration and anger consumed him. The Lord could do anything. So why hadn't he moved that car? Why couldn't he have made Ingrid leave 10 minutes later, or a second earlier or a second later? Why did three of his kids have to suffer through that?

As a player, he used to hear Rivers tell him the same thing, over and over: "Get past mad." But that was basketball; this was different. Now a lot of people were mad. Rivers certainly was. He wanted to prosecute someone. Seek justice. The other woman was the one who stole a life. How could you not be mad?

Monty focused on just making it through the memorial service, on February 18. Then maybe he'd take the kids and bolt to some state where no one knew him. Wyoming. South Dakota. Just hunker down and disappear.

First, though, he had to survive the week. He wished Ingrid were there. She'd know what to do. She always had.

They met in 1989, at a freshman mixer at Notre Dame. Monty was tall and skinny, with short hair and sleepy eyes. She was tiny, with dark hair, an electric smile, and catlike brown eyes. Different, that's the word Monty comes back to. The girl drinking water instead of beer. The one not afraid to talk about her faith, right off the bat, but who never proselytized. To be on the outside who she was on the inside.

So what did Monty do? Like an idiot, he acted too cool, trying to play the role of the big-time hoops recruit. He even tried to set her up with a buddy instead. "Can you believe it?" he says now. "Dumb old Mont."

But he knows that's who he was then: dumb in so many ways. He'd grown up in Oxon Hill, Maryland, outside D.C., a neighborhood where, as Monty says, "you could either hustle and sell drugs or just not have." Often, the Williams family didn't have. His parents split when he was seven—Monty says he has "no real relationship" with his father. He was raised by his mom, Joyce, a strict, devout woman who worked as a data entry clerk. Sometimes she wondered about her only child; give the boy lunch money and, to her consternation, he'd often give it away to another kid who had none, then come home hungry. Still, he was well-liked and grew into a formidable small forward, fluid and athletic, averaging 30 points and 16 rebounds as a senior and leading Potomac High to the Class AAA state championship. He also graduated with a 4.0. "Never saw that boy take a bite of food without blessing it first," says his coach, Taft Hickman. "Even at McDonald's."

And yet Monty says he was putting on an act. Inside he was prideful, self-critical, and prone to bouts of darkness. He spoke of faith but his was, he says, "nominal at best." When adults weren't around, he cussed up a storm. And when he prayed, what did he pray for? An NBA contract and fast cars.

For a young man who could go days without seeing a white
face, who barely read a book a month, Notre Dame was a shock.
Plato, genetics, philosophy, calculus? He just wanted to play ball.
He failed his first test, then the next, then the one after that, after
which he called his mom to say that maybe Notre Dame wasn't for
him. Joyce wasn't having any of it. She hung up.

And if it weren't for Ingrid, he might not have lasted in South
Bend. But a few weeks later he saw her on campus and did the
smart thing: apologized. The next time they saw each other, at a
party, they spent the whole night talking.

Next came joint study sessions. Though really, it was more like
Ingrid teaching Monty how to study. Lay your books and notes in a
semicircle, left to right. Prioritize. On breaks they took long walks
around campus. She told him about her brother and her parents,
blue-collar folks who worked in the automotive industry back in
Michigan. She became his anchor in an unfamiliar world. Slowly,
his test scores rose. It would be the first of many times she would
save him.

His new teammates couldn't believe it. Who gets to college and
immediately falls for a girl? What a rookie move. Monty didn't care.
He knew this was someone worth holding on to. Ingrid wanted to
take it slow. One afternoon he asked for a good-bye kiss after she
walked him to practice and she pecked his cheek. A few days later
she tippy-toed up to do it again and Monty pivoted.

The ensuing months were some of the best of Monty's life. Neither of them had much money, so date nights were at the dorm.
Pizza from the basement snack bar, Corn Nuts and soda from the
vending machines, then sit and talk. That summer he stayed on
campus, while Ingrid went back home to Michigan. They wrote
letters, hers arriving in envelopes covered in colorful drawings.

At the time he was just a smitten 18-year-old. It wasn't until later
that Monty would realize that he hadn't just met the love of his
life at Notre Dame, but he had discovered all the things he would
become, through her. He'd joke about how his players got sick of
him talking about Ingrid all the time, using her as an example,
over and over. How when he met new players for the first time,
he introduced her even if she wasn't there: "Hi, I'm Monty and
you'll meet my wife, Ingrid." But who else was he going to talk
about?

*

The day of the memorial happened also to be the NBA trade dead-line. So Sam Presti, the Thunder general manager, told the rest of the league that he had his own deadline, at 1 p.m., an hour before the service. He ended up dealing two players that day, D. J. Augustin and Steve Novak. Both still showed up with their wives at Crossings Community Church, along with nearly a thousand others. Ingrid's life—their life—was there in the pews. Family and friends, of course, but also women from the ministry where she volunteered. Local police. A contingent from the Spurs, including Popovich, Duncan, and David West, who flew in on the team plane even though they played later that night in L.A. Their opponents, the Clippers, were also represented, led by Rivers, his son Austin, and Chris Paul. And on it went: Jeff Van Gundy and Brett Brown and P. J. Carlesimo and Kevin Durant, along with the whole Thunder organization. Members of the Pelicans—the team that fired Monty as coach less than a year earlier—folded themselves into a row. "Tallest funeral I've ever seen," says pastor Bil Gebhardt.

A little after 2:30, Monty walked to the dais, wearing a black suit and tie, his shaved head gleaming. At 6-foot-8, and still fit at 44, he looked young enough to be a player. He placed a folded coach's card, containing some notes and scriptures, on the lectern. Then he took a deep breath and looked up.

Van Gundy wondered if it was a good idea for Monty to be speaking publicly. Monty had long been a pessimist, given to de-spair at times, and this could be too much. Others wondered if—even hoped that—he would condemn the other driver, as a coach calls out a player.

Monty had promised himself he wouldn't cry, the way he had the night before during the run-through with his family. "I'm thankful for all the people that showed up today," he began, his voice deep and more powerful than he expected. "It's a pretty tough time, not just for me but for all of you as well. I'm mindful of that."

He looked around the room but his only audience was his five children. He needed to show the way. "This is hard for my family, but this will work out," he continued. "And my wife would punch me if I were to sit up here and whine about what's going on. That doesn't take away the pain. But it will work out because God causes all things to work out. You just can't quit." He paused, looked around. "You can't give in."

*

You can't give in. How many times had she told him that? Like on that day in the doctor's office during his sophomore year, only a few weeks after Hickman had called to tell Monty that he was hearing he might be a first-round pick—not eventually, but next year. Now, Monty listened to a doctor tell him he had hypertrophic cardiomyopathy. A thickening of his left ventricle. Irregular heartbeat. Potentially fatal. All Monty heard was No more basketball. Not now, not next year, not ever.

Anger and depression consumed him. He pulled away from his teammates, his coaches, even Joyce. He got in fights. Punched through walls. He thought about transferring or dropping out, and at one point he even entertained the thought of taking his own life. For the next two years he became, as his mom says now, "not the nicest person" and "a different child."

Throughout, Ingrid was the one person who calmed him, "the one person I didn't want to hurt, no matter what." To leave school, or worse, would mean leaving her, and he couldn't bear that. If anything, they spent more time together: walking the campus, past the lake, stopping to pray at the Notre Dame Grotto. "The Lord will heal your heart," she told him, and something about the way she said it—so confident—made him believe her. So he poured himself into prayer, if for desperate, selfish reasons.

Ingrid's faith was different, though. Never convenient, never for show. Every week she disappeared for hours at a time in the afternoon. Finally, he asked where. So she brought him along and Monty watched, confused, as Ingrid spent two hours at a nursing home with a woman named Helen, one he was pretty sure was suffering from Alzheimer's. Ingrid brushed Helen's hair, talked with her, bathed her. As an athlete, Monty had been taught to perform charitable acts for the camera. But here was Ingrid, a young black woman, caring for an old white one, not for the cameras or a pat on the back. When he asked Ingrid why she did it, she looked at him funny. Wasn't this what Christ taught us to do? Monty was floored. "It was so real, and raw," he says.

For a while he accompanied her. Began to find his faith becoming more authentic. And then, in 1992, a Notre Dame trainer told him about an experimental test to determine if he could play with HCM. So he flew to the National Institutes of Health in Bethesda, Maryland. Five days of poking and prodding led to a final, frightening test. *We're going to stop your heart on purpose,* the doctors told him. *Trigger an arrhythmic episode. If it doesn't go well, it could kill you. You and your mom need to sign this waiver.*

What choice did Monty have? In his mind, there was no Plan B. For two years he'd gone against doctor's orders, working out furiously and playing in pickup games. In his mind it was basketball or nothing. Besides, he wasn't afraid of death. Or maybe, he'd later realize, he just didn't understand it yet.

Five doctors stood around the bed, just in case. Hours passed. Monty drifted in and out of consciousness. When he awoke, a doctor warned him not to sit up, or a vein could burst. Then he said there was something Monty should know. He was okay. Not just okay, but great. He could play ball again.

Monty sobbed. He had his life back. And can you blame him if his pride returned with it? He averaged 22.4 points and 8.2 boards for the Irish in 1993–1994. After the Knicks picked him 24th, he spent his money on cars and lived like the big star he always thought he'd be.

But Ingrid? She never changed, not really. She told him the cars were a waste of money; "you can only drive one at a time," she'd say. They'd gotten married after his rookie season then moved city to city—five teams in nine years as a player. When he got the head job in New Orleans, she was eight months pregnant with Micah and yet she seamlessly integrated into another community. Players like Anthony Davis later described her as a "second mother." Along with Monty, she spoke to inmates, distributing copies of "Look Again 52," the Bible study book they'd written together. They worked at a shelter for abused kids, donated shoes and equipment to the poor. In the off-season they went to South Africa with Basketball Without Borders.

Monty stresses that Ingrid was by no means perfect. She could be stubborn and headstrong. She could cut you down with one look. She was a loud talker, Monty always reminding her that "Hey honey, I'm sitting right next to you," to which she'd fume, because he was supposed to be listening to the message, not the delivery. And good luck changing her mind once she was set on an opinion. But all Monty knows is that when people have praised him for things in his life, it's usually Ingrid who was his ballast. Like in 2013, when Gia Allemand, the girlfriend of Ryan Anderson, committed suicide, and Ryan was the first one to find her, at her apartment. Hysterical, he called Gia's mom, then the police, and then, as Ryan says, "the one person I knew in New Orleans that would be there for me no matter what." Monty arrived to find Ryan on the floor, a mixture of sweat and tears. The coach dropped to his knees, unsure what to do, and began hugging Ryan, rocking slightly.

When Monty finally got him into his truck, he thought about how he couldn't mess this up—how these are the tests that really matter. Back home, Ingrid had already taken control. She'd moved the kids upstairs and put them to bed, with instructions not to come downstairs for anything. After her own brother's unexpected suicide in 2003, she knew that the only thing to do was just be there for Ryan. So she and Monty sat with him in the family room, praying. When it got late and Monty tried to come to bed, she redirected him: No, you're sleeping downstairs, right next to Ryan. And so he did, on a mattress next to the couch. When Ryan wanted to talk, they talked. When it was quiet, it was quiet. Monty followed Ingrid's advice: just listen.

Just listen. That Monty could do. It's what he'd done as a Trail Blazers assistant, after Nate McMillan hired him in 2005. Monty's was the door that was always open at the team hotel. He was the coach who had players over for dinner. The guy sharing his own mistakes. Because that's how a real connection grows.

To ask people around the league about Monty is to have your calls returned immediately, to have people cry on the phone, to hear a string of testimonials. Durant, who worked with Monty for a season in Oklahoma City, says, "He'll hate that I say this, but he's the best man that I know. And that's no slight to my dad, my godfather, my uncle, or any coaches that I've had." For Durant, lots of men have tried to fill the role of mentor. Most had lots of advice; few wanted to listen. Fewer still shared the hiccups in their own life. "Monty listens, allows you to vent," Durant says, "but then he'll bring you back in and keep it real with you."

Which is why when Durant needed advice last summer, while trying to decide whether to sign with the Warriors, he called Williams. A man most recently employed by the team he was considering leaving. (Williams didn't try to sway him: "The only way I could help was to say, 'Look, don't let anybody else make this decision for you. Your family or your boys or your shoe company. It's your decision.'")

Says Durant, "I was on the phone with him the second I made

the decision, right after, right before. A lot of people keep their mind in this basketball bubble and he looked at the whole life. He was there for me as a friend first."

All those people who flew out for the service? Maybe you're starting to understand why. They'd come to support Monty and to honor Ingrid's life. Still, most had no idea what to expect when he spoke.

Watching in the audience, Presti tried to keep it together. He had been the first to receive a call on the night of the accident, awoken at 2 a.m. by the hospital pastor. Presti had first met Monty in 2004, when they were both with San Antonio. Both men had moved on but, as with so many, remained part of the Spurs family. So Presti had thrown on some clothes and hurried to the hospital. In the hours to come, he'd sit with Monty all night, rubbing his back so hard that "it was like I was trying to start a fire." Throughout, Presti thought about everyone he now represented and how he felt "a huge amount of responsibility to make sure I was handling this the way Pop would handle it. This was on my watch, and I had to live up to the standard that Pop expects of us all. I had to fulfill an obligation that's much greater than basketball." In Monty's case, his indoctrination to the Spurs had come in 1996, when San Antonio traded for him, hoping for scoring. ("Turns out he couldn't shoot a lick," says Popovich.) He and Pop didn't get along at first. Monty chafed at Pop's tirades, thought he deserved more playing time, more touches. Pop saw him as a role player. Pop also noticed a darkness to the young man. "He was kind of a Debbie Downer, always expecting the worst to happen," Popovich recalls.

Still, Monty responded to the Spurs' culture. Bible study with David Robinson and Avery Johnson. Postgame parties at Sean Elliott's house. In particular he bonded with Duncan, the player he would come to hold up as the standard as a teammate and a leader. A man who became so close with the Williams family that he coined a nickname for Ingrid on account of how she juggled the kids and everything else, and always put Monty in his place: Legend.

Then, before the 1998 season, the Spurs let Monty go. He ended up sitting on his couch in June, crying as he watched San Antonio celebrate the first of five titles, filled with regret. In the years that followed, Monty and Popovich stayed in touch. Despite what Monty may have thought, Pop always liked the young man, thought he was intelligent and a hard worker. "And we're always looking for those kind of guys," says Popovich, "because you can't teach intelligence and it's pretty tough to get someone to have a work ethic if they don't already have one." So when Monty called him in 2004, despondent after bad knees had forced him to stop playing, Pop encouraged Monty to come hang out around the team. See if you like it. Soon enough, Pop slapped a label on him: coaching intern. Meanwhile Pop, a sucker for projects, pushed Monty to take chances, try new stuff. He introduced him to different foods, talked to him about politics, and reveled in cursing around Monty, who never cusses. ("That's his way of saying I love you," Monty explains.)

Monty learned what so many others already had. Once you joined the Spurs you were in for life, as long as you operated by certain principles. It was never about you. Pay it forward. Basketball is important, but not as important as family and relationships. In June 2005 the Spurs won their third title, the one that had eluded Monty as a player. As the confetti fell, he stood behind the bench, part of the team but still feeling like an outsider, when he felt someone tackle him from the side. He turned to see a grinning Pop. "You got one," Popovich shouted. "You missed out before, but now you got one."

Funny then, that Monty's most important game as a head coach, on the last day of the 2014–2015 season, was a win over Pop's Spurs that put the Pelicans in the playoffs. Afterward, as players celebrated and Ingrid brought the kids onto the court, Pop and Monty embraced at midcourt. It felt like a crowning moment.

It'd be easy to see it as karma of sorts: good things happen to good people, right? But in this case, not long after the Pelicans lost to the title-bound Warriors in the first round, Monty was fired. That same day, a TV reporter knocked on Monty's front door. Monty came out in a T-shirt and spoke for four minutes. He said a lot, thanking the city for its support and the ownership for the opportunity, but one line stood out. "Life's not fair," Monty said. "Don't expect it to be."

And now here was Monty, a guy who always expected the worst, confronted with about the worst situation imaginable. Yet he stood up on stage, projecting calm as he built to what he termed "the most important thing we need to understand." That's what drew the millions who would later watch video of the speech. What led to all those packages and letters, the ones that continued for half a year, flooding the Thunder offices. What led Popovich to decide that he needed to show the eulogy, in its entirety, to his players.

"Everybody's praying for me and my family, which is right," Monty said, left hand jammed in his pocket like an anchor. "But let us not forget that there were two people in this situation. And that family needs prayer as well." He paused. "That family didn't wake up wanting to hurt my wife.

"Life is hard. It is very hard. And that was tough, but we hold no ill will toward the Donaldson family, and we"—he made a circling motion with his right hand, indicating the whole room—"as a group, brothers united in unity, should be praying for that family because they grieve as well. So let's not lose sight of what's important."

Not long after, he wrapped up with a simple message: "And when we walk away from this place today, let's celebrate because my wife is where we all need to be. And I'm envious of that. But I've got five crumb-snatchers that I need to deal with."

Monty paused as some in the crowd chuckled. "I love you guys for taking time out of your day to celebrate my wife. We didn't lose her. When you lose something, you can't find it. I know exactly where my wife is."

As he left the stage, Monty didn't notice the reaction in the room, or if he did, he doesn't remember it. But those who were there describe a stunned silence. "He was saying to us what we should have been saying to him," says R. C. Buford, the San Antonio GM. David West turned contemplative. "We always talk about physical strength, but it's nothing compared to mental and emotional strength," West says. "You realize your own deficiencies, because I don't have that type of courage or strength or fortitude to stand as courageously as he did in that moment." Later, on the plane ride home, Popovich told West and Duncan that it would be "years before we understand the totality of that moment." Says Popovich now, "I was in awe. I could not believe that a human being could muster the control and command of his feelings and at the same time be as loving and magnanimous."

The theme at the heart of the speech—forgiveness—was simple, and not unique. Still, the effect was profound. Maybe it was Monty's delivery; it felt sincere. Maybe it's because, right or wrong, we don't always expect such empathy from professional athletes. Maybe it was that, for a message steeped in faith, it never felt preachy. In the weeks that followed, video of the memorial spread, and the reaction was immediate. Oklahoma City staffers made pins embossed with w7—that's what people always called the Williams family. Donations poured into Faithworks, the nonprofit Ingrid believed in so much, from strangers, from a half-dozen teams, from players Monty had never met.

Meanwhile, concerned friends offered help. All those people he and Ingrid had poured into over the years? "Now we all wanted to pour back into him," says Durant. His phone beeped constantly, only Monty didn't want any advice or help. On the exterior, he may have appeared strong, and in control. Inside, he was falling apart. He just wanted everyone to leave.

Everyone who loses a loved one processes grief differently. Some focus on coping mechanisms. Disbelief. Denial. Others become disorganized, acting out of character and making rash decisions. Still others try to "intellectualize" the loss, analyzing the situation leading to a loved one's death in intricate detail. To Monty, the world lost its grays; everything was either pitch black or blinding white. One moment he was fine; the next, a tiny thing would set him off. His appetite disappeared and sleep became impossible on many nights. He wanted to lash out, even feared that he'd hurt others. So he did what he'd always done and closed up, turning away from the world to only his family. After all, he and Ingrid had never needed help before. He didn't need it now.

Friends worried.

"I got this," he told Popovich.

"No, you don't have this," Pop answered. "You're going to have days you're pissed off and want to punch a wall, and you have to let it go. And other days when you'll be more together and in both situations you're going to need people, and friends and mentors, and it's okay, it's okay, you're not a f— island."

Still, he tried to go it alone. He woke at 5:30 for Bible study, then he got the kids up and was out of the house by 7:30. He wandered the aisles of the grocery store, in search of the darn bread. Fought with the laundry. At 11 he picked up Micah from nursery school, and then he was with the kids all afternoon, driving around Edmond, Oklahoma—to basketball, track, school, plays, doctors. He could handle breakfast and lunch, but many nights, dinner was Chick-fil-A. By the end of the day, he was so exhausted he'd fall asleep by 9:30.

Meanwhile, people kept saying he needed to take time for himself. It made him mad sometimes. Time? He didn't have time. And what did that even mean, anyway? What was he going to do, go get a massage?

The nights were the worst, once the kids were in bed but before sleep took hold. That's when the darker thoughts emerged. Popovich remembers talking to him in such moments, and how Monty sounded "like a wounded animal."

Many days Monty fought the urge to check out. And he might have if it weren't for Ingrid's voice in his head. Just take care of the kids. Just take care of the kids.

How in the world is this my life?

The pain and confusion never goes away, this is what Monty's learned. But it does recede. It's now January of 2017, and he ticks off the milestones. The first birthday without Ingrid, the first Thanksgiving, the first graduation. All that's left now is the anniversary of the crash itself.

It's a warm afternoon and he's driving back from practice in San Antonio, where he moved the family in June, to get away from the memories in Oklahoma City and to be closer to Ingrid's parents. He is back with the Spurs for the third time, now as executive VP of operations—"basically a job I made up for Monty," says Pop. He doesn't travel, so he can be home at night. After practices he can often be seen playing one-on-one with Duncan, whose friendship has been instrumental in helping Monty regain some sense of normalcy. Eventually, Pop just gave the two of them their own lockers in the coaches' room, next to each other.

The final month in Oklahoma City wasn't easy. He got through it on his faith and the generosity of others. It was Lawson, coming over to do the stuff that bewildered him, taking the girls shopping for bras. It was Presti and coach Billy Donovan, checking on him, and Pop calling, and Ingrid's parents, and Pastor Bil, reminding him that, "grief is the price of love." It was Tonja Ward, an old friend, pushing him until he hired a cook, to ease his burden.

Teams had reached out about coaching vacancies, and the kids had pushed him to get back into it, thinking it would make their dad happy. But it was too soon.

In August he'd lived a dream, serving as an assistant for the U.S. Olympic team. Upon returning from Rio, he developed something resembling a rhythm. Exercise to work out his anger. Focus on being a dad. Work toward being ready to coach again. Be okay delegating: to a cook, a cleaner, his in-laws.

To visit his home now is to enter a whirl of activity. There are the two boys, running outside to shoot hoops in the driveway, Monty stopping Micah—"Put some socks and shoes on, dude!"—and then turning to Elijah. "What do I always tell you?" Monty asks.

"Do. Not. Dominate him," Elijah responds. Monty nods, makes him repeat it again.

In the kitchen Faith makes herself a snack. Ingrid's mom, Veda, stops by—Monty says she has become his best friend over the last year. She brims with life, just like Ingrid, laughing and hugging and ribbing Monty because, after all these years of giving her grief, suddenly he's drinking coffee. (The Spurs' sports science people told him it was good for him.) Monty lets out the family's dog, a border collie named TZ.

To walk the halls is to see memories everywhere. Just off the entrance, a large framed picture of Monty with a grinning Popovich in the back of a limo while wine-tasting in Napa with friends, another of Pop's attempts to force Monty to liven up a bit ("You're not gonna order iced tea, you're gonna sit at dinner and try the damn wine and sit and talk with us"). Photos of the family line the walls. All seven of them, most in white, at a picnic in Oklahoma City. Monty and the kids, in the Turks and Caicos, their first vacation after Ingrid's death. He leads the way to his study. A tiny blue pair of Micah's shoes rests next to other mementos: nerf rims Elijah has broken, all-district plaques from the girls, Ziploc bags containing first lost teeth. A collection of framed photos of Ingrid occupies one corner. Next to it is his wedding ring. For a while he wore it, then put it on a chain around his neck. But that began to feel wrong. He's 44 with five kids. He has half his life ahead of him. He knows he won't stay single forever. She'd be upset if he did.

He puts on a good face, but talking about what happened, as he does over the course of the next three days, often pausing for minutes at a time, remains difficult. "I just couldn't understand it," he says. "And never will. But my faith in God never wavered. Just, sometimes your faith and your feelings don't line up."

He tries to put the grief in its place, as Pop always advises him to do. Compartmentalize. Still, he sometimes texts her, even though he knows she won't respond. Other times, he looks up, thinking she'll walk around a corner. "I can't say that I feel her presence. I just see so much of her in the kids and so many things remind me of her," Monty says. Sometimes he goes outside and talks to her. "And I don't even know what that's about. I just—I'm not grieving for her, you know. She's in heaven, she's with the Lord, she's like, balling right now. You grieve because you don't have what you had."

Moving forward, for Monty, means returning to the bench. He thinks he's ready, that it will center him. Indeed, he'll start getting more calls. In March, after making it through the first anniversary of her death with the help of friends, he'll turn down the top job at Illinois, wishing to focus on the NBA. People around the league will say it's a matter of time—perhaps by the time you read this story—until he's offered a head coaching job.

It will be weird, coaching without her. She was his sounding board, "his battery pack," as West puts it. But that's the reality of loss. You never fill certain voids.

Besides, he's still learning from her, even now. For example, Monty hates candy. Has ever since he suffered toothaches as a kid. So he made a rule: no candy in the house. Still, every once in a while, he'd be cleaning and find a bag of Snickers or M&Ms. "What's this?" he'd ask the kids. They'd hem and haw and finally one of the girls would answer. "Mom lets us have these when you're gone."

When he'd confront Ingrid, she'd stand her ground, as she always did. "Back off," she'd say. "They need to live."

Now if you go into the kitchen and open the cabinet, you'll find the stash. Lollipops and chocolate. It's a small thing, but it's something. They need to live. So he made certain Lael—the one everyone says is so much like Ingrid and who'd been a rock the week of the funeral, making medical decisions, caring for her sisters, and helping plan the service—went off to college at Wheaton, rather than stay home. And he guards against becoming too protective. By no means does he have it figured out, but he's trying.

That's why Monty hates when people call him a role model.

He's just a guy who's been tested, again and again. A guy trying to make it through, like all of us.

So maybe it's best to focus on Monty in the real, human moments, like this one. It's early evening and the winter sun is going down. The boys are getting a little crazy—"Dude, calm down," he yells. He still needs to check on homework, and pick up the bombs that the dog left out in the yard, and figure out what to do about the pool, which is on the fritz. He turns to a visitor, watching, and apologizes. "Sorry, man," he says. "I need to go deal with all this."

And so he does.

STEVE FRIEDMAN

Should Stop. Must Stop.
Can't Stop.

FROM RUNNER'S WORLD

AT 9:41 A.M., on July 27, 2001, Shannon Farar-Griefer jogged through a knot of cheering people in a pine forest clearing at the base of California's Mount Whitney. She had been running—and limping, puking, cramping, and crying—for 135 miles. After almost 52 hours, her feet were covered with oozing blisters. Five toenails were black.

Like most runners who tackle ultramarathons (any race longer than 26.2 miles), Shannon had endured without complaint, though she didn't like the bats swarming above her at night. But she had a knack for suffering, even by the standards of ultrarunners, for whom stoicism, if not masochism, is a way of life.

All of the 71 Badwater 135 ultramarathon competitors had started at Death Valley—at 280 feet below sea level, the lowest point in North America—and the 55 finishers (Shannon was 38th) had ended the race here, among the pines, at 8,300 feet. But Shannon wanted to keep going. Before race organizers, park officials, and, one imagines, commonsense concerns about death and liability conspired to shorten the course in 1990, Badwater had finished at the summit of Mount Whitney, the highest point in the contiguous United States. Some runners groused about overcautious race directors; Shannon, though, had her own idea. Now that she had finished the current course, she wanted to finish the former one. She intended to climb Mount Whitney, some 11 miles farther and 6,100 feet higher than where she stood.

Her plan would have been alarming under ordinary circumstances. With the threat of storms on the mountain, a ranger told her, it was out of the question. So she caught a ride to a friend's house in nearby Lone Pine to rest. Which to her meant popping blisters, gobbling veggie pizza, and checking weather reports. But not sleeping. It might be too hard to get back up.

At midnight she returned to what sensible ultrarunners call a finish line. And at 2 a.m., she started ascending the mountain. Roughly 24 hours later, she returned to the base. Waiting for her were her husband, Alan, and her boys, 11-year-old Moe and 8-year-old Ben. Ben was crying. He wanted to go home. He wanted everyone to go home.

She held him, stroked his head. She pictured the drive back home, lying down in the backseat with Ben, legs elevated, her battered feet hanging out the window. Instead, she slept a few hours at a hotel with Ben in her arms, her first real sleep in three days. Then she told her husband to get the boys in the car. She'd meet them later. She needed to do something. Ben was wailing: why couldn't she stop?

It would take years before she knew the answer. "In order to not feel pain," she wrote in a journal in 2015, a time when she began to make the sticky connection between what had happened to her as a child and her adult behavior. "I needed to find a place, a familiar place. A place I had to go . . ."

She watched her family drive away, then yanked three blackened toenails off her right foot, two off her left. She wanted to "double" the route—the entire original route—which meant that she had 135 more miles to go. She ran back toward Death Valley, back to where she had started.

Now 55, Shannon was born four months after her mother, Jackie, left Shannon's father. Jackie was 19, already the mother of an 11-month-old boy. She worked as a teller at a bank in Palm Springs and, for extra money, as a dancer for a television show with a handsome producer. His name was Yale Farar, and he and Jackie started dating when Shannon was three. When they married a few years later, Farar adopted Shannon. The couple then moved to the San Fernando Valley and had two more children, a girl and a boy.

When Shannon was 11 years old, the family took in an acquaintance. He was old and frail and told funny stories and asked Shannon about her schoolwork.

He stayed in the bedroom next to Shannon's. One afternoon when Shannon came home from fifth grade, he called to her to come into his room. He wanted to tell her a story. Shannon's mother had taken her little sister somewhere; her brother was playing outside.

The old man was in bed, on top of his bedspread, which was a dull, faded gold. She remembers that. And she remembers his thin plaid pajamas. She stood in the doorway, as he told the story, but he motioned her closer. Before long she was lying next to him, and his voice had lowered to a husky murmur and the story was making no sense. He put his hand on her stomach as he talked. She looked out the only window in the room. It was small and square, and if she had been standing she could have seen into the neighbor's yard, and maybe she would have seen her little brother playing outside, but all she could see was sky. She stared at it. As he was touching her, he touched himself too, faster until he grunted and became very quiet. Shannon kept staring at the sky. He told her to get up, and then he told her he loved her and that now they had a little secret and she couldn't tell anyone. No one would believe her, and someone might get hurt. As she was leaving, the old man reached into his bedside drawer, pulled out his wallet, and handed her a five-dollar bill.

It continued for months, until he left. She learned to focus on the sky, to take herself somewhere else. She wondered what she had done that caused him to do these things to her. She told no one.

Eventually the family moved to Northridge. Shannon's body started changing at 13. For a time she dressed like a boy to hide it, and avoided men. But by the time she was 16, she was frequenting television studio sets, where she was discovered by hard-core Hollywood partiers. Soon she was hanging out with producers and rock-and-roll stars, accepting invitations on private jets and yachts. She surfed at Malibu, drank too much, stopped eating, binged and purged. She worked as a salesperson at a Jack LaLanne Health Spa and took small acting roles on *CHiPs, Hunter,* and *Hill Street Blues.* She was 5-foot-2, weighed 90 pounds, drove a white convertible MG MGB, and smoked Marlboro Reds. Most nights started at clubs and ended at the house of a friend whose parents had a full bar. If her friend wasn't around, Shannon drank NyQuil.

She dropped out of school in 11th grade. At 17, her parents kicked her out, though Farar rented her an apartment around the corner, hoping it might help her settle down. Instead she found a boyfriend, a real estate mogul who drove a dark blue Mercedes-Benz 450. She smoked pot on a yacht with a movie star in his fifties. She watched a rock-and-roll idol inject himself with heroin.

She didn't tell her parents about the old man, she didn't tell the real estate mogul. She didn't tell the therapist she saw. She tried not to think about it.

Then she got a job selling a Velcro-like fabric, mostly to surf companies who used it for leashes, and soon she had landed some of their biggest accounts. Her boss called a friend and said that he had to come by and get a load of his new firecracker sales gal.

When Shannon met Alan Griefer, she thought, *This is the man I will marry. This is the man who'll give me children.*

This is the man who will save me.

A good wife looked pretty. She dressed nice. A good wife was a doting mother. A good wife did not spend her nights dancing with real estate moguls then knocking herself out with NyQuil.

Shannon took a professional cooking course at UCLA—a good wife cooked delicious and nutritious meals—and on the first day of class, the other students, all men, introduced themselves. "I'm Buck, and I've been studying in Tuscany," said one. "I'm Alfredo, and I've been working under a Michelin three-star chef in France," said another.

There was so much Shannon never could talk about. Now she had something she wanted everyone to know.

"I'm Shannon," she said, "and I'm getting married!" She returned from her honeymoon pregnant, and then three years after Moe, Ben was born.

Griefer worked in real estate, then started a credit card processing company. Times were good. He and Shannon each had American Express Black Cards. Together, they owned eight cars, including a Porsche 911 Carrera and a Ferrari. The family lived in a four-bedroom house on an acre of land in a gated hamlet called Hidden Hills, near Calabasas. They had a swimming pool with waterfalls, a fitness center, a barn, a screening room, and a guest cottage, where the housekeeper and the man who took care of Shannon's four horses lived. A lot of residents had horses. Many had screening rooms and wine cellars. Will Smith was a neighbor. So was Alex Van Halen and his family. And Howie Mandel. It was usually the wives who picked up the children at the elementary school just outside the gates. Shannon saw how young they seemed, how slim, how put-together.

Shannon was friendly, but she didn't speak much about her previous life—even with Griefer. She sometimes cut her time at the Mommy and Me group short, but not because everyone seemed to be dressed for the Academy Awards. She sometimes walked away because the women told each other secrets and talked about their pasts. She couldn't risk anyone discovering hers.

She started running when the boys were toddlers, to lose weight. She made it a mile, and a mile turned to three, then to six. She entered and finished a few 5Ks. She ran 15 miles sometimes. She entered more 5Ks and 10Ks and then half-marathons. She replaced her collection of crystal perfume bottles with race bibs and ribbons and medals. When she was 33, in March 1995, she finished the Los Angeles Marathon. It was her first 26.2-mile race.

Before she crossed the finish line, she would write in her journal, "I was a child of shame and pain, a high school dropout." After, though, "I felt free. I just found a new sense of 'me.' My life had changed that day; the once insecure, frightened girl is now a mom with two beautiful sons, a loyal husband . . . a freaking marathoner."

The next year, she became an ultramarathoner, finishing the Bulldog 50K in Calabasas. She finished it in 1997 and 1998 too. That year, she ran one 50-miler and four 50Ks. She ran another 50K and three 50-milers the next year, along with her first 100-miler. She discovered that when other marathoners started hurting at about mile 20, she started feeling better. What stopped other runners—blisters, twisted ankles, nausea—was no big deal to her. When she was sexually assaulted as a child, she had dissociated, taken her mind outside the window of the old man's room, into the sky. She used the same technique to manage the exhaustion and pain of her newfound obsession. That ability to dissociate allowed her to run distances most people would never imagine walking.

And it almost killed her. On September 25, 2004, Shannon

entered her sixth 100-miler, the Angeles Crest 100 Mile Endurance Run in Wrightwood, California. She vomited at mile 10. She tried to stay nourished by gobbling peanut butter, pretzels, and chocolate, and she drank water. Lots of water. By mile 20 she had stopped urinating and, though she didn't know it, was gaining weight. She was suffering from acute hyponatremia, or the rapid fall of sodium levels in the blood due to drinking too much water. Her kidneys were shutting down.

She passed out at mile 46. A runner roused her and ran with her the next two miles to a checkpoint / medical tent. After taking her vitals, the medical aide left to call for help. Shannon jumped up and ran into the darkness, back to the race. Nothing some water and snacks couldn't solve. She passed out again after less than a mile.

She woke up with IVs in her arms, electrodes attached to her chest.

A doctor at the Providence Tarzana Medical Center ER told her if she had spent 10 minutes more on the ground, she'd have gone into cardiac arrest. She was confused. "What's wrong?" she asked. "Didn't I run a good race?" She thought she was still at the race. "Where are the other finishers?"

Griefer and the doctor exchanged glances and walked away. While they were gone, Shannon considered what she'd do different next time. Start slower. Pace herself. Fuel more efficiently.

Her husband returned without the doctor, flanked by two serious-looking children. She didn't want to embarrass them, so she motioned her husband closer, where she whispered to him.

"Who are they?" she asked.

"Those are our sons," he said.

Two weeks later, a nurse from Ben's school called. The boy was complaining of stomachaches nearly every day. Shannon took him to a doctor, who suggested a therapist. Ben told the therapist that every day when his mother went for a run, he thought she might die. So for the next three months, instead of running her usual five or 10 or 15 miles in the mountains after she took the boys to school, she ran in the Bay Laurel Elementary School parking lot, for hours at a time, past Porsches and Bentleys, past pure-bred poodles with $200 haircuts. Sometimes she would look up and see Ben staring at her out his classroom window.

When she returned to the mountains, she approached training

like she had approached cooking class and marriage and selling fabric and partying. All in. That approach, and her remarkable endurance, buzzing energy, and striking good looks, brought her notice. SlimFast put her in commercials. Newspapers ran stories, magazines featured her in photo spreads. She was a regular on ESPN's *Cory Everson's Gotta Sweat,* which was pretty much what it sounds like. When she was put on bed rest while pregnant, she started a business, Moeben (named after her two sons), producing multihued arm sleeves for runners.

One of her neighbors, Stine Van Halen, asked Shannon to help her train for a marathon. Another neighbor asked the same thing. Then another, and another. More than a few had grown children, very wealthy spouses, and time on their hands. Soon Shannon was leading as many as 25 runners through the mountains that climbed from the border of Hidden Hills. Four days a week, anywhere from five to 15 miles. Everyone started out with a five-mile run. "Not to punish them," Shannon explains. "I just wanted them to see that being outside for an hour and a half wasn't going to kill them."

A few complained. A few stopped, said after a mile or so that they couldn't continue. Okay, Shannon said, barely slowing down, no problem. She hoped they'd all make it safely back home, out of the mountains, the wildcat-lurking, snake- and scorpion-infested mountains. That got them going again.

Shannon called the group the Calabitches, and that caught on, then they became the Hidden Hills Hos. Shannon was Head Ho, naturally. A woman who got dolled up beyond even Hidden Hills dolling-up standards was Posh Ho. The unassuming kindergarten teacher was Sweet Ho, even after she showed up one day with a new set of breasts. A woman who had been married to a well-known personality was Rock Star Ho. Another, always lagging behind the pack, was Back Ho.

Shannon told would-be runners they could join, and she would run a marathon with them, as long as they found a charity to run for, as long as they found sponsors and raised money. It seemed everyone who ran with the Hos even a single time finished a marathon.

Shannon was in her midtwenties before she told her mother about the molestation. Her mother cried, saying, "I wish I could take your pain." Shannon didn't tell Griefer. Certainly not the Hos, as much as she liked them. They wouldn't understand. How could they, with their wealth and grace and perfect lives? She didn't need to tell anyone, though. Not as long as she kept running.

In the autumn of 2005, Shannon felt an unusual burning sensation in her legs during the Javelina Jundred 100-miler in Arizona, causing her to drop out of the race. A few weeks later, she awoke just past midnight curled in a fetal position. Her legs felt like they were on fire. She didn't have sunburn, or any broken bones. She went to her computer. She found symptoms "that freaked me out, things I've never heard of and didn't want to know about."

She saw a doctor, who sent her to a neurologist. The neurologist sent her for a brain scan, and two days later she was back in his office for the results.

She and her mother, Jackie, sat while the doctor pointed at Shannon's MRI. Did they see those white spots? They didn't, not really. He told them they were lesions characteristic of multiple sclerosis, a rare and chronic disease in which one's immune system breaks down the protective covering of nerve fibers of the brain and spinal cord, replacing it with plaque, or "sclerotic" tissue. That in turn interferes with the transmission of nerve impulses, and it was almost certainly responsible for the burning pain in Shannon's legs.

That was December 2005. The first Saturday of 2006 she got out of bed and ran 20 miles. The next day she took the Hos for a 16-mile training run for the upcoming Los Angeles Marathon. If she had MS, how could she do that?

The next week, she was too weak to get out of bed. There was burning all along her right side. She felt like an elephant was sitting on her right arm.

Another neurologist, more tests. More brain lesions. It was early spring now and he would do a final round of testing in August, to be absolutely positive, but he was confident she had an aggressive form of MS and recommended starting treatment immediately. Some people with MS are relatively symptom-free most of their lives, while others suffer severe and/or chronic symptoms. Shannon would turn out to have the most common form of the disease, Relapsing-Remitting MS (RRMS), which is marked by attacks that include fatigue, numbness, muscle spasms, vision problems, loss of memory and attention, trouble breathing and swallowing, and impairment of motor function. The attacks are followed by periods of remission, when all symptoms sometimes stop. No one knows the cause of or cure for MS, or why most people with RRMS get progressively worse, or why some have more or fewer attacks than others.

The doctor wrote a prescription for Copaxone, one of a dozen or so drugs approved by the U.S. Food and Drug Administration for managing RRMS. He told Shannon she would have to inject herself daily, alternating between left quadriceps, right quadriceps, left arm, right arm, left hip, right hip, and abdomen. And she should be prepared for pain, redness, and swelling at the places she injected herself, as well as flushing, shortness of breath, and possibly chest pain.

Copaxone can reduce the frequency and severity of attacks, as well as slow accumulation of brain lesions. The MS Coalition, a group of independent organizations including the Multiple Sclerosis Association of America and the Multiple Sclerosis Foundation, advises starting treatment immediately after diagnosis and continuing indefinitely, unless side effects are intolerable or "a person is unable to follow the recommended treatment regimen."

Shannon asked what would happen if she delayed the shots and concentrated on eating a healthy diet and taking care of her body. What would be the risk in putting off the medication?

If she didn't take the treatment, the doctor promised, she'd be in a wheelchair in a year. She asked if he objected to her entering a footrace before the final round of tests. She didn't tell him the race she had in mind was Badwater. He said not only was it okay, he encouraged it. But what he said next worried her: it would probably be her last race.

Shannon decided to postpone starting Copaxone until she ran her third Badwater in July. Afterward Griefer took her and the boys to Bora-Bora for two weeks. Shannon wasn't sure if it was a reward for her grit, or a consolation for her disease, or even partly a celebration that by necessity she would be spending more time at home. After the South Pacific, she promised, she would start taking her medicine.

But at night, inhaling the scent of tropical flowers, listening to the waves, she wondered if she needed to. She'd just finished one of the toughest races in the world, for the third time, and felt okay. *Maybe there will be a miracle.*

There was, of a sort. Back home in Hidden Hills, late at night, just days before the final tests were to begin, Shannon woke Griefer. She asked him to go to the kitchen and bring her some jack cheese and sour pickles.

The MRIs and treatment would have to be postponed during the pregnancy.

When Jet was born in April 2007, Shannon stayed overnight in the hospital. "Are you an athlete?" a nurse said.

"Yes, why do you ask?" Shannon said.

"Because you just gave birth by C-section and your pulse is 38."

Shannon wasn't taking her medicine and she felt fine. She felt better than fine. She had nursed Moe and Ben till they were two, and she decided to nurse Jet for a long time too. She couldn't take Copaxone while she was nursing.

Eventually, when Jet was older, she started giving herself the shots. But she didn't like them. They hurt. They left welts, and made her feel run-down. They made her too weak to run. So she took them only sporadically. If she had a really bad attack, she could get an IV drip of steroids to reduce her inflammation and lessen the pain.

And so it went. Over the next 10 years, Shannon finished eleven 50-kilometer races, ten 50-milers, one 100-K, seven 100-milers, and three 135-milers, the longest events all through Death Valley, in large part without taking the medicine. Who said running didn't strengthen her immune system, and that running and a healthy diet hadn't helped slow down the MS? She wasn't paralyzed or in a wheelchair, was she?

Nicholas G. LaRocca, PhD, vice president of health care delivery and policy research at the National Multiple Sclerosis Society in New York City, allows that the disease affects different people in different ways, and each person copes with MS in their own way.

Shannon's friends are even more accepting. Record-setting ultrarunner Jenn Shelton says, "Shannon's decision is between herself, her sons, her doctors, and whatever god she believes in. But mainly it is a decision for herself. In her case her self-care seems to do as good a job as the best Western medicine money can buy. And when she is doing well, I'm happy for her. I'm not there to tell her how to manage her disease. I'm there to be her friend and listen when she wants to talk. I just love her. Even if she is a triflin' ho."

U.S. Olympic bronze medalist and record-setting marathoner Deena Kastor, another good friend, has privately suggested to

Shannon that she be more conscientious about her medication but won't judge. "She is an inspiration," Kastor says. "And she has touched more lives than she can imagine."

Everyone who knows Shannon says running makes her happier. She says she can't imagine living without it. And the National MS Society, which encourages exercise as a way to manage many symptoms of the disease, offers only this caveat: "Periods of exercise should be carefully timed to avoid the hotter periods of the day and prevent excessive fatigue."

Shannon has gone years without taking a single shot. She has run despite cramps and passing out and IVs. She has run even when she had difficulty swallowing. She has visited the ER so many times that she has lost count.

On one such visit, in October 2014, Shannon lay on a bed at West Hills Hospital & Medical Center, in the San Fernando Valley, gasping like a trout.

Doctors were confused. Her heart was fine. Her vital signs belonged to a serious athlete half her age. They thought the breathing difficulties might be caused by MS, but weren't sure, and wanted her to stay at the hospital, at least overnight. She said she'd rather go home. It was 11 p.m. A doctor asked if she knew what "AMA" meant. She did. Against medical advice.

In the weeks after, she caught up with three girlfriends, all ultrarunners. Yes, she told them, it was still on. Of course, she still wanted them to come. Hell, yes, she still thought it was a good idea. She'd entered and failed to finish four 100-milers in the past four years. But they knew she'd try this one, with or without them. So on July 28, 2015, in the height of a very hot summer, they met in Death Valley, at the hottest spot in North America, Furnace Creek. There, Shannon would run Badwater a final time—the last ultra of her life.

Jenn Shelton and Connie Gardner, another good friend, wanted to support Shannon in the race, to offer support and to assist in case of a medical emergency, which both believed likely. They thought Shannon wouldn't make it past the second checkpoint at 42 miles, at the tiny desert town of Stovepipe Wells, so they made plans to climb Telescope Peak that day while Shannon recovered in a motel room. Deena Kastor would drive from Mammoth Lakes and meet the gang on Wednesday.

Shannon started running at 8 p.m. on Tuesday, July 28. A month earlier she had suffered a bad episode of muscle pain and paralysis, and her left arm was numb and in a sling. She was 10 pounds heavier than usual, because of the three-day steroid drip she had received. She knew, she later wrote in her journal, "that I would soon have to detach . . . going to that place where I know I will endure 135 miles of pain." She knew she could do it. She had been doing it since "I was 11 years old when The Monster was about to attack."

More than 10 hours and some 42 miles later, after having vomited much of the night (while moving; it's a skill ultrarunners develop), she arrived at Stovepipe Wells with Shelton and Gardner. Kastor joined at mile 56. The women took turns running with Shannon, talking about children and marriage and love. Shannon still wore her sling. In it, she had a water bottle.

At mile 72, the third checkpoint, Shelton and Gardner had made peace with the fact that they wouldn't be climbing Telescope Peak. They, and Kastor, had learned not to be shocked at Shannon's absurd ability to endure. Still, they knew the limits of flesh. Shannon asked someone to pinch each of her toes, then stick a needle through bloodstained tape and squeeze out all the liquid. Shelton and Gardner retired to the van to doze. Kastor had headed out hours earlier.

Resting at the checkpoint, Shannon sat in a chair munching a veggie burger and fries, thinking. Running had cost her, she knew. The sprains and blisters, dehydration, and vomiting had been the least of it. It had cost her time, and that had affected relationships. Both of her husbands (she and Griefer were divorced in 2014; she remarried shortly thereafter and was divorced from her second husband last year) asked her to cut back to spend more time at home, and when she didn't, they weren't happy. She knew running had taken her away from her sons at times, even though she always scheduled it around soccer and Little League games, and it had been hard, especially for Ben, who is now estranged from Shannon. Moe, an avid surfer, says he accepts his mother's obsession; Jet has only known her during the time when she hasn't trained as often. She worries about them—especially Ben.

She also thought of all that running had given her. Keeping her fit, generating endorphins, those were far from the most important things. It had brought her friends. It had brought her community. Running had allowed her to block out the trauma of her past, a trauma that had given her the means to run through enormous pain. Running had given her a sense of worth, a sense of self. Before running, she'd been a daughter and wild child, then a wife and mother. Running was all hers. It was who she was. If she couldn't run . . . she couldn't even think of it.

Shannon knew that few people expected her to finish this Badwater. She knew how easy it would be to stay where she was, then drive home with her friends. She knew no one would fault her.

She got up from the chair.

I'm not the sick runner with MS, she thought. *I'm Shannon the ultrarunner!*

She climbed 18 miles, to Darwin, past huge faces of Hillary Clinton and E.T. (the extraterrestrial) bulging from the hillside. Sleep-deprivation had induced hallucinations. She watched a runner fall down, convulsing, while his wife shouted, "Open your eyes, open your eyes!" That wasn't a hallucination.

By mile 120, Shannon was weaving, and Gardner was pulling her off the road away from traffic, to the shoulder, where Shannon face-planted. Gardner woke her, scolded her, pulled her up.

At mile 121 Shannon turned onto Highway 395, a mile from the next checkpoint. She thought of her boys. Maybe this Badwater was less magnificent obsession, more self-destructive and selfish stunt. Profile in courage or idiotic delusion? Sometimes she wondered.

That's when she heard honking, and someone screaming. "This is your carrot, baby! You're going to make it!" It was Kastor, crying, dangling a bottle of champagne out a car window. She'd been following Shannon's progress by computer since she had left. When Kastor saw that Shannon had made it to mile 90, she drove back. "You're going to make it!" Kastor shouted again.

Shannon made it to the Lone Pine checkpoint by running a 10-minute mile on 122-mile legs. Sick, in her final Badwater, defiant, she crossed the finish line right after a cleansing rainstorm, slightly more than four and a half hours after she'd left Lone Pine. It was the fastest she had ever covered that leg of the race.

On a sunny fall day in 2015, Shannon listened to only a few words before she stabbed the "decline" button on the telephone panel in her gleaming silver Audi SUV. It was CVS on the line, telling

Shannon that her medicine was ready to be delivered. She had been hitting the decline button, off and on, for the past decade.

The story of her life, the way Shannon saw it, driving to her therapist's office in Encino, is one of fast times and forward motion, a rollicking saga of close calls and outrageous adventures. She's raised almost half a million dollars for charity. She started a successful business. Her photo has been in dozens of magazines. She's active on the event committee of the Race to Erase MS organization. She's done jumping jacks on national television.

She has suffered a few flare-ups of MS since finishing her sixth Badwater, which she decided wouldn't be her last one after all. She has been rushed to the ER a few more times. When she's feeling well, she doesn't stop talking or running, cooking, writing, driving, laughing—anything other than sitting still. During flare-ups, though, she is so weak she can't walk, so fatigued she can barely get out of bed.

A few days before her therapy appointment, she had seen a pulmonologist at Cedars-Sinai Medical Group in Beverly Hills who had diagnosed her with respiratory muscle weakness. When she told him she was planning to stop taking her medication altogether, he had said, "You are your own worst enemy. Athletes think they can outrun disease, but they can't. Even psychiatrists get depression, and when they do, they need treatment. You need to take your medicine."

Her current internist, Robert Goodman, MD, in Tarzana, is less sure. "She's got MS, but it's relatively quiescent," he says. "Her heart is strong, her blood pressure is okay." He's not crazy about Shannon running ultras, but doesn't see any real reason for her to stop. As for Copaxone, he adds: "I'm not that impressed with it —there's not much in the way of medication that really works for MS."

Shannon pulled into the parking garage at her therapist's office, clambered swiftly out of her SUV. She was cracking jokes, moving fast. Tonight she'd cook dinner for her mother and Moe and Jet. Her hazel eyes were flashing. She'd run five miles earlier. She's been talking nonstop for much of the previous three days. She'd been reviewing the same story with her therapist, Candice Slobin, for two years. Now she was in Slobin's office.

"You have said out loud, to me, that you're super-independent," Slobin said.

Shannon nodded.

"You've said, 'I'm not going to be dependent on other people or on medicine.'"

Shannon nodded again. In the past year, there had been a handful of times when she hadn't been able to get out of bed for days at a time. But when she could make it to her feet, she ran in the mountains. She tries to run five to 10 miles, five days a week. When she couldn't run, she walked. If she fell, she made sure to take a cane the next time, and she limped a shorter route. "But you are, right?" Slobin said. "You are dependent on others now?"

Shannon made a small noise. Running had given her agency, it had given her strength. And there was no proof that the Copaxone would slow her disease, was there? And hadn't she shown everyone what could be accomplished by just putting one foot in front of the other, over and over again? She was the one who helped others, not the other way around. Shannon would continue to run, she told her therapist, with medicine or without.

"Can I say something?" Slobin asked.

Shannon nodded.

"You are brilliantly capable of manipulating yourself out of acknowledgment of pain. What allows you to run are the psychological tools you developed as a child."

Shannon said nothing.

"Your gift has saved you," Slobin said. "But it has crippled your ability to deal with your disease."

She suggested that Shannon continue to attend running events, and if the medicine made it too difficult to participate, that she volunteer. She could be part of the running world without running.

"But people there have always seen me as a runner," Shannon said.

Now it was Slobin's turn to say nothing.

"Now they see me as a sick runner," said Shannon. "I don't want to be Shannon, the sick runner."

"But you are sick."

That's when Shannon cried. She would eventually find another therapist.

In the year or so since, Shannon moved to a different house in Hidden Hills, and has been working on a cookbook, a lifestyle book, and a memoir. She has continued to log 30 miles a week running (or walking or limping) in the nearby mountains. She has finished a 30K race, two 50Ks, and a 50-miler. When she finished the Javelina Jundred last October, "it felt like redemption." She started strength-training and receives regular massage and chiropractic care. She researched the connection between diet and inflammation, experimented with different spices. She only takes Copaxone when she has flare-ups, "which seem like they're shorter and farther apart." She says her doctors scold her, so she stopped making as many appointments. "They said I'm in denial, and yeah, I'm in total denial when I feel well. But the treatment made me feel like I was succumbing. I know I need to be on consistent treatment soon, but I feel the tools I developed through ultrarunning—the ability to ride out the storm through fatigue and pain—have helped me take on this disease in a different way, until I find an alternative treatment. I know the flare-ups will pass, just like mile 80 in a 100-miler."

Shannon is planning to run Badwater again this year. There will be a couple more after that, too. She wants to be a 10-time finisher. If she didn't have a goal, who would she be? She thinks about that a lot. When she takes her medicine, who will she be? She might be sick. And if she is sick, she might not be able to run.

If she can't run, who will she be?

JANE BERNSTEIN

Still Running

FROM THE SUN

I START TO RUN in 1973 on a track above the basketball court
at the McBurney YMCA in New York City. Twenty laps to a mile.
T-shirt, cutoff jeans, denim sneakers with orange laces—flat and
heavy, like low-cut basketball shoes.

The Y sells a lap counter, a metal gizmo that fits into my palm:
one click for each time around. Using it means I no longer have
to count the laps, and my mind can wander while my legs do the
work. I can be both *of* my body and *apart from* it, present and far
away.

Before I stepped onto this track, I thought of myself as unath-
letic. Hadn't ever played sports. There were no teams for girls in
my big suburban high school, only gym class, with its daunting
pommel horses I could not mount and ropes I was afraid to climb.
Never the absolute last to be chosen but one of the stragglers, a
restless, fumble-fingered klutz in an ugly blue gym suit.

Now it's as if a switch has been flicked, and the whirring restless-
ness inside me has turned into purpose. I can run!

I buy real running shoes—white Adidas with three green stripes
—and run in the street. Never again will I run indoors.

A woman runner is a rare sight. Men call out when I jog by:
"Where's the fire?"

They run beside me for a few steps or trot in an exaggerated
way, pumping their arms.

"Who's chasing you?" they shout.

*

Marriage. In-laws in Florida: "She wants to *what?*"

My father-in-law watches me lace up my running shoes, then follows me out of the house, warning me about the rattlesnakes that slither in the sandy far reaches of their development. He stands on the doorstep when I leave, shaking his head and chuckling, and when I return, he's still at the door, still shaking his head, still chuckling. "That takes the cake," he says.

All that week he keeps shaking his head and chuckling in benign disbelief: "That really takes the cake."

My husband's former girlfriend Ginger asks if she can join me on a morning run in New York City. Too shy to say no, I agree to meet her on Bleecker Street, midway between our Greenwich Village apartments. We head southwest, toward Canal Street, run up the ramp onto the remaining stretch of the elevated West Side Highway (closed to traffic), exit at the Battery, and continue home.

Our short Saturday runs become longer, more-frequent "training runs." We continue down to City Hall and over the Brooklyn Bridge, and later around the lower perimeter of Manhattan. We run on the East Side and the West Side, and sometimes we join a group that runs a 17-mile course at night up Riverside Park to the George Washington Bridge and back. Ginger and I log hundreds of hours of conversation, running side by side, talk that grows more intimate as the miles pass.

The first time we meet for dinner, I barely recognize her in street clothes. Our conversation is awkward and disjointed. We've never sat across from each other, never looked in each other's eyes. It takes a while to adjust.

First road race. Ginger and I stand at the starting line in Central Park with fifty or so others on a frigid fall morning.

My husband cheers for me at the finish line.

He wants children badly, but I'm ambivalent. "No matter what," he says, "I promise I'll always make sure you can run." This is how he gets me to agree.

What can a pregnant runner wear? In desperation I buy a tennis outfit—a sleeveless, empire-waisted top and bloomers with an elastic waist. It's all I can find.

You look like a float in a Memorial Day parade," my husband says.

There is no cheering when I galumph down the street, no tubas or drums or applause—just the occasional dumbstruck pedestrian pausing to watch. I imagine him thinking, *That really takes the cake.*

First daughter: Charlotte.
First marathon: New York.
First line of first published novel: "Lydia ran."

My heroes in those days:

Kathrine Switzer, the first woman to officially enter the Boston Marathon. She wasn't looking to make history; she only wanted to run. But in 1967 the marathon was closed to women. So she entered as "K. V. Switzer" and ran in disguise for four miles until the race director, Jock Semple, jumped off the press truck and shouted, "Get the hell out of my race!" The picture of him trying to rip the number off her chest made headlines.

Grete Waitz, the first woman to run a marathon in under two and a half hours.

Miki Gorman, who won the Boston and New York Marathons twice each.

Toshiko d'Elia, who was born in wartime Japan. "We starved," she told a reporter. "My mother would stand on food lines all day and come home with a cucumber to feed a family of six. I dreamed of being a bird so I could fly away." She started running at the age of 44, waking at 5 a.m. to set out before work. I remember seeing her: tiny, hair in pigtails, flying beside the earthbound others.

I loved these women, who were not encouraged to run; loved watching them float, fly, set records—gracefully, silently, defiantly.

The 1980s are the boom years. Everyone is running. Sweat-wicking fabric. Shoes with gel cushioning and waffle soles. Sports drinks. Orthotics for every ache below the knees.

Men wear running shoes with tuxedos.

Running can improve your sex life, body image, and mental health, I read. Run to feel centered and empowered, to shed extra pounds.

I don't know: I just love it. I need no other reason to run.

*

Our move from New York to New Jersey is wrenching and inevitable. There's so much I'll miss about the city—most of all my regular runs with Ginger.

Tamaques Park, in the town where we move, is like a bus depot on Saturday mornings: groups of runners leave every 15 minutes, starting at 6 a.m. I fit into a pack made up of middle-aged men, including a psychiatrist who tells all his patients to run.

After a long run in the winter, tiny balls of ice hang from their facial hair like Christmas decorations. In the summer their nipples bleed from rubbing against their shirts.

My second toe is longer than my first, a condition known as Morton's toe. If the toe box of my running shoe isn't broad enough, the toenail pushes against the shoe, bruises, blackens, and falls off.

How often has this happened to me? Ten times? Twenty?

In Maine, where we have a cottage, I call the local sporting-goods store to see if they know of any women who run long-distance. They put me in touch with Evelyn, who was co-captain of the cross-country team at Bowdoin College with Olympian Joan Benoit.

I run with Evelyn and her fiancé, a lobsterman, and with their friends and cousins. I run with carpenters and fishers of Irish moss and sometimes with strangers. "Where are you running?" I ask. "What's your pace? Can I join you?"

"I saw you running," people say to me often.

"Yes!" I say.

And that's it. Nothing ever follows this exchange.

My husband keeps his promise, even after the marriage begins to fail.

Now, though, if I linger too long around him, he says in irritation, "Go running, will you?" Translation: *Go straight to hell.*

You cannot cry and run at the same time. It's one or the other. Crying tightens your chest and makes your breathing jagged. You can either give in to the grief or let it go.

In this period, when there are no arms that can placate me, nothing to make me feel better, all I can do is go outside, take in the familiar streets and woods, and run. After a few minutes I begin to feel a heightened awareness of the world around me, a sense of connectedness.

And pleasure. Something sweet that cuts through the grief.

Then they stop, most of the runners I know. Their reasons are many:

My knees gave out. ("And so will yours.")

My back went bad.

My hip.

Plantar fasciitis.

A torn meniscus.

My sciatica was killing me.

Surgery for my ACL.

The kids.

So *boring*.

The arthritis in my toe.

Who has time?

And then I fell.

I got hit by a car.

So I gave it up.

The unspoken message: *And so will you.*

I cannot imagine it. I cannot imagine the day I will sit on the floor to lace my running shoes for a last time.

It's 1995. I'm in a new city: Pittsburgh, Pennsylvania. A single parent. Divorced. I have a couple of running friends, but mostly I run alone in the city's big woodland parks.

I no longer designate a single day of the week to do hill work. Every day is hill work.

The woods become my holy place.

Maybe it's because I am alone. Because I've stopped keeping training logs. Because I am older. Because these hilly parks are so beautiful that I become exquisitely aware of my *self* on these rutted trails: the rustling leaves, the sky, my breathing, the hill I mount, the squawking crow—all of it part of the same fabric. This is what I have loved above all else, only now I feel it more fully than ever before.

*

My daughter Charlotte is a teenager, and rebellious. Later, when she recalls these years, the punch line of every incident will be my turquoise spandex tights:

She leaves a note to tell me she's run away from home. I figure out she's at a coffee shop called the Beehive, and when I stomp inside and find her with a backpack full of beer, I'm wearing my *turquoise spandex tights.*

She's forgotten to bring a check for her high school ski club on the last possible day to register, so I tuck the check in my pocket and go by the school on the way back from my run. She is standing beneath a tree, smoking with her friends, when she sees me running toward her in my *turquoise spandex tights.*

Fifty years old. Sinewy. I keep tights, a T-shirt, and a spare pair of running shoes in the trunk of my car. You never know. Like the postman, I run through rain, snow, and sleet. But not ice.

Falling:

On wet leaves, on ice, on roots, on broken sidewalk.

On cement, years back, when I was seven months pregnant with my second daughter.

On the bridle path in Central Park, where I slid on the dirt like a baseball player trying to steal a base.

Always stunned. Always getting up and saying, "I'm okay! I'm fine!"

On the metal grate over the Gowanus Canal in Brooklyn. A medical student sits on the curb with me while her boyfriend runs to get napkins for the blood that spurts from my chin and knee. My hand throbs.

"I'm fine!" I insist. "I'm okay."

They pay for a taxi to take me home.

I ice my knee, try to stop the bleeding, think as I always do: *One day I will fall, and that will be it.*

And then: *I wonder if I'll be able to run tomorrow.*

By 2003 running is no longer fun. The problem is my ass, my tuchis, my keister, my behind.

It has a name, this not-at-all-funny pain in the butt: piriformis syndrome. Common among runners and people who sit for hours —bus drivers, writers, cops.

Sitting hurts worse than running. The radiating pain makes me feel like an animal with a limb caught in a trap. I want to chew off my leg.

I get MRIs, physical therapy, cortisone shots, new diagnoses.

I buy a wedge cushion, more-cushioned running shoes. I give up desk chairs and running on asphalt.

I wait to feel joy. Run, limp, wait some more.

I think of Jock Semple shoving and clawing at Kathrine Switzer —and she ran on.

I think of all the injuries that plagued the women runners I admire, all the tendons and muscles and ligaments torn and repaired. I think of my friend Ginger's countless surgeries—and she ran on.

I think of Toshiko d'Elia, eight months after a cancer diagnosis, completing a marathon in under three hours, setting a world record for women over 50.

A year passes. In this limping, aching period I buy a new house three minutes from a 644-acre woodland park with plenty of hilly trails.

Start doing yoga every morning.

Carry my wedge cushion with me when I travel.

The pain begins to dissipate.

And then one day an awareness: I ran and nothing hurt.

Sixty. In running clothes I look like a plucked chicken.

"I saw you running," an acquaintance says.

"Yes," I tell her.

Slowly, I think.

But the joy has returned.

Until close to the end of her life, Toshiko d'Elia was in the pool every morning at 7 a.m. She swam a mile, ran in the water, did yoga. Then, in the afternoon, she ran three to five miles. "That was her day, until the day she couldn't," said her daughter in her *New York Times* obituary.

Sixty-seven. I am still running.

JOHN BRANCH

Cheers on a Soccer Field, Far from Las Vegas

FROM THE NEW YORK TIMES

I WAS ON THE sideline of a soccer field two Saturdays ago, watching my 12-year-old daughter and her Novato teammates. I don't remember much about that game, but Novato won, and one of the goals was scored by the smallest girl on the team, a quick and feisty forward who wears a long ponytail and jersey No. 8. We whooped and cheered her name. I found out later that her parents weren't there that afternoon. They were in Las Vegas for a getaway weekend.

About 36 hours later, I was on my way to Las Vegas myself, rushing to join my *New York Times* colleagues to cover the latest mass shooting, maybe bigger than them all. I hadn't covered one of them since 1999, when I was in the wrong place at the right time and rushed into the aftermath of Columbine.

A colleague of mine and I checked into a massive suite at Mandalay Bay Resort and Casino, 11 floors directly below that of the shooter. It had the same view of the concert ground across the Strip, where investigators in the daylight were picking through the carnage of the night before. That was about when my wife sent me a text. That little soccer player's mom was at the concert the night before, she said. She's missing.

But Stacee Etcheber was not my story. The gunman was. I spent a week mostly about 100 feet below where the shooter committed mass murder, trying to solve the mystery of what he'd done. I talked to people, followed every lead, and wrote stories. It's what reporters do. It was a news story, as horrific as they come, and we're trained to keep our emotional distance from the things that we cover.

Late that night, I stood in front of the window, the same one that a madman broke 11 floors above and used as a perch to shoot hundreds of people he did not know. The body count was on its way to 58. I thought about home.

Stacee's family soon announced that she died. My wife and I didn't really know Stacee much—obviously not well enough to notice that she was not among the few dozen people at a rec-level girls' soccer game. But some of our closest friends were dear friends of hers, and our town is small enough that there was probably no more than two degrees of separation to the family.

My family was among the hundreds of people, friends and strangers, who crowded onto the grounds of an elementary school and held candles aloft during the vigil. My daughter was one of the dozens of kids who solemnly held roses in her honor, and she hugged her classmate and teammate when it ended. She and a couple of friends made a cake and delivered it to the Etchebers' house the next day.

Orange was Stacee's favorite color, and on Friday, after people bought as much orange ribbon as they could find at all the local craft stores, an army tied ribbons all around town, from the trees on downtown's Grant Avenue to the posts in front of Pioneer Park. My wife and her friends tied them around the trees in front of the middle school where Stacee's daughter goes to school, along with mine.

I missed it all. I was as close to the site of the shooting as you could get, and yet felt fully disconnected from the effect of the tragedy. One night I walked to the memorial that sprang up in the median of South Las Vegas Boulevard, the kind of now-familiar post-shooting memorial that I saw at Columbine almost two decades before, with balloons and flowers and candles. I found a photo of Stacee that had been placed in the middle of it all, and took a picture and sent it home.

In Las Vegas, Stacee was just one in a crowd, part of a list. But she and her family were all anyone talked or thought about back in Novato, and that is where I got my news. I heard that Stacee's husband, a San Francisco police officer, was running with Stacee through the barrage of gunfire when he stopped to help someone;

he told his wife to go on and never saw her alive again. I heard that television news trucks were parked in front of the house. I heard stories of friends pulling over in their cars to cry at the weight and nearness of it all. There were beautiful and crushingly sad Facebook posts in Stacee's honor, the kind you see after every tragedy, except these were written by people I knew well.

I heard my wife, who grew up in a nearby town, tell me that she had never been more proud to call Novato home.

I checked out of that Mandalay Bay suite on Saturday morning, excused from reporting duties, and flew home in the hopes of making my daughter's soccer game. I found the red rose from the vigil, starting to fade and wilt, in a vase on the kitchen counter. When we got to the game, we and the other parents were somewhat surprised to see Stacee's husband and extended family there too. Warming up with the girls was No. 8, with her long ponytail.

We all wore orange ribbons, attached by safety pins, including the girls on both teams. The Novato team wore orange armbands with the initials "s.e." Before kickoff, both squads came across the field to the spectator side and lined up in straight lines. Our team's coach asked the parents to stand for 30 seconds of silence. And then two of the league's better teams played a rather meaningless soccer game, only this one felt about as meaningful as anything I've ever watched.

And it was late in the second half when the ball suddenly swung from one end to the other, and Stacee's daughter gave chase through three retreating opponents and beat them all to the ball. And in one blink-and-you-missed-it moment, she booted the ball into the corner of the net for what held on as the winning goal.

Her teammates chased her and swarmed her, and they and she looked as free and happy as girls can be on a sunny fall Saturday afternoon with their friends. The parents jumped and cheered as loudly as I've heard parents cheer at a kids' soccer game. Behind my sunglasses, I was bawling. It was the first time I'd cried all week.

WRIGHT THOMPSON

Pat Riley's Final Test

FROM ESPN: THE MAGAZINE

THE DIGITAL CLOCK above the door in Pat Riley's presidential suite counts down the minutes to tip-off. The room is in a back hallway underneath the arena, a few feet from the secret path beneath the bleachers that he takes to his seat. I sit on the couch and read a laminated prayer card the team made for the game. Nobody else is here; his wife, Chris, is out blessing different parts of the arena. Tip-off is 29 minutes away, the last game of the season. The Heat need to win and see one of two other teams lose to make the playoffs. Still no sign of Riley. For the past two months, he and I have spoken nearly every day, which continues to shock his wife, who knows how private he can be. But earlier today, someone with the Heat suggested I tread lightly. The boss is in a mood. A peak state of Rileyness.

Then my phone buzzes.

"R u here?" Riley texts.

He sends his assistant, Karen, down to get me.

"It's tense," she says as we climb the stairs and approach the glass walls of his office, where he sits in an easy chair near the sofa, alone. It's quiet and dark, the blinds half-drawn, blocking out the view of the water. A three- or four-day growth on his face makes him look gaunt and tired. Around him, he's got the talismans that might bring him luck: a strange statue of Buddha reimagined as a Heat fan, and a Bob Dylan lyric taped to his bookshelf: "When you got nothing, you got nothing to lose."

Karen hands him a coffee, in one of those thin green Gatorade cups.

He sighs, and shifts his weight, and sips.

These past months have been an emotional time to be around him; the public highs and lows have been mirrored by the most difficult private challenge he's ever faced. Not long ago he said the scariest thing in the world was "extinction," or the emptiness that might swallow him if he ever managed to leave basketball behind, which he's considering. Waiting out the start of the game, we circle a familiar subject: there are changes he'd like to make in his life, if he could ever escape the seductive rhythms of the NBA calendar. The prayer cards being passed out downstairs have a quote on the back, part of which asks: *Will I lie down or will I fight?* For the past 50 years, and especially this season, that question has been central to Riley's daily life, a man perpetually seeking out opportunities to prove himself worthy of his reputation. The problem is that every time he proves himself, he puts off his future by another day.

A horn sounds somewhere below, breaking the stillness of his office.

"Watch the time," Karen says.

"What time is it?" he asks.

"Three minutes to eight," she says.

Riley slips on his jacket, and we walk past the empty offices. His feet don't make any sound on the soft red and black carpet in the back stairway down to the court. The noise of the arena gets louder the closer he gets, thumping bass at first, then the high-pitched whine of a packed house. He loves these gladiatorial walks, a feeling few people ever know, the pounding adrenaline and the roaring, unseen crowd. Minutes from tip-off, he passes the empty locker room. His team is on the floor. There's a mural there in the hall, a blown-up photograph of Ray Allen's famous 2013 buzzer beater in the Finals, and he stops to stare for a moment. He looks at the fans in the background of the photo, studying the desperation in their faces, he says, like he's looking in a mirror at himself.

This season has challenged Riley as much as any in the past 50 years. The troubles began swirling three years ago, in the summer of 2014. Behind the Big Three—LeBron James, Dwyane Wade, and Chris Bosh—the Heat had been to four straight Finals, winning two titles, and Riley felt as if he had built something greater than his Showtime Lakers, something to rival even the Bill Russell–led Celtics. But James was a free agent that summer, and Riley and his guys flew out to Las Vegas to make their case for him to stay in Miami.

Riley told his lieutenant, Andy Elisburg, to get the two championship trophies LeBron had won and pack them in their hardshell carrying cases. Elisburg also brought charts and an easel for a presentation about the free agents the Heat would pursue. The day of the meeting, a hotel bellhop followed them with a luggage cart carrying the presentation and the two trophies. Riley brought wine from a Napa vineyard named Promise. It was the same label Maverick Carter had presented Riley with when they did the deal four years earlier. Riley respects Carter, and when he walked into the suite and saw James with agent Rich Paul and friend Randy Mims but no Maverick, part of him knew the meeting wasn't sincere. He told Elisburg to keep the trophies and easel in the hall. James and his associates were watching a World Cup game, which they kept glancing at during the presentation. At one point, Riley asked if they'd mute the TV.

Riley flew home worried and got a text telling him to be ready for a call. About 15 minutes later, his phone rang and Paul was on the other end. The agent handed the phone to LeBron, who started by saying, "I want to thank you for four years . . ."

"I was silent," Riley says. "I didn't say anything. My mind began to just go. And it was over. I was very angry when LeBron left. It was personal for me. It just was. I had a very good friend who talked me off the ledge and kept me from going out there and saying something like Dan Gilbert. I'm glad I didn't do it."

The next year, the Heat missed the playoffs, Riley consumed with self-doubt, his own mind whispering that he'd stayed too long. Then last season Miami lost Bosh to blood clots, but the team still fought to the playoffs, falling to the Raptors in seven in the Eastern Conference semifinals. On the flight back from Toronto, Riley and his staff drank wine and debated the free agents they'd get to join Wade for another deep playoff run.

The beginning of July, all that fell apart.

Wade decided to leave Miami, his bond with Riley fractured. They'd been like family once, with Wade visiting Riley at home and Riley a guest at Wade's wedding. But with Bosh's return in grave doubt, Wade saw an uncertain future in Miami—and just like that, the Big Three had disintegrated. Hurt and wounded, Riley and his wife booked a last-minute trip to Paris, leaving three days later for a reprieve and a few Bruce Springsteen shows. During the first one, Springsteen played Riley's favorite song: "Land of Hope and Dreams." It's an anthem for Riley, because he spends a lot of time imagining the future he might have, when all his battles have been fought and won. He dreams of a different life, and not in an abstract way. He *sees* it, down to the taste of the dinner he'll eat and the music he'll play.

That night, standing close to the stage, he sang along. The people who recognized him in the general admission pit saw the exterior: good-looking, tanned, and well-dressed. Most can't see past that image, which is perhaps its point. His inside is as messy and complex as his outside is manicured and defined. Chris Riley has always viewed any issue, including the pain over losing Wade, through her intimate knowledge of her husband's hidden motivations and scars: it'd been 60 years since he scored 19 points as a sixth-grader, and the same nun who locked him in the church basement, forgetting him there with the rats and cobwebs, gave him a standing ovation after the buzzer, setting into motion all the urges that sent him running to Paris.

Back home, his friends wondered how he might be handling such a public failure. Two pals from various yacht trips over the years, Dick Butera and Peter Gubar, ran into each other during the off-season, their conversation recounted by Butera.

"Have you seen Pat?" Dick asked. "Is he gonna stay?"

"Pat will be always be Pat," Peter said.

"You mean the contest is still on?" Dick asked.

"The game is never gonna be over," Peter said.

His friends know him well. Eight days after returning from Paris, Riley went to Erik Spoelstra's wedding, at an old mansion and gardens on the water in Miami. Randy Pfund, who left his job as Heat GM after Riley stopped coaching in 2008, walked over to his table to say hello. Riley didn't open with tales of Paris or gushing praise for the flowers or bride. Almost immediately, he started giving his side of the Wade departure.

"Within 15 seconds," Pfund says.

Even as he obsesses over the Heat, in this or any other year, part of Riley's mind is never far from his estate on the Pacific in Malibu. Sometimes he checks the live security cameras just to feel close to the place. He and Chris spend about a month there at the end of every off-season, surrounded by their oldest friends. She calls it their "heart home."

Last year he took the most concrete action he's ever taken to make that dreamed future a reality. He signed a new five-year contract, with the understanding that he can work anywhere, including his perch overlooking the Pacific. His friends have been wondering for years when he'd head west, all of them following the internal conflict they've come to know as Miami versus Malibu. "I love the schism because that's all he talks about," says his friend, the actor Michael Douglas. "That's all he talks about, getting back to Malibu to that house."

When Douglas discusses Riley's life in Florida, and the one he might live in California, he's not talking about geography. Each place serves as an easy code to describe the competing sides of Riley's personality. Miami represents the man living six inches in front of his face, Douglas says. One of many examples: near the end of his last season with the Lakers, in 1990, he screamed at the players in a hotel ballroom and punched a mirror, shattering it and cutting his hand so deeply that bright red blood covered the sleeve of his crisp white shirt. He has punched mirrors and walls, wept and raged and trashed locker rooms. He has carried and nursed grudges. "Is Pat a dick?" Pfund says, repeating a question. "I know hundreds and hundreds of people who would say worse than that."

The other Riley loves emojis—texting hearts, smiley faces and sunsets, praying hands, cute baby heads, and palm trees. He has written six unproduced screenplays. Enamored with his five-year-old grandson, he's teaching him about old cars and buying him toys that play the Motown classic "My Girl." There's a contagious joy in his eyes. At bar mitzvahs, he's been the only adult on the dance floor of kids, leaving when the music stops and he's covered in sweat. He shows up for people who matter to him; when his college teammate Tommy Kron died, the family walked into the church that morning to find two people: the priest and a grieving Riley. He's been all over the world with friends on boats; he's often the one with binoculars scanning coasts for little bars where they can surrender for an afternoon and night. "They drink and they sing and they play music," says actress Lynda Carter, a longtime friend best known for playing Wonder Woman. "And he loves Springsteen and Motown and doo-wop. He and my daughter, Jess, were singing these duets, 'Red Dirt Road,' by Brooks & Dunn. They are crooning together and playing air guitar."

The flexibility in his contract about Malibu, then, isn't about distance. It's a vow he's making—about the kind of person he can still be, even as a 72-year-old man. The entire estate, from the porches with the million-dollar views to the bocce ball court near the beach, is full of little promises.

He's got a guitar collection out there, because one day he swears he will learn to play "My Girl" for Chris. He dreams of strumming her that song, and she dreams of planting a garden, and they both dream of hammocks on the beach. He's planning to move half his antique cars—he's got nearly a dozen—out to Malibu. Five minutes from the estate, he found a storage facility to keep them all. He rented every available bay, so they're all sitting there empty, waiting. The owner called him not long ago, worried that one person had all his space and wasn't using it, wanting a long-term tenant and not some fickle rich guy who might up and leave.

"What is your plan?" the man asked.

"These are going to be filled one day," Riley said.

He owns three houses in a row, purchased one at a time starting in the Showtime days when his kids were young. One of his many dreams is for the family to have a compound, for Pat and Chris to have a house, and for James and Elisabeth to each have one too. That vision got him through many long seasons and those lonely nights in hotel bars—the belief that he wasn't giving up a life, just postponing it a bit. For 30 years, he's told himself a story about the man he will be, about the family he will have, once he reaches his destination. But now his kids are grown, 32 and 28, with lives of their own and no time for a compound. They're busy.

He waited too long.

Pat Riley began his NBA playing career in 1967. In October, when the 2016–2017 campaign began, it marked the 50th year he's lived by the code of Riley: when the team sucks, *he* sucks. And the Heat suck. They suck in ways big and small. The team blows a 19-point lead in the home opener. Wade beats the Heat in his return to Miami, off an infuriating and iffy foul call. On December 12, they are third to last in the conference, 7-17, when the Riley family gets news that makes all that losing cease to matter.

Lis, their 28-year-old daughter who'd gotten married the year before and moved to Denver, notices she has massively swollen lymph nodes. Pat and Chris rush to Denver, where a doctor tells them what they'd feared the most: it looks like cancer, lymphoma, and they should schedule a procedure and then wait for confirmation.

The Heat lose four of five, but Pat's mind is elsewhere. For all his children's lives, he has felt as if he could solve any problem they encountered. When his son, James, went to boarding school, Pat flew up early to make sure the young man's room was arranged perfectly, likely in search of a grand gesture to ease his guilt for all he'd missed. The morning James was scheduled to report, Pat found the dorm locked around 5 a.m., so he climbed in the window and went over everything again, down to the space between shirts in the closet. On the day of Elisabeth's wedding, he raised hell with the planners, making them redo the draping and piping on a table minutes before rushing to change clothes and walk her down the aisle.

"He was hysterical," his close friend Steve Chabre says. "He was almost manic."

But illness he cannot fix.

"A father's worst feeling," Riley says, "is the feeling of helplessness when his little girl is exactly that: helpless."

On Christmas Eve, Pat and Chris fly to Denver to see Lis and her husband, Paul. The four of them pile into a hotel suite. Pat opens a few bottles of Screaming Eagle, a cabernet they love. Lis gives them matching red-and-black-checked pajamas, so Pat and Chris put them on and all four curl up to watch movies, like they did when the kids were young. Outside, the snow comes down. Chris holds Lis on the couch, while Pat and his son-in-law sit on sofas on either side, all eight feet on the same ottoman. In the hotel suite, Pat thinks about game days when the kids were growing up. It's funny what comes back when you're scared. Chris would keep the children occupied so he could nap, and then he'd get up and come down to the big center landing and whistle. He can really whistle—once he randomly saw Magic Johnson walking down a beach in the Bahamas and hid behind a dune and let out a loud one, watching the star jump and swivel—and when he whistled for his kids, he'd yell, "Triple kisses!" They'd come running and give him a kiss good luck. Sitting on a couch, wondering if his daughter might have lymphoma, he remembers triple kisses.

*

The memories come, Lis in her wedding dress, the day they brought James home, stopping first at the Pacific Ocean so the baby boy could see the wonder and the power Pat and Chris loved so much. Sliding back, his own wedding, the yellow 1967 Corvette he drove when he met Chris, the last time he spoke to his father, his bench-warming in the pros, everybody's All-American at Kentucky, back to the streets of Schenectady, New York. He can smell the high school gymnasium.

Maybe it was his senior year. He drove the lane and thought he'd been fouled. When the referee called a charge, he turned and headed the other way. The gym got murmuring and tense, and Riley didn't see his father running drunk onto the court—exactly like the scene in *Hoosiers,* he'd tell people years later, on the rare occasion when he'd share the story—and going after the ref. Lee Riley had been a baseball player and often blamed people for his unrealized dreams, including this particular official, who'd umpired the minor league games he managed. Pat didn't even know his dad was at the game, Lee having hidden beneath the bleachers, and Pat saw his beloved high school coach, Walt Przybylo, take charge and escort Lee off the court so the game could resume.

Riley adored Walt, later hiring one of his sons as a scout for the Heat. The night before Kentucky's NCAA final against Texas Western in 1966, stress caused Pat's feet to break out in painful sores. While Pat tried to sleep, Walt sat up all night gently soaking his feet, an act almost biblical in its devotion.

Lee and Mary Riley did not come to the game. They never saw him play a single time in college or the NBA. They never explained why.

Lee played for 17 minor league teams in 16 seasons and quit in 1943 to work in a factory during the war. A year later, the Phillies offered him a major league contract, and for four glorious games, he was delivered this miracle of a second chance. He got one hit in 12 at-bats, on April 30, 1944. The next day the organization bought a minor league team in upstate New York and sent Lee to play for it. Pat was born 10 months later. In 1952, when Lee was managing a minor league club, he got suspended 90 days for stalling during a game. He quit professional baseball. When he got home, he burned all his gear and memorabilia and rarely spoke of those lost years. In 1970, he died, leaving many things unsaid. "I can't remember my father ever telling me he loved me," Pat says. "Not much from my mother either."

In his mind, Pat finds himself pulled toward 58 Spruce Street.

He remembers it as a dark place, loud with unspoken words. The Rileys didn't talk about anything. Pat had a sister die in infancy 10 years before he was born, according to a book about World War II baseball, which dedicated a section to Lee Riley. Until I brought this to his attention, Pat had never heard the story of his infant sister. It's possible the book is wrong, he says, or that his parents kept the secret to themselves. His mom rarely left the house, and he'd come home to find her sitting downstairs, on top of the only heat register, trying to stay warm. Another family lives in the house now, but there remains a worn spot on the floor and wall in the shape of Mary Riley.

He remembers his trips back home through the years and how every single time, he would find himself driving past all these places, his house, Walt's house, the bar where his dad drank away a decade, the high school gymnasium. Once he accidentally set off the alarm in the gym, which is now named after him. He remembers his greatest games and the time his dad ran onto the court to defend him. That's how he decided to eventually tell that story, cleaning up his father whenever he could, even to himself. Riley talked about Lee to his players, to schoolkids and corporate executives. Over time, he rewrote his own father, punching up stories and inventing others, a mixture of Lee and Walt and the books Pat read for inspiration. Imagination and willpower were always Pat's two most important gifts, and along the way he used both to create the man he thought Lee Riley deserved to be. Before one speech in 1997, at the ceremony naming the high school gym in Riley's honor, a friend's video camera catches Pat and his mom talking.

"Make sure you don't tell anybody when I'm not telling the truth," he said.

His mom and older sister burst out laughing, and he went onstage.

He told that auditorium of students about his dad coming into his room at night to give him wisdom, telling him he was made of special stuff. Chris Riley, a trained therapist, saw through him then and sees through him now. Over the years, she's watched her husband construct the dad he wanted. There were no fatherly bedside chats on Spruce Street.

"Are you kidding me?" she says. "It was so much bleaker than that."

Out in Denver, in the dark of the hotel suite, they watch movies, a Christmas special, then *The Accountant* and *Deepwater Horizon*. Everybody sleeps in the next morning. Nothing matters but the wait, not the losses piling up, not anything, until January 11, when the doctors deliver surprising news.

No cancer.

A month later, a perfect Sunday, Pat Riley cranks his black 1971 Chevelle, wanting to escape the busy streets of Miami Beach, aiming toward the vast nothingness to the southwest. He downshifts, the 502-horsepower Chevelle bucking and roaring under the yoke of the lower gear. The sound blasts off the art deco facades. Since his daughter's news, the Heat have, improbably, gone on a winning streak. The team won at home and on the road, knocking off the Warriors with a last-second shot, fighting out of an 18-point fourth-quarter hole to beat the Nets. They've run off 13 straight victories, transforming themselves from a team that was better off tanking to a playoff contender.

Now on the road, Riley is exhaling.

The stereo plays "Listen to the Music," then "Born to Run," and he turns up the volume. He laughs and talks to people a lane over in traffic when he accidentally grinds the gears. A circle of sweat spreads on the back of his shirt. He seems light and happy, and he says he's been reborn.

His arm hangs out the window.

"I owe everybody a lot," he says. "A lot. I owe them all a lot, but . . ."

He pauses, considering how many times he's climbed a mountain only to get knocked down and start climbing again. "I don't owe them anything anymore," he says, forcefully, as if conviction will make the words true. He's trying, still deeply invested in the positive parts of building and running a team but saying he's free at last from the negative motivations he's never been able to control. In two days, he and Chris are flying to the Bahamas to sail around on a boat with their oldest and best friends, a break after the stress and joy of the past two months. He would have never done that 10 years ago, he says.

His slicked-back hair is white now and a little fluffy on the sides.

The outskirts of Miami pass in a blur of car dealerships, no-cover strip clubs, and canals. He shifts gears and accelerates, hurtling away from the city where he's worked these past 22 years.

"I don't have to get pulled back into this one more time," he says.

He almost got away. That's the thing. Four years ago, he missed his chance. Now, of course, he sees the lost moment so clearly. He remembers the night, August 10, 2013, his 50th high school reunion, a party decades in the making, part of the Schenectady he's carried with him: intense loyalty for the people who held him up, and a loneliness Chris could sense when they met. He longed to go back—to the time and the place—and two months after the 2013 Finals, flush with back-to-back titles, he did.

He served as social chair for the event, booking the Four Tops *and* the Temptations. No detail escaped his attention; he even stopped at a local production studio to review the short video that would play during the event. His close friends Paul Heiner and Warren DeSantis oversaw logistics. Riley demanded to pay for all of it, a bill that eventually topped $160,000.

"This f—ing ridiculous reunion of yours," Heiner came to lovingly call it.

Stage lights bathed the gymnasium in purple. The music started, one familiar hit after another. Pat and Chris danced right up in front. If it's possible for an entire life to lead to a single moment, this was it: back-to-back titles for the second time in Riley's career, listening to the music he and his wife loved, in the place where his journey began. He couldn't remember a happier time, and somewhere in the revelry, he realized he should walk away from basketball. "I thought this is what life should be," he says. "Friends, family, and fun. A lot of thought about enough is enough. A time to leave with all debts paid to the game and nothing to suck me back in."

The Four Tops came out for a duet with the Temps and called Pat up onstage.

The band kicked into "My Girl."

A yellow spotlight pointed down on him when the last verse came around. "I don't need no money, fortune, or fame . . . ," he sang, a little shaky. "I got all the riches, baby, one man can claim."

He pointed at Chris in the front row, and for just a little while, it seemed as if he might get out, a legend by any definition, with nine rings as a player, assistant coach, head coach, and president, his marriage and family intact, nothing to prove.

He stayed.

It's mid-February, and even as the Heat push toward the eighth and final spot in the playoffs, the rise and fall of the Big Three shadows the season. The week before the All-Star break, Dwyane Wade appears on Yahoo's popular basketball podcast. For the first time, he says a driving reason for his departure from Miami was hurt feelings over Riley never calling him. Wade says Riley didn't reach out, and Dwyane felt he deserved respect after helping deliver three titles. Heat PR man and longtime consigliere Tim Donovan doesn't alert Riley to the interview, but Pat has clearly heard about it because he shows up late for a lunch and immediately wants to tell his side.

When the conversation naturally drifts toward other topics, he steers it back.

Riley says that Wade's agent asked to deal directly with the owners instead of Pat, so he merely honored that request. Mostly, he just wishes the whole thing had gone differently. "I know he feels I didn't fight hard enough for him," he says. "I was very, very sad when Dwyane said no. I wish I could have been there and told him why I didn't really fight for him at the end . . . I fought for the team. The one thing I wanted to do for him, and maybe this is what obscured my vision, but I wanted to get him another player so he could end his career competitive."

When he describes his reaction to Wade's leaving, it's always in terms of how sad it makes him feel, and while his emotions toward James's return to Cleveland were primal in the months, and even years, afterward, now he understands why LeBron had to leave.

"He went home because he had to go home," he says. "It was time. It was really time for him to go home, in his prime. If he's ever gonna do anything in Akron again, this was the time to do it. Otherwise, he'd have had a scarlet letter on his back the rest of his whole life."

But of course, Riley says, almost immediately after LeBron left, Bosh's camp wanted to reopen a deal they'd just finished, knowing the Heat had money and felt vulnerable. Bosh threatened to sign with the Rockets. In the end, Riley gave Bosh what he wanted. Now he wishes he'd said no to Bosh's max deal and given all that money to Wade. (James and Bosh declined to comment for this story. Wade issued a statement thanking Riley for their years together.)

"You never think it's gonna end," Riley says. "Then it always ends."

The Heat's climb into playoff contention hits a spot in Riley's brain nothing else can hit. *You've still got it, Riley. One more time.* It starts as a whisper, which these days he says he chooses not to hear. With the team clawing toward that eighth and final seed in the East, he says, "I've let go of all the stuff that used to hold me to the grind." He and Chris sit at a back table at a South Beach steakhouse, looking out at the water. A staff member calls him Coach.

"Am I different?" Pat asks.

"He's on his way," Chris says.

"I'm on my way," he says, smiling.

"I can't say the craziness isn't still there," she says.

"I wanna win, honey," he says. "We both wanna win."

Reaching into her purse, Chris hands him a small ziplock bag of pills, a cocktail of homeopathic medicine and vitamins they take to ward off the kudzu creep of time. Both preach the effectiveness of Eastern medicine. Although Pat went to a therapist only once —five minutes into the session, he burst into tears, stood up, and never returned—Chris says he's done a lot of soul-searching about many things, mainly his father, the taproot of his drive and his inability to stop driving.

She stops and starts, trying to articulate her thoughts.

She exhales.

"He's good," she says finally. "He's much better. He's clearly forgiven his father. That's the peace he's made. Now, whether he comes to peace with himself with that is another thing."

She hears what he says about not owing anyone anything anymore.

"He's talking about it," she says. "Do I trust it?"

She's right to be skeptical. Sitting on his desk at the arena, he's got a monitor with a live video feed from the practice court. On a random Tuesday during the second half of the season, around 4:30 in the afternoon, he works at his desk. With the team on the road and no players to watch, he leans over a piece of paper, grinding on a task he should probably delegate, drawing up the seating charts for a charity dinner.

"He's putting in 12 to 14 hours," she says.

He insists he's different, and while Chris Riley believes he's sincere in his desire, she understands his personal code, perhaps even better than he does: the better the Heat play, the louder the siren song of more becomes.

"How do you change what got you everything you've got?" she says.

"It's embedded," he says.

When she looks at him, she sees a man with an incredible tolerance for pain and work, but she also sees a sixth-grader getting a standing ovation from the nuns.

"You perform to get your goodies," Chris says. "You can psychologically know your issues, but the key is: can you change the habits?"

The stretch run is a test. With just 20 games left in the season, Riley has done the math. The Heat need to go 13-7 to beat out the Pacers and Bulls for the eighth seed. Tonight, in March, Cleveland is in the building, photographers hanging in the private underground concourses, trying to snap a photo of LeBron. Watching the digital clock in his suite, Riley leans back on a red chair with his arms crossed. He's holding court with one of his oldest friends, Peter Gubar, who sits on a low-slung couch to his left. The playoffs are within reach.

"You've crept up from the bottom," Gubar says. "You're right on the cusp."

"Are we really the 11-30 team or the 17-4 team?" Riley says.

LeBron doesn't play, resting, and the Heat blow out the Cavs. There's almost a fight at the end of the game, and after it, Miami flies to Cleveland for an immediate rematch. Already, Riley is thinking about setting the table one last time, not necessarily winning a title but putting the pieces in place. He isn't going to Cleveland, he says when asked, because that time in his life has passed. In 1985, for Game 6 of the Finals, he wanted to wear a white tuxedo and a shamrock bow tie in Boston—"a lot more hubris then," he says—but now that belongs to Spoelstra and the players.

"I will go work in the garden and pick some fresh vegetables and play with my grandson while they battle," he says. "We will have a great meal as we watch the game on TV."

"You have a garden?"

"A major plan," he replies. "Right now all imagery, but I see it."

He sees the vegetables, with Chris in those thick gloves with a shovel, yet he also sees one more title run. The competing visions leave him conflicted. "I NEED ONE MORE," he writes in a text message immediately after talking about the garden. "AND I KNOW THIS WILL BE THE TOUGHEST TO GET."

The team wins that night in Cleveland and keeps winning, muscling past Chicago and Detroit. On the second full day of the NCAA tournament, the Heat finally make it to eighth place alone.

Riley flies west to scout games.

That first night, he stops over in Malibu before a flight to Sacramento in the morning. He lounges on the deck. The clock on his phone says 4:48 p.m. It's the "golden hour," as he calls it, which usually means he turns on the "R&B 2" playlist, watching the sun set to a soundtrack of the Chi-Lites and Frankie Beverly. But today, he listens to just a few songs on repeat, by singer-songwriter Jason Isbell, "Something More Than Free" and "Traveling Alone."

They're about loneliness and labor and the emptiness of being made to travel a road not of your choosing. *I've grown tired of traveling alone.* The ocean is close enough that the waves drone white noise instead of rising and falling swells. His two lives flash through his mind, the one he keeps dreaming about and the one he's actually living. The songs repeat again. He calls Chris to talk about what he feels. Three decades ago, they planned a life here, in their heart home with this view every day. He wants more Malibu and less Miami, feeling his "tipping point" close at hand, as he puts it, but there's another flight to catch in the morning. He stares out at the sunset.

"Instead of this," he says, "I go to work!"

The memories come again, punching walls in Miami after losing a playoff series, unable to face the team; headlines in New York when he left—"Pat the Rat"—back to 1985, a cramped, un-air-conditioned locker room beneath the Boston Garden. The Lakers screamed and poured champagne. They'd finally beaten the Celtics—and in Boston—avoiding three straight Finals losses and the likely end of Riley's career. No more newspaper stories about

the "LA Fakers." Pat had wanted only to find Chris. *Where was she?*
Then he saw her, leaning against the wall by the training room. "I
was across the room by the shower entrance," he says years later,
"but noticed she was watching and waiting for me all the time to
free myself of the others. When we finally locked eyes and moved
toward each other, that path opened like the Red Sea. The tears
just flowed before we could embrace. Tears just flowing with happiness, joy, and relief at the sight of each other and this big moment. We embraced hard, and I lifted her up. My Girl Chris, man.
She said we earned this. She said this is ours forever."

These things come to him on a barstool on the next-to-last day
of the 2016–2017 season.

He orders a double martini.

The story doesn't end with the embrace, he says.

He stirs his drink with a spear of olives.

Twenty-one years later, in 2006, he mistakenly threw away the
ring he won that night, along with all his Lakers rings, the real
ones mixed together with dozens of worthless samples for the
Heat championship ring he was designing. The company gave him
exact replicas, but they felt too shiny, with not enough dents and
scratches, so he put them in a bag and beat them against a wall.
Instead of adding scars and patina, he just knocked loose a bunch
of diamonds. When he got them fixed, he locked the replicas in
a safe at home. With Pat Riley, there's no self-curated shrine to
his own former glories. The past can't possibly compete with the
season he's living and breathing today, waiting out the next-to-last
afternoon with a martini in a South Beach bar.

It's April 11, five days since the Heat slipped out of that eighth
playoff spot they'd worked so hard to earn. He feels tired and depressed. The losses and the shrinking math have pushed Riley into
a hole, drowning in the darkness. He hates how a loss, even after
all these years, crushes the joy he'd felt hours earlier playing with
his grandson. One game remains, tomorrow night. Miami needs
to win, then hope for Chicago or Indiana to lose. Inside, he already knows the truth. In about 18 hours, they will come up one
victory short of the playoffs—all these months culminating in exactly nothing, just a guy coming home and staring at a quote on
his mirror: Warriors don't live in the past; the past is dead; life is
now and the future is waiting.

Over drinks, the day before that 82nd and final game, next season comes into focus. They're not good enough to beat the Warriors with the current lineup. *He's* not good enough. The team needs at least one star, and probably two, to compete.

The sun makes the waterfront room feel light and easy.

A bartender talks with a singsong Dublin lilt.

Sitting on his stool, Riley tells stories about the Native American chief Tecumseh, and about an old thoroughbred horse who broke his leg in the homestretch and got a bullet to the head instead of a garland of roses. Finished with his martini, Riley orders one more before heading home to dinner, planning his good-bye speech to this team he's grown to love. The simplicity of tomorrow clarifies him. He smiles. In the late-afternoon happy hour glow, he sees himself clearly, not as he wants to be but as he is. No roses for him, just a long stretch of track and a bullet with his name on it, one day, when he can't run anymore.

"You know the greatest lie in the world?" he says, starting to laugh. "Pat's retiring to Malibu."

SALLY JENKINS

Manning Adds Some Meaning to a Final Game Without Much

FROM THE WASHINGTON POST

THERE WAS A glaze of ice over everything, a cold slippery sheen that made it hard to get a purchase and invited benumbed feet to quit trying. Only a few durable souls tailgated in the parking lot, hunched over grills that poured out smoke along with breath vapor, and a gusting wind blew it around and seemed to suggest everyone should just go home. Inside MetLife Stadium, two hopeless teams played a pointless game. Yet that was what made it so unexpectedly interesting because there is an integrity in what players do when it counts the least, and so Eli Manning was worth watching on this worthless day.

"It was cold, and we were not playing for much," Manning said later.

For his entire 14-year career, Manning's easy, undemonstrative demeanor has been mistaken for complacency. It has subtly undermined him, made it harder for his critics to value him on his best days despite two Super Bowl victories and made it easy to denigrate him on his bad ones, of which this was one. But respect had to be paid as he fought through this day, fought the wind chill, fought the injuries that decimated the New York Giants, fought all the uncertainty over his future and fought for an 18–10 victory over the Washington Redskins that lifted the Giants' record to 3-13. When it was over and he was jogging off the field, after completing just 10 of his 28 passes for 132 yards, a faint noise came from that thin shivering crowd. They were chanting his name.

"It's probably been my toughest year of football," he said.

The final tally for this season: the Giants started 0-5; lost 21 players to injured reserve, including their three top receivers; briefly benched Manning in favor of Geno Smith; and fired their head coach and general manager. They began the day tied for third in the NFL in dropped passes, 31st in scoring offense, and 32nd in total defense. Manning absorbed it all, as he usually does, with those slouching shoulders and that falling, self-effacing voice and kept coming back for more with that easy temperament of his. Which was why after it was all over, interim coach Steve Spagnuolo waited on the field to catch him as he jogged off and hugged him for a long moment.

"We've both been through a lot and none more so than him with this season, but he never changed," Spagnuolo said. "He's had the highest of highs, and this was certainly very, very low, but he's a tremendous competitor, and I appreciate him greatly."

If there is a silver lining for Manning, it may be that he finally gets some credit for his grit, which is continually underestimated but allowed him to start 210 straight games. Over the years his shambling, nonchalant-seeming body language has made it easy to misread him; he can seem passive or easily defeated.

"I always heard them say Eli doesn't care," his father, Archie, said once. "Eli cares. But Eli doesn't worry."

This season, though, there was worry. The injuries mounted around him: he lost every member of the starting offensive line, and when Odell Beckham Jr., Brandon Marshall, and Dwayne Harris all had to undergo surgery, there went 1,342 catches and 128 touchdowns. He was left with some talented but unrehearsed young strangers at the receiver positions. "Hard to be on rhythm and on time," he said. It made everyone look bad—and Manning picked up the tab for it.

Manning will turn 37 years old this week, and the sand is running out. But he insists there still is enough in him to compete. "I think I still have good football in me," he said earlier in the week. "I don't want to stop playing football. This is all I want to do. I don't have a backup plan, I don't have something I'm looking forward to doing when this is done."

Whether the new Giants management believes that remains to be seen. The Giants have the No. 2 pick in the NFL draft and may well look for their future quarterback in it. Though newly appointed general manager Dave Gettleman has suggested publicly the Giants want to keep Manning, nothing is promised, as Manning noted. "I think we've just got to see what happens," he said. "I always think the talks in person are more important than what's said in the media."

It would be a mistake for the Giants to let him out of the building.

Even in one of his worst seasons as a pro, Manning defined professionalism and resilience. He never wavered in the face of criticism, still exercised his devotion to craft, still found a way to throw for more touchdowns than interceptions. He regained the starting job after the indignity of his benching. And after all that, he managed to win an unlikely game. A meaningless one that somehow meant everything to him.

"I believe he's got some football left—a lot of football in him," Spagnuolo said. "He's a competitor. Competitors—they last in this league. And you need them."

LARS ANDERSON

The Death of a Teenage Quarterback

FROM B/R MAG

THE MOTHER WALKS through the midnight darkness of the upstairs hallway in their New Jersey home, pushing open the door to
her only child's bedroom. She checks his closet—sometimes she'll
put on his clothes to feel close to him, to smell him, to *be* with him
—and then examines his books on a shelf. Her boy had a way with
words and wanted to become a writer, and now the mother is looking for a message from him, a clue, even though she knows she'll
never really find one.

The coach ambles onto the football field in western New Jersey
where it all went so terribly wrong two autumns ago. He comes
here now, in the rolling green foothills of the Pocono Mountains,
to be close to the spot where he last saw the quarterback who was
unlike any other player in his 37-year coaching career. He's still
trying to understand the cruelness of it all, the meaning of that last
game, even though he knows he never really will.

The best friend sits on a wooden bench in the park where they
played together and dreamed together. He closes his eyes and
replays it all again on the grainy film of memory: the basketball
games in this park, the football, the soccer, the skinned elbows,
the laughter. The bench is the best friend's favorite place in the
world, and on many summer nights when he's home from college
he'll come here and, alone in the pines, rehash the final hours of
the life of Evan Murray, wondering if football is to blame, trying

to make sense of his best friend's death at age 17, even though he
knows he never really will.

The last day begins when the alarm on Evan Murray's bedroom
nightstand buzzes at 5:45 a.m. It's September 25, 2015. He lifts
his 6-foot-2, 190-pound frame out of his bed and touches his size-
13 feet to the carpeted floor. Already, the high school senior is
excited by the promise of this Friday: it's game day between Warren Hills Regional High—where Evan is the starting quarterback
—and Summit (New Jersey) High. Kickoff is 13 hours away.

He presses on his iPod and blares Chance the Rapper, the beat
so loud it practically shakes the upstairs windows in the four-bedroom house on this quiet street with lush lawns and soaring oaks.
He showers, slips on his blue-and-white No. 18 jersey—he wears
it in honor of Peyton Manning, who he had recently profiled for
an English class—and slides into his 2010 Volkswagen Passat. It is
now 6:30 a.m.

He swings by the house of a teammate, Shane Plenge, and
the two drive to Muheisen's Bagel & Deli. Evan orders his usual
French toast bagel with cream cheese and a plain bagel with cream
cheese. He washes them down with a tall carton of chocolate milk.
As the teammates eat breakfast in the car, Evan seems quieter than
usual, but Plenge chalks it up to game-day anticipation.

The two drive to school, with Evan steering the silver Passat
through the cloudless early morning. Evan's father, Tom, had
given him the Volkswagen only two weeks earlier, replacing the
family minivan Evan had been driving. Oh man, Evan's friends
loved to mock his "middle-age mom's minivan," as they called it,
but he embraced how uncool he looked behind the wheel, always
motoring into the school parking lot with his sunglasses on, windows down, rap music thumping, and the slyest of smiles lighting
his face. That was Evan being Evan, a goofball's goofball.

He guides his Passat into the high school parking lot and turns
into stall No. 287—his assigned spot. The starting quarterback for
the Blue Streaks then grabs his backpack and strides into school,
his gait steady and strong, the easy glide of a star athlete. Evan
had once considered quitting football if he wasn't named the starting quarterback—he had no desire to ride the bench and could
be as impetuous as any teenager—but now was living his hal-

cyon days. A student tells him to "kick some ass" against Summit High.

Kelly Murray, Evan's mother, is in St. Clair, Michigan, moving her own mother into the hospice care wing at a nursing home. Kelly hasn't seen Evan for eight days. She sends him a text message early in the morning.

"Good luck bud," the text reads. "Be safe. I love you."

Evan texts back: "I love you too."

She always grew so terrified on fall Friday nights as she approached those lights, some 40 feet tall, that cast an amber glow onto the football field. Before home games at Warren Hills Regional High in Washington Township, Kelly Murray paced in the school parking lot as other parents tailgated and talked. Then, once the game began, she'd continue pacing across the walkways and stairs in the grandstands, unable to sit still.

"Evan, you know I'm not in favor of you playing football," Kelly told her son five years earlier, when he first signed up to play in a youth league. "I won't stop you, but I'll never feel good about it because it's so dangerous."

"It's going to be okay, Mom," replied Evan, then 12 years old. "I can get hurt playing basketball and in other sports too. Trust me, I'll be just fine."

Kelly took every precaution. Six weeks before Evan's final season, she drove him to a doctor's office for his annual precamp physical. She watched intently as the physician pushed on his stomach, listened to his heart, and flashed a light into his eyes.

Evan never complained about being sick. As a toddler, Kelly would realize he was ill only when he vomited. But then again, Evan's deal-with-it demeanor was evident right away: born 10 weeks early, he spent the first six weeks of his life in the neonatal intensive care unit, fighting for breath, rarely crying even then.

From then on he'd been a textbook overachiever; as a teenager, for instance, he'd read novels when most of his classmates were watching television, not just for the pleasure, but also because he understood it improved his writing and his relationship with words.

"Tell me if you're not feeling well," Kelly said on numerous occasions.

"Mom," Evan would reply, "I'm good just like always."

The doctor pronounced Evan fit to play after his 15-minute physical before his senior year, assuring Kelly that her son was a healthy young man.

Still, six weeks after that exam, Kelly is a mess of nerves as game time ticks closer. She tells a friend in Michigan, "I should be there with my son."

Seven hours before kickoff, Evan Murray is sitting in his government class, his head bobbing. Evan's big hazel eyes usually flash with curiosity, but now he has trouble keeping them open as he rests his head on his right hand, which is propped up by his elbow anchored to the desk. Evan is an A student—in his junior year he recorded the school's highest PSAT score in the English comprehension section—and no one in the class is accustomed to seeing him doze during a lecture.

The bell rings to signal the end of the period. The brightness in Evan's eyes suddenly returns. In the hall he nods at virtually every student he passes, his chin held high. Evan was named the starting quarterback late in his sophomore season, and now he knows how to play that role, projecting confidence and strength to every curious glance shot his way. This is what his hero Peyton Manning did, and this is what Evan does now.

Even when Evan was 15, he organized players-only practice sessions and tutored older players in the nuances of the playbook, which Evan seemed to memorize after one reading. Now he is usually the last player to head to the showers after practice. He lingers on the field, staying late with receivers and launching long, spiraling passes through the twilight. From their cars on Jackson Valley Road, locals driving home from work can see the silhouette of No. 18 striving to get better.

"I coached for over 35 years, and Evan was one of the hardestworking players I ever had," says Larry Dubiel, the longtime head football coach at Warren Hills. "A dream player—an absolute coach's dream."

Piloting a pro-style offense that features sprint-outs and bootlegs, Evan is a dual-threat quarterback. He has a strong arm—he consistently throws a 90-mile-per-hour fastball as a starting pitcher on the Warren Hills baseball team—and is a capable runner. In the season opener, Evan threw for 209 yards and a touchdown in

Warren Hills's 24–23 loss to Cranford. Eight days later, he passed for 290 yards and three touchdowns in the Blue Streaks' 28–21 win over Rahway.

Now six hours before kickoff against Summit High, Evan spots his head coach in the school hallway. They talk about an opposing cornerback they think they can beat on deep routes.

"I can't wait," Evan says. "This is going to be so much fun. We got this, Coach. We got this."

Evan knows his grandmother is sick. So three days before his final game, he sits at the desk in the study of his house and writes a letter, the love pouring from his pen.

Dear Grandma Margie,

It's Evan, your favorite Grandson (of course)! . . . Football is going well so far, even though we lost our first game 24–23. It was a great game, back and forth the whole time, and it came down to the final seconds. Even though we didn't come out on top, I was encouraged because I had over 200 yards passing, and the other team was favored by about 30 points. The next week we won 28–21, and I had another great game . . . School is challenging because I have lots of highlevel classes, but I'm doing well! Keep being strong Grandma, I love you so much!

Love,

Evan

The next morning, before driving to school, Evan addresses an envelope and affixes a stamp. The letter is mailed 36 hours before kickoff.

Five hours before kickoff, with classes out for the day, Evan drives a few friends to QuickChek convenience store—and they buy subs for themselves and teammates.

They return to the school cafeteria, where the players eat and the entire team watches a movie. At one point Evan leaves to use the restroom. When he sits back down with his friends, he remarks on the strange color of his urine.

The team holds a walkthrough practice on the Warren Hills basketball court, reviewing plays and formations and game strategies. Evan is his usual self, correcting mistakes by his teammates and explaining how important it will be to be precise in everything they do in just three hours out on the football field, across Jackson Valley Road from the school.

The players pull on their uniforms in the school locker room and, with kickoff 70 minutes away, walk toward the field. Evan leads the way.

Three nights before his final game, Evan sat down in the family study to tackle his English homework. The assignment was to write an essay for a pretend college application answering the following question: *Choose a community to which you belong and describe that community and your place within it.*

His head buried in a circle of lamplight, Evan tapped the keys on his computer for two hours, distilling his thoughts onto the computer screen. "The group that I am most proud to be a part of . . . is the football team," Evan wrote.

> I believe that I help bring all these groups in the Warren Hills community together for a short time. I play quarterback and am charged with leading the team on and off the field. Being in this position really puts my life in perspective and emphasizes what it means to be a Blue Streak, because I find myself being a spokesperson for our team everywhere I go.
>
>   . . .
>
> There is nothing like playing on Friday nights in front of the whole Blue Streak community, with all its groups and members coming together to cheer us on. After games, I talk to countless people about how the game went, and I find that so many people take a special interest in what we do, and that makes me truly feel like I make a small difference in the community. Bringing everybody together for one night in the week makes me proud to be a Blue Streak, and to be the leader of the group makes me feel even prouder.

Thirty hours before kickoff, Evan hands the essay to his teacher. He plans to send it along with his application to the University of Michigan.

The father takes his seat on top of the tiny wooden press box, papers and pens spread out before him on a table. Tom Murray, purchasing director for Bed Bath & Beyond, is a statistician for the Warren High football team. He does this not out of his love for numbers but to be closer to his only son. A stoic man, Tom can't suppress his pride in Evan.

With kickoff 20 minutes away on this sparkling fall night, Tom watches his son warm up from his perch above the field, a thin smile stretching across his face. With each passing week this summer and fall, the frontiers of what is possible have expanded for Evan, and no one is more aware of this than his father. His friends know not to bother him during games.

The stands begin to fill with about 1,500 fans, most clad in blue and white. Evan is hitting his receivers in stride during his pregame throws, the passes rarely touching the field turf. "We're expecting a big night from you," Coach Dubiel tells Evan. "You're our leader."

Tom Murray continues to watch his son. Six days earlier, the two had driven together to Pittsburgh, where Evan pitched for a baseball coach at the University of Pittsburgh. The Panthers are recruiting Evan to play baseball, but during his informal "tryout," Evan struggled with his velocity and control. When pressed by his father if he felt okay, Evan insisted he was fine. "Just a little tired," he said. "It's no big deal."

From his metal folding chair atop the press box, Tom studies his son carefully, analyzing his pregame movements and throws and mannerisms and countenance.

Evan looks absolutely wonderful.

Minutes before kickoff, 615 miles away in St. Clair, Michigan, Kelly Murray glances at her watch. A familiar feeling grips her—the queasiness of knowing her son is about to step between the white lines.

Kelly has always enjoyed the sleepy pace of life in St. Clair (population: 5,802), the town near where she grew up that now offers her a nice escape from the hustle of East Coast living. Located in the eastern "thumb" of the state, St. Clair is home to the longest freshwater boardwalk in the world, and Kelly has always enjoyed losing herself by taking leisurely, lovely strolls along the St. Clair River, gazing across the water into Canada. Here she feels safe.

She joins two friends at the River Crab restaurant on the St. Clair. She looks at her watch again. It reads 6:58. Two minutes later, she looks again.

"What's the matter?" a friend asks Kelly after they are seated at a riverside table. Outside the window, the evening sunlight dances on the water and glitters like diamonds. "Why are you so serious?"

"It's game time," Kelly says. "I've just got a funny feeling."
She wishes to be with her son.

Evan jogs onto the field for the Blue Streaks' first offensive possession. He looks to the sideline and receives the play call from
his head coach. He's alert in the huddle, his eyes gleaming, and
before the first snap he tells his teammates that this is their time,
their moment, their night.

Evan slings the ball all over the field during the game's first
20 minutes of clock time, some passes reaching his receivers, others falling incomplete. On a few plays, he is hit after he releases
the ball. On one third down, he drops back and runs to his right;
just as he unleashes a pass, a defender crashes into him, slamming
Evan's head and body to the turf.

Evan wobbles to the sideline, clutching his sternum beneath
his pads. The athletic trainer, Kevin Call, immediately checks him,
worried he is concussed. After a cursory exam, Call tells the coaching staff Evan is good to return to the game.

So he does. With about a minute remaining in the first half and
the ball at midfield, Evan receives a snap and rolls to his left. He
wants to attack the cornerback he and his coach had discussed
earlier. Evan rears back and rifles a ball deep, sending it high into
the September sky.

A defensive end wallops Evan after the ball leaves his fingertips,
and he slams Evan into the turf. The cornerback intercepts the
pass. Wanting to make the tackle, Evan pops up and, as he's an-
gling toward the cornerback, another defensive player rams into
him. The quarterback crumbles to the ground. Both hits are legal.

Evan rises and gingerly walks to the sideline. The trainer, Call,
moves immediately to Evan and escorts him to the bench.

One minute passes in real time, two—Evan appears fine, responding to coaches and the trainer. Then, as Call is still inspect-
ing him, Evan suddenly slumps on the bench and his limp body
slides sideways, like a seated mannequin tipping to its left. Evan
loses consciousness as he's caught by a teammate. Tom Murray,
atop the press box, is busily recording statistics when a family
friend yells for him: "Tom, something is wrong with Evan!"

Tom sprints down the grandstand. He leaps over the four-and-
a-half-foot chain-link fence behind the bench and is quickly at his

son's side on the bench, grasping his hand, looking into his sweat-beaded face.

Evan blinks his eyes open. The coaching and training staff, huddling over him, believe he has a concussion. They call for the ambulance, which is parked close to the locker room about 75 yards away.

About two minutes later, the first half ends with Warren Hills trailing 0–6. On his way to the locker room, Dubiel stops to talk to Evan, who is now sitting up on the sideline and waiting for the ambulance to move onto the field. "How are you doing?" Dubiel asks.

"I'll be fine," Evan says. "Go get this. We'll talk after the game."

The ambulance pulls near Evan, who is now on a gurney. Tom Murray hands his cell phone to his son as the teen is loaded into the back of the emergency vehicle.

Kelly is on the other end of the line. A concerned friend in the stands had texted her and told her to call Tom immediately.

"What happened?" Kelly asks.

"I don't know," Evan says. "I think I blacked out or something. I'm okay."

"I love you," Kelly says.

"I love you too," Evan replies.

Evan gives the phone back to his father. Lying on his back on the stretcher, he flashes a thumbs-up sign to the crowd, prompting a relieved round of applause. Evan, with eye-black smudged on his face, smiles.

He is lifted into the ambulance. Tom climbs into the front seat. The vehicle rumbles off the field and disappears down the dark two-lane road, red and white lights flashing as it passes the Victorian-style houses in the Jersey night.

Kelly trembles at the table. She tells her friends Evan has been injured. "Something's not right," she says. "Something's not right."

She orders her food. She calls her sister in Syracuse, New York, telling her in a panicked voice that her boy is hurt, that something is terribly wrong. She cannot eat.

Her friends drive her back to their house in Michigan. In the car Kelly is so scared she has trouble breathing.

*

From the front seat of the ambulance, Tom peers into the back at his son through a window. The driver is heading to a small hospital four miles from the football field.

The white ambulance cruises along a highway, the driver obeying the speed limits, believing his patient is in no grave danger.

But then, horror: Tom sees, through the window, the emergency medical technician performing chest compressions on Evan. His son has stopped breathing.

The driver changes course: Evan needs to go to Morristown Memorial Hospital, some 40 minutes away, because it houses a trauma unit. The driver flips on the siren and mashes the accelerator.

Tom stares at his boy.

The medic works feverishly, pumping hard on Evan's chest. Up and down, up and down, he pushes.

Tom stares at his boy.

Minutes and miles pass. The ambulance finally stops in front of the emergency room at Morristown Memorial. Tom rushes out of the passenger seat, eyes wide with terror.

Tom looks around but sees no medical personnel running out of the hospital to help his boy. "Where is everyone?" Tom yells. "Why aren't they waiting for us?"

The answer—the oh-my-God answer, the please-no-no-no answer—hits Tom at just past 9:15 p.m. ET, 135 minutes after kickoff.

Kelly steps out of the car at her friend's house and into the growing Michigan darkness. She's standing in the front lawn when her cell phone rings, the smell of freshly cut grass hanging in the cool air.

"He didn't make it," Tom says.

"What do you mean?!" Kelly yells. "What do you mean?!"

"He didn't make it," Tom says. "He's gone."

"What are you saying to me, Tom?!" Kelly yells. "Don't say that to me! Don't say that to me!"

One friend takes the phone from Kelly, who falls to the ground, wailing. She rips up the grass and continues to yell, the screams audible for blocks. Another friend picks her up and carries her into the house.

Kelly sits on a chair, unable to talk for 30 minutes, sobbing so hard that her friends quickly decide she is in no condition to fly home. She needs to be driven to her son immediately.

*

In a private room at Morristown Memorial, Tom wraps his arms around his son. Evan is on a gurney with a tube in his mouth and a brace around his neck. The time of death was around 9:30 p.m., two and a half hours after kickoff. The medical staff believes he suffered some sort of fatal brain injury.

For over an hour, Tom won't let go of his boy. A family friend arrives, hugs Tom tightly, and tells him a dozen students and parents are in the waiting room and deeply concerned. Tom briefly leaves Evan's side and quietly tells everyone, "We lost Evan." Then he returns and continues to hold and caress his boy.

Into the night and through the small hours of the morning, Tom doesn't let go—can't let go.

Kelly sits in the backseat of the car, her head resting on the shoulder of her brother-in-law. Her eyes are blank.

The countrysides of different states pass by—Michigan, Ohio, Pennsylvania. At one point she sees the first blush of the day's light ripple across the horizon and shoot across the farming fields of the Midwest. Gazing out the window at the sunrise, Kelly is reminded that the world will carry on, even if her son won't—and even if she can't.

Kelly is quiet in the backseat, with so many questions about Evan rolling through her mind: Did he suffer? Did he take one fatal hit? Was it a blow to the head? What caused him to die? Then she'd catch herself and think: *What's it all matter? My boy is gone. That's all. My boy is gone.*

The car pulls into her driveway 20 hours after kickoff. But now she can't bring herself to walk inside, not when her son isn't there. Tom eventually approaches; husband and wife collapse into each other's arms, moaning together in pain.

The entire football staff soon comes to the house. They form a line to hug and comfort Evan's parents. Tom can't stop blaming himself for his son's death, believing he could have done something to prevent it. "It's my fault," he says over and over. "My fault."

More than 300 students, teachers, coaches, and community members gather at the football field the day after, unsure of where else to go. They hug, cry, and share stories of Evan—stories of his love of drawing comic book heroes, stories of his silly high-pitched laughter, stories of how he was going to become a sportswriter, stories of his ability to drink more gallons of chocolate milk in a week than any other kid on the planet.

Friends also congregate in the school parking lot in space No. 287 and build a makeshift memorial. Within hours, this rectangle of asphalt is filled with flowers, balloons, candles, banners, written notes, cards, and photos. One handwritten missive reads: "We love you, Evan. You are so beautiful. Never, never will we forget you."

Two police officers arrive to deliver seven boxes of Dunkin' Donuts and enough coffee for everyone. Coach Dubiel, who had sped to the hospital to be by Tom's side, shuffles onto the field, his eyes red. He embraces each of the players, whispering in their ears that he loves them. He says the same thing to non-football players.

According to the Korey Stringer Institute at the University of Connecticut, named after the former Vikings offensive tackle who died from heat stroke complications during a practice in 2001, Evan was one of 13 U.S. high school students whose death was linked to playing football in 2015.

"But this isn't supposed to happen here," Coach Dubiel says. "Not in Hometown, USA."

The line stretches the length of several football fields out of Faith Discovery Church. Young and old, wealthy and poor, black and white, even little kids from across the region who never knew Evan yet dressed in their football uniforms—they all come to say goodbye at the visitation five days after Evan has died.

The family is the first to enter. Kelly still hasn't seen her son. Holding the hands of her husband and sister, she approaches the open casket. She loses all strength in her legs when she's two feet away.

She strokes his face, rubs his bearded chin. She wants to crawl in the casket with him and never let go. For the next nine hours, she clutches every last person in the line as they stream past Evan. One peewee football team kneels in front of the casket and says a quiet prayer. Even the 70 police officers and firefighters from Warren County assigned to work the visitation embrace Evan's mom. That night Kelly is so sore she can barely lift her arms.

The funeral is the next day. Evan is wearing a blue-and-green checkered shirt. Two days earlier, Tom had entered Evan's room to pick out the shirt—the last time Tom will walk into his boy's bedroom.

In the nursing home in Michigan, a family friend streams the funeral on her iPhone and plays it for Evan's grandmother, who is unconscious. She dies three days later.

The letter Evan wrote to her is sitting on her nightstand.

The medical examiner calls with the news: Evan's spleen was abnormally large, so big that it was literally hanging out of his rib cage. The spleen was lacerated; Evan bled to death within about 30 minutes of his final play on the football field. The examiner explains that he had mononucleosis, a condition that often causes the spleen to swell.

Most young people with mono don't have the energy to climb out of bed—this was the case for Kelly when she was struck with mono as a 16-year-old—but Evan was virtually asymptomatic and ignored the symptoms he did experience. He didn't allow the fatigue or dehydration (signaled by the strange-colored urine after school) to keep him from the football field. "An atypical case," the medical examiner calls it.

Tom is shocked by the information; he assumed a head injury had taken his son.

But the knowledge that there was nothing Tom could have done to prevent the sequence of events brings no relief to the father. His boy is still gone.

"It was Evan's tremendous work ethic that sadly led to his downfall," Dubiel says. "He never complained about anything. He was so tough, so determined. He never wanted anyone to worry about him."

In the days, weeks, and months following the funeral, thousands more cards and notes arrive in the Murrays' mailbox. Peyton Manning sends a signed jersey. Eli Manning pens a long letter. ("The pain of losing a child is unimaginable," Eli says now. "It's something you never get over, but when I think of Evan's family, I pray they have peace.") Coach Jim Harbaugh explains that he read Evan's college application essay to his players. Atlanta Falcons coach Dan Quinn writes, "Our team is thinking of you." And a mother in Illinois details how she lost her son to football too—he suffered a fatal head injury—and that she prays peace will come.

Kelly reads every last word.

She finds no peace.

*

It's a blue-gray summer afternoon in Washington, New Jersey, and Kelly is driving through the quaint downtown with her niece, Danielle Hobson.

It's been almost two years since her son lost his life, but blue-and-white ribbons are still attached to street signs and utility poles in Evan's memory. Kelly always counts the ribbons on her slow rides through downtown, desperately hoping none have blown away.

The family wants Evan's story told, to help their own healing and so that other football families, perhaps, can learn from their devastation. Kelly hasn't returned to her job as an in-home caregiver. Tom sometimes doesn't remember driving to work in the mornings, still searching for his magnetic north.

They haven't canceled the mobile plan for Evan's phone, because it comforts Kelly to know his voice is still alive, forever frozen at 17. Kelly still visits his room—which is just as Evan left it, down to the exact order of how he arranged his books on his bookcase—and lies in his bed at night, letting thoughts of her son wash over her.

Yet on this June afternoon, as Kelly cruises along Belvidere Avenue in her white Mazda CX-7, there is joy in the backseat—exactly 11.7 pounds of it. Strapped into a car seat is Adrian Evan Hobson, a baby boy Danielle gave birth to eight weeks ago. When Danielle told Kelly and Tom that she was going to pass along Evan's name to her firstborn, the still-grieving parents cried. But after a few moments they both smiled, as if sunlight had finally penetrated the fog.

"I don't want my son playing football," Danielle says. "It's dangerous. But will my wishes stop him? I don't know."

"Football didn't kill Evan," says Kathy Killgore, Kelly's sister. "He died because he was sick, and he was playing when he was sick, and nobody knew it."

Kelly, her niece, and little Adrian Evan pull into Meadow Breeze Park, the place where Evan grew up playing football, baseball, basketball, and soccer. A few parents bought a bench, engraved Evan's name into the wood, and placed it near the basketball court. Evan's best friend, A. J. Lea, often sits on the bench when he's home from college. Here, surrounded by blooming marigolds, the wind dusting his cheeks, he reads books and relives those crowded hours of happiness he shared with Evan.

"The bench is where I spend time with Evan," says Lea, now a sophomore at Cornell. "Evan and I pushed each other academically. We did a reading competition against each other in the third grade, and in high school we were in the National Honor Society together. We even edited each other's college essays. My life will never be the same without him."

Kelly steers the car toward the Warren Hills High football field, back to those haunting floodlights. Dubiel retired after the 2016 season, but he still returns to the stadium on Jackson Valley Road —and can still picture that last game with Evan, that final conversation on the field.

"You want to move on in life, but it hasn't been easy," he says. "I don't blame football. I blame this on life not always being fair."

Kelly parks outside of the stadium. She walks to the plaque that hangs on the outside wall of the locker room. The words from Evan's college essay are inscribed in bronze. Kelly examines every syllable, saying each word aloud, searching for . . . searching for . . . her son.

"I ask myself all the time, 'How should I feel about football?'" Kelly says, her fingers rubbing the plaque. "Some people think I should hate it, but I don't. Football put Evan in a compromising position, but it could have been on a basketball court where he took a hit or even in the school hallway messing around with his friends. But sometimes I think I should have made him stop. He'd be here now if I did. But how could I? He loved it so much. Just *loved* it."

For one minute, Kelly keeps her right hand on the plaque, two. Rain begins to fall.

Three minutes, four.

Her hand doesn't budge.

Five, six.

In stillness, she closes her eyes.

She is with her boy.

There's Nowhere to Run

FROM THE WASHINGTON POST

HE INCHES FORWARD, with jets overhead and the ground 50 stories below. Larry Johnson can feel it happening: the arrival, he calls it, of the demons.

They push him toward the barrier of a rooftop deck of an apartment building where he sometimes comes to visit a friend, and, in moments like these, there's a strengthening urge—an almost overwhelming curiosity, he describes it—to jump.

"One is telling you to do it; one is telling you don't," says Johnson, a former NFL running back. "One is telling you it'd be fun."

It is early November, less than two weeks before his 38th birthday. He played his last game in 2011, and he now believes he suffers from chronic traumatic encephalopathy, the degenerative brain disorder linked to more than 100 former football players. For now, CTE can be confirmed only after death, but Johnson says his symptoms—anxiety, paranoia, the occasional self-destructive impulse—are consistent with those of past victims.

On this afternoon, he shuffles closer to the ledge, past the drainage fixture a foot or so from the glass barrier. His body is tingling, he says; his thoughts are filled with static.

"They say when you die," Johnson says, looking down toward Southeast First Avenue, "you feel that euphoric feeling."

Closer now. He's frightened, less of the fall than the direction of his own mind.

"What would it be like," he says, "for this to be the day for people to find out you're not here?"

Fading Memories

At a red light back on terra firma, Johnson glances into the back-seat. "Let me see the homework," he tells Jaylen, his seven-year-old daughter. He flips through the stapled pages: math problems and reading comprehension about bicycles and roller coasters. The light changes, and Johnson hands the papers back and hits the gas on his Porsche SUV. For the next half-hour, Johnson—prone to fits of volatility, jarring mood swings, extreme periods of silence —will say almost nothing.

Johnson says father and daughter have many things in common, including a quiet personality and a running stride that made Johnson a 2002 Heisman Trophy finalist at Penn State and a two-time Pro Bowl honoree. He was a rusher so durable and fierce that, while playing for the Kansas City Chiefs in 2006, he set an NFL record with 416 carries. That same year, groundbreaking neurologist Bennet Omalu published additional concussion research that linked football-related head injuries with degenerative brain trauma, the beginning of an NFL crisis that still rages and one of the reasons Johnson's carries record probably will never be broken.

Jaylen doesn't know much about that part of her Papi's life, in part because Johnson thinks his daughter is too young to understand how football brought him both glory and ruin. But it's also because there are widening chunks of his career that he can't remember: two full NFL seasons have disappeared from his memory, he says, and even some of his most memorable plays have grown hazy.

Which is why, in the past few years, Johnson has begun making video compilations of his football highlights, in part as reminders to himself that he was involved in them—but also, when she's ready, as a time capsule for Jaylen.

Johnson fears that, by the time he's 50, he won't remember his own name. If that proves to be the case, Johnson is taking steps for Jaylen to watch her Papi run, to learn who he was, to maybe understand why he was so unpredictable—even, on occasion, with her.

"If I can't remember who I was, I've got YouTube; I've got music videos that I'm making for myself, so when I watch these things I can remember," he says. "I'm trying to get these things in order so she knows who I am and what I came from."

The project became urgent a few months ago, after a particularly severe case of CTE was discovered in the brain of Aaron Hernandez. The former New England Patriots tight end, with a history of erratic and explosive behavior, was convicted of first-degree murder in 2015 before hanging himself in his prison cell in April.

"I could be Aaron Hernandez," Johnson says, and indeed he sees the former Patriots star as a kindred spirit as much as a cautionary tale.

Like Hernandez, Johnson has a history of erratic behavior and violence: he has been arrested six times, and several of the incidents involved Johnson physically assaulting women. The ex-running back says his decision to publicly describe his darkest thoughts is meant not as a way to excuse his past but rather a way to begin a conversation with other former players who Johnson suspects are experiencing many of the same symptoms.

Johnson says he frequently gets brief but intense headaches, often triggered by bright lights or noise, and is increasingly jittery and forgetful. He has no idea how the Porsche's passenger-side mirror got smashed, nor can he remember the full sequence that led to the cluster of dents in the vehicle's rear hatch.

"Blank spots" are what Johnson calls the empty spaces in his memory, and there are seemingly more of them every year. But there's another similarity with Hernandez that scares him most.

Johnson says he has considered violence toward others and himself, and perhaps the only reason he hasn't acted on these impulses is sitting quietly in the backseat, looking out the window at the South Florida flatlands.

"Chicken, steak, or spaghetti?" Johnson asks, and Jaylen chooses spaghetti. Her voice is soft as a whisper. Her father believes it's also the only one, when the demons push him to the edge, strong enough to pull him back.

"Sometimes he was the reason"

Almost three decades ago, on a youth field in Oxon Hill, a nine-year-old kick returner caught the ball and sped toward the sideline.

Hoping he'd be tackled quickly and painlessly, young Larry kept running and tried to get out of bounds—but then an opponent crashed into him from the side, spinning his helmet sideways.

The boy got up, dizzy and with no idea where he was, and spent the rest of the game on the sideline with a headache. Though it was never diagnosed as a concussion—Johnson says, in 23 years of football, he was never diagnosed with one—he now suspects this was his first of many.

But more than the impact, he now says, he felt then that he had let his father down. Larry Johnson Sr., at the time a well-known high school coach in Maryland, was in the bleachers, and the boy felt he had shown everyone that the coach's son was soft.

"I didn't know how to redeem myself," Johnson says, though soon he was going into the family's basement for extra blocking drills, studying footage of prodigious NFL hitters Ronnie Lott and Mike Singletary, looking for any chance to prove his toughness.

He grew, and by middle school he was researching which opponents came from broken homes; those were the kids he'd taunt before plays and, for an extra psychological advantage, the ones he'd tackle from behind. If Johnson was benched, he'd blow up at coaches; if an opponent or teammate challenged him, Johnson wasn't above the cheap shot.

Then he'd look to the bleachers.

"I'd be like: 'Dad, you saw that?' It was a point of pride," he says now, and he came to believe, in an era that glamorized masculinity and intimidation, that "this is what tough means."

Larry Johnson Sr., now an assistant head coach at Ohio State, says that wasn't exactly the intention.

"He ran with rage, and it was just his way of saying, 'I'm not going to let this opportunity get away,'" the coach says. "It might have taken him to places he didn't think he would go."

Some of those places, as Johnson became a college player and eventually a pro, included the backs of police cars or disciplinary meetings with coaches. He says he began experiencing symptoms of depression in college, and he sought to prove his toughness in nightclubs and fights with women. He tried to numb himself with alcohol, which took him deeper into the shadows.

Months after Kansas City selected him in the first round of the 2003 draft, Johnson was arrested for aggravated assault and domes-

tic battery for an incident involving a woman. A misunderstand-
ing, Johnson would say. Less than two years later, he was arrested
again for shoving a different woman to the floor of a bar. An overly
aggressive local law, he'd say.

"There's always a reason" for Johnson's mistakes, says Tony
Johnson, the ex-player's brother and his day-to-day manager during his NFL career. "And sometimes he was the reason."

Johnson could be cheerful and social at times, sullen and iso-
lated at others. He collected slights and bad habits, to say nothing
of the guns he kept strapped to his shoulders at high-end restau-
rants or under the seat of his white Bentley. Some nights he'd fire
rounds into strangers' lawns or palm a pistol at a gas station, he
says, hoping someone would challenge him for a late-night lesson
in toughness.

"Me against everybody," he says, and on and off the field that
became his code, driving him to rush for a combined 3,539 yards
in 2005 and '06. His dominance and persona made him an A-list
celebrity and opened doors to a friendship with Jay-Z and dates
with R&B singer Mýa.

Whether it was brain injuries, immaturity, celebrity, or some
combination, Johnson says, aggression became "a switch I couldn't
shut off." After a while Jay-Z cut him off via email for being arrested so often, Johnson says, and Mýa once stopped him from
jumping from a window.

After two more arrests and a suspension, the Chiefs released
Johnson in 2009 after he insulted his head coach on Twitter and
for using gay slurs toward a fan and reporters. Years after trying
to adapt his personality to an unforgiving game, Johnson found
himself too volatile for the NFL. Over his final two seasons, with
Washington and Miami, he carried the ball six times.

"Those two combinations, of being angry and not being able
to shut that switch off, started to disrupt who I really was," he says.
"And it was just waiting to eat me up."

Sound and Fury

They're in the living room now, Papi and Jaylen, surrounded by
walls undecorated but for the blotchy spackling compound behind

them. That's where, a few years ago, Johnson punched through the drywall.

Jaylen was there, and Johnson says he sent her upstairs before making the hole. The way he describes it, the best he can do sometimes is to shield her view.

"Did you think it was something that you did?" Johnson recalls asking Jaylen afterward, and the girl nodded. "I had to explain it: It's never your fault."

But her little mind is expanding quickly, and he worries that these will be some of her earliest memories. And so he tries. It might not seem like it, he admits, but he tries.

On this afternoon, father and daughter play a racing game on Xbox—bright colors, loud sound effects, rapid movement—and after a few minutes, Johnson pauses the game and walks onto his balcony. He stands alone for a minute or two, hands clasped behind his head; he'll say later he felt the onset of a headache and needed to step away.

He returns, and now it's homework time. Johnson has high expectations for Jaylen, and he believes the universe was making a point when it gave him a daughter. How better to punish him for shoving or choking women than to assign him a girl to shepherd through a world filled with Larry Johnsons?

"My greatest fear is my daughter falling in love with somebody who's me," he'll say, and he believes if he's honest and tough with Jaylen, she'll never accept anyone treating her the way her father treated women.

With the sun filtering between the blinds, Johnson plays with her curly hair as she slides a finger across her sentences.

"All people," Jaylen reads aloud, and her father interrupts.

"No," he says. "Why would it say 'all people'? It . . ."

He stops, sighs, and presses two fingers into his eyelids. She looks back at him, and he tells her to keep reading. He rubs his hands, massages his forehead, checks his watch. He'll say he sometimes forgets she's only in second grade.

They move on to her page of math problems: 27 plus seven.

"How many tens?" he asks her.

"Two."

"And how many ones?"

"Seven."

"No," he says, visibly frustrated until Jaylen reaches the answer. Next: 57 plus seven. She stares at the page.

"So count," he says. "Count!"

Thirteen plus eight. Again staring at the numbers. Johnson's worst subject was math, another trait Jaylen inherited. But his empathy is sometimes drowned out by more dominant emotions.

"You start at thirteen and count eight ones," he tells her, and in the kitchen, a watch alarm begins to beep. Jaylen counts her fingers.

"No," her dad tells her, again rubbing his face. The beeping continues in the next room. "No!"

Abruptly, he stands and stomps out of the room without saying anything. Jaylen's eyes follow him, eyebrows raised, and she listens as her father swipes the beeping watch from a table, swings open the back door, and throws it into the courtyard.

In the minds of both father and daughter, it is impossible to know what's happening. Will she remember this, or has Johnson shielded her from something worse? Is he managing his impulses as well as he can, and even if he is, will Jaylen someday come to view moments such as these as emotional milestones?

For now, when her Papi returns, Jaylen's eyes dart back to the page.

"So what's the answer?" he says.

"A bittersweet thing"

Nighttime now, and Johnson takes a pull off his Stella longneck and hits "play" on the remote.

There he is, or more precisely there he was: a wrecking ball in Penn State blue, highlights of Johnson overpowering defenders interspersed with pictures of Jaylen. The background music, which he selected, is the Imagine Dragons song "I'm So Sorry."

"This is who I really am," he says is the intended message of his self-produced video. "I can't change who I am, regardless of who you are."

He points the remote again, and next is a video of some of his best moments in the NFL: cheers and chants and line-of-scrimmage assaults that, in this era of increased awareness, are both exciting and devastating. The background song is "War Pigs" by Black Sabbath.

In the fields the bodies burning
As the war machine keeps turning

Johnson lifts the remote again. "This may . . ." he says, choking up. "I get emotional."

He hits "play."

"I did this for her," he says, and a moment later the piano begins.

A few years ago, Johnson woke into a hangover and felt drawn to his computer, spending hours navigating a video-editing program. What emerged was more than a gift for Jaylen's second birthday, Johnson says; these next five minutes 17 seconds were meant to say good-bye.

Back then, the demons could be overpowering. Johnson, drifting in the months and years after his NFL career ended, went searching for a new identity. He was arrested again for an incident with an ex-girlfriend, and he cycled among peddling bootleg makeup kits on South Beach, being turned down for a job stocking shelves, researching how to join the military. Usually it was just easier to go to a nightclub and chase salvation down the neck of a tequila bottle.

Trying to spend his way into new friends or purpose, Johnson says he sometimes dropped $50,000 in a night, torching his savings. In 2007, he signed a contract with the Chiefs that included $19 million in guaranteed money, but now, he says, he has enough for Jaylen's college and for himself to get by, and not much more.

Then, he says, he sometimes began evenings with the intention of starting trouble. Other times, he could feel himself losing control—an approaching cloud, he says, impossible to stop. Alcohol and noise were kerosene on his smoldering patience, and friends became used to Johnson turning into, as one friend put it, the Incredible Hulk.

"You could see the mood swings, and they were drastic," says Chantel Cohen, who has known Johnson for most of the past decade. "He could be super happy one moment, and an hour later, he's just ready to blow up. You're like: What just went wrong?"

Once, Johnson says, he sat with a group at a crowded table, and a man he'd just met was being loud. Johnson says he asked, profanely, for the man to shut up; a second later they both stood, and Johnson says he experienced one of his blank spots.

"When I came to, he was already on the ground, like, leaned over, and I'm kind of like: 'Damn, I must have did that,'" he says. As Johnson tried to get away, the man went after him with a chair, and that's where the dents in the back of his Porsche came from.

He would call his parents at all hours, cursing and making strange accusations. Tony Johnson woke to so many worried texts from his brother's friends that he stopped checking his phone in the morning and made peace with how his brother's story might end.

And so did Johnson himself. Working on that video for Jaylen years ago, he was aware he was about to go destroy himself. Like the time he punched through the wall, he explains, he could delay the explosion, but he couldn't avoid it.

Now rewatching the video in his living room, he says he wasn't exactly considering suicide but that he was preparing to go away to stay. Prison was a possibility, and so were a few others, considering he'd decided that if he did something to get himself arrested, he wasn't planning on going quietly.

There was, he recalls, something calming about it.

"A bittersweet thing: I'm going to be free of everything that's holding me down," Johnson says now, and he wonders whether Hernandez experienced similarly intense feelings in his final days. "The same way Aaron thought: I'm going to be gone from this world, but I'm still going to be able to take care of my child, because that's all I care about."

A moment later, he continues. His voice cracks.

"When you're that down deep in it," he says, "you don't want to be talked out of it."

And so that day a few years ago, he worked on the video until it was perfect, the music and images and sequence just right. A text banner—"I will always Love you," it reads—flutters past near the beginning, and with the Christina Perri song "A Thousand Years" in the background, it closes with a photograph of Johnson kissing Jaylen. It pans out before fading.

Then he posted the video on Instagram before loading his pockets with painkillers and ecstasy, he says, and set off into the space beneath a dropping curtain.

"He definitely has something"

A few weekends ago, friends invited Johnson to join them at a bar, have a few drinks, meet a woman he might like.

He agreed, and indeed he was drawn to her. They talked, and so did the friends—a little too much, maybe—and after a while Johnson could feel the shadow falling. The Hulk was coming, so at one point he excused himself and, without explanation, just left.

Distrustful of his own mind, Johnson says now that he wasn't just annoyed by his chatty friends. He noticed himself staring at one of them, feeling a growing urge to punch him. Almost in a heartbeat, Johnson went from sociable and joyful to deeply angry and potentially violent—frightening, at least this time, only himself.

"Something so easily dismissed," he says. "But it's just—once I get in that mood, I can't stop it. And it comes out of nowhere."

Even so, is this truly a look at CTE's corrosive effects in real time? Or has Johnson, with his history of blame deflection and self-validating reasons, simply found an unimpeachable—and unprovable—excuse?

"Do I think he's a special breed? Yes," says Tony Johnson, who suggests the family will consider donating Larry's brain for study after his death. "Do I think he might have CTE? I just can't say."

Others, who point out the brain's frontal lobe is the portion that regulates judgment and behavior—and the region most under attack during on-field collisions—see it more Johnson's way.

"I'm pretty sure that he definitely has something going on," says longtime friend Cohen, who claims she knew Junior Seau, the Hall of Fame linebacker who in 2012 shot himself in the chest so that his brain could be studied; indeed, CTE was discovered in Seau's brain. Cohen sees some similarities in the behavior of Johnson and Seau.

Johnson says years ago he was diagnosed with type-1 bipolar disorder, a condition he blames on head injuries. Though this cannot be confirmed in Johnson's case, brain injury experts have found possible links between bipolar symptoms and midlife behavior issues and CTE.

"Certain things happen in your life," he says, "that you just can't come back from."

After making the video for Jaylen a few years back, Johnson says, he spent the next 72 hours cycling from one party to the next, daring bar patrons or police or even death to bring him down. When nothing did, he kept going.

At one point he sat on a sidewalk, exhausted and struggling to breathe, and thought of his daughter. She was living with her mother at the time; Jaylen's parents now share custody.

Johnson went home, slept it off, and not long afterward, he says, he sold his ownership stake in a club on South Beach and reduced his intake of hard liquor. He still found trouble sometimes, including a 2014 arrest for aggravated battery involving another man, and Johnson says he has since made more changes.

He moved out of a trendy high-rise in Miami and into a quiet townhouse in Fort Lauderdale, got rid of his guns, took a job with a nonprofit that uses the arts to mentor disadvantaged children. Johnson also quit therapy and refused to take his prescribed medication; he says it's because he's better equipped to manage his impulses himself. All these years later, it's still Johnson against everybody—even himself.

He has, more recently, filled his bookshelf not with reminders of his playing career but with photographs of Jaylen and her paintings. If friends invite him out, more and more he turns them down.

"You kind of create your own prison," Johnson says. "I've kind of barricaded myself in my surroundings [with] certain things that I can handle. That's kind of how I beat it."

That's easy when his daughter is here—Jaylen spends most weekends with her father and weekdays with her mother in a nearby town—and a challenge when she's not. On the nights he's alone, Johnson is more likely to sulk or drink or venture into the depths of his restless mind. If she's here, bedtime is at 8:30, and they play games or watch television or draw.

"She's, like, a good distraction I have," he says. "She sees something in me that most people will never see."

Occasionally they watch football together, Jaylen in her Penn State or Kansas City jersey, and she asks why the announcers sometimes say his name. He explains some of it, and very carefully he has begun to explain some of the rest.

"Papi," he says he tells her, "used to be really bad."

He doesn't offer much more, and though he's uncertain what

the future will bring, Johnson says he wants to tell her his whole story eventually.

Johnson figures that in seven more years, or when she's 14 or so, Jaylen will be old enough to absorb the paradoxical nature of her father: the life of the party and the introvert, a man capable of violence and tenderness, the person he actually is and the one he wants to be.

He wants his mind to hang out at least that long. Jaylen might not like what she learns, but he wants to be present for those conversations.

His biggest fear, if he were to disappear now, is that Jaylen wouldn't remember him; his second biggest is that she would.

"That scares me more than anything," he says. "Sometimes it scares me to tears."

Back to the Unknown

He's driving again, steering the Porsche south on a highway not long after sunrise. Jaylen, who like her Papi is not a morning person, is dozing off in the backseat.

Earlier, the vehicle's back latch wouldn't close, and in the 20 or so minutes since, Johnson hasn't said a word. He weaves through traffic, occasionally touching 90 miles per hour, and a radio commercial plays a doorbell sound. The tone repeats again. And again. Johnson jabs his finger into the preset button to change the station.

He cracks his knuckles, sighs loudly, checks his phone.

He looks behind him occasionally, Jaylen napping or drawing imaginary circles on the glass. She's spending the next few days with her mother, and Johnson is already nervous about the upcoming time by himself. What if friends call and ask him to go drinking? Or if someone crosses him at the wrong moment?

How will he react this time if the demons come?

For now, she's with him a few more minutes, so Johnson parks the Porsche and lifts her from the backseat. He carries her toward the elementary school and kisses her cheek as they cross the driveway and fall into a line of students.

The line starts moving, and he tucks in her shirt and kisses her again. "I'll see you this weekend, okay?" he says, and then he turns toward the crosswalk.

He's alone again, left to face the next few days—and whichever emotions and impulses are waiting—with his mind as his only company. He looks behind him to see Jaylen toddling toward the entrance, and with little more than uncertainty ahead, Johnson stands on the curb and waits for her to drift out of sight before stepping, finally, off the edge.

DAVID ROTH

Downward Spiral

FROM THE BAFFLER

WHEN THE PREGAME show after the first pregame show ended, there were of course commercials. After that, nearly 100 million Americans watched a quill pen being dipped into an inkwell. The camera pulls back to reveal the arm and powdered wig of the man holding the pen; his hand protrudes from a voluminous sleeve that seems to terminate in some kind of avant-garde doily. String tones and a lone plonking horn on the soundtrack set a properly capital-H Historical tone. We are already hearing voiceover, plummy and rounded and fakey. A wider shot reveals a pewter mug at the edge of the desk, with a half-dozen other quills sticking floofily out of it. The bewigged man with the avant-garde sleeves signs his name and the date: *Th. Jefferson, June 1776.*

It was almost time for the football game.

A record 97.5 million people were watching Fox TV that night, February 3, 2008, to see the last and most important game of the NFL season, between the New York Giants and the undefeated New England Patriots. But first, to what we might as well imagine was their moderate-to-great surprise, they were watching *this.* The millions looked on as, in the next sequence, actors done up in inexpensive-looking Founding Father finery materialize like jowly ghosts in the interior of Philadelphia's Independence Hall and deliver themselves of famous historical quotes to a camera tracking left to right. The lighting is gauzy, and a snare drum rum-dummy-dums under all of it.

"The tree of liberty is watered with the blood of patriots and tyrants both," the man playing Thomas Jefferson says. The actor's hair is in a severe middle part, and seen straight on he is thickish and pale and looks like a bartender in a Coen Brothers film. This concluded the Spectral Founder portion of the segment, which ran for six and a half minutes in all, and promptly gave way to something even stranger. The image dissolves to NFL Hall of Fame running back Jim Brown, in a full denim ensemble and what appears be a camouflage kufi, and he solemnly recites the first words of the Declaration of Independence. Only then did the broadcast of Super Bowl XLII reach the 90-second mark.

It improbably got weirder still from there, like, Peyton Manning grimly intoning 18th-century prose through his pipe-organ sinuses weird. But the most important thing to note here is that this was all real—at least in the sense that the NFL's self-dramatizing rites of civic belonging are now a real and autonomous part of our bedrock national saga. Less grandiosely, I guess, this was real in the sense that anything that happens on TV in America is automatically real.

The reality of all this is worth reiterating mostly because the sheer absurdity of it would otherwise be overwhelming. There was former commissioner Paul Tagliabue honking out his lines while standing at attention by the Jefferson Memorial; there was Giants defensive end Michael Strahan—well before his rebranding as a happy-talk daytime TV host—barking out the word "rectitude" while surrounded by firemen at Ground Zero. This was really on television, where millions of Americans who mostly wanted to watch a football game could see it. Something similar had happened in years before and has happened in years since. Fox started doing this with Super Bowl XXXVI, which was played five months after the attacks of September 11, 2001. Three years after those 97 million or so viewers watched Tedy Bruschi, Jack Kemp, Steve Largent, Roger Staubach, and Marie Tillman (the widow of Pat Tillman) do their best with their assigned chunks of the Declaration before Super Bowl XLII, another record viewership—111 million, this time for the Green Bay Packers and Pittsburgh Steelers in Super Bowl XLV—was treated to an iteration that began with former secretary of state Colin Powell and NFL commissioner Roger Goodell striding gravely through the National Archives.

This is not only real, but in the broader context of the NFL —the biggest, richest, and most luridly batshit sports league the world has ever seen—it is even something like *normal.*

Blood, Soil, and Pigskin

Not normal by any standard except for the one that prevails in the NFL, admittedly, but that's the one we're talking about here. We are talking about the NFL, which is to say that we are talking about a league that increasingly sees itself as presenting not only the most popular American sport—which football demonstrably is, at least going by television ratings and profits—but the most American American sport.

The sport's elephantine self-regard plays out in ways big and small—and in ways that transcend the obvious patriotic signifiers that the NFL grafts to every available surface of its exhaustively branded viewing experience. It's not just the booming fighter jet flyovers or the deployment of American flags visible from space when it's time for the national anthem, although there is all that. It's the bombastic anthem rituals—and the sidelong glances cast during that anthem to make sure that everyone around is revering the anthem appropriately. Some of that is the result of Colin Kaepernick's quiet and quite probably career-ending anthem-based act of protest, but the NFL's dedication to its specific and strange vision of conformity predated Kaepernick's political awakening. The NFL is selective and self-serving and alternately priggish and thuggish in how it goes about maintaining its strange brand, but it is always singular. Every mania of our broader moment, from those grandiose delusions to the million points of cheesy graft, is reflected in the NFL itself. In retrospect, it was inevitable that the NFL would come into conflict with President Trump—when it comes to honking overdetermined proxies for Maximum America, there can be only one.

So there are the flyovers and the performative patriotism, but there is also the fact that the NFL was, for years, *secretly billing* the Pentagon for all those color guards and Hometown Hero promotions. And it's maybe especially the fact that the commissioner's office expressed shocked dismay upon the exposure last year of all of this and contritely returned a small percentage of the money the teams had received.

To a culture that's addicted to spectacle and inured to dishonesty, the NFL delivers bulk loads of both: the pyrotechnically performative God-and-country stuff and the greasy profit-seeking,

the stilted recitation of the Declaration of Independence before
a football game, and then the batshit branded hijinks that follow
at the commercial breaks. There isn't much distance, in broadcast
time or pure blank weirdness, between those patriotic fife-and-
drum montages and the ads in which a lone Budweiser Clydesdale
convinces a small businessman not to commit suicide or a man
eating Doritos is comically rocked in the nuts by a snack-minded
Corgi or whatever. America, as the poet said, is hard to see. But
in watching the NFL, at the baroque phase on what appears to be
the back end of its zenith, we can see a reflection of the nation at
something like the same point.

The NFL is financially healthy and also pretty luridly out of its
mind, increasingly given to grandiose delusion and stubborn denial and spasms of executive sadism. And lately, it's declining—in
ways that are obvious for even casual viewers and evident during
an average Sunday's slate of games and in ways that the league
might not fully feel for generations.

It's America's game all right, and if the NFL is sick, if it is
even perhaps dying, it is for the most American of reasons—because it is increasingly ragged and rotten with corruption, and
because it can't quite come up with any other way that it would
rather be.

Life, Liberty, and the Pursuit of Impunity

There is a door that opens while watching a bad NFL game on TV,
a gateway into something very much like an out-of-body experience. It's not an especially desirable out-of-body experience, to be
sure, but there's something about being subjected to a NFL game
at its worst that grants even the most devout fans the opportunity
to see how football looks to people who absolutely hate football.
Witness enough off-tackle plunges for one-yard gains, then watch
as they are negated by offsetting penalties, and something reveals
itself, even to those of us who enjoy the game.

It is not pretty. The grunting, juddering, anti-flow of the broader
game, the rote brutality and steak-headed backwardness of the
action at the play-by-play level, the sudden blundering intrusion
of all those honking commercials—for achingly sincere domes-

tic macro-pilsners, for strapping trucks and their loud and swaggering drive-train warranties, for extremely emotional insurance companies and also weirdly ironic insurance companies—at every stoppage of play. In the most basic sense this is just what the average NFL game *is,* but more worrying for the lords of the league, it is also a description of what is an objectively not-great television show—one with the queasy pacing of rush-hour traffic, the jarring violence of a car accident, and the fuddy legalism of traffic court, and that somehow manages to be three hours long.

For people who don't like watching the NFL, every excruciating moment of every game looks like this. For those of us who enjoy it, against or despite our better political and aesthetic judgment, that description only fits the worst shitshow jackpot: muddy punt-offs in Cleveland, for example, or the groggy Sunday morning games that the NFL has lately played in front of rustling, uninterested crowds at London's Wembley Stadium as part of its stalled attempt to open international markets.

In recent years, though, the games resembling out-of-body experiences have become worryingly common. The sudden glut of ultra-shitty games probably isn't the greatest long-term problem facing the sport, but it's also the most obvious and inescapable challenge to all the solemn covenant-pageantry of the NFL; it's hard to civically sanctify the experience of being bored.

Not every game can be a classic, of course, or even competitive. But the palpable decline in game quality, week by week and 12–9 game by 12–9 game, is neither incidental nor accidental but happening seemingly by design—the natural result of teams taking cheap-out shortcuts in constructing their rosters, and a high-volume and highly conservative coaching style that emphasizes an empty efficiency over any of the unpredictabilities that make games worth watching.

Put another way, the specific nature of the league's declining ratings is a reflection of the limited appeal of spending three hours watching quarterbacks rack up four-yard completions. As *The Ringer*'s Kevin Clark points out, the absolute number of people watching NFL games hasn't declined, but those viewers are watching for increasingly brief periods of time. "Fans are tuning in and then tuning out," Clark writes. "If that doesn't scare the league, then nothing will."

Gladiators on the Make

Here's the thing, though: the NFL not only doesn't seem scared, it
doesn't seem to care at all. It's broadly understood that NFL football
is not terribly good at the moment. If you credit the lamentations
of the anonymous front-office types who tend to pop up in stories
complaining, always complaining, about how unprepared today's
college players are for the pro game or the dearth of NFL-ready
quarterbacks available through the NFL draft, the near future does
not look great either. Factor in a steady decline in youth football
participation that extends back to the first stories about the link
between football and brain injuries (such as chronic traumatic encephalopathy) more than a decade ago and it's tough to feel great
about the long-term outlook.

Rich television deals ensure that profitability is locked in for the
foreseeable future, and ratings are only slightly off their old Olympian standard. But the NFL currently feels very much like a league
in decline—the league seems in a real way to have lost interest
in football, or in trying to stop the league's broader skid. There
are and will always be bad teams, but the NFL in 2017 is remarkable for the number of teams that appear not even to be trying
to compete. This includes not just teams embarking on variously
forward-thinking tank schemes to gain advantageous position in
upcoming drafts, or the roughly equal number of teams that are
plainly institutionally incompetent. The ones that stand out most
dramatically are those that are plainly not trying to do anything
but bump along the bottoms of their divisions and collect their
share of the $39.6 billion in television revenues that the league's
32 teams will divide between 2014 and 2022.

Fans will put up with a lot, but such overt and unapologetic
indifference is an insult that's hard to ignore. The NFL has always prioritized the profits of the men who own the league's teams
above any other end and has only rarely bothered to conceal that
fact. In its simultaneously sincere and delirious self-performance,
the NFL rhymes perfectly both with our Trump-y moment and the
man himself, from its valorizing of not just money but greed, its
blank devotion to bigness, its endless capacity to take offense at
every outrage against itself, by "anti-football" doctors revealing the

damage the game does to the people who play it, to the kneeling Kaepernick. It makes sense that Trump once owned a football team of his own, the New Jersey Generals of the short-lived USFL; it's a nice Trumpian touch that the USFL only realized a modest financial return when Trump and his fellow team owners negotiated a buyout at the expense of their far richer NFL counterparts. That the same NFL owners who donated more than any other sports executives to Trump's inauguration celebration, according to FEC filings, recoil righteously from Kaepernick vulgarly "politicizing" their American Sunday tradition is, mostly, unsurprising. That Trump, in a characteristically beefy ad-lib at a late-September rally for Alabama senator Luther Strange, said he would "love to see one of these NFL owners, when somebody disrespects our flag, to say, 'Get that son of a bitch off the field right now, out, he's fired,'" was, in retrospect, probably inevitable. That he kept mashing away at that (popular) sentiment whenever his poll numbers turned down in the months afterward spoke not just to Trump's well-documented animal shamelessness but also to the risks of the NFL's long, strange campaign against its players.

It's not quite sufficient to say that the NFL is an owners' league. It absolutely is, in the sense that every decision the league makes is made to advance the financial interests and flatter the various vanities of the owners. But, on a more mundane level, the league's current deemphasizing of the game of football in favor of oafish executive theater—the protean expansion of the league's metastatic rulebook, the endless rounds of stern but vague disciplinary action that issue from the commissioner's office—is more than the owners dictating the way that their sport is overseen and organized. It is the owners making the league more explicitly about them: not just what they want, but what they do.

From a fan's perspective, this is a bad choice for a bunch of reasons, starting with the fact that the people playing football in today's NFL are stronger and faster than any people who have ever played the game before and that the owners are interchangeable soft pink guys whiffing on high-fives in their luxury boxes. Those are the bosses, though, and so the league's appeal to fans is increasingly less about strength than *power*—less about the physical geniuses tossing or catching 40-yard lasers than the proper management and, where necessary, punishment of those players. The fantasy the league sells is less about the vicarious experience of a superhuman specimen like Odell Beckham Jr. than the vicarious experience of *controlling* such a specimen—whether on a fantasy team or through taking a hard line in real-world salary negotiations.

It's possible to see this collective will-to-power as part of a slick and subtle bit of anti-labor propagandizing on the part of a caste whose most deeply held ideal has always been paying players as little as possible. But it's just as easy to see it as a simple failure of imagination by rich men who have come to believe that they are more important and more interesting than the strange, violent, astonishing game on which this is all leveraged. Again, you may detect a Trumpian echo to all this.

The Bosses Barrel Downfield

A certain significant subset of NFL fans plainly has no problem with owners taking a high- and heavy-handed approach to the league's labor relations and disciplinary enforcement. The relationship between the league's owners and its players—who are, at the risk of pointing out the obvious, both the league's labor force and its product—has been characterized by enmity and aggression for generations, and remains notably lopsided. For a certain part of the league's fan base, this reflexive authoritarianism is more feature than bug.

The formal expression of that authoritarianism might have changed through the years, but its underlying substance is as unyielding as, well, the language of the Declaration of Independence. Where Dallas Cowboys president Tex Schramm told NFL Players Association head Gene Upshaw, "You guys are cattle, and we're the ranchers," in 1987, today's owners prefer the involuted Trumpian rhetoric of outrage and redress. "We signed a shitty [labor] deal last time," Jerry Richardson, the owner of the Carolina Panthers, told his peers at the NFL's annual owners meeting in 2010, exhorting them toward a 2011 lockout that lasted for 132 days. "And we're going to stick together and take back our league and fucking do something about it." Documents later revealed that, in the season before Richardson and his fellow owners succeeded in reduc-

ing the share of league revenues devoted to player salaries from 50
to 47 percent, the Panthers showed an operating profit of $78.7
million. They went 2-14 that year.

Some of the NFL's current crisis of mediocrity can be attributed
to the league's owners standing on their debauched principles to
the detriment of the teams they put on the field. The Houston
Texans, for instance, began the 2017 season without star offensive
tackle Duane Brown in large part because they refused to guar-
antee his salary for this season. But, strange as that decision is
when considered on its own dubious merits, it's neither new nor
remotely unique to the NFL. While we can probably assume that
owners would rather win games than lose them, they will only put
themselves out so far to that end.

Why? Well, because they don't have to. NFL owners are fundamentally unaccountable even to their team's fans, and that means
that they're free to do whatever they want. And so they do: the
Rams and Chargers ditched St. Louis and San Diego, respectively,
for Los Angeles, where they now lose games in front of a smattering of apathetic fans in a city that never seemed especially en-
thused about bringing even one team to town. Here, too, we can
readily document the warping effect of all this compounding unaccountability in anemic ticket sales. In-person game attendance
represents a small and decreasing portion of how teams make
money—and despite that trend, Rams owner Stan Kroenke saw
his team's valuation double immediately upon making the move;
the franchise's last winning season was in 2003, but they are now
the sixth-most-valuable team in the league.

This summer, though, NFL owners showed off their ability to
do whatever they want by deciding, in a soft sort of blackball, *not*
to do something they didn't want to do. And that was sign Colin
Kaepernick.

Anyone but Kaepernick

Kaepernick, of course, has been a symbol of athletic and celebrity
protest against police killings of black Americans for more than a
year. But in terms of the NFL's oligarchic structure, he represents
something broader—the notion that players possess not just their

own voices but their own dissenting opinions in the debate over the administration of apartheid-style justice in America. To paraphrase Schramm's simile, it was like awakening on your ranch to hear your cattle not only talking, but loudly plotting your overthrow.

So the obvious solution for the NFL cartel was to transform an accomplished quarterback into a league-wide pariah. Consider the surreal course of Kaepernick's off-season. In late July, the Baltimore Ravens signed a quarterback out of an arena football league that exists a notch below the actual Arena Football League. David Olson spent four years as a backup at Stanford and never threw a pass in an actual game; he graduated and transferred to Clemson, where he spent one season with the team as a graduate student and completed one of the three passes he attempted. This is the sort of thing that happens at the end of July when teams need extra arms in training camp, and as it turned out, Olson only lasted three days with the Ravens. On the last day of July, they released him and signed a similarly obscure quarterback named Josh Woodrum. The *Sporting News* headline for the transaction—"Ravens waive David Olson, sign another QB who isn't Colin Kaepernick"— succinctly tells the story of why any of this was even briefly and tenuously news.

By that point in the off-season, the league's all-but-official omerta on the hiring of Kaepernick had long since exited its plausible deniability stage. Kaepernick had, after an early career flirtation with stardom upon taking the 49ers to the Super Bowl in 2013, settled in as a middling NFL quarterback. This looks like fainter praise than it is; only a couple dozen people on earth can capably play football's most important position at the highest level, and while Kaepernick was at the lower end of that group, his production and his game tape both suggest that he was indeed in it.

Given that the NFL has 32 teams, and given that Kaepernick was coming off a solid season, it remains hard to understand his unemployment as anything but the result of the understated protest he began staging on NFL sidelines in 2016. When NFL teams rolled out the honor guard and an American flag the size of a football field for the National Anthem, Kaepernick sat. He did this for a while without anyone noticing; when NFL.com reporter Steve

Wyche eventually did take note of the gesture and asked him why, Kaepernick said, "I am not going to stand up to show pride in a flag for a country that oppresses black people and people of color. To me, this is bigger than football and it would be selfish on my part to look the other way. There are bodies in the street."

Kaepernick then decided to kneel during the anthem and was later joined in this protest by players throughout the league; police unions and owners issued the statements you'd expect, and the usual sports media wind machines roared at jet-engine volume. At the end of the season, Kaepernick opted out of his contract with the 49ers and became a free agent. Well into the new NFL season, he still was.

"He's a really good football player," Ravens coach John Harbaugh said of Kaepernick right before his team signed Olson. "I believe he's a really good person. It all depends on a lot of things. It depends on Colin first of all and what's his passion, what's his priority, what's [*sic*] he want to do." This was less of a mystery than Harbaugh seemed to think. Kaepernick was both clear about his desire and readiness to play in the NFL and consistent in his determination to use his public role in the service of social activism. And while Kaepernick reportedly planned to end his anthem protest in 2017, he has remained active on social justice issues as a donor and an advocate. "I don't think it's different for us than any other team," Harbaugh concluded.

It's hard to argue with that last bit. The Ravens, and every other team, have found excuses not to sign Kaepernick; the Seattle Seahawks were the only team that invited him to compete for a backup job. It says something about how the league went about performing its slow-motion blackballing of Kaepernick that Harbaugh's perfectly circular comment qualifies as an unusually forthright statement. Owners were dismissive; those same anonymous front-office types offered quotes framing Kaepernick as an enemy of the state at worst and a "distraction" at best. The Seahawks, for their part, explained their decision to bring in an inferior player after working out Kaepernick by more or less saying Kaepernick was too good to be a backup. Overall, it was a lot of work to avoid speaking aloud something that was otherwise quite easy to grasp —the NFL's owners are not going to do anything but what they want to do.

Sudden Death

In the grand scheme of the NFL, the unjustified unemployment of a mid-tier quarterback wouldn't seem to be a terribly significant story. It's not really a new one. Chris Kluwe was a solid punter for the Minnesota Vikings until his activism in favor of gay rights drew criticism from his coaches. When the Vikings let him go in 2013 he spoke out against his homophobic coaches; he hasn't worked in the NFL since. Kerry Rhodes was an above-average NFL starting safety for eight seasons, but never even got a tryout with a NFL team after a man claiming to be his ex-boyfriend outed him on a gossip site. (For whatever it's worth, Rhodes, who's now a successful film actor, was married to Australian actress Nicky Whelan this spring.)

But the confluence of a number of factors worked to turn Kaepernick and his protest into the target of an inquisition unlike any prior crusade in NFL history. The nature of Kaepernick's grievances and the pointed symbolism of his protest; the broader spirit of unease in the country and the specific impunities of the NFL and its corporate culture; the strangeness of seeing a player in the most popular and theatrically authority-positive league take such a stance—any one of these things, by itself, would have been enough to attract notice, and probably enough to seal Kaepernick's fate. But taken together, they created that strangest of NFL spectacles: a league-wide backlash against Kaepernick as a thought criminal. This was no small irony, of course, for a sport that had appointed itself the televisual guardian of the very idea of American independence. As is often the case with the NFL, the tangle of hypocrisies and contradictions and weird umbrage unravels cleanly when you remember that this is all mostly about power. For the NFL's most powerful people, being seen to be in charge isn't everything—it's the only thing.

And, for better or worse, they're still very much in charge. But Kaepernick's protest and banishment, more than any of the NFL's other indicators of decline, point to divergent futures for the league. On the one hand, there is the nascent movement of protest among African American players that Kaepernick left behind, which is modest but expanding despite the disapproval of the league elite—indeed, there was no small tremor of discontent within that elite when the early weeks of the NFL season saw *white players* joining the National Anthem protests. Meanwhile, the NFLPA, long the most ineffectual union in pro sports, has lately shown at least a rhetorical disposition to organize another work stoppage around the expiration of the next collective bargaining agreement in 2021. In a league as change-averse as the NFL, even these vague stirrings qualify as progress.

And on the other hand, there is all that familiar unaccountability. The NFL that we have serves its owners much better than it serves anyone else, and those owners' refusal to budge from their feather-bedding management style has clearly done the league a great deal of harm in a number of areas, from the way the league's long-running quest for parity has settled into sludgy, shrugging mediocrity to protecting the safety of their players and the long-term viability of the league. The owners aren't likely to recognize any of this, of course, until the flailing status quo starts costing them money. But that inability or unwillingness to reckon with the NFL's increasingly untenable present becomes more risky by the day.

There's a new pomposity—to say nothing of a perverse and shortsighted shamelessness—to the league as it wheels past its peak, but the NFL remains fundamentally what it has long been. The league has been retrograde and proudly plutocratic for as long as it has existed, and it's hard to picture a future in which its owners act like anything but who and what they are. It's more difficult, though, to imagine a future for the NFL that looks like the present. The league's signature corruptions have unmistakably diminished both the quality of the games and the broader health of the sport; things just can't go on this way. It does not take a fighter jet flyover to be reminded of how discomfitingly well this feeling lines up with our broader American moment.

It couldn't be any other way. As the league's patriotic play-acting so stridently reminds us, football is a uniquely American game, in ways that both flatter and put the lie to a number of treasured national myths. But after its decadent zenith, the league is showing signs of a very particular and very particularly American kind of decline. In the ways that blank greed and unaccountability have warped and weakened both the league and the sport itself, we can see a funhouse refraction of what corruption does to societies. In both cases, rich men's self-serving smallness and single-minded dedication to their own narrow interests have put a broader future at direct and dire risk. In both the NFL and the similarly beleaguered American republic, change has never seemed more urgent or necessary, or more difficult to bring to pass. And in both venues of bloated, wobbling patriotic spectacle, the last and greatest reason for hope is the certainty that a present that so poorly serves so many cannot also be the future.

TYLER TYNES

There Is No Escape from Politics

FROM SB NATION

I. "By the way, everyone wanted to be here today"

IT IS THE day Donald Trump is meeting with the Stanley Cup
champion Pittsburgh Penguins, and I am sitting in the basement
of the White House with a group of black folks. The group is made
up of journalists, cameramen—all here to watch the day unfold.

The mood is light; we talk; joke. But it's hard not to recognize
how surreal this scene is. Here we are on this October afternoon,
black, in a house built by slaves—a house where the first black
president used to dance with his black wife, laugh with his black
kids, and enjoy the company of his black friends.

That was then. Now, upstairs lives a president who is there
largely because he *is not* black, whose campaign was built upon
thinly veiled promises to return power to the majority; to make
things the way they were before a black man was president.

We eventually walk inside the East Room, listening to the president speak, his words twisting in the pretzel logic we've somehow
gotten used to. I can't help but think how weird this all is. Gone
are the days of Obama dancing with Northsiders and Cubs on one
of the last days of his administration. The White House felt warm,
inviting, even loving under Obama for folks like me. This place
feels cold, aggressive, and devoid of anything harboring black joy.

"By the way, everyone wanted to be here today," Trump says,
smiling. "And I know why."

His smile is one I recognize. It's one that doesn't quite involve
his eyes.

There is constant cheering. Trump calls the hockey players handsome. He says they are incredible patriots, embodying values all young Americans needed to see. It's unclear if Trump realizes how many of these young men weren't born in the U.S.

It's also clear that these hockey stars aren't being celebrated for what they have accomplished. Trump's White House has not rushed to invite any other teams who have won championships, including the Golden State Warriors. It took Stephen Curry saying he wasn't interested in going to the White House for Trump to say the invitation was rescinded—in truth, no invitation had ever been sent to the team. The only other team Trump has welcomed has been the Chicago Cubs, whose co-owner, Todd Ricketts, was a Trump supporter and had been considered for Deputy Secretary of Commerce.

The Penguins are welcomed with open arms as a display of how white athletes are meant to behave. The president can't put aside his own agenda, even for a moment. Trump brought the team here to reinforce his attacks against the black people he deems dishonorable, the football players who have protested police brutality, and who Trump has made his latest adversaries in his never-ending culture war.

The white audience seems unaware or uncaring. The blackness in the room or watching on TV is being taunted. Trump is taking a victory lap with his chosen champions, gaslighting nonbelievers and smiling while they squirm.

These political gymnastics are exhausting. For the entirety of this charade, I have felt disoriented. How can no one address this?

In this moment, I remember where I'd seen that smile.

II. The Day of Reckoning

It was a few weeks before that day at the White House, September 25, when Dallas and Arizona faced off in a *Monday Night Football* game.

All weekend, NFL players had kneeled during "The Star-Spangled Banner," some in support of Colin Kaepernick and his original protest against the police killing of black people. Others were responding to Trump, who implored NFL owners to "get that son of a bitch off the field right now" if a player kneeled during the National Anthem at a rally earlier that week.

While some NFL owners supported their players and were vocally against Trump's vulgar tirade, reports had come out that the majority of NFL owners were scrambling to find a way to stop the protests, or at least quiet them down enough to make football the story again.

Ahead of *Monday Night Football,* there was little talk of what would happen in the game. It was all about what would happen before the kickoff, during the playing of "The Star-Spangled Banner." Sports fans, culture warriors, and America tuned in as Cowboys owner Jerry Jones walked out with his players. I'll admit: I did not, in my wildest thoughts, think I'd see ol'Jerruh, practically a caricature of a rich white man, walk out with these men.

Then, before "The Star-Spangled Banner" began, they all kneeled, arms locked, Jones right in the middle. Jones kept his head down while fans booed. He did not care. His plan was already in motion. He finally looked up. The cameras moved closer. He looked directly into the lens and there it was: the smile. That same, soulless smile.

Then, just before the song, Jones and the rest of the Cowboys stood. It was a protest without any teeth. His smile had been a clear signal to white America: *Don't worry. Jerry will take care of this. We're going to put them in their place.*

What was funny about all this was that Jones, certainly by accident, actually showed hypocrisy on the part of the white people he was trying to send a signal to. He exposed the lie that kneeling was about "The Star-Spangled Banner" or patriotism or Trump. He knelt *before the song played* and was still booed.

If Jones's demonstration was inartful, it was at least emphatic. Jones has made no mistake about his belief that players should stand for the National Anthem, even threatening to lead a coup against Commissioner Roger Goodell in part because Goodell wouldn't place any mandate on players. Even within a group of 31 owners who had collectively donated millions to Trump's campaign, Jones was a hard-liner, and he was lockstep with Trump that Goodell should have nipped the protests in the bud. Via ESPN:

At first, some in the room admired Jones' pure bravado, the mix of folksy politician and visionary salesman he has perfected. But he was angry. He said the owners had to take the business impact seriously, as the league was threatened by a polarizing issue it couldn't contain or control. To some in the room, it was clear Jones was trying to build momentum for an anthem mandate resolution, and in the words of one owner, "he brought up a lot of fair points."

Jones couldn't get exactly what he wanted—what Trump had demanded—in part because the movement was too big. Watching black bodies defy power in prime time was unexpected. Players reacting so quickly and strongly was unexpected and beautiful, and the league was too overwhelmed to react. The weekend had a chance to be historic. Jones needed to usurp the cause somehow, and he found a way. That moment when Jones smiled, I felt that beauty slip away.

That smile haunts me. It was in that moment I understood that this movement would be taken over and killed. This was the white owner reasserting control.

This was the co-opting of a black message. This was a smile equivalent to a death sentence, signaling the fate of Colin Kaepernick's movement—the end of an international moment staked in black pride.

This is something we have seen time and time again in the history of American sport: the use of the black body for popular entertainment; black men and women using that popularity to speak out, then white gatekeepers (either owner, audience, or overseer) co-opting that message or striking it down, often violently.

Truthfully, football was never meant to serve the black body, which has been abused for generations. America watched as men they perceive as property begged for a voice and were muzzled. This is a cycle America has always known. It is no wonder these NFL players did not get far.

III. *"Those wild and low sports"*

Maybe it was destiny that led Tom Molineaux to Copthorne Common on a blustery December afternoon in 1810 to fight Tom Cribb.

Molineaux, a man newspapers called the "American Othello,"

was a freed slave from a Virginia plantation whose family taught him to box. Cribb was the champion of England and white. Molineaux had sailed from America just six months prior to start a new life as a prize fighter.

Englishmen thought he was a lamb being led to slaughter. Though the English were sympathetic to abolitionism, a slave wasn't supposed to swing against his white master. By the ninth round, Cribb was being pummeled. After 30 minutes, fans rioted. They thought Molineaux was cheating. By some accounts, they even broke his fingers.

After 39 rounds, Molineaux conceded, finally succumbing to exhaustion. He appeared to knock out Cribb in the 28th round, but no one could hear the referee call "time!" to indicate that Molineaux had won in the chaos that ensued. Cribb recovered and the fight continued. It was a brilliant fight by all accounts, yet there wasn't much to read about Molineaux's exploits in America outside of a small clipping in a North Carolina newspaper.

Molineaux was a symbol of a possibility that was deadly to the white world back then. If black people could prove they are equal in one arena, who's to say they shouldn't be equal in every arena?

Sports were the thing that kept Molineaux enslaved *and* his tool for liberation. Sports were created on the plantation as diversions to help slavers control the revolutionary urges of slaves. Frederick Douglass, who fought off his owner and ran to freedom, was a critic of sports on the plantation. In Douglass's autobiography, he said Southern plantation owners deployed "those wild and low sports" in an effort to keep black slaves "civilized."

What Douglass wrote is, foolishly, why owners expect athletes to know their place. It is why no one expected a Day of Reckoning to begin with. What Douglass missed, and what black athletes discovered, was the expressionism sports allowed. As Molineaux demonstrated, sports create room for protest because they hold the minds of the white consumers hostage during play.

White people showed up to watch Cribb beat Molineaux, and instead were held captive as Molineaux upended their expectations. Similarly, they did not think, both owners and fans, that black football players were capable of revolt. And just as Molineaux helped establish a norm, NFL players have made protest commonplace. To restore the old order would require intervention, co-option—violence of a nonphysical sort. That was the reason behind ol'Jerruh's smile. If order was to be reinstated, pain of some kind would have to be established.

IV. "Coach, a Negro boy can't play football with white fellers"

It took seven minutes for Oklahoma A&M—the university now named Oklahoma State—to try to kill Johnny Bright, Drake University's black Heisman candidate. It was 1951. Bright was knocked unconscious three times, often without the ball. The third was the most brutal. A large, white defensive end named Wilbanks Smith saw Bright, looking left, throwing a pass. Seconds later—some say as many as six—Smith leapt from his feet and cracked Bright's jaw with a forceful elbow. Bright's trainer and another player carried him to the bench. A penalty hadn't been called all day.

Maury White, who wrote about the attack for the *Des Moines Register*, said, "You could feel the bones move." Photos of Bright are kept in the Drake Heritage Collection. They show images of Bright pulling his mouth apart, wires keeping his jaw straight, the reason his college career was upended. The "Great Negro Flash" would never make it to the NFL.

Local accounts before the game had students saying Bright "would not be around at the end of the game." Three students told the *Register* that A&M's head coach was seen yelling "get that nigger" when the scout team was running Bright's plays. Bright told the paper in 1980: "There's no way it couldn't have been racially motivated."

Smith, the white man who tried to kill Bright, said in 2012 he had "nothing to apologize for." Within two days after the incident, Smith received hundreds of letters of support. Half of the messages begged him to run for office in Louisiana or lead local Klan startups.

"If it wasn't Wilbanks Smith, it would have been someone else," the A&M basketball player Dean Nims told the *Register* in 1980. "They were determined to stop Bright."

Oklahoma State waited 22 years after Bright died to express sympathy.

Violence was the price of being black in these spaces. It is important to understanding the Day of Reckoning. Players are not simply millionaires asking for attention. They have received death threats, their parents have lost their jobs, their jerseys have been burned from New York to Oakland, their likenesses are being used as tackling dummies before games, and their coaches are called "no-good niggers."

A few years before Bright had his jaw demolished in front of the country, Levi Jackson, the first black football captain at Yale, was playing in a high school exhibition. His body had been thrashed for hours, and he was ready to quit. In this era, it was common for white players to attack black players between the whistles. Jackson, however, was fed up. Reading his words, I assume he knew what this sport could do to us. The message was there: white sympathy was not for us unless we were willing to get over race.

"Coach, a Negro boy can't play football with white fellers," he said, according to *Sport Magazine* in November 1949. "You saw what they did to me today. I'm turning in my suit. It's not sport."

V. *"Nothing more than a mere picnic"*

After the Day of Reckoning, the NFL responded by promoting a message of "Unity." I have grown so tired of hearing about "unity" that I no longer believe it's real. What is unity? What are we unifying against? It doesn't appear to be racism. It has never appeared to be racism. When the concept of unity was offered to these black athletes, it felt comedic.

Look at all these white men. They do not look afraid, as I have. They do not seem tired, as I am.

And the black athletes who felt the same way were often labeled as ungrateful millionaires. "Ungrateful is the new uppity," Jelani Cobb wrote in the wake of the president's attack on players.

For the current revolting black athlete, this certainly seems the case. By co-opting the message of the protests, NFL owners like Jones were able to make still-unsatisfied athletes seem bitter and greedy in a certain light. Thus, Jones's performative wokeness successfully play-actioned protests about police brutality into something lesser that many players felt obligated to accept or else be ostracized even more.

This sort of transformation of messaging angered Bill Russell, one of America's great social agitators in sports. By the time the March on Washington came to the capital in 1963, Russell was disenchanted with the civil rights movement. He was sick of compromises. He said the day became "nothing more than a mere picnic" because whites marched. The message changed, and the voice of the oppressed was not one with the oppressor at his shoulder.

"The March on Washington was brilliantly conceived and badly executed," Russell recalled in *Go Up for Glory* in 1965. "The bigots will make something of this. But I concur with what Malcolm X said: 'They merely marched from the feet of one dead president to the feet of another.'"

Acts of "Unity" have been the fodder making America's heart swell. Hand-holding in the face of a president who believes people of color are inhuman plays into America's often misguided ideals of egalitarianism. Our nation loves to see black hands holding white hands but has never stopped to gauge what it accomplishes. We are not postracial by any means, and we will not get there soon by evading America's insidious nature.

Co-option is a powerful tool. So is money. This year, Eagles safety Malcolm Jenkins said he would stop protesting after NFL owners met with the Players Coalition—a group Jenkins cofounded—and agreed to give $89 million over seven years to charitable groups working toward criminal justice reform and better relationships between community and law enforcement. Several members of the Players Coalition, including 49ers safety Eric Reid, publicly announced their decision to leave the group when the announcement was made.

NFL owners didn't have to look far for a lesson in how to stifle a movement.

In 1961, the Baltimore Colts played the Pittsburgh Steelers in an exhibition game in Roanoke, Virginia. Virginia State Police were enforcing Jim Crow seating. Local NAACP chapters filed lawsuits. For days state courts didn't hear the suit. Telegrams were sent to black players on both teams. Coaches asked them what they would do if the game proceeded, and many said they wouldn't play if segregated seating was enforced. Roanoke officials gathered and said they would ignore the segregationist law to keep peace with players. Pete Rozelle, the NFL commissioner, even sent out a press release.

Newspapers labeled the day a victory before it began. Then Lenny Moore, a star tailback for the Colts, walked inside the stadium and saw that the gatekeepers had lied. Jim Crow seating was enforced, just like any other day.

"I had to reach through the chain-link fence in order to shake their hands," Moore said in his autobiography. "No image had ever made me realize, with such force, just what blacks have been up against all through American history: We have always been on the outside looking in."

The lesson here is to be wary of white folks; to know that football is fun, but it is also work. You must maim your body for the happiness of your owner, fans, and America. Or you will be fired. You will be cast aside. And you will go back to being an unknown number in a country that does not love you.

VI. *"What they are saying is don't upset the system"*

As we leave the East Room back on that October afternoon, I think to myself that this did not happen by chance. The concerns of black constituents, black footballers calling for an end to police brutality, none of these is as mighty as the man attacking them to get praise from white Americans.

Only under Trump could the Day of Reckoning have happened. If Obama's presidency was a result of a second era of Black Reconstruction, then Trump, as the journalist Adam Serwer and the author Ta-Nehisi Coates have noted, sparked a second wave of white redemption.

Trump's white identity politics are stronger than concerns about his temperament, his sanity, or the people who inhabit his administration. They are stronger than the black athletes at odds with him. If white Americans of virtually every economic background were willing to elect a man like this, one whose political identity is tailored for white nationalism, then there is no place for black, protesting football players.

Trump will always attack black athletes because they pose a threat to this white power dynamic, and because it is the easiest way to signal to his base that that they are right to feel threatened. They are evidence that the gatekeeper's control is slipping. To suppress that idea, Trump must dismiss them and dehumanize them. As an added bonus for Trump, this excites the base—the large swath of the country that created this moment.

"If you look very carefully you will see that they are the same people who are quite happy with the situation as it is," the Nigerian novelist Chinua Achebe told James Baldwin in 1980. "What they are saying is not don't introduce politics. What they are saying is don't upset the system. They are just as political as any of us. It's only that they are on the other side."

I can understand why the gatekeepers claim these footballers are unpatriotic, because they don't see us as citizens of their states. This can be an argument about the flag if you don't believe it represents folks like me.

Near the manicured lawn of the White House, Mike Sullivan, the Penguins coach, begins speaking to gathered press. Sullivan reinforces the lie of the afternoon: he says he felt no pressure accepting an invitation here because it wasn't political. This was only a celebration, he said.

At this point in our history, it seems foolish that someone could offer this misconceived belief unless they are too nonchalant to care or very careful to preserve their position of power. Either feels like cowardice.

"Does it matter that, regardless of [what you've said], the president is using you and your team as a prop in this culture war against other black leagues?" I ask. "Because you can kind of say it as many times as you want, but the appearance is that you are complicit."

"See, you're suggesting that that's the case," Sullivan says. "We don't believe that."

It was that moment when I knew, despite anything said, that my initial thought was correct. This shit was weird. Trump and whiteness had won the Day of Reckoning. To be passive in the face of the crime is as dangerous as the transparent attack. To be willfully ignorant about race perpetuates and enables racism in America. I can't help but think that they are all too afraid, too scared to challenge white power, to do what is just, to show a shred of morality for the unprivileged.

And while it is weird, by this point Sullivan's words are expected. Yes, all of this is still insulting. Yet since black people were kidnapped and dragged here, four violent centuries says all of this is the American normal.

Jerry Jones provided the smile that killed football's latest revolt. He is no ally. He is not smiling to me. He is smiling to them: the rest of America. I'm sure they are at ease. His message to them is one that we have heard from white people in power for centuries: *Don't worry. The black men had their fun and are back, reset, ready for servitude, docile once more.* How dastardly. How American. What a rush.

VII. "We gon' be alright"

Talking to black people in this country about the last two years since Kaepernick ignited protest in football and elsewhere, it is easy to become despondent. Folks truly, honestly, wanted to believe something could be done, that we could be saved, and that progress, the same progress we have always clamored for, was possible.

Look around. There is no better. There is no hope. This movie ends in tragedy. The idea that white folks think black folks have reason to believe in change is deflating.

There is no reason for optimism when the first black president was followed by a man looking to destroy his legacy and belittle the achievements and advancements of people who he sees as less than. That includes the men in pads who look as I do.

How can I enjoy optimism while a country pays black people for entertainment, appropriates our culture, then spits in their faces when they say anything other than "thank you"?

Optimism is not for me, though it is beautiful to dream. There is no hope for the black body in modern America. But neither am I despondent.

Black protesters turned football players should not be hopeful. They also should not compromise. They did not win. Whiteness won. It always wins. But there is space to be positive. Blackness has become indefatigable even if our existence here and on the football field fighting for equality is Sisyphean and disheartening.

Thinking of this often makes me think of Kendrick Lamar and his anthems about Black America. On his 2015 album *To Pimp a Butterfly,* Kendrick examines the emotions we can have being

American. In the past 15 months, I found myself doing this, going back to these affirmations, humming them during "The Star-
Spangled Banner."

"Nigga, we gon' be alright," Kendrick promises.

These words, in repetition, are like a proverb. Black people
were kidnapped and tortured on the way to this country, built its
infrastructure, and became its greatest athletes and entertainers.
We are the culture, the sound, its consciousness—the heartbeat of
America and somehow also its biggest enemy. Kendrick's ghetto
lullaby reminds me of that. The toot of that saxophone, the ping
of that high hat, the rasp of his Compton attitude: it's all soothing.

Our culture, our beauty, allows us—throughout this tortured
cycle of protest and destruction—to keep our pride. There is fire
shut up in our bones. We have shown how mighty we are. Listen
to the song. Kendrick keeps saying, "Nigga, we gon' be alright."

Well.

Nigga, maybe you right. Maybe one day we actually will.

SAM BORDEN

Eternal Champions

FROM ESPN: THE MAGAZINE

THERE IS RAIN in Chiquinho's pockets. Rain running down his shoulders. Rain squishing through his shoes. The rain is so loud, he barely hears the music. The rain is so thick, he barely sees the coffins.

Chiquinho tries to focus. He has a job. He is the groundskeeper. He takes care of the undersoil and the topsoil. He takes care of the field. This stadium is his home. The members of the club are his friends.

One of the goalkeepers, Danilo, used to joke with Chiquinho about the bare patch down at the end of the field. All that mowing and feeding and watering in the warm Brazilian sun and Chiquinho still couldn't get grass to grow there. "Where is the grass?" Danilo would ask with a sparkle in his eyes, and Chiquinho's leathery face would crinkle.

One of the team's trainers, Anderson Paixão, used to talk with Chiquinho about the stray dog Chiquinho found lying outside the gates one morning a few years back. The dog was hurt and whimpering—a boy nearby said he thought it might have been hit by a car—and Chiquinho and his crew took it in. They gave the dog dried meat and bought it medicine. They rubbed its belly and cleaned its black fur. They got it a leash and built it a tiny house out near the shed with the rakes. They named it Pitico, which is Portuguese for "something little."

Before training, Paixão would pet Pitico and wrestle Pitico and kick soccer balls for Pitico, like a game of fetch, except Pitico would skip right past the balls because he was more interested in chasing the birds swooping low near the sidewalls. Pitico would nuzzle Paixão, and Paixão would giggle, and Chiquinho, watching from the side, would take pictures on his phone that he could look at during his long bus ride home every night around dusk. Chiquinho took pictures of the players before each game too.

But now Pitico is missing. And Paixão, Chiquinho's friend, is in a box coming toward him, and Danilo is in one too, and the water that has been running off Chiquinho's neck all day is suddenly rising through the grass on the field like a bathtub with the stopper dropped in. Big puddles are forming, and water is splashing everywhere, and Chiquinho the groundskeeper is scared.

There are tens of thousands of people watching Brazilian servicemen carry in one coffin after another. The coffins are heavy. What if a soldier carrying Danilo or Paixão slips? What if a coffin gets covered in mud?

Chiquinho cannot allow this. There are 50 coffins today. Fifty. And it is Chiquinho's field. He even laid out the floral wreaths and tied the bunting through the holes in the metal fences. He doesn't know anything about flowers or colors or bunting, but he wanted to make it nice. He wanted it to be respectful. He knows the coffins must stay dry. He has to fix the flooding.

As the processional continues, he runs toward the end of the stadium. There must be a blockage. One of the drainpipes again. He bows his shoulders and slides into the concrete bunker under the stands where all the pipes snake together. It is quiet in there: nothing is draining.

Chiquinho bangs on a pipe, testing to see whether he can hear which valve is stopped up. He bangs on another and another, twisting and whirling around to test as many as he can. He can't figure out which one is jammed. He slams the pipes with his hand. His cheeks are wet.

He has no choice. Chiquinho takes a saw and begins hacking. He cuts through one pipe and a second and a third, destroying the drainage system. He cuts another pipe. And another. And another. His blade flails in all directions.

Finally, Chiquinho cuts the right pipe. Gunky water gushes everywhere. His pants and shirt are sopping. Chiquinho stumbles out of the bunker and back onto the field. The pooling in the grass begins to ebb. He exhales.

Then he straightens up and stands at attention, clutching the saw in his fist. He stares as the rest of the coffins are carried in. Everyone else in the arena watches too. Some watch the military men. Some watch the widows or the mothers or the fathers who scream and hold each other through plastic ponchos. Some watch the children, who fidget and fuss and might or might not understand exactly why an entire city in the interior of Brazil has come together at a soccer stadium to mourn in the rain.

Chiquinho just watches all the feet. He cannot help it. He is praying no one slips.

It is November 23, 2016 — 10 days earlier. It is hot and dry. The winds are calm. The sunlight glints off the stained glass of Santo Antônio Cathedral, which sits up high on one of the hills. The rain feels far away.

As afternoon shades toward evening, the people of Chapecó crowd the streets wearing green and white. Vendors set up carts selling water and beer. Fans park their cars and lean against the open trunks. More than 800 miles southwest of Rio de Janeiro, this dusty city known for its slaughterhouses and its farmland is preparing for the most important soccer game in its history.

Inside the stadium, Chiquinho waters the grass constantly in temperatures that rise toward 90 degrees. Down the street, at the Hotel Bertaso, the players of Chapecoense, which everyone just shortens to Chape (CHAH-pay), compose themselves. Before every home game, the players spend the night in this hotel together in "concentration." They go over tactics and scouting. They talk about formations and strategy. Then, when they are done with all that, they pass the time.

The hotel gives the team the entire second floor, and the players spread out. Danilo, the goalkeeper with the kind eyes, is chatty. Kempes, the striker with the frizzy Afro, plays his *pandeiro,* which is a tiny tambourine. Tiaguinho, a young winger with a dimple, cannot put down his phone.

The mood is buoyant. The game tonight is against San Lorenzo, a team from Argentina, and it is the second leg of a two-match semifinal in the Copa Sudamericana, the South American Cup. In the first match of the aggregate series, in Buenos Aires, the teams tied 1–1. Tonight all Chape needs to do is tie 0–0, because the tiebreaker in this tournament is goals scored in the opponent's stadium. If Chape advances, it will go to the final of one of the continent's most important tournaments. For a team from a city like Chapecó, a team that was founded in 1973 and was in the lowest division in Brazil as recently as 2009, it is fantasy.

The players get ready to leave for the stadium, but Tiaguinho cannot stop texting his wife, Graziele. She is only 19, but they grew up in the same town and have been in love for years, ever since the day Tiaguinho sat next to her on a bench in grade school and showed her his arm. He had written her name on it in marker, over and over from elbow to wrist. He said, "See how much I like you?" and she laughed.

A day earlier, not long after the players arrived at the hotel to begin concentration, Tiaguinho was sitting in the hall outside his room. Two teammates, Matheus Biteco and Caramelo, approached him. "We have a present for you," they told him, and Biteco gave him a gift bag. Tiaguinho took the bag and looked up at them, wary.

"It is from a female fan who likes you," Biteco said, and Tiaguinho dropped the bag as if it were on fire. He did not want his friends to see him interested in anyone but Graziele. "Just open it, man," Caramelo said, nudging it back, and Tiaguinho grudgingly pulled out a tiny box with a shiny ribbon and card. His eyes went wide. It was from Graziele.

Tiaguinho furrowed his brow. He opened the card and read it slowly, tracing his finger over some of the words. Then he closed it, took a deep breath, and opened it again. Biteco leaned in, hovering over his friend, and Tiaguinho shot up from the floor, shouting and dancing and hugging everyone around him. He showed them what was inside the box: tiny shoes. Then he rocked an imaginary baby in his arms while his teammates howled.

Since that moment, Tiaguinho has been floating. Even now, just hours before this match against San Lorenzo, he is texting Graziele about names. They both like Maitê for a girl; it means "beloved." For a boy, Tiaguinho pushes for Santiago, which is a family name. Finally his teammates tell him it is time to go. He cannot resist and texts once more, telling Graziele that he loves her.

The game begins around 7. Arena Condá thrums. The fans chant and cheer and sing, standing together on the concrete bleachers or crowding up against the fence that separates the walkway from the team benches. In the press box, Chape's radio play-by-play announcer, Rafael Henzel, holds up his phone to take a video of the energy just before kickoff, even as he narrates the action live.

Rafael is 43, with a flat face and thin hair and glasses. He works with several other announcers, including his partner, Renan Agnolin, but he is the team's voice. He has been coming to Chape games since he was little. As a child, he would arrive at the arena with no money and wait outside the gates. Once everyone had gone in and the game started, he could find an entrance that was unattended and slip in for free. He cheered for the team when it was still playing in the amateur leagues. He became a broadcaster at age 15. When Chape finally qualified for Brazil's top division in 2013, he cried in his radio booth.

Tonight, with a place in the final at stake, Rafael is even more dynamic than usual. The Chape players know what they have to do: just avoid conceding a goal. They do not need to score, and San Lorenzo's players are more talented anyway. San Lorenzo has three players who played in England's Premier League. It has a regular for Argentina's national team. It has players who play for Uruguay and Paraguay.

Chape has only the one away goal it scored in the first game that it wants to protect.

After the first 15 minutes, the Chape players—and the crowd —grow more confident. Danilo dives to his left to push away a shot, and the fans erupt. Dener, a midfielder, flicks the ball over his head to elude an opponent, and the spectators shout a mocking "Oh!" as the San Lorenzo player gives chase.

Chape occasionally presses forward in attack, and there is one sequence, about half an hour into the game, when Chape nearly scores. A free kick comes in, and Willian Thiego, a stout central defender, lashes the ball into the goal. He turns away to celebrate, wanting desperately to share the emotion with his teammates on the bench. He does not see the offside flag raised. When he does, he stops his gyrations mid-jiggle, shakes his head, and runs back up the field.

Mostly, Chape just defends. A San Lorenzo player's header hits the post and bounces out. Danilo slides out quickly to block a shot. A long-range blast goes wide.

The minutes creep by. Seventy. Eighty. Eighty-five. Eighty-eight. Eighty-nine. It is still 0–0. The fans are frothing as it appears Chape will do it. The stadium is shaking. With seconds left, San Lorenzo gets a free kick and lofts the ball toward Chape's goal. Even with all the defenders there, it ricochets around and falls at the feet of Marcos Angeleri, an experienced Argentine. Angeleri is directly in front of the goal, 18 feet away. All he has to do is shoot the ball into the net, which is 24 feet wide, and San Lorenzo will steal the game, go to the final, and keep Chape home. Danilo, the goal-keeper, looks helpless. Rafael, in the radio booth, puts his hands to his head. He fears the worst: at the last breath, Chape will lose.

But as Angeleri prepares to shoot, Danilo rises up like a lion on its back legs. And somehow, with his right foot splayed sideways, he blocks Angeleri's blast from close range. For a beat, it is as if the fans cannot fathom what has happened. But then the roar is long and loud, and Danilo thumps his chest with glee.

Rafael, in his radio booth, calls out Danilo's name, over and over. Except he changes it. Instead of saying "Danilo!" he wails, "Deus-nilo! Deus-nilo! Deus-nilo!" When the referee blows the whistle to end the game and officially send Chape to the final, he bellows it once more. "Deus-nilo! Deus-nilo! Deus-nilo!"

In Portuguese, *Deus* is the word for God.

The celebration begins in the hot and sticky locker room. The players form a circle and scream out the team song, the one the fans sing whenever something good happens or something bad happens or, really, anything happens: "Ohhhhhh! Vamos-vamos-Cha-pay! Vamos-vamos-Cha-pay! Vamos-vamos-Cha-paaaa-aay!"

They are delirious. Ananias, an attacking midfielder, jumps up and down on the seat in front of his cubby. Bruno Rangel, the team's leading scorer, is shirtless and claps his hands over his head. Sérgio Manoel, one of the only players still wearing his full uniform, dances through the middle of it all. Jackson Follmann, the backup goalkeeper, bangs his hands against the frame of his locker. Even the mayor of Chapecó, Luciano Buligon, holding a paper cup in his hand, shouts along.

The party moves to Spettus, a restaurant in town where the team often goes. Paixão, the trainer, has a *cavaquinho,* or four-string gui-tar. Willian Thiego has a *surdo,* a large Brazilian bass drum. Waiters circulate, cutting thick slices of sirloin from towering skewers. The players relive the match. There is a toast to Danilo for his miracu-lous save. The wives and girlfriends sit together and talk about how they have never seen their men like this.

The women of Chape are close. The men are always playing or training or in concentration before they play again, so genuine friendships among the women are natural. When Graziele received the results of her pregnancy test—before she surprised Tiaguinho with the news—she went with Geisa, who is Caramelo's wife, and Val, who is married to defensive midfielder Gil. They had not known one another long, but when the results came back positive, the women hugged Graziele and congratulated her and told her she was so young to be having a baby.

At Spettus, the women talk about the future. About the championship game, yes, but only a little bit. They talk about Graziele's baby and about a trip that many of the families are planning to take to the Dominican Republic after the season. They talk about bathing suits and how they will go to the beach together. They talk about relaxing.

Aline Machado joins in but cannot stop looking at her husband, Filipe. He has never been this happy, not when he was playing in Iran or elsewhere in the Middle East or for other clubs in Brazil. Not even when he was making good money. "He looks fulfilled," she says to one of her friends.

Over the next few days, nothing changes. In the morning, Filipe leaves a love note for Aline on a napkin in the kitchen. When he begins packing for the trip to São Paulo, where Chape will play a Brazilian league game and then, from there, go to Medellín, Colombia, for the first leg of the Copa Sudamericana final, Filipe puts their two-year-old daughter, Antonella, up on top of the suitcase as he wheels it around the apartment.

Antonella squeals and grabs her father's arms. Filipe and Aline talk about the team and the winning and the trip to the Dominican Republic and about Antonella's love of the problem-solving dogs on the TV cartoon *Paw Patrol*. As Filipe is about to leave, Aline kisses him and tells him, "Go now, go and take this moment."

At Tiaguinho and Graziele's apartment, Tiaguinho puts his bag down by the door and caresses Graziele's belly. At their wedding, she wore a sleek white gown with a floor-length veil and a headband with crystal butterflies on it and looked like a princess. Now she tells him she hopes she will start having strange cravings soon, like pickles or sausage, instead of just feeling nauseous all the time. He hugs her and talks to the baby, telling it he is going to teach it how to play soccer and take it onto the field with him before a

big game someday. Tiaguinho nuzzles Graziele's stomach before
he walks out the door and says, "Love, take care of our little baby."

Alan Ruschel, a left back for Chape, has a more frenetic departure. A misplaced passport leaves him and his fiancée, Marina,
scrambling, and Marina is worried it is some sort of sign, a harbin-
ger about her fiancé's chance to play well in an important final.
But the passport is found, and Alan can leave, and Marina feels an
exaggerated sensation of comfort and calm come over her when
she is in the shower the next morning. It is an unusual feeling for
her; she likes energy and pace. She was in beauty pageants when
she was younger and sometimes wears a nose ring and highlights
her hair lighter or darker depending on her particular mood. She
is working on designing her own clothing line and likes walking
the couple's dog, even though the dog has an affinity for chewing
everything from shoes to furniture.

She is not used to serenity. She tells Alan about this feeling, and
he chuckles at her. "What do you think it means?" he asks, and
she hesitates. She cannot place the sensation; she knows only that
it makes her feel warm. "I think something very good is going to
happen to you," she says finally. "I think maybe you are going to
score a goal."

The flight to Medellín takes off at 6:18 p.m. local time. It is delayed slightly because one of the players asks, just as the doors are
closing, whether he can get his bag back from the luggage hold.
He left his video game player inside. Many jokes are made, but the
bag is retrieved.

It is retrieved because this is a charter flight operated by LaMia
Airlines and not a regular commercial flight. LaMia is a Bolivian
company that has flown many other soccer clubs to important
games. Just a few weeks ago, on the same plane, it flew Lionel
Messi and the Argentine national team to a World Cup qualifier.
A Bolivian airline cannot legally operate a flight from Brazil to Colombia, so the Chape traveling party first takes a commercial flight
from São Paulo (where the team loses 1–0 to Palmeiras in that
Brazilian league game) to Santa Cruz de la Sierra, a Bolivian town.
LaMia will then take the team from there to Medellín for the first
match of the Copa Sudamericana final against Atlético Nacional.

While waiting for the flight, Alan Ruschel does magic tricks. He correctly guesses which card a teammate picks from the deck and makes a card disappear right in front of everyone's eyes. Danilo tries some tricks too, but he is better as a member of the audience because he gets visibly startled when Alan suddenly makes the card appear again.

Everyone is giddy. A Bolivian television crew does interviews before departure, and one of the flight crew members says to the camera, "I think we'll return with good results." Kempes, the striker, gestures to the crew member and grins, saying, "Everything is fine because he is in charge." The team used LaMia for a trip earlier in the Copa Sudamericana, and Caio Júnior, the head coach, tells the interviewer that traveling via Bolivia "gives us good luck."

Once in the air, the players deal cards and play samba. One of the staff members tries to teach a flight attendant Portuguese. Caio Júnior sits up front with most of the coaches. Kempes sits on the right side by a window. Two rows from the back, Rafael Henzel sits in a middle seat among the other journalists. Alan sits next to Follmann, the backup goalkeeper, in the center of the plane; Alan was originally in the rear but moved up when the journalists gathered there. Follmann grabbed him and pulled him into his row.

The flight is long. Some players eat. Some doze. Some keep their headphones on the entire time. At about 9:30 p.m. local time, the plane begins its descent. A different aircraft, flying from Bogotá to San Andrés, has just been diverted to Medellín because of a mechanical issue, so Chape's flight is directed into a holding pattern. At 9:49 p.m., the pilot on Chape's flight requests priority to land from the air traffic controller.

In the cabin, Rafael asks a flight attendant when they will be on the ground. Ten minutes. Ten minutes, he is told. He notices that the flight attendant looks worried. At 9:52 p.m., the air traffic controller tells the pilot there is another plane also holding just below them and asks whether they can wait a few more minutes for clearance.

At 9:53 p.m., one of the four engines on the British-made Avro RJ85 plane fails. Thirteen seconds later, the second engine fails. At 9:55 p.m., the third engine fails. Fourteen seconds after that, the fourth engine fails. The lights in the cabin go out, and the air circulator goes quiet. There is no turbulence or shaking; it feels instead as if the plane is floating toward the ground.

Using the standard phonetic alphabet to refer to LaMia's call letters of LMI, the pilot shouts into his radio at the female air traffic controller: "Señorita, Lima Mike India 2933 is in total failure!"

About 30 seconds later, the pilot calls again: "Lima Mike India, vectors! Vectors, señorita! Vectors to the runway!"

He is asking for directions. The controller answers that the plane has disappeared from her radar. She tries to guide the pilot toward the runway anyway and asks for the plane's altitude. The pilot shouts, "9,000 feet, señorita. Vectors, vectors!" The controller tells the pilot how far the plane is from the runway. There is a pause. Then the controller hears the word "Jesus" over the radio. She asks again for the pilot to call his altitude, and the radio is silent.

At 9:59 p.m. local time on November 28, the Chape flight, traveling at about 150 miles per hour, crashes into Cerro Gordo, a mountain with an elevation of 8,500 feet. On impact, the plane shears into two pieces. The tail embeds on the south side of the crest. The nose shoots over the edge and finishes on the north side, nearly 500 feet away. One of the engines catches in the branches of an uprooted tree. There is no explosion, no fire at the site, only twisted metal and debris.

The temperature at Cerro Gordo is 66 degrees. There are cloudy skies and thunder in the distance. It is, by most measures, an unremarkable night in Colombia. After traveling four hours and roughly 1,800 miles, Chape's plane plunges to the ground just 11 miles from the runway at José María Córdova International Airport outside Medellín.

Aline Machado is sleeping, but it is the sleep of a parent with a toddler nearby. When the phone rings in the early morning, she answers it immediately. It is her mother.

At first, Aline does not understand what her mother is saying. Then she hears the words "airplane" and "Chape." Her head starts pounding. She sits up in bed and turns on the television. There are confusing reports about something happening.

She feels sick. She calls Antonella's nanny to come over so she won't be alone. The text-message group of Chape wives and girlfriends buzzes on her phone over and over. No one knows what is going on. No one knows what to believe. One woman says that someone from Colombia has messaged her on Facebook but that she is not sure if it is reliable. The person says there are no fatalities, that it was just an emergency landing. There is hope. The television and radio voices keep talking but not saying anything for certain. Then the reports begin mentioning "some" survivors, and the phone buzzes more.

Aline believes Filipe is alive. She believes she can feel him. She has known Filipe since they were children. On their first date, he took her to see pigs. Some of her friends thought it was strange, but she understood. The pigs were at a farm his family owned on the outskirts of Gravataí, near Porto Alegre. Filipe imagined that someday he would turn the farm into a soccer field for the community. He would build the locker rooms himself. He would put up goals, and children would come and play. He would run camps and clinics. It would be his to share.

So on that first date, when they were just teenagers, Filipe was showing Aline his dream. She felt his passion, his ambition that day. She felt his enthusiasm. And now, in the middle of the night, she still feels it. When the TV says a defender is among the survivors, she is sure it is Filipe. She is sure of it. When the TV says it is Neto, she is happy because it means one of Filipe's friends survived too.

She goes to Rosangela's house. Rosangela is married to Cléber Santana, the captain of the team. Filipe and Cléber Santana are close; when Cléber Santana was substituted late in the game against São Paulo, Filipe took the captain's armband and finished the game as the team's leader.

Aline is going to pick up Rosangela, and the two of them will go to the stadium together to wait for more news with the other wives. When Aline comes into Rosangela's living room, the TV is on. Rosangela is sitting there. Aline looks at her and then looks at the TV and hears the reporter say, "There are no more survivors." She stares at the TV for a beat or two or three. Then Aline wails and collapses to the ground.

After 20 minutes, Aline and Rosangela collect themselves and go to the stadium. They sit in the locker room with wives and girlfriends and mothers and fathers. Everyone connected to the club has come to the stadium because no one knows where else to go. Even Chiquinho is there. Graziele is hysterical. Someone says, "Be strong, Grazi, for the baby." A locker room attendant begins to gather the players' clothing, putting things in bags.

In one corner is Marina. She feels torn. Val, Aline, Rosangela
—they are all crying. Marina is crying too, but her fiancé, Alan
Ruschel, is alive. The team doctor took Marina aside and told her
Alan was in surgery in Colombia. Marina does not know the details
of the surgery, but she knows Alan is alive. She tries to comfort her
friends, to hold them and hug them, but they know her partner is
not dead like theirs. They know she is not left alone, and already
it is different.

When the man collecting clothes from the lockers comes
around to Alan's, Marina stops him. He seems confused. She looks
around and tries to whisper. "No," she says under her breath. "No.
Don't take these."

Rafael Henzel does not know what happened. He does not know
where he is, exactly. But he sees lights moving and hears strange
voices and tries to call out. "I'm here!" he shouts. "I'm here!"

He calls out for his radio colleague, his friend. "Renan? Renan?" Renan Agnolin, his partner, was sitting next to him on the
plane. But Rafael cannot see him anymore. He calls Renan's name
again and again, but there is no answer.

Slowly, Rafael begins to realize there are trees around him.
Then he sees faces. There are five or six men. There is a woman.
They are talking to him and pulling at his clothes. He yells at them,
"Don't rip my shirt! Don't cut my trousers!" He is worried he will
lose the only change of clothes he has in Colombia. They tell him
he is going to be okay, that they are going to help him. One keeps
shouting, "Don't go to sleep, Rafa! Don't go to sleep!"

Rafael does not know he was in the back piece of the plane, the
one that plunged into the soft earth on the near side of the mountain. He does not know that the elevation and the fog and the mud
made it impossible for helicopters to land at the crash site, and
that it took hours before rescue workers could arrive. He does not
know that he will be extracted from the site in the back of a pickup
truck because ambulances cannot get to him.

Once he reaches the hospital, he has a vague understanding of
what has happened but knows no specifics. He knows the plane
crashed, but the doctors do not tell him how many people are
dead. He does not know that Alan Ruschel kept asking the doctors, "Where are my friends?" as he was wheeled into surgery. He
does not know that Follmann, the backup goalkeeper, will have his

leg amputated below the knee or that one physician will describe Neto to a television station as "currently" alive because he does not want to be presumptuous. Rafael does not know that Danilo survived the crash and was rescued, only to die at the hospital.

A day later, Rafael's wife arrives and traces her finger over his face, where a tree branch or a piece of wreckage has gouged a wound above his right eye. He has a swollen abdomen from his seven broken ribs and a tube down his throat, and he is sedated. She looks at him and says, "I came to get you," and his eyes grow moist.

She wants Rafael to focus on himself, on his own recovery, so she and the doctors tell him the story in stages. Three days after the crash, Rafael learns that there are only a few survivors. No one tells him about exactly how the plane went down. No one tells him that there are so many coffins in the San Vicente funeral home in Medellín that they have to be kept in the parking garage because there is no room inside. No one tells him that two days of school have been canceled in Chapecó and that residents are holding vigils all day at the stadium and that children have written cards and drawn pictures that are piling up outside the gates. No one tells him the city is in mourning.

On Saturday, five days after the crash, Rafael finally looks at the list, finally reads all the names. That morning, three C-130 Hercules aircraft from the Brazilian air force arrive in Chapecó with all the bodies. The coffins are loaded onto several open-sided box trucks, a dozen or more in each, and driven from the airport to the stadium. Shrouded in white and wrapped in plastic because of the rain, the coffins are carried in by the soldiers.

Chiquinho and his men have set out the flowers and the bunting. They have also left only one set of goalposts on the field—the one Danilo was guarding when he made the save against San Lorenzo that sent Chape to the final. Danilo's wife places a picture of Danilo in the goalmouth. The godfather of Danilo's son pounds the crossbar with Danilo's gloves. Under the tent, Danilo's mother hugs Filipe's father and whispers, "Why did he have to make that save in the last minute?"

The president of Brazil is there. The FIFA president is there. Nearly 100,000 people, about half the population of the city, are inside the Arena Condá or directly outside. There is coverage of the memorial all over the world.

There were 77 people on the plane. Twenty-two were Chapecoense players, and three survived. Twenty-three more were coaches or team staff, and there were two team guests. There were 21 journalists, including Rafael, and there was the flight crew, all of whom perished except for one flight attendant and a maintenance technician. Of the 71 who died, there were 64 Brazilians, five Bolivians, one Venezuelan, and one Paraguayan. Fifty coffins come to the wake in Chapecó; the rest are flown elsewhere for separate services.

In the hospital, Rafael does not watch any of the memorial on television. He does not see the stadium's exterior wrapped in a giant black ribbon. He does not listen to the speeches in which the mayor likens the rain to God's tears. He can't bear any of it. It is too fresh. Instead, he just looks at the list, reading the names of his friends over and over.

Aline Machado goes to the airport to see Filipe's coffin come off the military plane, and then she goes to the stadium. But she does not want to be around people from Chape, does not want to talk about how the club must be *força, força,* or strong in the face of tragedy. Aline does not want to be strong. She is angry.

She has so many questions, so many things that do not make sense to her. Two stand out: Why did a Brazilian team hire a Bolivian airline to take it to Colombia? And what was the pilot thinking?

Filipe's father, Osmar, is mad too. Filipe died on Osmar's birthday, and Osmar cannot stop reading news reports about LaMia and the pilot. Within days, he reads that LaMia was a twice-failed Venezuelan airline whose name was sold to Bolivian investors and relaunched in 2015. He learns that it had three planes and that only one was operational. He learns that the pilot, Miguel Quiroga, was in trouble with the Bolivian air force for leaving his military service early with no explanation. And he learns that Miguel Quiroga was also one of the owners of LaMia.

This infuriates him. He tells Aline, "The pilot is a murderer," as he hears more and more on television and the radio. Most crashes involve a massive fire because the fuel explodes, but investigators say all the LaMia fuel gauges found in the wreckage were "below zero," so there was no fire, no explosion. The official flight plan Quiroga filed is scrutinized, and investigators believe that Quiroga might have underreported the weight of the flight. Also, the maxi-

mum flying time before fuel ran out—four hours, 22 minutes—
was listed as the exact same amount of time as the expected trip
time, with no safety buffer for things such as the plane circling the
arrival airport to let another plane land in front of it.

Why did the plane crash? Osmar cringes when he says it: it ran
out of gas.

The club makes statements about how LaMia had flown other
soccer teams in South America and was reputable. There was only
a day or two between winning the semifinal and leaving for the
trip, it says, so the time to make decisions about the travel plans was
short. The team had flown with LaMia earlier in the tournament
and had been satisfied. It liked the way LaMia put Chape's logo on
the plane and on the headrests of the seats. Using a charter airline
was more efficient as well, the club says, because it meant the team
could leave right after the game and get back sooner than if it had
to wait for a commercial flight the next day.

It does not add up for Osmar or Aline, and Osmar seethes as
he reads about a few other LaMia employees being questioned by
Bolivian police. An investigation into the flight controller is under
way too. There is no official word from LaMia yet, but to Osmar it
feels so simple: it was about money. Chape flew with LaMia, he tells
his family, because it was a little bit cheaper than chartering with
Gol or another Brazilian commercial airline. And Quiroga did not
stop to refuel when he should have, Osmar says, because it would
have taken money out of his own pocket. Quiroga tried to push it
to save a little, and so Filipe is dead.

Aline talks to a lawyer. There are discussions about lawsuits,
about legal action. There are meetings. Some other wives and family members are interested, but many just want to move on, to try
to figure out how to put their lives back together without their
husband or son or brother.

Aline wants to move on too, but every time she leaves the room,
Antonella tenses up. Every time she goes to the store, Antonella
cries nervously. At the *Paw Patrol* birthday party, Aline will be
alone. And at Filipe's farm, the locker room isn't finished, and the
grass needs cutting, and the field still needs lines. Every time Aline
goes there, to let Antonella run around or to simply look out over
the countryside, she feels as if she is looking at a story that ends in
the middle of a sentence.

That is why Aline cannot just move on. And so she keeps talking to the lawyer, keeps asking questions, even though there are no answers. Whenever she tries to ask anyone at the club about what happened, she is told that all the directors at Chape who made the decision to use LaMia were on the plane. She is told that all the directors who made the decision are dead.

Fifty-four days after the crash, Rafael Henzel walks back into his radio booth. It is January 21, 2017, and he is wearing a light shirt and hat with a green lanyard holding his credential around his neck. His seven broken ribs are still healing, but his lungs are strong. Before he puts on his headset, he sits in his seat and pauses; he thinks of Renan Agnolin, who was next to him on the plane.

There is a game today. It is a preseason match, Chape against Palmeiras, the reigning national champion, at Arena Condá. The stadium is full. Chiquinho has spent hours on the field, determined to make it a palace. It feels strange—a new team, a new time—but Chiquinho wants to make it nice, even if he doesn't know these players. Pitico is missing and hasn't been seen since the tragedy, and Chiquinho wonders whether it is because the dog does not recognize the new players either.

Before the match, there is a ceremony. Alan Ruschel and Neto and Follmann come out onto the field. Neto has a scar on the back of his head, his hair shaved away in a patch. Follmann is in a wheelchair, his right stump wrapped in beige dressing. He wears a black neck brace. Alan puts one hand on the back of Follmann's chair and walks gingerly, still stiff and sore after spinal surgery.

The fans sing and wave paper origami with the club's crest on it. The surviving players join members of their teammates' families in the middle of the field. Atlético Nacional conceded the Copa Sudamericana final to Chape, so the Chape players are now *campeões eternos*—eternal champions.

Winners' medals are draped over the necks of widows and children. Many of the wives wear their husbands' jerseys backward, so that the names are on the front. From his chair, Follmann lifts the trophy through tears. When Barbara, the wife of Ananias, receives his medal, she cries out and raises her hands and points with two fingers to the sky.

The new players walk out of the tunnel and onto the field. Chape's board has been reconstituted, and a new president has been elected. A new coach, Vágner Mancini, has been recruited.

A new front office is in place, and in six weeks the team has been rebuilt: 25 players signed, a group of coaches brought in, and a support staff hired.

Some teams lend players to Chape to help. Some who played for the team earlier in their careers feel a pull to return. Túlio de Melo, a renowned forward, had played briefly for Chape in 2015 and is supposed to play for a team in Qatar in 2017. The salary is big and the destination intriguing. Then he receives a message from his friend Neto while Neto is still in the hospital after the crash. It says, "The club needs you," and Túlio de Melo comes to Chape instead.

The game begins. The fans behind the goal brandish their flags as usual. It feels good to cheer. Palmeiras scores the first goal, but then Chape bends in a free kick, and the ball is nodded across the goalmouth, and Douglas Grolli, a player who grew up in Chape's youth academy and has come back to help it rebuild, nudges it over the line.

There is a *whoosh* of energy, as if the whole stadium has welled up together. Some fans scream. Others cry. Many in the stands are wearing tiny earpieces so they can hear Rafael describe what is happening right in front of them. In his booth, Rafael's eyes go wide and he bellows, "Goooooooooooal!"

He takes a breath. "My heart overflows! My heart overflows!" he shouts. "Chapecoense! The team of our heart is reborn with a goal from its past!"

Graziele takes the baby pants out of the drawer. There are tiny blue jeans, pastel slacks, and striped shorts. She folds them, organizing them in different stacks. Then she puts them back in the drawer and takes out the baby shoes to evaluate.

She does this every day. It is her therapy. She likes to organize the baby clothes and the baby shoes while she feels the baby kick. She likes to be in the baby's room, where there are giraffes on the wall and a soccer ball in the mobile and pictures of Tiaguinho beside the diaper-changing pad. She likes to make a mess so that she has to tidy up again.

Her therapist tells her it is okay. It is okay for her to have a photo of Tiaguinho on the wall above her bed so she can feel him watching her sleep. It is okay for her to have a collage of their pictures covering the wall near the baby's room so she can feel as if she is not alone. It is okay for her to believe that her husband is going to be reborn as her son. At the body-scan ultrasound, she sees the baby's features and is relieved. She tells her mother, "The baby has his eyes."

The baby will be born in July. Tiaguinho hoped it would be born on July 22 because that was his father's birthday, and now Graziele hopes it will be then too. She has also decided that the baby's name will be Tiago. It was so obvious; in January, her friends and family had a gender-reveal party for her, and when she cut the cake and saw that the inside was blue, everyone shouted out "Tiago!" and threw confetti. Graziele cried. She wants to take a picture of Tiaguinho with her to the delivery room. She wants her husband to be there too.

Graziele does not love soccer. She follows Chape a little, but she lives in Bom Jardim now, her hometown about three hours northwest of Rio. She does not stay in close touch with the other Chape wives. She has her parents and Tiaguinho's parents nearby. She has Tiago in her belly. She has her pictures. She has voice messages from Tiaguinho on her phone that she listens to under the covers.

Aline Machado leaves Chapecó too. Aline is in Gravataí with Antonella. She plays *Paw Patrol* with her, and when Antonella asks about Filipe, she tells her that Filipe is in heaven. Aline says he is with Nina's daddy and Julia's daddy so that Antonella doesn't feel as if she is the only one. Sometimes at night before bed, Antonella looks out the window and points to a star and says, "Look at Daddy."

Aline's life and Graziele's life go on without Chape. So do Rosangela's and Val's and the lives of so many others. They move away because of the crash. They have to.

Others stay. Chiquinho still takes care of the undersoil and the topsoil, still keeps an eye on the drainage system when it rains. After a few weeks, he and his men put away the blankets, throw away the dog food, and take down the tiny house out near the shed with the rakes. Their dog, Pitico, disappeared after the crash, and Chiquinho understands. But every evening around dusk, as he rides the bus home from work, Chiquinho looks out the window anyway, craning his neck in the hope he might catch one more glimpse of Pitico, somewhere else in the city running and playing and chasing the birds that swoop low.

Follmann stays too. His neck brace is off, and he has a German prosthesis and already walks easily on it, so he doesn't need a wheelchair. He goes on a Brazilian television morning show and shows off his singing voice. He laughs, just as he did before the crash, and says he is eyeing a career as a Paralympian. He jokes that it should be no problem because his iron leg never gets tired.

Alan Ruschel and Neto stay as well. They rehab and train, sweating through extra work on the side during practices. They watch the new players revel in the crowds at Arena Condá, energized by the chants and the songs and the ritual, in the 71st minute of every game, when the fans shout "Vamos-vamos-Chape!" over and over, in homage to the 71 people who died in the crash.

They watch the team win or tie 20 of its first 24 games, and they work harder. Marina is nervous about Alan's spine, but she goes to the games with him and watches and chants in the 71st minute too, because she knows he is unbowed; team trainers think he might be ready to play by the middle of summer. Rafael Henzel has told Alan and Neto that he cannot wait to call their names again.

Inside the team, the coaches make a decision: they do not talk about the tragedy anymore. They did for a month or so, but then they decide the locker room needs to look forward. "We need to write our own history," the new coach tells the new players, even if it is with some of the old pieces.

That is why, before every home game, Chape still does concentration at Hotel Bertaso. The coaches still talk about strategy and tactics. The players still sit in the hall on the second floor, playing music and texting and filling the time until the bus leaves for the short ride to the arena. And then, as kickoff approaches, they still run out to play on the same field of those who came before them, the field that Chiquinho prepares by seeding and mowing and watering that bare patch down at the end.

TIM BROWN

There Are Hundreds of Baseball Journeymen, but Only One Cody Decker

FROM YAHOO SPORTS

CODY DECKER IS a 30-year-old professional baseball player with 11 major league at-bats and, because minor leaguers are expected to be poor and grateful for it, a running tab with his parents. When he does become a regular big leaguer, and he will too, just ask him, the first check he writes will have their names on it.

We're standing one morning in the parking lot at UCLA's Jackie Robinson Stadium, where he played in college. There are banners on poles around the complex. His name is on one of the banners. He's wrapping his bats in wax paper so the pine tar doesn't get all over everything in the back of his Ford Explorer and over the dull crinkling of the wax paper he's quoting a character from a movie, some movie, who'd said, "I don't want to see the past. I want to see where we're going."

He smiled.

"I love that line."

He is today a Milwaukee Brewer, they being organization number five in the past 15 months, assuming, as he said a few times this morning, they remember they signed him, because nobody'd told him yet when he was supposed to report for spring training.

Over three hours that felt planned to the minute and wholly frantic at the same time, Decker had hit off a tee and hit short flips and hit regular batting practice and took grounders from his knees and took grounders from his feet and caught bare-handed flips from a catcher's squat then put on all the gear and caught a full bullpen and then took off the gear and drove across the complex to a small gym, where he squatted lots of weight and deadlifted lots of weight and jumped rope and swung a kettlebell between his legs and slammed a medicine ball to the ground and did these spidery things across the floor and probably that wasn't all, it was hard to keep up.

He'd talked almost the whole time, in part because I'd been asking a lot of questions. I had the sense he would have been talking anyway, like that perfect line drive four feet to the left of the exit sign in the batting cage, that line drive that came off the bat barrel just right because he'd kept his body parts connected and stayed inside the ball and driven through the ball, that perfect line drive wouldn't have been real unless it were narrated too.

"That's the one, Skip," he'd shouted, and the man throwing batting practice, 69-year-old Rick Magnante, said, "Yeah it was," while heaving another pitch from behind a screen.

"Eh, that wasn't it, Skip."

"Nah, it wasn't."

There'd been a handful of other players around the complex. A few ex-Bruins, mostly minor leaguers. There was a man rocking a baby carriage while playing catch with Lucas Giolito, the former first-rounder who two months before had been dealt from the Washington Nationals to the Chicago White Sox. Brad Miller, the shortstop–first baseman (–second baseman?) for the Tampa Bay Rays too. And Cody Decker, sweated up from three hours of baseball, with still a three-mile run ahead of him, and with a single goal still out there.

"I just want to play baseball for the rest of my life," he says. "That's all."

Then he looks at you, like, *And you can't talk me out of it.*

He's 30.

"No," he says. "I'm not done."

He has just those 11 at-bats, those wonderful few weeks with the San Diego Padres two Septembers ago. Those can't be it.

"Not even close," he says. "I have a lot more to do."

This he knows.

"Because I belong there," he says. "I've spent my entire life do-ing this, to do that."

Because the minor league hits and home runs were real. Be-cause surely there's somebody out there who can see that. Because this is what he is if not who he is—but maybe who he is too some-times—and just because the game seems to have one opinion of him does not mean that is real, not today and not tomorrow. So he's going to play baseball for the rest of his life.

"Because I said so," he says. "Because I decided it's not enough yet."

So he does what he must, and that means getting after it at UCLA almost every day and choosing to believe and, after years of being a corner outfielder and infielder who could catch some too, he's recast—and retrained—himself as a catcher who could play some corner outfield and infield too. It's also meant gigs selling comic books and pouring drinks and checking IDs at the door and driv-ing Uber and acting and writing and making movies and emceeing a trivia night—Antihero Trivia Night, officially, and it's a raunchy, charming, hilarious kick in the pants that devolves/evolves into dance contests, karaoke jags, and full conversations using only Ric Flair "woos"—at a joint on Wilshire Boulevard in Santa Monica.

There are more like Cody Decker. Not exactly like him, be-cause, seriously, look at that last paragraph. Most haven't hit 173 minor league home runs, for one. But they're out there, and they're packing for spring training too, and they're not done ei-ther, just ask them. Maybe they can run. Maybe they can defend. Maybe they're just good guys to have around. Maybe they've been unlucky, the right guy at the wrong time in the wrong organiza-tion. There's no telling, no explanation, really, for the borderline cruelty of the ballplayer who tops out in Triple A, who's told, yeah, he's really very good at the game but, whoa, not so fast, he's also never going to be a regular big leaguer and never going to make any money at it. This is not to say Decker is one of those, not yet, because that Decker is here at all says something about who he is.

"This kid," said Pat Murphy, who managed Decker for most of three summers with the Padres and is the bench coach in Milwau-kee, "was not a high-end prospect in terms of how scouts do it. This kid taught himself to hit. And just when you think he can't play a position—it doesn't look perfect, maybe—but he gets it done."

Murphy considered Decker, the whole of Decker, chuckled, and said, "If he ever got a shot, he just might do something. I know this, he ain't quittin'."

It is to say every day, every decision, and every at-bat begin to carry the weight of the past 30 years, or at least the last 10 or so, and then it becomes easier to root for a man such as Cody Decker, who—damn it—is trying to get there and have a good time getting there and has had it with the notion he won't hit major league pitching when he's almost always hit all pitching and, besides, maybe a guy deserves more than 11 shots at getting a big-league hit.

Beyond that, beyond believing he's good enough and that the Brewers will understand that soon enough if they don't already, Decker loves a good story. So when I asked him why baseball and not, say, football or accounting or chemistry or something, he said, "You ever see *The Natural*? Baseball's the only thing of all those things that's just magical."

I asked if he'd read *The Natural*, a book that ends not with fireworks and happy tears but with, "When Roy looked into the boy's eyes he wanted to say it wasn't but couldn't, and he lifted his hands to his face and wept many bitter tears." He said he had and much preferred the movie, because no good story ends with bitter tears.

Beyond the good story, he loves a happy ending to the good story, and there's hardly a better ending to a good story than the guy with 11 big-league at-bats on his 30th birthday hitting (and catching) his way into a few more at-bats and making a decent living from them. That would mean Cody Decker was right about what his bat could do given the chance, and also that the good guy —that being him—won in the end, which is the point of this whole thing. That and paying back his parents.

Meantime, he quotes more movies. He runs through the entire history of KISS, the band, when a KISS song comes on in the weight room, and finishes by calling Paul Stanley "the best front man ever," and maybe he's joking and maybe he's not. He tells of being incredibly moved by his recent trip to Israel—Decker is Jewish and is playing for Israel in the World Baseball Classic. He replays the past 15 months—Padres to Kansas City Royals to Colorado Rockies to Boston Red Sox to Brewers, and admits to them being, at times, unnerving. When I ask if he's scared it's close to over, if all the moving around is a bad sign, if he thinks maybe he's only holding a spot for the next guy and the next guy isn't too far off, he grins and summons a line from Doc Holliday in *Tombstone*.

"Not me," he says. "I'm in my prime."

We shake hands and he goes to run those three miles. Spring's coming and there's a good story out there somewhere.

BRYAN SMITH

The Ballad of Ed "Bad Boy" Brown

FROM CHICAGO MAGAZINE

LEAVE. PLEASE, ED. *Pack your shit, say your good-byes, and get outta here. Your family, your girlfriend, your fellow boxers, your managers—especially your managers: we're scared for you. Too much craziness in these streets. You've already been shot three times. What, you think you're bulletproof?*

Well, he kinda was, wasn't he? He'd taken gunshots to his neck, his knee, his ankle—body looking like a connect-the-dots game. *Bulletproof.* If he didn't already have a nickname, he might have copped that one, stitched it right on his boxing trunks instead of the one everybody knew him by. Ed "Bad Boy" Brown. Pride of Garfield Park, future champ, silly, joke-crackin', handsome as Ali, with a right-left combo that hit so hard your whole family would need a standing eight.

"Bulletproof" was sorta funny, when you thought about it. But Brown knew as well as anyone that death doesn't play. And definitely doesn't heed a nickname. He knew at just 11 years old, the evening his mother kissed him good night and went to E2, the club on Michigan Avenue, to celebrate her boyfriend's birthday and never came home—killed with 20 others in a stampede after a security guard tried to break up a fight with pepper spray. "She was a good mama," Ed would tell the papers the next day, his younger brother crying beside him.

He knew from last October, when his girlfriend's brother, a guy he'd come to regard as his own sibling, got clipped sitting in a car, not doing anything. He sure knew from his mornings at the boxing gym, when he'd hear other boxers talking—"Did you hear . . . ?"—or see them pull their shirts up to show their own bullet wounds. He knew from the gym wall, papered with memorial announcements and photos of young men just like him: fists up, hard looks. Bulletproof. Dead.

His comanager and his promoter, one of the biggest in the sport, were offering to stake him to a new life in Vegas, California, anywhere but here. If he'd just say the word.

All right, he vowed. At 25, he had a record of 20-0, with maybe one more fight to get his ranking up and earn some big paydays. Enough to take along his three-year-old daughter and his girlfriend and maybe even his father, who was back from prison. One more fight and he'd get them all outta here. He'd do what everyone asked. *Leave.*

But now here he was. Just after 1 a.m. on a Saturday. The streets of Garfield Park spooling past his backseat window like a documentary, a grainy indictment of all that was wrong with the city, *his* city. *Leave.*

The car slowed. His female cousin driving, his friend next to her up front. She eased into a parking spot under the pale cone of a streetlight. *Damn.* It was getting late. He had to be up early to work out. No half stepping. Too much riding on this next fight.

Then the silver sedan rolled up, slowing just as it reached his cousin's car. The windows glided down, the gun barrels emerged like snake heads. *Aw, no. No.*

"Work, work, work. Trabajo! *Trabajo. Fuerza, fuerza!*" says the short, bald middle-aged man with the salt-and-pepper broom mustache. "The fuck you doin'? You standing there! You ain't gonna win no fights on the ropes."

Two young boxers, red-faced and glistening under foam headgear, shirts soaked, stalk each other around the ring, lunging, lurching, jabbing, feinting, parrying, punching, then dancing away. One, in a TEAM SHORTY T-shirt, stood up by a hard right, unleashes a barrage that sends the other boomeranging off the ropes.

"That's a freight train," the man says approvingly from the skirt of the ring. As if looking for confirmation, he turns his head to a smattering of other boxers below the ring in various stages of their workouts: shadow punching, skipping rope, pumping crunches.

At first glance, the Chicago Park District boxing gym in East

Garfield Park seems little more than a modest-size, high-ceilinged room marooned at the end of a dim hallway, the ghost of some long-ago administrative headquarters. But a few steps in, the sepia richness of its storied past begins to reveal itself. The space is dominated by the ring, a 24-by-24-foot square of sky-blue canvas bearing the words CORONA EXTRA and set about four feet off the floor, the corner poles resting on dingy, barf-beige industrial tile littered with boxing gear. From an adjacent room comes the *da-da-ta-da-da-ta-da-da-ta* of a speed bag being worked. From another, the thuds of a heavy bag.

Roaring above all, though, is the ringside commentary—a mix of drill sergeant commands, professorial patter, and stand-up routine—of the middle-aged man, George Hernandez. Dressed in striped Adidas track pants and a Chicago Park District polo, this West Side Mussolini looks every bit the part of the bellicose trainer–slash–father figure that has made him an icon in local boxing circles. The City of Chicago might technically run the place, but this is his gym, just ask.

"This ain't no goddamn democracy," he bellows to no one in particular. "What I say goes up in this motherfucker!"

One of the boxers launches a sharp flurry that recaptures his attention.

"More of that, more of that, *there* you go!"

And then: "You tired, aren't you? Took the week off. All you do is fuck and eat. All that pussy got your legs fucked up. You better get your shit together. Donald Trump might deport your ass."

"I got my papers," the boxer shoots back.

It was at this same gym, nearly 20 years ago, that a skinny six-year-old named Ed Brown appeared with his two cousins, arriving like so many boys who find their way here: uncertain, wide-eyed, intimidated, self-conscious—and desperate to hide any hint of that.

The trio were from the neighborhood, long considered one of the city's poorest and most gang-ridden. With rare exception, its appearance matches the statistical gloom: a wrecked landscape of vacant lots and boarded-up houses and caved-in graystones, unrelieved stretches of blasted wasteland studded with gardens of broken glass and clusters of young men on street corners.

From the heart of the desolation rises what at first seems a glittering mirage, a dome gilded with 23-karat gold tiles crowning a

splendidly carved Spanish baroque edifice. Flanked by lagoons
and blessed with a panoramic view of the downtown skyline, some
seven miles off, the structure was originally built in 1928 as the
headquarters for the West Park Commission. Like much of the
neighborhood, it succumbed to blight and neglect, crumbling
brick and falling plaster, but was rescued from demolition at the
last moment in the early '90s. Today, situated next to the Garfield
Park Conservatory, it houses a gymnasium, an auditorium, a dance
studio, a fitness center, a grand ballroom, and—calling out to kids
in need of positive, not to mention safe, places to hang out—a
boxing gym.

Of the three boys who walked in that day in 1997, only Brown
stuck. Hernandez is fuzzy on his first encounter with him ("So
many come in here," he says), but it isn't hard to imagine the
moment. "These are tough boys from tough neighborhoods," he
says. "Some are coming from prison, some are dope fiends, gang-
bangers. I've taken guns away from kids. I can't come off like, 'Hi,
how are you?' When they come through that door, I have to let
them know I'm nobody to play with. I'm the only bully here. You
bring that gangbangin' shit in here and out you go. You don't do
what I say, out you go. You think you know better, out you go."

Hernandez's approach derived from his own adversity, which
included growing up without parents. After separating from Hernandez's mother, his father dropped him and his three brothers
off at a police station, declaring that he didn't want them anymore.
Hernandez became a ward of the state, joined the Army, then studied criminal justice and fine arts at Loyola. He learned to fight by
fending for himself growing up in group homes.

The blunt-force welcome he unloads on newcomers is intentional—a first chance to take a kid's measure. "You don't got no
heart, no balls, we run you out of here," he says. The payoff for
those who don't get scared off or pissed off is acceptance into a
sort of surrogate family. "What you can't find at home, I try to give
them here," Hernandez says.

Ed Brown ingratiated himself from the get-go: "He was really
funny and goofy, already cussing up a storm at six years old," Hernandez recalls. He was also eager to learn. "He was like a sponge.
He would pick up everything."

Even as a boy, Brown was fierce, "always getting into fights at
the park—and winning," says boxing writer Bill Hillman, a former

Golden Gloves champion who began tracking Brown's career early on. That's why Brown's family steered him toward Hernandez and the gym. "They thought they could turn that anger into something positive."

And they did. At age eight, Brown, weighing 60 pounds, won a Silver Gloves title, the under-16 equivalent of the Golden Gloves. He also claimed an Illinois Junior Olympic championship. For him boxing was, at first, just something to do. It was only when he saw he had a gift for it, he told a television interviewer years later, that he fully committed: "It gave me confidence."

The shattering news of his mother's death, however, upended everything. Hernandez dropped any pretense of tough love. "We just started becoming close," he says. "He started hanging out more. I was feeding him every day." With Brown's father in and out of prison, the boy's grandmother took custody. But Brown also sometimes stayed with Hernandez and his wife. "I wanted to be the parents he didn't have," the trainer says.

At the gym, Hernandez sought to refine Brown's boxing skills, which were becoming more evident by the month. "He was skinny and tall, but, man, he could hit," remembers DeShawn "Hurricane" Boyd, who was 11 when he began sparring with a 14-year-old Brown. "It felt like he had bricks in his gloves."

Brown's leanness wasn't the only thing at odds with his toughness in the ring. "A lot of people would say, 'If I didn't know who Ed was and I just saw him on the street, I'd be like, 'Is this the goof you all been talking about?'" Boyd recalls. "But when it was time to get serious and he put on them gloves and he hit you, you would be like, That boy can hit."

Over the years, Boyd developed a tight bond with Brown. "We grew this big-brother, little-brother relationship," he says. "He was always in the gym, pushing me to be better. If I was slacking off, he'd always be on me."

The contrasts within Brown—caring, charismatic kid one minute, ferocious fighter the next—drew Hillmann to him. "I was always fascinated because there was this bad-boy thing he had, but also he was a kind, nice person and everybody just fell in love with him," he says. "They cared about him almost instantly, and the same thing happened to me."

Brown and his clique of boxers began calling themselves the Broke Team—a play on Floyd Mayweather Jr.'s the Money Team—

because of their raggedy equipment and Hernandez's beater van, which hauled them to fights and sometimes doubled as parking-lot sleeping quarters. They reveled in their underdog status, in how people underestimated them. Brown might have had to fight in borrowed headgear and a donated mouth guard, but he was proving himself in the ring, pummeling opponents in local matches. Neighborhood folks, family, friends, and fellow boxers would pack his fights.

He loved it. But he was also drawn to another kind of rush: the streets. Trouble surfaced just as his boxing reputation was growing. He slid into what would become his favorite vice: gambling. He smoked weed. He began to slack off on his training.

Hernandez noticed the changes. "I was beside myself," he says. "I'd worry about him every time he left the gym. Where is this guy?" He remembers driving the streets one time looking for Brown and finding him huddled with a group slinging dice. At one point, when Brown was 16, Hernandez had had enough: "I told him to get the fuck out of the gym."

The banishment didn't last long, and Brown's behavior improved enough for Hernandez to take him back. But Brown had by no means turned his life around. He was, by his own admission, a "gangbanger." Hernandez and others close to Brown have refuted this. But in a recorded interview with Hillmann, a copy of which he shared with *Chicago,* Brown used that word to describe himself. Criminal records detailing charges ranging from marijuana possession and gambling to gun possession—eight in all—list Brown as a member of the Black Souls, a West Side gang.

He dropped out of Al Raby High School, a few blocks from the gym, in 2009—just half a credit short of graduating. Then, not long after turning 19, he came into a hefty chunk of money. The owners of the E2 nightclub had agreed to a settlement that, according to Brown, brought him $140,000.

It was, needless to say, more money than he had ever seen. But within nine months, it was gone. In interviews with Hillmann years later, Brown said he squandered it on guns and cars. "I was young," Brown told him. "I was living the lifestyle. It was stupid, but I did it."

Despite the distractions, Brown flourished in the ring. He won the Chicago Golden Gloves title in 2010 and 2011. Brutal punches became his trademark. "He knocked one guy's mouthpiece out,"

Hillmann recalls. "He ripped another guy's headgear off. I had never seen that in all my life in boxing. Right then, I was like, 'This is for real.'"

The flip side of being a success in the ring, of being handsome, well dressed, liked by the ladies, and looked up to by young boys is that it made him a potential target for neighborhood rivals. "They find any little thing to pick on people that got something going for themselves," says Boyd. That Brown could fight only put him more at risk. "Boxers have to watch out," says Boyd, "because if someone tries to start something with us, they know we will whoop their ass, so they will come back on us with a gun."

Truth is, in Garfield Park, you don't have to be targeted to catch a bullet. In 2011, while training for the Olympic trials, Brown was shot in a drive-by on his block. "I got caught in the crossfire," he would later tell Hillmann. "It hit me in the neck. The doctors said I would have died if I wasn't in such good shape from boxing." He survived. His Olympic dream did not.

Still, Brown pushed on, and in December 2012, he made his professional debut. The fight took place at Cicero Stadium, a 1,500-seat arena that has long been home to the local Golden Gloves tournament, where boxers like Joe Louis, Sonny Liston, and Cassius Clay made names for themselves.

The night was a festive coming-out party for the 6-foot-1 Brown, who fought as a 147-pound welterweight. He danced into the ring with an eight-piece marching band and to the roar of fans waiting to see what he could do in the pro ranks—against a far more experienced fighter by the name of Dontre King.

Within the first minute, Brown landed a left hook to the body that was so hard, Hillmann recalls, "I swear I could hear King's ribs breaking from where I was sitting." Brown knocked King out in the first round.

The joy vanished less than two weeks later. Out at a club, Brown got into an altercation and was shot—again in the neck and also in the knee. Talking about the incident later to Hillmann, he shrugged it off, even though he'd nearly died: "It didn't hit any major organs, but I was out for a minute."

Actually, he was out of boxing for the better part of four months. But when he stepped back into the ring in April 2013, he showed little rust, winning his next two fights by TKO.

Then, more bullets. In November 2013, he and some friends had just stepped off a "party bus"—a tricked-out rented shuttle bus with a dance floor and bar—in North Lawndale around 4 a.m. That's when two men approached and began shooting. Brown was hit twice in the ankle.

Nine months later, just as he was ready to resume his career, he faced yet another major setback: he was arrested on charges serious enough to put him in prison. He had been convicted of a felony before—in 2012 for possession of ecstasy—but had managed to avoid serving time. In this case, he wasn't so lucky. In August 2014, police caught him on an East Garfield Park corner with a .22-caliber gun, and he was charged with six felony counts. One of Chicago's most promising boxers was now in jail awaiting trial, his career in jeopardy. All that, coupled with the reality of life behind bars, hit Brown hard, say Hernandez and Boyd, who visited him in Cook County Jail. "Man, I hate it up in here," Boyd recalls Brown saying. "People tell you when to eat, sleep, what you can and can't do. This is not what I want."

In February 2015, after six months in jail, Brown pleaded guilty to a felony gun possession charge. He was sentenced to a year but given credit for time served and released on parole.

Now back at home, Brown had added motivation to straighten up: a year-old daughter, Kayla. The relationship with her mother hadn't lasted, but by all accounts, Brown doted on his baby girl, lavishing her with gifts and as much time as he could spare.

He also began to take his boxing career more seriously. At 24, he was still young enough to make a legitimate run at the big time. But he had to push. He needed a proper manager, someone who could get him fights—good fights—against increasingly accomplished opponents to build his résumé.

Mike Cericola, a fight promoter and manager out of Bridgeport who had taken an interest in Brown since the boxer was about 19, made a case for himself. The clincher was when he was able to persuade Cameron Dunkin, one of the sport's top promoters, to manage Brown as well. Over three decades, the Las Vegas–based Dunkin has worked with 34 world champions, and he currently reps three titleholders—junior welterweight Terence Crawford, junior featherweight Nonito Donaire, and welterweight Jessie Vargas. Having Dunkin aboard would mean instant credibility.

"I told him there's a kid in Chicago that's really doing well in the gym. He's down on his luck, but he's 3-0," Cericola recalls of his conversation with Dunkin. "And when I said it was Ed Brown, Cameron paused for a minute, like, 'Where do I know that name?' Then it came to him: He knew Ed from a tournament years back, and he remembered how impressed he was. He said, 'Wow, I forgot about that kid! I gotta get him.'"

He did, and over the next 18 months—from May 2015 to November 2016—the promoter arranged a staggering 17 bouts for Brown. The newest addition to Dunkin's stable didn't disappoint. Brown not only won every one of those fights but dominated them, taking 14 by knockout or TKO and the other three by unanimous decision. "I pride myself on accurately judging talent, and I think my track record proves that," Dunkin said at the time. "So believe me when I say Ed Brown is the goods. He is on the road to become boxing's next big thing."

Brown's run caught the eye of executives at premium cable networks like Showtime and had him on the cusp of a world ranking. Nate Jones, a former Olympic and professional boxer and an assistant trainer to Mayweather, agreed with Dunkin. "He was three fights away from fighting for the world championship. Three fights away," Jones would later tell the *Chicago Sun-Times*. Big purses, the kind that could dwarf Brown's E2 settlement, seemed within reach.

Brown's rapid ascent, his team believes, largely grew out of the positive changes in his life. He'd made a concerted effort to surround himself with better influences. "He would tell me, 'You can't survive with negative people around you or bad things are going to happen,'" Hillmann recalls. One benefit of fighting so many bouts in such a compressed time was that he was always training. "When you're a hundred percent committed to being a boxer, you don't have time to be in the street," Hillmann says.

Outside of the gym, Brown kept to himself more. "He was staying in the house," says Boyd. "But the problem is, when you are popular, sometimes trouble follows you."

That reality was stark enough that when Cericola started giving Brown rides back and forth to the gym, he learned that the direct route was not always best—not when Brown was trying to stay clear of rival gangs. "He would tell me, 'Don't drive down this street, don't drive down that street,'" says Cericola. "Every morning when I'd pick him up, he was looking over his shoulder, worried who was watching. I could see the stress on him."

The ring remained Brown's haven. "To him, it was the safest place, the one place he couldn't be hurt," says Cericola. "When he got in the ring, he knew he was okay."

As 2015 bled into 2016, Brown found himself mentoring other boxers, helping them avoid the pitfalls that nearly sank his career. Boyd, for one, was on the verge of abandoning his dream of fighting professionally, but Brown talked him out of it. "I wasn't really feeling boxing like that no more," Boyd recalls. "I had a lot going on. Two of my friends got killed, and I lost some cousins. Ed was there through it all. He kept pushing me, especially when he found out I had a daughter on the way. He was like, 'Man, you got to step it up now and do what you got to do.' That's why our relationship was so tight. He knew how life is out here in Chicago, how hard it is to stay out of trouble. He made me feel that I could do something because *he* was. He gave me hope."

By this time, two major developments reinforced Brown's new outlook. The first was that he'd formed a deeper bond with his father, Ed Brown Sr., who had been in and out of prison for much of his son's life, mostly on drug-dealing convictions. The father had become a fixture at the boxing gym and at bouts. He hounded his son to leave the streets behind, not make the same mistakes he had. "He'd get so angry," says Tamika Rainey, the elder Brown's sister. "He had a fear, like a clock was ticking" (a "death doom," she calls it) for his son. "Little Ed would always laugh and say, 'What's the matter with you, Daddy?'"

The second was Brown's ongoing relationship with Tiana Phillips, a young woman he met at a Burger King drive-through. Brown was "so goofy," she recalls. "He would order all this food he wouldn't even eat just to talk to me. I finally gave him my phone number." She started going to most of his fights, even to ones in Los Angeles and Philadelphia, and he moved in with her and her mother. Immediately, he was "the life of the house," Phillips says.

Even with Brown turning things around, Cericola and Dunkin fretted. The streets were still the streets. Bullets could still find him.

In October 2015, they nearly did again. Brown and some friends had rented another party bus, this time to celebrate his 25th birthday. "Him and I agreed that he shouldn't be out clubbing," recalls Cericola. The bus was a compromise. The group parked on Jef-

ferson Street in the South Loop, near the Roosevelt Road corridor
of big-box stores. At some point, according to the police, an argument broke out and gunfire erupted. Three men were shot. Brown
escaped without injury, but the incident was another reminder of
the threats Chicago presented.

To Cericola and Dunkin, the solution seemed simple: leave.
"You know we can send you somewhere," Cericola told Brown
at one point. "We could put you in the mountains, training with
other fighters. We could put you in California. We could put you
almost anywhere, with Cameron's connections."

Remaining in Chicago—in Garfield Park—was begging for
trouble. Who knew that better than Brown? He wore the scars.
How many friends had he lost?

"I tried every way to get him to leave," Dunkin says. "He wasn't
doing anything bad, didn't break the law. But I had told him, 'You
can be walking down the street there [and be in danger]. You're
living in a war zone. Why do you want to stay?'"

It's easy to ask that from the outside. But shedding everything
you know, what you've grown up around all your life, is not so
simple. "A lot of these kids have never even left their neighborhood, let alone gotten on a plane," says Cericola. Adds Hillmann:
"Leaving would have been such a monstrous step for Ed. Leaving
Chicago is essentially leaving George as a trainer and a father figure. That's really hard. George really, really loves his fighters, and
those fighters love him."

Brown would flirt with the idea of moving, but then . . . what
about his daughter? She was the most important thing in his life.
How could he leave her? And what about Tiana? This wasn't a casual thing. He loved her, her family. And he was only now getting
to know his own father.

"If it was me—and this is the honest truth—I wouldn't leave either," says Boyd. "Not a chance until I knew I got enough money to
take my mama and my brothers and my sisters with me, my daughter and the mother of my child with me. In Chicago, you wouldn't
just want to leave your people behind. That's like somebody in a
scary movie leaving their family in the woods with the killer."

Brown's wavering sparked tension between his manager and his
trainer. "George and I would fight every day about it," Cericola
says. For his part, Hernandez insists that he wasn't holding Brown

back and that he actually encouraged him to leave—but only if the promises Dunkin was making, about a place to live and training support, were put on paper.

Brown continued to vacillate until an October night in 2016. That evening, Phillips's brother—who had become one of Brown's best friends—was shot and killed in an apparent drive-by.

Friends say that his death fundamentally changed Brown. Boyd recalls a conversation he had with the boxer not long afterward. Gone for good, it seemed, was the goofy Ed Brown, the man-child with the bulletproof swagger. "Li'l bro," Brown told Boyd, "I'm just trying to better my life so me and my family and all of us can get up out of here. That street shit ain't where it's at no more."

And then Brown said something Boyd will never forget: "The next time I get shot, I might not make it."

One more fight, maybe two, and he'd be out of Chicago.

Friday, December 2, 2016, began for Brown the way most all of his recent days had. He woke up at 8 a.m. and headed out to the gym for a few hours, Tiana giving him the good-bye she always did: "Be careful. I love you."

That night, he met up with Boyd for a second workout. Brown seemed unusually reflective, Boyd recalls. As they were leaving the gym around 7:30, Brown hugged Boyd and put his hands affectionately on the back of his friend's head.

"I ain't the best fighter you know?" Brown asked.

"Yeah, you know you the best fighter I know."

Brown then declared that Boyd was going to win a Golden Gloves title.

"All right, li'l bro, I'll see you in the morning," Brown added.

But what Boyd remembers most about that conversation is what didn't get said. "It's something we always say in Chicago before we leave somebody: 'Love. Keep your head up.' I said, 'Keep your head up, big bro.' I was going to say 'love,' but then George started talking to us. When I walked away, I was like, Dang, I didn't get to tell bro 'love.' Then he was already in the car, gone."

Somebody knows why Ed Brown was out that night, on the street at that hour. Somebody knows why he was in the backseat of a sedan with his cousin at the wheel and beside her a friend who'd been with Brown at least two times he was shot.

And somebody knows why death couldn't wait for him to get out of the city, as so many people had begged him to do. *Go before it's too late. Leave.*

The police report put the time of the incident at 1:10 a.m., the location as the 3200 block of West Warren Boulevard in East Garfield Park, a few blocks from the gym. The cousin told police she had just pulled up to the curb on Warren when a silver sedan crept up and its occupants started shooting. Brown was hit in the head, left hand, and butt. His cousin took a bullet to the leg, but nothing life-threatening.

Brown was rushed to nearby Mount Sinai Hospital, where doctors operated to reduce the swelling in his brain. He was placed on life support, on which he would remain throughout the night, the next day, and into the day after.

Cericola found out that Brown had been shot shortly after noticing two missed calls. "As soon as I saw that his dad called me two minutes after his girlfriend, I knew something was up," he says. "The first call I made was to George. He answered the phone and said, 'Is he dead?' That's how he answered, 'Is he dead?' I'll never forget it."

Boyd received his own call from a friend. "I just had that feeling, especially when they told me he got shot in the head, like, 'Dang, bro, you just going to leave me like this?'"

Cericola rushed to the hospital. "There was a big crowd outside," he says. "The police let family and people close to him sit in the emergency room. It wasn't until the next day that we were able to actually go up, two by two, and see him."

When he entered, Cericola recalls, Brown was hooked up to machines and tubes. The manager approached his boxer's bed and whispered, "Fight. Just fight. We love you." But it was clear to Cericola: "He was already, you know, he was already gone."

At 4 p.m. on Sunday, December 4—39 hours after the shooting —Brown was declared dead.

Brown's friends still have questions: Was it a random drive-by? Did a rival gang recognize the car Brown was in and move on him? Was he set up somehow? No arrests have been made, and police have refused to comment on a possible motive.

"You never know why a person might be trying to kill you out here," says Boyd. "The hate and the envy, that is a big thing out of Chicago. Somebody see you doing good, and they not doing good

—they ain't got nothing or ain't doing nothing. That's just how Chicago is."

Hernandez was so distraught about Brown's death that he considered retiring—but was talked out of it by his Park District bosses. "I've got too much work to do," he says. Hillmann, too, has thought about Brown's death a lot and found no solace, no easy answers. "He was conflicted like all of us," Hillmann says. "The darkness and the light inside of him were at war. All of it might be why he was such a great fighter. Because his whole life was a war, even when he was alone looking at himself in the mirror."

In January, a little over a month after Brown's death and nearly 20 years after he first stepped into the boxing gym in East Garfield Park, a tall young man of about 19 wandered through the door of that same building and took in the ring. He was here to see Hernandez, he said. But as hard as he worked to put on a brave face, he was clearly nervous, especially after Hernandez's welcome, a version of which he's given to hundreds of young men over the years:

"What the fuck? Who are you?" Hernandez briefly regarded the lanky newcomer, who had a scratchy goatee, baggy sweats, and scuffed high-tops. "This ain't no amateur hour. These are professionals up in here."

"I know."

"You know. What you know? Sheeeeiiit."

"I can take a punch."

"Take a punch? You want to give a punch, not take a punch, motherfucker. Can you hang is my real question."

"I can hang."

Hernandez put a smirk in his voice. "I got a feeling you can't. Get dressed. *Que paso!* I ain't got time to wait!"

A short while later, after a horn blast, the young man pounded his gloves together and walked toward his opponent, one of the gym pros trained by Hernandez. He parried the first few blows and even landed a couple, but a straight right popped his mouthpiece out. He fought on, even as some of the other fighters yelled at Hernandez to stop the contest. Hernandez waved his hand. *Let him go.* A few seconds later, the newcomer was on his butt.

He scrambled to his feet and threw a few more punches, then clinched for dear life as blows continued to rain down. When the horn blasted again, a second fighter replaced the first and began pummeling the newcomer, whose white T-shirt was now speckled with blood. Hernandez pretended not to pay attention, chatting with another boxer just outside the ring about a fight from the weekend. When the horn sounded a third time, the newcomer lurched toward the corner, his nose a crimson blossom. "I'm good," he said as a corner man cleaned him up. After a few minutes, the horn sounded again, and he was back in the ring. Overhead, a pair of black shorts with "BAD BOY" stitched across the waistband hung from a wire.

Hernandez watched out of the corner of his eye for a bit. Then he went into his office and lit a cigar next to that wall filled with photos—photos of bulletproof boys.

LEE JENKINS

Don't Try to Change Jimmy Butler

FROM SPORTS ILLUSTRATED

THE SELF-TITLED Garbage Guy from small-town Texas who grew up on Spam and syrup sandwiches, who waited tables at Denny's and mowed lawns in basketball shoes, who played one game of AAU ("travel ball," he called it) and never left the bench, who received a single scholarship offer out of high school from Centenary and a partial from Quinnipiac, who started in junior college only after two regulars failed drug tests, and who faxed his letter of intent to Marquette from a McDonald's sinks into a tan leather banquette on a Gulfstream III bound for Silicon Valley. Jimmy Butler is on the phone with his new head coach in Minnesota, Tom Thibodeau, who of course was also his old head coach in Chicago. They talk every day, often multiple times, about what food the Timberwolves should order for training-camp spreads and what hotel they should book in New Orleans. Butler prattles on about rush-hour traffic patterns.

But this August afternoon they are evaluating free-agent backup point guards, and Butler makes the case for a veteran he has been courting. "We spoke today," Butler says. "He's ready. He'll do everything I do. He can live in my house if he wants." The engine whirs, the plane rises, and Butler tells Thibodeau he will call back when his private flight from Los Angeles lands in San Jose. Butler is a bold-faced headliner now with 24-hour access to the coach and team president, two rented houses in the Minneapolis suburbs, dominoes engraved with JIMMY BUCKETS, and practice basketballs etched with the question, CAN A KID FROM TOMBALL BE MVP? Chicago is where Butler became a two-way wing and three-time All-Star, but he felt like the Bulls still looked at him as the 30th pick in the draft, that anxious rookie who chirped from the bench, just loud enough to hear, "I can guard that dude! I can do this!" The Wolves, on the other hand, viewed him purely as the keystone of the NBA's next contender.

How Butler sees himself is more complicated. On a short stroll through downtown Palo Alto, in search of a caramel macchiato with an extra espresso shot, strangers whisper his name as he passes. Most hoop elites are identified by no more than two syllables: LeBron. KD. Steph. Russ. Kawhi. CP. Beard. "I'm always *Jimmybutler*," he muses. The formality suits him, a superstar who used to be a sideman and still grapples with the transition. "How is a star treated?" he wonders. "I don't know. I'm learning like everyone else, and it's a helluva curve." Butler flies in a Gulfstream but drives a Toyota minivan with a BABY ON BOARD sticker across the back, even though he is single with no children. He put up 52 points in a game last season against the Hornets and 40 in a *half* the season before against the Raptors, but his preferred final score is 2–0. His favorite time of year is "grimy season," an unspecified stretch of summer and fall when he braids his hair, grows his beard and works out twice a day, hot yoga in between. "Bandannas and buckets," he crows. "That's the heart. That's the hustle."

Butler grinds in the middle of a Western Conference crucible. Instead of lying down for the dominant Warriors, several clubs geared up, the Thunder pairing Russell Westbrook with Paul George, the Rockets flanking James Harden with Chris Paul, and the Timberwolves combining Karl-Anthony Towns with Butler. While George and Paul are upcoming free agents, Butler is under contract for two years, giving the T-Wolves a rare opportunity to dent the West hierarchy.

On the eve of his introductory press conference in Minnesota, Butler stewed over reports claiming he had been a stormy presence and abrasive leader in Chicago, the kind of accusation big-market franchises traditionally leak about exiled alphas after mindless trades. "I ought to go out there tomorrow and be like, 'If you got a problem, here's my number, call me,'" Butler vented. Ifeanyi Koggu, a close friend who handles Butler's business phone, laughed nervously. "That would be funny," Koggu replied, "but not a good idea." Butler commandeered the iPhone 7 in their suite at the Loews the next morning and changed the outgoing voice-mail message from an automated greeting to a personal one. "Jimmy Butler, sorry I couldn't get to the phone, but leave your name and number and I'll hit you back. If you got any beef, definitely leave a message." During his presser at Mall of America, in front of 2,500 hungry souls waiting on the second coming of Kevin Garnett, Butler broadcast the digits to the world.

"Everybody is entitled to their opinion," he began. "But with that being said, my phone is in my back pocket. Whoever has anything to say to me, feel free: 773-899-6071." The phone was not actually in Butler's back pocket. It was in the front pocket of Koggu's jeans. "Once he got to the last digit, I could feel my hip vibrate," Koggu recalls. "And it didn't stop." Within five minutes, the mailbox was full, and within 10, he couldn't answer a call if he tried. "There were too many coming in at the same time," Koggu explains. "Calls and texts, but also cameras popping up with Facetime requests. You could never get to the main screen." The phone became too hot to hold, so Koggu shut it down before restarting it. On a private plane to Los Angeles, Butler chatted with two fans on Facetime, including a boy who spent 45 seconds running around his house hollering for his older brother. Then the device froze for good.

After the plane landed at Van Nuys Airport, Koggu rushed to a Verizon Wireless store in Westlake Village where bewildered employees eyed the bleating gadget as if it were 1985. They reported that the phone had received more than 10,000 texts, 700 calls, and 500 Facetimes in a seven-hour span. Butler was expecting a couple hundred, max. "I'm moving you up in line because we need to change your number," a manager told Koggu. "But first I have to ask, 'Why is this happening?'" Koggu thought about his funny, edgy, and excitable friend who once told Derrick Rose, "Don't throw me the ball because I don't want to f— up," and is now recognizable enough to scramble a cell simply by saying the number out loud. "Man," Koggu told the Verizon guy, "it's a long story."

The minivan sets Butler apart from the NBA's superstar class, as does the sound blaring from its speakers, a foreign twang that prompts violent convulsions among his peers. When Butler was at Marquette, he grew so weary of the hip-hop leaking from teammates' headphones that one day he blasted Tim McGraw's "Don't Take the Girl" in the locker room, mainly to annoy them. Butler was moved enough by the heart-wrenching ballad that he sampled more country music, and soon he was showing up backstage at Luke Bryan, Thomas Rhett, and Florida Georgia Line concerts. "They didn't know who I was, but there aren't a lot of 6-foot-8 black guys at country shows," Butler says. "They damn sure couldn't forget my face, especially with this dumbass hairdo."

Butler spends his vacations in tour buses across the heartland with Bryan and FGL. He disdains Miami, New York City, and Las Vegas, the NBA's natural habitats. He actually considered rejecting an invitation from the U.S. Olympic team because the squad trains in Sin City. He summers in L.A., but not really. The Spanish compound he rents in Calabasas sits over a creek and off a gravel road 45 minutes from Hollywood, out of cell reception. "I like it because it gives me an excuse," Butler says. "'Oh, big party tonight, everybody's going to be there? Sorry, I'd really love to go, but I'm all the way out here in the middle of nowhere.'" He doesn't watch League Pass, doesn't know his NBA2K rating, and hasn't tweeted in almost a year. He recently went two and a half months without turning on his television, which he realized only when a guest discovered that his remote control was missing its batteries.

He keeps a strict daily schedule: wake up at 6 a.m., work out at 7, turkey bacon and oatmeal with berries for breakfast at 8. Lunch is a chicken, rice, and lettuce bowl from Chipotle. Before bed, Butler spends 10 minutes writing in a leather-bound journal given to him by his coach at Marquette, Buzz Williams. One entry may be trivial, about a table he spotted at Target that he might buy for his apartment in San Diego. Another is sentimental, about a mom-and-pop restaurant that served him dinner even though the kitchen was closed. (Butler invited the chef to sit with him and drink a beer.) He passes time playing touch football—although he won't take the field unless he's wearing a regulation NFL jersey with cleats—and dominoes, the game that taught him to count. He and his crew can flip tiles for five straight hours, trash-talking in a language only they understand. *Put that Dak on him*, a reference to the Cowboys quarterback, means somebody turned a 4. *Trees fell on him* is a 15 and must be followed by the refrain, *On his neck.*

For years Butler refused to work out alongside any pro not on his own roster, once recusing himself from a regularly scheduled session with D. J. Augustin after the point guard bolted the Bulls for the Pistons. He has relaxed his policy a bit, but his primary training partner is Mike Smith, who met Butler as a senior at Fenwick High School in Chicago during a Jordan Brand event. "I want to learn," said Smith, whose high fade reminded Butler of his own distinctive hairstyle. Smith, now a close-cropped sophomore guard at Columbia, lives with Butler in the off-season and is often behind the wheel of the minivan. "You own a Rolls-Royce and an Escalade!" Smith gripes. "Why do we always have to take this big-ass soccer mom car and listen to Garth Brooks?"

Butler seethes in the backseat. "First of all," he sighs, "it's Josh Turner."

The minivan and the baby sticker are partly aspirational. Butler yearns to start a family. "When you get to the NBA, you want the most beautiful girl you can find," he says. "But I'm thinking more about kids now, what they're going to be like, and maybe she doesn't have to be the most beautiful if she's 5-foot-11." He and Smith have just completed their morning workout at Pepperdine, and as Butler finished firing turnaround jumpers, the women's volleyball team trickled in for practice, their leggy presence prompting his genetic ruminations.

Butler's own itinerant childhood has been well-chronicled: At 13, his single mother kicked him out of her home in the Houston exurb of Tomball, starting a four-year couch-surfing odyssey that ended when a friend's family took him in. He is not interested in reliving many of the details, but he remembers all of them. Over oatmeal and bacon at Ollo, his breakfast haunt in Malibu, the sight of a silk tie reminds him of a clip-on he bought at Walmart for his sixth-grade basketball banquet. "Everybody made fun of me," he recounts. "I was like, 'At my 10-year reunion, I'm going to land a helicopter on the 50-yard-line of the f— football field.'"

He didn't make the reunion, let alone rent the chopper, but he did visit Mrs. Putney. She taught Butler's first-period government class at Tomball High, and on all his homework assignments, he wrote Tracy McGrady's name atop the paper instead of his own. Alarmed, Mrs. Putney hung a poster on the wall that cited the astronomical odds of becoming a professional athlete. "Every day I had to read it out loud in front of everybody," Butler recalls. "One in a billion, or something close." After Butler reached the NBA, he returned to Tomball High and discovered that Mrs. Putney had moved to the new school in town, Tomball Memorial. When he finally found her classroom, he asked for the poster because he wanted to frame it. "She told me it was lost," Butler says. "I think she was lying."

Butler's high school team was not impressive—"Me and four guys who look like you," he tells a 5-foot-9 reporter—but he still scored an invitation to join the Houston Superstars AAU program. His first game was against the Hoops, memorable only because one of the Hoops' best players threw his shoe at a referee. Butler took a DNP in the game, but he wasn't discouraged until afterward, when he saw his coach chatting up the shoe-tosser outside the gym. The Hoops didn't want the kid anymore. The Superstars, wary of their new wing from Tomball, were desperate. Butler's travel-ball career was over.

His freshman year at Tyler (Texas) Community College did not start any better. Coach Mike Marquis imposed a rule mandating that cell phones be turned off in the locker room, and during his first meeting the phone rang in Reggie Nelson's locker, next to Butler's. "Whose phone is it?" Marquis asked. He made both players sprint the length of the court 10 times each. *Whose phone is it?* He made them do 500 push-ups. *Whose phone is it?* Nelson never copped and Butler never squealed. Marquis was impressed, Butler shone, and a year later he was in Milwaukee swiping winter clothes from Wesley Matthews's closet.

Butler was a source of curiosity at Marquette, and not just because he arrived in the upper Midwest with nothing but T-shirts and shorts. At practice, he stood off to the side of the court when he was tired, legs crossed and a hand atop his head. Williams, then the Golden Eagles' coach, exploded at the sight of his flamingo pose. But the eruptions did not alienate Butler. To the contrary, they hooked him. He studied Williams, how the regimented coach always woke up at 4:30 a.m., used 10 colored pens to take notes, ate at Cracker Barrel on the road. A child of chaos, Butler gravitated to discipline and order. He developed his own routine, including a turkey sandwich with mustard and banana peppers from Subway that he scarfed down every day for lunch while watching video of Marquette's upcoming opponent. "How do I fit here?" Butler asked graduate manager Jamie McNeilly, over his foot-long sub. "How do I find a way to stick?"

He was a survivor, not a standout. At first McNeilly told him to grab two or three offensive rebounds per game, and he did that. Then, McNeilly told him to smother the other team's best player, and he did that. Before a game against Connecticut, McNeilly asked if he wanted to check clips of Jeremy Lamb, an obvious matchup. But the Huskies' best player was a 6-foot-1 point guard, not a 6-foot-5 wing. "No," Butler replied. "Kemba Walker."

"He gets obsessed," McNeilly explains, "and when he's done obsessing over one thing, he obsesses over something else." At Marquette, Butler fixated on his three-pointer to an unhealthy extent, spewing a stream of profanity after each miss. He was so eager to see the ball drop through the net that he rushed line drives at the front of the rim. The problem, coaches concluded, was not mechanical. It was mental. In shooting games, they deducted points for every expletive to chill him out. Eventually, he regained his stroke and found other areas to fret about. During practice, he'd halt a four-man fast-break drill if he caught a ball with one hand instead of two, insisting his group start over. "What are you doing?" teammates asked. "No one even saw." Didn't matter. He saw.

"It was a kind of self-inflicted pain," says McNeilly, now an assistant to Williams at Virginia Tech. "By the time Jimmy left, he was calling out mistakes just as much as Buzz. They were more than player and coach. They were like family." Williams did not know Thibodeau personally, but he recognized the telltale signs of a kindred coaching spirit: long hours, loud voices, tough love. Before the 2011 draft, Williams contacted Bulls general manager Gar Forman and played matchmaker. Butler and Thibs, he believed, would be family too. "With Jimmy, it won't work if you're proper, if you're too tactical or technical," Williams says. "You have to be hard-core. That's how he learned to eat."

The marriage started the way so many everlasting unions do. "We couldn't stand each other," Butler says. It was December 2011, and Thibodeau had a lot on his mind: Derrick Rose, Joakim Noah, a lockout-condensed schedule, and Miami's Big Three. Butler, the last pick of the first round, was not a priority. At practice, Bulls assistant coach Adrian Griffin would tell Butler to make 20 corner threes and the rookie would bristle: "Why? It won't matter, anyway. Thibs doesn't want me here. I'm not going to play tomorrow. I'm not going to play the game after that. I'm not going to play 10 games after that." He was sure he'd spend the next decade in Turkey. At halftime Butler would trail Griffin to the locker room and plead, "Talk to Thibs! Tell him I'm ready!" Once, Griffin persuaded Thibodeau to put the rook in a game and call a pick-and-roll. Butler promptly turned the ball over. "See!" Thibodeau barked at Griffin. "I told you!"

In a midwinter game against the Knicks at Madison Square Garden, starting small forward Luol Deng was injured and Chicago needed somebody to defend Carmelo Anthony. "Go guard Carmelo," Thibodeau grumbled, and Butler assumed he should do nothing else. "If I just guard Carmelo," he reasoned, "I can't f— up. So if anybody passes me the ball, I'm going to pass it right back." On one possession, the Knicks doubled Rose, who swung the ball to Butler. He immediately returned it. In the ensuing time-out, Rose told Butler, "Yo, when I give you the ball, look to score." Butler shook his head. "No," he replied, "I'm only guarding Carmelo."

Here was a rookie Thibodeau could appreciate, and a coach Butler could respect. He challenged himself to get to the team's facility before Thibodeau. "I pull up at 6 a.m.—'I'm gonna beat his ass today!'—and I see that damn black Range Rover parked out front. Next morning I get there at 5:45—'I'm *definitely* gonna beat his ass today!'—and there it is again. Then late at night I come back to shoot with Luol, and it's still parked in that same spot. It's like, 'Okay, forget it, I can't beat the guy. So I'm just gonna run through a wall for this motherf—.'" From 2013 through '15, Butler averaged the most minutes per game in the NBA, and he could not complain. "Hey, you asked to play," Thibodeau reminded him at the first trace of fatigue. "So you'll play 48 minutes." Butler beamed.

He built an offensive arsenal with trainer Chris Johnson in grimy season, from June to October, miming the midrange mastery of Dwyane Wade and Kobe Bryant: back-to-the-basket fadeaways, one-dribble pull-ups, elbow jumpers. But at his first All-Star Game, he still pestered Chris Paul for 94 feet, lest anyone think he'd lost his blunt edge. "God made me a dog," Butler coos. God, Thibs, and Buzz, not necessarily in that order. "He became an All-Star and that didn't change him," Thibodeau says. "He became an Olympian and that didn't change him. He got paid and that didn't change him. I don't think you can change him."

In the spring of '15, as Butler finally replaced Rose atop the

United Center marquee, Thibodeau was fired in favor of Fred Hoiberg. Teams were trying to parrot the Warriors, with all their sunshine and rainbows. Thibodeau's style—heavy on defense, discipline, and 90-minute shootarounds—was out of fashion. "Of course I missed him," Butler says. "I missed the way he went about things: 'Get up on the ball screen! I told you one time and I don't want to tell you again!' I don't need a coach who is going to be like, 'Oh, Jimmy, it's okay,' after I go 0 for 10. 'No! It's not okay! And you can tell me it's not okay!'" He never asked the Bulls to trade him, and up until the end he expressed a desire to stay. When Thibodeau called on draft night to break news of the deal, Butler was playing spades in Paris. He braced for a two-hour conversation about Minnesota's flimsy pick-and-roll coverage. In truth, he craved it.

"Thibs, I'm so happy to be with you again," Butler started. "I'm training. I'm excited. I'm ready to show the world. I'm ready to motherf— go!" Thibodeau let him rant. "Okay, Jimmy," he said. "We'll talk. Enjoy your time in Paris." Butler looked dumbfounded at the phone, as if an impersonator were on the other line. *Enjoy your time in Paris. Hmm,* Butler thought. *That's weird.* The next day he ate dinner at Chez l'Ami Louis, a 93-year-old bistro with a dozen tables that was recommended by Mark Wahlberg. Over escargot he broke up laughing at the ludicrousness of his working life, which started back at Denny's in Tomball, where he quit on his first day after accidentally dousing a table of customers with a tray of drinks.

Now 28, Butler averages 23.9 points, shoots 45.5 percent, and tours Silicon Valley startups, the kind of thing modern basketball stars do. At STRIVR, where Virtual Reality helps athletes train, Butler was uncharacteristically quiet until he glimpsed VR footage of a Stanford basketball practice. "Oh, buddy, what a terrible closeout," he groaned at a lead-footed Cardinal forward. "Thibs wouldn't like that at all. If you're closing out to somebody on the baseline, you never let them go middle. You have to force them down to the defender on the baseline. If he gets middle, everybody collapses and he kicks out. At all costs, he can't get middle!"

Andrew Wiggins, Karl-Anthony Towns, and the Timberwolves can expect to hear a similar mantra for the next six months. Butler believes Thibodeau has mellowed a bit since the Chicago days ("He's still up and yelling, don't get me wrong, but he's gained this whole *human element*") and ponders whether he can do the same. Criticism of Butler's leadership in Chicago was poorly timed, but not unfounded. His tongue-lashings can actually be harsher than Thibodeau's. Butler gives an example: "What are you doing right now? What is going on in your mind? Who the f— do you think you are? If you shoot that ball again, I'm throwing it upside your head." Butler pauses to assess his words. "Okay, that's what I'd want to hear. But not everybody is the same, and right now, you're probably scared of me and want to be left alone."

Former Bulls guard Michael Carter-Williams forced Butler to reconsider his delivery during a meeting last season, when Carter-Williams suggested that encouragement could produce better results than outrage. On the Gulfstream back to Los Angeles from San Jose, Butler tests the diplomatic approach with his agent, Bernie Lee. "If I think Bernie is ugly, I can tell him, 'Bernie, you're the ugliest thing I've ever seen.' Or I can say, 'Bernie, did you do something different with your hair today?'" Butler is proud of his progress. Regardless, it's probably good that the mild-mannered Wiggins and the fun-loving Towns already spent a year with Kevin Garnett howling in their eardrums.

Like K.G. with Flip Saunders, Butler can address Thibodeau on the sideline and channel him in the locker room. "I'm able to tell Thibs, 'Chill out, I'll talk to Karl,'" Butler says. "And I'm able to tell Karl, 'If you come off the ball screen, I need you to be up, I can't have you back. That's what Thibs wants.'" The Timberwolves, despite their glut of young talent, did not resemble a Thibodeau team in year one. They finished 20 games under .500 and 28th in field goal percentage defense. Enter Butler, a stopper, scorer, and emerging playmaker who transforms a promising collective into a potent core. "Great intensity, great passion," Towns says. "I just don't know if I'm going to listen to the country."

By day three of training camp in San Diego, Butler has found new fixations. He urges the T-Wolves to talk more on D, reminds power forward Taj Gibson to catch with two hands, and begs the big men to stop inbounding the ball directly under the rim. "We're not the Warriors," Butler explains later. "We have to do the little things. It's 100–100, five seconds left, we've got possession. Our point guard is denied, he spins out, and we throw the pass off the goal. You've got to take it out to the side of the basket."

He resists the temptation to share this elaborate hypothetical with the group. "I'm not going to do what I did before," Butler vows. "I can't be like, 'Look, motherf—, here's what we're gonna do.' I was too emotional, too confrontational." He is perched behind the wheel of his white Rolls-Royce, braids tucked under a black mesh hat, Michael Jordan splayed across his T-shirt. He sings along with his buddy Luke Bryan — *If you wanna call me, call me, call me you don't have to worry 'bout it baby / You can wake me up in the dead of the night; wreck my plans, baby that's alright* — as the GPS guides him along the Del Mar coastline to a sandwich shop, where he places his college order: turkey with mustard and banana peppers.

The Rolls gleams in the parking lot. The minivan is back in Minnesota. "I miss it," Butler says. "Unfortunately, we have to use this thing just a little longer." He shrugs with the slightest hint of irony.

Grimy season never ends.

CHANTEL JENNINGS

Dante Pettis's Reading List: Defenses, and Then the Definitive Works

FROM THE ATHLETIC

DANTE PETTIS KNOWS his route.

Through the doors and to the left, past the new releases and the best-sellers, he takes a quick right and turns the corner into a thin row of books. At its tallest, the shelves are above eye level for Pettis, making it easy for him to take stock of some suggested reads and newly-placed novels.

"This guy is crazy good," he says, pulling Junot Díaz's connective short story collection *This Is How You Lose Her* off the shelf, going into an explanation of how it took him a year to read the first few short stories before finishing the book in a few weeks. Now, he's cruising through another Díaz novel, *The Brief Wondrous Life of Oscar Wao*. After this, he'll add yet another from the author to his ever-growing pile of books to read (current status: 11 books).

On the field, he's intentional with each of his movements, pacing the No. 9 Washington Huskies in receiving yardage and on special teams.

But here, in his favorite bookstore, with no end zones to find or defensive players to break, he allows himself to slow down, to find his pace in a way that he isn't able to otherwise.

Life will change dramatically for Pettis in the next few weeks. Soon, his college career will come to an end and he'll have NFL decisions to make. As busy as life has been for him at Washington, the stakes will be raised. He has prepared himself for that time on the football field, but he has also prepared for that lifestyle in this bookstore.

"Have you read any of his other books?" he says as he takes Paulo Coelho's classic read *The Alchemist* off the shelf. "I connected with *By the River Piedra I Sat Down and Wept* more, I guess."

Pettis spots *The Great Gatsby,* his all-time favorite piece of literature.

"The way F. Scott Fitzgerald writes, I feel like it's so poetic," he says. "He puts together these huge sentences that he doesn't have to, he could easily say it in a different way. But he strings them together and it comes out still."

This past summer Pettis found a list online entitled "The 100 Books You Should Read Before You Die."

He made it through 10 before football season started.

From the fiction section, he moves on to a small shelf of poetry, his favorite genre, and then makes a swing by the young adult shelves.

"I heard this was good, but I didn't like it," he says, taking one novel off the shelf. "It wasn't captivating."

One back cover review reads: *What it feels like to be young and in love.*

"Yeah," he says, putting it back. "I did *not* feel that way."

From there he makes his way to the art section. He has tried his hand at several crafts: writing poetry and short stories as a creative writing major at Washington, learning photography, even picking up drawing this fall ("I am the absolute beginner," he says, holding the book he bought before fall camp—*Drawing for the Absolute Beginner*).

"Every single day you're playing football, so it has the capability to just take over to where you're not even thinking about anything else," Pettis says. "I think that's when people get in trouble because once they're done playing the sport, it's like, 'Well, all I've done is this, what am I supposed to do now?'"

So, what does Pettis do?

He reads.

Pettis jokes that the reason he wanted to become a collegiate All-American in the first place was that during his freshman season he realized former Husky Shaq Thompson didn't have to share a room during Washington's bowl trip that year.

The reason why was simple: Thompson was an All-American. So, Pettis figured, all he had to do to get his own room for a bowl trip was to become one of the 25 best players in the country.

In four seasons, at least as a specialist, where Pettis now holds the NCAA record in career punt return touchdowns (nine), Pettis has almost certainly secured himself a spot.

But an equally impressive stat to co-offensive coordinator and wide receivers coach Matt Lubick is that Pettis still has managed to read two novels this football season, and he's working his way through three books of poetry now.

"That balance puts football in perspective for him," Lubick said. "He has a lot better balance than I had when I was in college. It helps him withstand the ebbs and flows."

This season those ebbs and flows have come in the form of injuries. Washington has lost three starters on the offense alone (wide receiver Chico McClatcher, left tackle Trey Adams, tight end Hunter Bryant) and has struggled to find fast starts in most of its games. The Huskies dropped one to Arizona State in week seven, a game that the College Football Playoff committee is unlikely to let slide.

Through all that, Pettis has led the Huskies with seven touchdowns on 49 receptions. But, he has—because of injuries, inexperience, and the departure of the speedy John Ross—been a bit of a one-man band. Last season, the Huskies were No. 1 in the nation with 47 passing touchdowns. This season, they're at 45th.

But the Pac-12 title, the only benchmark Pettis really set for himself when he got to Washington, is still within reach for the second season in a row.

Pettis's top-five all time books:
1. *The Great Gatsby,* F. Scott Fitzgerald
2. *This Is How You Lose Her,* Junot Díaz
3. *By the River Piedra I Sat Down and Wept,* Paulo Coelho
4. *The Perks of Being a Wallflower,* Stephen Chbosky
5. *Me and Earl and the Dying Girl,* Jesse Andrews

In most meetings Lubick has with Pettis or on the occasions when the two sit next to one another on flights, Pettis tends to recommend novels or collections of poetry to Lubick that, Lubick admits, he has yet to read.

But right now, the book Lubick sees as one of the most important for Pettis this season has been the notebook that Pettis has kept to detail the minutiae of each matchup and scheme the Huskies have faced this season.

"He brings his notepad everywhere he goes and writes things down and then recopies it," Lubick said. "I think there's a big correlation to why he doesn't make a lot of mental mistakes."

Lubick, who arrived at Washington in February after spending four seasons with Oregon and three with Duke before that, has coached plenty of talented wide receivers, but he said he has never seen someone four years into the system take notes as Pettis has this year.

For Pettis, who already loves words and books, the reasoning is simple—everything can make more sense when it's written down. It's just one more book in his collection.

"There are so many things that go into being a receiver that most guys underestimate," Pettis said. "Simple things like understanding the whole play concept, or knowing what yard the route is supposed to be run at—stuff like that. If you write it down, it makes it way easier to remember."

One NFL scouting source, speaking on condition of anonymity for competitive reasons, compared Pettis's physical and mental skill set to that of the Texans' Will Fuller, and said that Pettis's talent in special teams could give his draft stock a boost similar to the way Adoree' Jackson's did.

"A guy like him who's not only talented enough to play inside and out," the source said of Pettis, "but also smart enough that he can handle the mental aspect of the game . . . he's the kind of guy that's going to prepare well, do all of the little things right, and keep finding ways to get better."

And for Pettis, who's currently working his way through three separate books of poetry— *Whiskey, Words, and a Shovel* (R. H. Sin), *What We Talk about When We Talk about Love* (Raymond Carver), and *Citizen: An American Lyric* (Claudia Rankine)—one of the ways he knows he's going to keep getting better in football is by spending time away from the field, specifically in a book.

Or three.

MICHAEL LANANNA

Born to Be a VandyBoy

FROM BASEBALL AMERICA

THANK YOU TEDDY and Susan—I am honored to speak about your son . . . and our teammate.

Cars never drove down the street in front of Forney Abbott's house.

Born in Houston and raised in 1940s Palestine (No, not the Middle East. Palestine, Texas. Pronounced PaleSTEEN), Abbott's formative years came before cell phones and Xboxes and color TVs. He didn't even have a diamond nearby to play on, no chalky foul lines or fertile grass, just the white lines and the hot, black asphalt of a mostly deserted street.

When he was seven, eight years old, Abbott would take a baseball and march onto that street like he was Joe DiMaggio and it was Yankee Stadium. Instead of throwing from foul pole to foul pole, he'd go light pole to light pole, hurling the ball as far as he could over the power lines that stretched above his head and aiming for the pole 100 yards away.

He did this every day, until one day, a car did drive down the street in front of Forney Abbott's house. And inside that car were two scouts for Major League Baseball teams, one for the Pirates and one for the Cardinals. Abbott, now 77, doesn't remember their names—a few too many blows to the head in the boxing matches of his youth sapped him of those memories. But he remembers them stopping their car, on their way to some recruiting mission in nearby Houston or Tyler, and talking to this seven-, eight-year-old kid out on the street and watching him throw. That car would continue to stop, usually once every month or so, and the Pirates scout

—who lived in a small town about 15 or 20 miles away—would give the young Abbott pointers. Okay, here's how to throw a baseball.

The scout kept coming by until Abbott was 11 years old. For that, he's always been thankful. Still, as a teenager, playing for his high school team and summer league teams, Abbott would draw criticism for the way he threw. Other kids would always tell him he was throwing the wrong way. But he knew they were the ones who were wrong. He knew he threw hard. He didn't have a radar gun to prove it, but he always felt as though God had granted him the ability to throw a baseball with velocity.

Abbott never had the chance to test his arm in the professional ranks. He joined the Army. Served in the Korean War. And when he returned, he moved to Clarksville, Tennessee. He turned his attention to coaching kids, just like that Pirates scout once coached him. He felt, again, as though God had given him this gift for a reason. God wanted him to share it.

Over his adult life, Abbott has helped thousands of kids—and some of those kids' kids. At any time, he could have several 11- or 12-year-olds out in his front yard—instead of in the street like he was—working on drills to strengthen their bodies, arms, and minds.

There was one kid, among those thousands, who was different. One kid that no uppercut to the jaw could ever jostle free from his memory.

Abbott will never forget Donny Everett. He gets emotional thinking about him now.

"I was glad to know Donny," Abbott says. "It was one of the best things that ever happened to me."

Abbott still remembers the day Donny and his father, Teddy Everett, pulled up in front of Abbott's carport about eight years ago. Donny stepped out of the passenger's side with the widest smile, a younger, spitting image of his burly blond-haired father. Together with Teddy, the 11-year-old Donny strolled toward the 70-year-old Abbott, who was sitting outside, and introduced himself.

"Mr. Forney," Donny began. He always called him Mr. Forney. Never Mr. Abbott. Never coach. Just Mr. Forney. "Can you help me?"

"Son, I don't know," Mr. Forney said, "What do you need me to help you with?"

"He wants to be a baseball player," Teddy interjected.

"Well," Mr. Forney laughed. "What does he do?"

"He pitches."

"Okay, if he pitches, that's good," Mr. Forney said. "What does he want to do with this if he wants to be a pitcher?"

Abbott will never forget the look in the 11-year-old Donny's eyes after he asked that question—the urgent sense of determination, the desire, a simmering dream on the precipice of reality. Abbott knew, in that moment, that Donny would get to where he wanted to go, that this kid was going to be something special. He was already special.

"Mr. Forney," Donny said, looking up at the 70-year-old man in front of him. "I want to be a major league baseball player."

The eyes in the Soddy Daisy (Tennessee) High dugout didn't blink as the 6-foot-2, 230-pound linebacker of a 17-year-old lumbered by them, bat in one hand, glove in the other, shaking the ground beneath him.

"That's Donny Everett!" their eyes seemed to scream in adulation. They weren't expecting this—THE Donny Everett running toward the bullpen. No. 14 wasn't supposed to pitch today.

It was March 21, 2015—the fifth inning of a game between a loaded Soddy Daisy team and Everett's visiting Clarksville Wildcats. Everett was playing first base and batting cleanup, his Wildcats down, 3–1, to the Trojans. Standing in the hole, Everett saw his head coach Brian Hetland, who was coaching third base, motion for him to head toward the bullpen. Hetland and his senior star had discussed the possibility of Everett, the Clarksville ace, making a relief appearance in this game in lieu of a standard side session; now, Hetland was pulling the trigger.

Everett took his bat to the bullpen, running past the astonished Trojans dugout, and only managed to throw eight or 10 warm-up pitches before he heard Hetland yelling, "Donny, Donny, come on! You gotta go! You gotta go!" Two batters had reached. There was a helmet waiting for Everett at home plate. It was his turn to bat.

Everett ran back onto the field, dug into the batter's box, and didn't waste a single breath. The right-handed hitter muscled the very first pitch he saw well over the left-field fence. A no-doubt, go-ahead three-run home run. Everett trotted around the bases, stepped on home plate, pivoted, and immediately sprinted back

toward the bullpen. This time, every player in Soddy Daisy's dugout was on his feet, staring in awe at the titan who thundered by
them. Soddy Daisy coach Jared Hensley grabbed three baseballs
out of a bucket in the dugout, waved them tauntingly at his players, and yelled, "Hey, do you want him to sign these balls for you
too?"

The next inning, Everett took the mound. Three batters faced.
Three strikeouts. A fastball touching 98 miles per hour.

That's just one Donny Everett story, of many. The very next
game, he touched 101 miles per hour.

"I've been in this area for 28 years," said Hetland from his office
along the first-base line of the Clarksville High baseball field. "He's
definitely the best high school talent and player and pitcher that's
ever come through Clarksville in that time period, for sure—and
maybe forever.

"Because there's not many who can throw 100 miles per hour,
and know where it's going."

Hetland remembers the 101-mile-per-hour game clearly—
March 23, 2015, on a cool night at nearby Northwest High in
Clarksville. There might've been more Stalker radar guns than
fans in the stands that night.

Everett shoved, striking out 14 and allowing two runs (one
earned) in six innings. The Herculean right-hander never liked
coming out of a game—that night especially. Hetland remembers
his mound visit being like a Joe Frazier–Muhammad Ali fight when
Everett finally reached his pitch count.

All night, the stands were buzzing. The fans couldn't help but
see the numbers flashing on the guns in front of them. At one
point an alum in the crowd went up to the Northwest High coach
between innings and said, "You're not going to believe what I just
saw."

Some guns had 99. Some had 100. Some had 101. It was all the
same to Northwest hitters. They couldn't touch it.

Mike Wagner, an area scout for the Yankees based in Tennessee,
had seen Everett the week before throwing four to five miles per
hour slower. Wagner had followed the right-hander closely, had
done a home visit, gotten to know him and his family intimately.
Wagner wasn't in the stands that night. But his bosses were. Scouting director Damon Oppenheimer and national cross-checker
Brian Barber.

"As an area scout, that's as good a feeling as you can have—on your scouting director's radar gun, the prospect that you like and they're there to see, is up to 100 miles an hour," Wagner recalled, laughing. "That was a great night. It was one of those nights I won't forget.

"Because I had just seen him in Alabama the week before and saw him pitch 94–96, and I thought I'd seen him throw about as good as a high school prospect can throw a baseball, and my director went in and saw him throw better. We don't get many of those nights."

That kind of night became routine for Everett in his senior year. He went 9-1, 0.94 that season with a PlayStation-like 125 strikeouts to eight walks in 67 innings. He won the Gatorade Player of the Year Award in the state of Tennessee. Hetland still has that see-through trophy sitting on the upper-most shelf in the corner of his office.

In truth, Everett's entire high school career was video game–like. He came to school as a precociously strong, physically mature freshman—some opposing coaches joked he looked more like a junior. The right-hander pitched in the upper 80s then, but he quickly earned the trust of his coaching staff, starting on the mound against rival Rossview High as a freshman—the most important game of the season. Hetland remembers Everett starting in the first game of the district tournament later that year and —unbeknownst to him—Everett played with the flu. He threw five no-hit innings, then hit an inside-the-park home run off the top of the center-field wall in the bottom of the fifth, crossed home plate, ran behind the dugout, and vomited. Everett sat out the rest of the tournament, and Hetland made the rest of his players all get flu shots.

Over the next few years, Everett's stuff progressively ticked up. He worked in the low 90s his sophomore year, routinely touched 95-plus as a junior, and flirted with triple digits as a senior. His breaking ball began to show flashes of becoming an effective pitch that senior year. His command improved, as well.

The Wildcats lost only two games Everett started his junior and senior year—both 1–0 games. One loss came in extra innings, in the other, the lone run scored on a balk.

"You get so many players who give you one inning here or one inning there. What I loved about Donny is he never gave you one inning—he gave you everything he had," said a national cross-checker whose club had significant interest in Everett. "It doesn't mean he was good every time. It doesn't mean he was the best. It doesn't mean he dominated for seven innings. I think it probably spoke to what was going on in the inside that he wanted to give you six or seven innings. He never took the ball thinking, 'I'm just going to go out for one inning and go home.'

"He went out there for his team and he gave it to you . . . There was no pitch count. He just said, 'It's my time to pitch, and I'm going to give it to you.' And I loved that about him."

"Donny, I can help you," Mr. Forney told the 11-year-old golden-haired boy in his backyard, after Abbott had watched him throw for a few minutes.

Even at Donny's young age, Mr. Forney could see the quickness of his arm and the untapped potential in his highly projectable body. He had a future, although he had no way of knowing just how bright.

"If your goal is to be a major league ballplayer, you have to do everything we tell you to do," Mr. Forney told Donny. "And this is going to be a six-day affair. You've gotta work out six days a week, and one day you have to take off because that's how God made our bodies to work.

"If you understand that, we can keep going."

Donny nodded his head.

"The other thing you have to do is your dad has to agree to be with you until you get into college," Mr. Forney continued. "Somebody has to be with you to help you with this stuff, because it's a lot of movement and a lot of different things that's going to accumulate and allow you to be a major league ballplayer.

"Are you sure your dad's going to be with you every day?"

"Yes, Mr. Forney."

"Now then there's one more thing to this equation," Mr. Forney said, "and that's your mother."

"My mother?"

"Yes. She's got to agree to cook everything you eat from now until you graduate high school. If she don't agree to cook and feed you what you need to eat, then you're not going to be able to do what you want to do, so all of this is off."

Donny didn't hesitate.

"My mother will do that."

Susan met Teddy in a public park in Clarksville in 1987.

Growing up with a father in the military, Susan had spent most of her life in Clarksville, near Fort Campbell. Teddy was born and raised in Louisville, Kentucky, but after joining the Army, he was initially stationed at Fort Campbell too.

After that first meeting in the park, Susan and Teddy dated for three years, married in July of 1990, and have been together ever since. Teddy Everett was a sergeant, a crew chief on a CH-47 helicopter—a large copter with tandem rotors. He spent 10 years in the military, serving in Korea, Desert Storm, Desert Shield, and more. At one point, he was stationed in Italy, where he and Susan lived together until they moved back to Clarksville in 1995.

All the while, Susan and Teddy were trying to have a child. They tried for seven years. "We didn't think we were going to have children, actually," Teddy said. "We had pretty much given up."

Then, on April 16, 1997, Donny Everett came into the world —born into a home that couldn't have possibly been more loving.

"I was very, very excited," Teddy said. "Very, very excited. I was."

Even as an infant, Donny rarely gave Susan or Teddy any problems. He'd sleep through the night without much of a stir. In high school, he'd still go to bed around 8 p.m. most nights and wake up at the crack of dawn.

"We'd never have to go upstairs and be like, 'Get up!'" said Susan, laughing.

From a young age, Donny also displayed a clear affinity for sports.

"Even from the time he was just a baby—couldn't even walk yet —he'd throw a ball," Teddy said. "I told Susan, 'Well, he's going to grow up and throw a ball. I don't know what it's going to be, but it's going to be a ball of some sort.'

"We would spend hours. I'd be on a chair, and he'd be on his knees and throw a ball to me, and I would just catch it and throw it back to him, and it would go forever and ever and ever, and then I would take it and chuck it through the house and he'd go crawling off and getting it and coming back, and then we'd go again. We'd do that for hours."

As he grew older, Donny channeled that love for throwing into a love for baseball. He'd spend many days over at Susan's father's house and help his grandparents with yardwork and various chores. He'd also watch Red Sox games with his grandpa. His grandpa explained to Donny the intricacies of the game.

When Donny started playing organized baseball, he separated himself almost immediately. His Little League and middle school coach Rod Streeter remembers how ecstatic he felt when he had the opportunity to coach Donny. And that excitement was based solely on seeing Donny play in Pee Wee baseball as a seven-year-old.

"It's just something you feel about a certain kid," Streeter said. "He was bigger than everybody for his age, but he was one of the youngest of his age group. And when I say 'big,' I mean tall. You look at a kid and you project what he's going to look like in the future, that was one thing. And then as he got older, the work ethic he put into it. The wanting to stay longer after practice. The wanting to get there early.

"Some days when you're done with practice, you want to go home. When he got to be 11 or 12, he just had that motivation. You knew that he was going to work to get to where he wanted to be. To me, I could just tell that you weren't going to stop him. He was going to get to where he wanted to go."

It was also around that age when Teddy realized Donny had advanced to a point where he couldn't help him any more—at least, not with baseball.

"I was like, 'Rod, do you know anybody I can send Donny to work with?'" Teddy said.

Streeter did know someone—the same man in Clarksville who had helped him more than 20 years prior, when he was a pitcher at Austin Peay, and the same man who had helped almost every aspiring young pitcher who came through Clarksville.

"Yeah," Streeter replied. "This guy's a little older—but he knows what he's talking about."

June 8, 2015. Draft night at the Everett house.

Teddy and Rod Streeter were sitting in the bonus room, back behind the couch, where Donny was sprawled. They were watching MLB Network, listening to the names called—Vanderbilt shortstop Dansby Swanson was the first player off the board that year. They knew that, at any point, one of the names out of MLB commissioner Rob Manfred's mouth could be "Donny Everett."

Suddenly, Donny's phone rang, and he stood up from the couch and left the room. He returned 30 minutes later.

"Well," Donny told them, almost matter-of-factly, "I just turned down $2.5 million."

Teddy and Rod exchange a glance, eyes wide.

"It was like 'wow,'" Rod remembered, nearly two years later. "This kid—it made me have even more respect for him . . . I just remember thinking, 'Who would turn that down as an 18-year-old kid? And what parent would allow their kid to make that decision?' I think a lot of parents would be like, 'Take it, take it! Go!'

"But they left that decision up to Donny, and I have so much respect, even more respect, that he wanted to go to school and get that college experience, and that money wasn't everything."

Money was not everything. In fact, Donny's very next move that night, mere minutes after turning down the offer, was to start playing games with Rod's then-eight-year-old daughter Tessa.

"He went from making that decision to, 'Do you want to play foosball?'" Rod said, laughing.

But that was Donny. And that was the Everett family. Donny always valued relationships over finances, the collective over the individual, and Teddy and Susan valued their son's independence. Certainly, both of them weighed in and were heavily involved throughout the draft process; they wanted nothing but the best for their son. But they left the final decision—the most important decision of Donny's young life—up to the person who'd have to live with it.

Scouts in the area said that even during in-home visits, Donny would do the majority of the talking—he'd run the show—while his parents played a more complementary role. Usually it's the other way around. Donny's ability to handle himself, his maturity, garnered him even more respect among the scouting community. His makeup might've ultimately graded higher than his fastball. The club that offered him $2.5 million on draft day (the club wished to remain anonymous out of respect for the family) took that gamble, in part, because of its faith in Donny's mettle.

Had he accepted, Donny would've been drafted in the latter

half of the first round. But Donny had a number in his head going into draft day, and the $2.5 figure fell just short. He slid, instead, to the 29th round to the Brewers. But he wasn't going to sign.

"He finally said, 'I made a commitment, and I want to keep it,'" Susan said.

Added Teddy: "A big thing he always harped on was players not wanting to make a commitment, and he always felt like he wanted to do that."

That commitment was to Vanderbilt, a school about 45 minutes down I-24 East.

Donny fell in love with the program when he was 10 years old, playing in the same youth tournament as future Commodores ace and Dodgers draftee Jordan Sheffield. Commodores head coach Tim Corbin made a speech at that tournament, and when Donny heard it, he told his parents right then and there, "I'd really like to go to Vanderbilt."

Vanderbilt fell in love with Donny a few years later, when the Commodores hosted the Kansas City Royals Scout Team for a game at Hawkins Field. Then–recruiting coordinator Travis Jewett was sitting in his office at the ballpark when he saw a kid larger than any other on the mound. When he heard the ear-shattering pop of the catcher's mitt, Jewett knew he needed to act. Fast.

"They FBI'd us in the back parking lot," Teddy said, laughing. "Donny was driving and he went to put it in reverse and a black SUV pulls up and all four doors open up, and all these people were getting out, and we're like, 'What in the world is going on?' It was all the coaching staff here at Vanderbilt."

Thus began Vanderbilt's recruiting of Donny Everett—not that it was a tough sell. Donny wore a Vandy sweatshirt on his first official visit.

Still, the admiration was mutual. Both Jewett and Corbin could see quickly that Donny had the kind of character they look for in recruits. He didn't just fit the VandyBoy mold—he was the embodiment of it.

"I think those people who are inside the walls, they understand what a VandyBoy is," said Jewett, now in his first year as Tulane's head coach. "People who have that kind of character—people who are selfless, serving others, good teammates, humble. This kid was a heck of a good competitor, but even at a young age, you could see him fitting in.

"Everyone liked him. He had an infectious smile. Obviously, he was big and strong and all of those things, but yet soft and nurtured in terms of who he was as a person."

Added Corbin: "He was just a real, in my opinion, Midwestern, American kid with tremendous values but happy-go-lucky and just went through life as if it was a game and he was having fun with it."

Donny had this joyful, carefree aura about him; he was brimming with life. He collected nicknames like baseball cards: The Don, Big Bird, Sweaty Goat (he earned that one in middle school, when he had the dual habit of sweating profusely on the mound, while also chewing peanuts with the shell intact). Donny could take a ribbing in good humor, but he could also dish it out, with his trademark dry one-liners. He wasn't afraid to be self-deprecating. The two teeth inside his eyeteeth never came in; he had to wear a retainer, with two false teeth, until he was old enough to get dental implants. He'd always play around with people when he first met them, especially during meals. He'd pop out his teeth at the restaurant and place them right on the table—often to the surprise of his eating companions.

Donny paired his jovial nature with a voracious work ethic. He was blue-collar in his love for hard labor; for creating things with his own hands. He was never the type to lose days in front of the TV. One of Donny's favorite hobbies was building model trains. In fact, the Everetts turned the spare bedroom of their house into a display room for those trains; the homemade platform fills the room. Donny would spend entire winters—when he had to take a break from throwing—in that room, constructing and tinkering; sometimes his parents wouldn't see him for hours.

When Donny was 14, he convinced his father to restore a 1979 Ford F-100 truck that Teddy had purchased for $150 from a co-worker—solely for the engine. Teddy and Donny worked on that truck for nearly a year, refurbishing it from a junkyard shell into a mint-green beauty. Donny cherished that truck like it was his offspring. He always hated to see his classmates get new cars, only to mistreat them.

Donny had an appreciation for the intricacies of life, for the effort behind the results, for his roots. Even when he went to Vanderbilt, Donny never lost sight of where he came from.

Streeter remembers a day in late May of Donny's freshman year at Vandy—May 28 to be exact—when Donny and Teddy came over to visit. His son Ryan, one of Donny's best friends, was home too. The day before, Vanderbilt had been eliminated from the Southeastern Conference tournament in Hoover, Alabama. Now, together, the Streeters and the Everetts watched the remaining SEC tournament games on TV.

All of a sudden, while watching the games, Streeter's youngest daughter, Tessa, walked into the living room and said, "Hey, who wants to play catch with me?"

"I'm sitting there, I don't get up, my son doesn't get up, but Donny gets up," Streeter said. "He doesn't say a word and goes out and plays catch with her out in the front yard. And it's getting dark. And I'm thinking, 'This kid just got done pitching in the SEC tournament, and he's out front playing catch with a nine-year-old girl who doesn't play softball, who doesn't catch very well, but he's out there, and he doesn't have to be here doing that.'"

Donny had pitched in the SEC tournament four days prior, a scoreless ninth inning against Missouri to close out a 7–0 win. The final pitch of that game was the last pitch Donny Everett would ever throw. On the Hoover Metropolitan Stadium scoreboard, the radar reading flashed three digits:

One. Zero. One.

A tobacco barn, a woodstove, a cow mat with a strike zone painted on it, a makeshift mound constructed out of plywood—this was Donny's and Mr. Forney's playground, their weight room, their boxing ring.

Mr. Forney had warned the boy that this was going to be hard, that this would be grueling, that it would be six days of sheer, brutal, sweat-drenched intensity every week. He wasn't lying. Mr. Forney made Donny agree that he couldn't change a single part of the routine—unless Mr. Forney, Teddy, and Susan all agreed on it.

"When we get started, everybody's gonna want to change you," Mr. Forney told Donny that very first day in his yard. "But we can't let that happen. You have to continue on the course we start on because you can't deviate from this or you're not going to do what you want to do.

"You're going to lose a lot of friends."

"I don't want to lose any friends," 11-year-old Donny replied. "But if that's what I gotta do, that's what we'll do."

Mr. Forney's teachings were less about angles and hand placement and more about feeling, more about getting the ball to where Donny wanted it to go—not just in the strike zone, but in a precise location within the zone. Mr. Forney designed drills to build up Donny's body, particularly his lower body, to catch up with the strength of his arm. He prescribed him a very specific diet too, to facilitate growth—which was where Susan came in. She'd make Donny a high-protein breakfast every morning before school, scrambled eggs with spinach, bacon, ham. Sometimes even salmon.

Donny would take a shake to school, mixed with vegetables and protein powder (100 percent protein. Mr. Forney was very particular about that). He kept a giant jar of peanut butter by his bed (creamy, he liked it creamy) and he'd eat it nightly by the spoonful. For good measure, Mr. Forney insisted Susan cook all of Donny's meals with coconut oil. That diet, combined with Donny's hard labor, began to yield results.

Even still, Donny would grow frustrated at times, barking at Mr. Forney if Forney tweaked one of their drills or added additional steps. He would say, "Mr. Forney, I gotta go." He always said that. And then he would leave.

The next day, he'd come back, and he'd work twice as hard.

"He was just such a good kid," Mr. Forney said. "I know there's more out there. They show up all the time. But they don't have the will that he did—to fight through all the pain and struggle that it took to get him where he had to go."

Mr. Forney and Donny remained connected through middle school, through high school, even when Donny went off to Vanderbilt.

Whenever Donny experienced any sort of problem, if he was ever struggling or aggravated or stressed, he'd call Abbott and say, "Mr. Forney, can I come by?" And the two would sit on the swing outside of Mr. Forney's carport and talk about life, just life, rarely anything about baseball. They would talk the most about fishing—Donny loved to fish. And after hours on that swing, Donny would get up and say, like he always did, "Mr. Forney, I gotta go."

Mr. Forney would usually respond, "But what about the problem?"

One day, in the middle of Donny's freshman season at Vanderbilt, he came by Mr. Forney's place seeking advice. Donny hadn't pitched a single inning with the Commodores—sidelined with a lat injury—and he had begun to worry. Mr. Forney assured him it was only a minor setback. He would be fine.

"Donny, you like to fish and all that?" Mr. Forney asked.

"Yeah."

Mr. Forney grabbed a couple of rods and some reels, handed them to Donny, and told him to go fishing with his father, to take his mind off of baseball and his injury. No stress. No pressure. Just a boat, a rod, and the open water.

"To me," Mr. Forney says now, "it's the worst thing I did."

Months later, at Donny's funeral in Clarksville, Teddy and Susan asked Mr. Forney if he would be willing to say a few words about their son, but he just couldn't bring himself to do it. All he could muster was a single sentence, something private and personal—something he knew Donny would hear and would understand.

"Donny," Mr. Forney said, "It's my time to say 'I gotta go.'"

II

"Donny, what do you got?"

That phrase is common coach speak from me to one of the players. I ask, and they respond—how they respond, you never know. I am essentially asking them, "How are you? What are you doing? What are you working on today? What do you got?"

For Donny, it was rhetorical.

"Donny, what do you got?"

He would just look at me with that crooked smile that leaned to the left and say, "What do YOU got?" and then just dance off with that lumbering jog of his . . .

Sitting behind home plate in late January, inside the offices at Hawkins Field, Collin Snider points to his left hand, tracing the area of his palm where his thumb and left index finger connect.

"My hand was bruised all the time," Snider says, with a chuckle. "Right up in this area."

A few inches below that area, on his wrist, is a tattoo: "DE41," along with a date, in Roman numerals. June 2, 2016.

Snider remembers the day clearly. They all do. How could they forget? They can't. They won't.

June 2, 2016, was a sunny day in Nashville, with a high of 88 degrees. A practice day. Vanderbilt was getting ready to host UC

Santa Barbara, Washington, and Xavier in an NCAA regional—slated to begin the next day. A little before 10 a.m., Vanderbilt pitchers gathered on the turf football field next to Hawkins Field to get loose and participate in long toss, Snider included.

Snider, then a sophomore, loved Donny Everett as a teammate, as a friend, as a person—but he hated catching him. "[It was] the scariest thing I did every single day," he said, laughing. Snider had the bruises and battle scars to prove it. Donny threw so hard and with so much movement, Snider at times simply couldn't see it, especially once they got to the portion of the drill when they were 60 feet apart and Snider had to squat down like he was a catcher. One day, Snider was so rattled, he stood up and said he couldn't catch Donny anymore. Pitching coach Scott Brown (colloquially known as "Brownie"), told Snider to get back into his squat, then turned to the 6-foot-2, 230-pound freshman across from him and said, "Donny, that tells you everything you need to know."

On June 2, 2016, Snider took extra precautions. He asked junior catcher Jason Delay if he could borrow his catcher's mitt —just for a little extra padding—and Delay obliged. Even still, Snider squirmed uncomfortably in his simulated catcher's squat. Near the end of the workout, about an hour and 15 minutes later, Donny held up two fingers, as if to say, "Two more fastballs, then I'm done."

As he walked up and down the field to monitor all of his pitchers, Vanderbilt coach Tim Corbin saw Donny's two fingers out of the corner of his eye and decided to move closer to the comically mismatched Snider-Everett battery. As Corbin inched closer, within batter's box range, Donny threw one high and tight—very close to the coach's body. Corbin glared at him, but Donny never made eye contact.

Fastball No. 1.

Now, Corbin was curious. He stepped even closer to Snider —standing firmly within the hypothetical batter's box. Snider's thinking, *Is Donny actually doing this to him right now?* but Corbin just smiled. Donny threw this next one even harder—and closer —just under Corbin's chin, and the head coach flinched and fell back on his heels.

Fastball No. 2.

Workout over. Donny walked up to Snider and shook hands, still not making eye contact with Corbin—out of a sense of masculine pride. Then, Corbin asked Donny his signature question, the question he asks every player, every day, and the question Donny rarely took seriously.

"Donny, what do you got?"

Donny looked at Corbin with a sly smile and winked—a look Corbin will never forget.

"You got nothing, Coach."

Corbin loved it—the confidence, the self-assurance, the competitive edge. In his eyes, that was a moment of growth, and it was the last moment the coach and his freshman phenom would share.

Around 11:15 a.m., practice ended and the team dispersed, players free to spend their afternoon however they chose, as long as they were back to their dorms by curfew.

Donny, fellow freshman right-hander Chandler Day, redshirt junior left-hander Ryan Johnson, and two of Donny's Clarksville friends went to Chipotle for lunch, then went back to their dorms, gathered their fishing gear, and drove about 70 miles southeast to Normandy Lake, near the city of Tullahoma in Coffee County.

Corbin stayed put, preparing for the next day's postseason action. At about a quarter to eight, when he had finished his NCAA meetings and was done poring over film, Corbin picked up his wife, Maggie, and the couple started driving toward Sam's Sports Grill for dinner.

As they drove, Corbin's phone began to ring. It was junior ace Jordan Sheffield. That was odd. Corbin's players rarely, if ever, call him at night.

Corbin answered the phone.

"Coach, I just want you to know something. I'm not trying to alert you, but—"

It was too late for that.

Every pitch, any thrilling play or moment, even some routine plays, just for laughs—"Write it down, Donny!"

For the first two months of his freshman season at Vanderbilt, Donny was sidelined by a lat injury—nothing terribly serious—but serious enough to keep him off the mound until April 12. He ended up making just six appearances all year—two starts—going 0-1, 1.50 in 12 innings. As such, Donny had to find other ways to integrate himself with his new teammates, to be of some use. One way was through pitch charting; he became an avid pitch charter. Every day, whoever had the charts in his hands, Donny would come up to him and take them, and he'd write down every small detail during games. His teammates soon caught on to this. Even his coaches.

"'Write it down, Donny!' They loved that because it just became an expression," pitching coach Scott Brown said, laughing. "Someone would get a time on [a base runner], and they'd just be like, 'Write that down, Donny!'

"They loved to tease him. And he would just take it and kind of smirk it off and laugh. It was almost like he was saying, 'Yeah, whatever.' But he would laugh about it, and they knew it was getting under his skin just a little bit, so they just continued it . . . He was at the center of poking fun because he just had that teddy-bear type personality."

The VandyBoy veterans all made sure Donny's head never got too big—not that that was ever a problem, anyway.

"We would never let him know that he threw hard," joked junior right-hander Kyle Wright. "We would always make sure that he knew that we threw a pitch harder than him . . . If he hit 95-plus, we'd say the gun was hot or he hit the hot spot."

A couple of Vanderbilt flamethrowers would always gather at the end of the stretch line, in a sort of exclusive club. They'd call it "Velo Valley." For months, they didn't let Donny join; at least, not until he threw his first collegiate pitch. He touched 97 miles per hour in his first appearance, against Middle Tennessee State in April. Only then was he allowed in the Valley. Reluctantly.

As much as Donny's teammates would make fun of him, they truly did relish his company. His lightheartedness was a form of social glue, even as a freshman. He'd routinely go fishing with teammates—Day, Johnson, Penn Murfee, and others. An avid Tennessee Titans fan and a season-ticket holder, he brought Wright with him to a couple of NFL games. If any player on the team had an issue with his car, Donny would happily be there to repair it. A group of players often played *Call of Duty* on their PlayStation 4s online, and Donny would jump into those online matches from his dorm room—sometimes to their confusion ("Who's this Sweaty Goat guy who keeps wanting to get into all our games?").

Perhaps Donny's greatest cultural impact, though, was one the coaching staff wasn't aware of for some time. The Fast Food Crew.

Donny, Snider, Wright, Day, Johnson, and Hayden Stone (on occasion; he'd never admit to being a member) would get together on the weekends after a team workout and eat fast food —Taco Bell, Wendy's, Chick-fil-A. "Sometimes Sonic—on special occasions," Snider said, laughing.

"We used it as an excuse for velo," Wright added with a sly smile. "'This is how we're going to throw harder.'"

The specific term that the Fast Food Crew loved to use was "velo pouch." They'd eat to build up their velo pouches.

"That doesn't come from me," Brown said. "I think they all took the old 'mass times acceleration equals force,' and I think they took the 'mass' part to heart, where they were like, 'I can put a little extra mass right down there.'"

While not every member of the group participated every time, Donny always did. Sometimes, he'd even go by himself. Together with Day, a subcommittee of the Fast Food Crew was soon formed.

The White Castle Clan.

"In the spring, we started a Sunday tradition of going to White Castle," Day wrote in a Twitter tribute to Donny last June (Day was not made available for comment). "We ordered six cheese sliders, five-piece mozzarella sticks, and a large Big Red creme soda.

"The best part was you [Donny] setting your retainer on the counter and the looks you would get. Still had the most affectionate smile without those two teeth."

Donny loved Day; he had met the Granville, Ohio, native before college, on the showcase circuit. He loved his teammates. He loved Vanderbilt. He only threw 12 innings due to his injury, but there were no regrets for his decision not to sign. He rarely came home, which is what his parents had wanted; they wanted him to find a place where he was happy, where he could truly thrive. Even though he was there for only a few months, they marveled at how quickly their 19-year-old son grew into a man.

"I'd say, 'You can bring your laundry home!' Because I'd miss just doing stuff for him," Susan said. "And he'd say, 'I got it. It's my responsibility.' And I was like, 'I don't mind, bring it home!'"

One time Teddy and Susan came to Vanderbilt to visit, but they made the mistake of coming on a Sunday. A White Castle Sunday.

"No, Mom," Donny said, "I can't go to eat with you. I'm going to eat with Chandler. It's our date."

She understood.

"Donny loved Chandler so much," Susan said, tearfully. "I texted his mom a picture, and I'll never forget because she said, 'They're going to make great memories together.'"

Jordan Sheffield wasn't trying to worry his head coach. But he did.

As Corbin continued driving with Maggie by his side, Sheffield told Corbin that his mom had heard something disturbing on the police scanner—that a Vanderbilt baseball player had gone fishing and drowned in a lake near Tullahoma.

"But I don't see how that can be, Coach," Sheffield said. "It can't be a Vanderbilt player. It must be a mix-up."

"Everyone's back, right?" Corbin responded.

"Almost everyone."

"Who's missing?"

Sheffield proceeded to tell Corbin that Donny, Chandler, and Ryan had gone fishing after practice, but they had said they'd be back at the Towers—the dorm where the players were staying—by 8 o'clock.

At this point, a twinge of panic set in. More than a twinge.

"Can you try to find out where Donny is, and the rest of the boys?"

Corbin hung up the phone and immediately called the sheriff's office. He got the dispatcher.

"Can I speak to the sheriff there?"

"I'll have him call you back. What's your number?"

Five minutes later, Corbin and Maggie were in the parking lot outside of Sam's, sitting in the car. Waiting. It was about 8:30. They hadn't eaten.

The phone rang.

The sheriff, in as calm a voice as he could muster, began speaking on the other line.

"Coach," he said, introducing himself. "I just want to let you know that Donny Everett was found dead tonight in 25 feet of water."

Time stopped. Earth stopped spinning. Corbin stopped listening. Maggie could hear the sheriff's voice from the passenger's seat. Silence. Cold silence. What do you do? What do you say? What do you feel? What can you do?

Corbin called Sheffield back.

"Could you please gather the kids in the dorm?"

Deputy Charles Taylor of the Coffee County Sheriff's Department received a call just before 5 p.m. on June 2, 2016. Another deputy, Brandon Reed, soon joined him on the scene.

Five young men—Donny Everett, Chandler Day, Ryan Johnson, and two of Donny's Clarksville friends were fishing at Normandy Lake near Fire Lake Bridge on Mountain View Road, according to a release from the department. Everett's four fishing companions told police that Everett was on the west side of that bridge and had decided to go into the water in an attempt to swim to the other side.

Everett made it halfway across before he started to ask for help. He was smiling, and his friends thought he was "joking around," according to the report.

At one point, one of the boys jumped into the water and pulled Everett several feet, but he told police he wasn't a good swimmer and was struggling to stay afloat. When it seemed like Everett was no longer struggling, the boy let go and swam back to shore. The group, as a collective, still thought Everett was joking.

When the boy looked back, Everett had gone underwater. He didn't resurface.

"He went fishing with those rods I gave him," Forney Abbott said. "And he decided to swim, and not being familiar with cold water and mountain lakes, he was thinking summertime, it was warm, he could get in the water and go across. Well, I'm sure that cold water shut him down. Because it's 50-degree water and his muscles just didn't work, and the others didn't understand what was happening to him."

When Reed arrived on scene a little after 5 p.m., he went into the water and tried to locate Everett, with no luck. The sheriff's department launched a boat to help with the search. Divers from the Coffee County Rescue Squad entered the water at 6:38 p.m. to search for Everett, according to the report. At 6:47 they dove again, and at 6:49 they found Everett's body in 25 feet of water, about 15 feet from the shore line.

"People say, 'Why the heck did he try to swim across?'" his old high school coach, Brian Hetland, said. "He was carefree. He was Donny. It was in the late afternoon, getting ready to close it up and go on back and get ready for the game. It wasn't like he was there at midnight, or swimming at 1 in the morning, all crazy and messed up.

"It wasn't nothing like that. It was just being a normal teenager. Doing normal stuff. Doing what he liked to do."

Teddy Everett had to work in the morning. He'd always get up at 3 a.m., make the 45-minute drive to the post office in Nashville, and work the early shift. He and Susan were already in bed when the sheriff knocked.

It was 9:30 p.m. The sheriff kept knocking. And knocking. And knocking. And knocking. And knocking.

Susan remembers every little detail from that day, June 2, 2016. She remembers calling Donny. She remembers texting him. She remembers not hearing back. She remembers telling Teddy she thought something was wrong. She remembers thinking something had to be wrong. She remembers the sound of the knocking on the front door. She remembers the feeling of dread.

Teddy remembers nothing.

Corbin and Maggie never got out of their car. Tim pulled out of the parking lot outside of the restaurant and started driving back toward Vanderbilt's campus.

As he drove, Maggie's phone rang. Tim could hear the wailing on the other line. It was Chandler Day and Ryan Johnson. They were standing in Tim and Maggie's front yard.

"Tell those boys to get over to the dorm," Tim said to Maggie, "and we'll be waiting on them."

As Corbin prepared to enter the Towers, he had flashbacks to the early 1990s, his final season as the head coach at Presbyterian. One of his players, Marcus Miller, died in a car accident. He remembers bringing his players into his apartment and telling them the news. That doesn't help. Experience doesn't help. There's no preparation for this. There's no 10-step guide for Dealing with Devastation. It doesn't get easier the second time. Not in the slightest.

"It's so toxic because you don't know what to do, what to say," Corbin said. "Because at that point right there, when you share that news with them, they've gone somewhere else. They've just gone to their emotion."

Corbin didn't even need to say a word as he entered the lobby of the Towers. They could tell from his body language.

"Corbs comes in," Snider said, "and I don't remember if he even said anything."

"He knew that we had all kind of heard rumors as to what possibly happened," Wright said. "He came in and basically said one thing, 'Yeah,' and that was pretty much kind of it. And then from there, guys just kind of broke down. There really wasn't a whole lot of talking. It was more just silence. Because it was still just a disbelief-type thing. We were with him literally six hours earlier in the day, practicing and getting ready for the regional."

No one wanted to sleep that night. No one wanted to be alone. No one wanted to talk. No one wanted to think about the regional the next day. No one wanted to think about the NCAA tournament. No one wanted to think about the postseason. No one wanted to think about baseball. No one wanted to think about a game.

Finally, at 4 a.m., Corbin told his players to get to their rooms. Try to get some sleep. If some of them wanted to sleep in the same room, they could. Many players did just that. Some didn't sleep at all.

The next morning, the Commodores boarded a bus and made the 45-minute ride to Clarksville. Teddy and Susan were waiting in their front yard, arms open wide, a Vanderbilt flag displayed proudly in front of their house. Players circled around them, hugged them, cried together, mourned together.

At one point, Teddy and Susan approached the two teammates who were with Donny at the lake—Chandler Day and Ryan Johnson. They embraced them. They didn't want them to carry an unnecessary burden. They didn't want them to blame themselves. They knew this was Donny's decision.

The first words out of Mr. and Mrs. Everett's mouths:

"This wasn't your fault."

"No words can express how I feel for the Everett family," Chandler Day tweeted at 5:22 p.m. on June 3, 2016.

"I met Donny at Team USA and East Coast Pro. I only knew him as a ballplayer then. When we first came to Vanderbilt, I started to know Donny as a person.

"In the fall we had English together, and we sat next to each other every day. I always hated that class, but you made it go by fast with your attitude and personality.

"In the spring we started a Sunday tradition of going to White Castle. We ordered six cheese sliders, five-piece mozzarella sticks, and a large Big Red creme soda. The best part was you setting your retainer on the counter and the looks you would get. Still had the most affectionate smile without those two teeth. You bet your ass I'm ordering seven whenever I go, and that one will be for you.

"Our fishing trips, hanging out in the dorms, our drives together. Those are the things I will cherish the most. Life was too short for you, but I will live both of ours to the fullest.

"I miss you. I will continue to miss you, and I love you forever, man.

"White Castle Clan out. Rest in peace, my friend."

The clubhouse was divided—to play or not to play? How could they play? But then, how could they not play? Donny would've played. Shouldn't they play for him?

Corbin called three team leaders—Ro Coleman, Tyler Campbell, and Kyle Smith—into his office on the morning of June 3, 2016. The morning after.

"Fellas," he said, "we're going to go on and we're going to play, because I think at this point the baseball field and the locker room is a safe haven for you guys. If we're going to mourn, let's mourn together. If we're going to grieve, let's grieve together, but let's do this."

Fate intervened. The Nashville skies opened and rain washed away Vanderbilt's NCAA regional-opening game against Xavier. It was hardly a reprieve. Another sleepless night. Another night of mourning. Saturday, June 4, was just as gray. Saturday, June 4, was just as rainy.

The flags at Hawkins Field flew at half-mast. Donny's No. 41 jersey hung in the home dugout. The Commodores left a space for Donny down the foul line as they lined up for the national anthem. Every player wrote "DE41" on his hat.

Corbin and his coaching staff did their best to manage their players' emotions—to lend them some morsel of strength. But it was still all so raw. The tears still flowed freely. There was still that sense of disbelief, that excruciating grapple with reality.

"Hey, listen," Corbin told them, trying to alleviate at least some of the pressure, "don't be afraid to smile or laugh. You're not being disrespectful. There's a human side to this where your emotions have to play out a little bit. You're in competition now. So whatever emotions come through competition, let them play out. Don't be afraid."

When freshman Ethan Paul singled in Vanderbilt's first run of the game in the fifth, to tie the score at 1–1, the Commodores ran out of the dugout to celebrate, like he had just hit a walk-off grand slam. At that moment of exultant catharsis, the Commodores bore some resemblance to the Vanderbilt team that had won 43 games in the regular season. But the illusion quickly shattered. Behind ace Jordan Sheffield, Vanderbilt made an uncharacteristic four errors, fueling an explosive 13-run seventh inning. The Musketeers won, 15–1. The shaken Commodores suddenly were staring at an elimination game. Cruelly, they'd have to play for a second time that day.

When Kyle Wright took the mound that night against Washington, he had barely slept, going to bed at 4 a.m. the previous two nights. He was running on pure, unadulterated adrenaline. Through the first three innings, that seemed to be enough to carry him. He kept the Huskies off the board, while Vanderbilt established a 1–0 lead. Then it began to unravel.

"My first three innings, they were really good, and then I found myself drifting back and forth between the game and thinking about Donny," Wright said. "It was kind of an emotional roller coaster for me. I was very emotional. I was yelling more. I was all over the place more.

"Usually, I'm a very calm pitcher. I don't let a whole lot of things affect me. But that game, I specifically remember being out of whack, just because I wanted to win so badly for him, but at the same time, the mind-set wasn't right."

Down 8–2 in the sixth, the Huskies led a spirited comeback, knocking out Wright in the seventh inning and taking a 9–8 lead in the eighth on a two-run home run by outfielder Jack Meggs.

That score would hold.

Vanderbilt's season ended. Abruptly. Painfully.

"It sucked, because I think I gave up seven runs," Wright said. "I didn't feel great about myself because the hitters gave me a great chance to win the game and I was kind of lost a little bit . . . But at the same time, after the game was lost, we all kind of realized that it's bigger than baseball, and that kind of helped me get over the fact that I could've pitched better.

"All the guys were so great. I specifically remember [reliever] Ben Bowden put his arm around me after the game and told me, 'It's not your fault.' That kind of helped make me feel better about it."

After that final game ended, no one said a word in the Hawkins Field dugout. The Commodores sat there for an hour, silent, encircling coach Corbin. Snider remembers looking up at the No. 41 jersey hanging on the jacket rack and crying. He had wanted to win with every fiber of his being. They had all wanted to.

But the truth was—as Corbin later shared with his team—Vanderbilt wasn't meant to win that day. This was life's way of saying they needed to direct their attention and love elsewhere—completely and fully toward Donny.

"We were thinking about Donny the entire day. I think the kids are probably saying, 'Did this really happen? That really happened?' It's replay in your mind," Corbin said. "And we've all had dreams and we've all had nightmares, and you wake up and you say to yourself, 'Boy, that dream was so real, and I'm glad it never happened.' And then you continue to try to wake up from this, and you're up, or at least you think you're up because—what is life?

"Life might be one huge dream for all I know, but whatever we're doing at the time, you wake up and it keeps replaying itself, 'Yes, this did happen; yes, this did happen; yes, this did happen; but I have an at-bat here. Yes, this did happen; yes, this did happen; yes, this did happen; but I've got to throw a pitch here, but yes, this did happen.' And it just keeps coming.

"People outside go, 'That must be so difficult to do.' Difficult is not the word. It's not doable. The game of baseball was not overpowering. That was not our opponent. Grief was our opponent. And grief just says, 'I don't care what you have for me, I will eat you up, I will move you to the side, you can throw anything my way,' but grief always wins. Grief's undefeated—unless you don't have a heartbeat.

"Quite frankly, when grief ate us, it just did the best thing it could've done for Vanderbilt baseball at that moment. It just made us stop playing a sport and then turn our attention to Donny, and that's what we needed to do, and that was healthier than winning two baseball games."

Three days later, Vanderbilt's team bus unloaded outside of Faith Outreach Church in Clarksville. The community poured into the church to honor Donny Everett—every person he had ever touched filled its expansive interior. Even Vanderbilt players Donny never played with—Dansby Swanson, Carson Fulmer, Rhett Wiseman—came to offer their condolences. Eight players served as pallbearers, Snider and Wright included. Representing his teammates, Snider made a touching eulogy, describing Donny as the "ultimate VandyBoy."

"Everything you think about Vanderbilt baseball," Snider said, "Donny had."

Tim Corbin made his own eulogy, a moving reflection on Donny's carefree Midwest American values, his positive life force, and his biting wit.

Corbin still has that eulogy saved in a Word document on his office computer. It's 10 pages long.

JIM OWCZARSKI

Cincinnati Bengals Great Tim Krumrie's Brain: A Work in Progress

FROM THE CINCINNATI ENQUIRER

THE TAN LEATHER of the steering wheel of his Ford F-250 slides through Tim Krumrie's thick hands. He jokes he'll break yours if he wants. He wheels the truck down his favorite back way, the less trafficked Howelsen Parkway along the Yampa River to the base of sun-splashed Emerald Mountain. Here, on the eastern side of the Rockies, are hiking and biking trails, a ski slope, and the home of a pro rodeo series.

It's where he goes to walk. A place to drift into a reverie.

It's good to daydream, he says.

An hour earlier the smile had faded for a few minutes, the jokes subdued. His eyes intensified. His night visions once weren't so beautiful.

"Bad dreams. Wrong dreams. Can't repeat 'em. Wake up and wonder if you did something wrong."

He set his jaw. Just below his bottom lip, but above his chin, there's a quiver.

"Ugly."

Such terrors are symptoms of a damaged frontal lobe, which resulted from a 12-year NFL career with the Cincinnati Bengals, two years of wrestling and four years of football at the University of Wisconsin that put him in the College Football Hall of Fame, and playing linebacker and wrestling in his youth.

He sure as hell doesn't want any pity.

Instead he wants to talk about it.

"It was just sleeping. Just sitting there. Doing nothing," he said of his brain. "The blood flow wasn't getting there. The people have to understand you have to get educated on some of this a little bit. I am not a doctor. All I'm doing is telling you my story. And this s— is true. I don't know the fancy words or all that other stuff. That's not my job. My job is to tell the people of the world it's okay. This stuff happens. Until you come over across the tracks and say hey, I have a problem. I have a problem, I'm screwed up.

"You have to get the correct doctor and find out. So we found out."

Poster Boy

The eyes say it all.

Well, almost.

Toss in the broken nose, the blood. That says it all.

The color photo is huge, life-sized, if that can be believed.

Now 57, Krumrie is a fit 226 pounds. He'll steel his gaze and challenge anyone to give him a shot to the oblique. Stone, he says. A few hundred crunches will do that. Voted the third best player in the 50-year history of the franchise and a five-time team leader in tackles, he's wearing a black Bengals hat, a thin, long-sleeved performance Bengals shirt, jeans, and cowboy boots.

"A bad day at the office," he laughs, looking at the print of himself in his workout room.

This is where his two Pro Bowl jerseys are framed. There's a scarred Bengals helmet. The 1988 Super Bowl champion Wheaties Box that never was. The photo faces the treadmill, the bike, and the resistance bands, right around the corner from the rack that holds over a dozen cowboy hats.

It's where he lost 60 pounds in 100 days. It's where he rehabbed a double knee replacement in 2013, a surgery where the surgeons tried, and failed, to wrench out the 15-inch titanium rod in his left leg. He returned to coach the East-West Shrine Game nine weeks later.

He never missed a game in his life, from high school through the moment he rode off the turf at Riverfront Stadium on a Harley Davidson gifted from Mike Brown. He is most famous for suffering the worst injury at the worst time: the shattered left tibia, fibula, and ankle on the choppy turf of Super Bowl XXIII at Joe Robbie Stadium in Florida on January 22, 1989.

There are no regrets. He proudly accepts the costs of his life's work. And he'd do it again.

"In a second. In a second," he said. "You put me in the Super Bowl you can break my leg—two of 'em! It's that important."

He loves football. He loves the National Football League. You'd be hard-pressed to find a bigger advocate for the sport.

"He is so pro-NFL," his wife, Cheryl, said. "He talks to [NFL executive vice president] Jeff Miller. He talks to [executive vice president] Troy Vincent. He talks to [commissioner] Roger [Goodell]. He just loves the game and he loves the league. He wears his NFL hat all the time because that's the shield and [you] always protect the shield. He doesn't want to play the blame game.

"I would love for him to be the poster boy for this, the poster boy for saying 'go and take care of yourself, figure out how to live and how not to be mad.'"

A Hard Truth Discovered

Tim Krumrie is into his third year of a new chapter of his life, one he hopes can be an example for those stuck in the early drafts of theirs.

He sets his jaw again. The quiver returns too.

"Do you go to the doctor if you get the flu? Yes. You break your leg? You go to the doctor? Yes. Why can't you go to the doctor to see if your brain is okay?" he said. "Why can't you do that? Nothing wrong with it."

Make no mistake. It took some time for him to come to that realization.

The Krumries say they first noticed symptoms of brain trauma after Tim wasn't able to find another coaching job after his contract with Kansas City expired after the 2010 season. He had coached the defensive lines in Cincinnati, Buffalo, and Kansas City for 15 years. A nearly three-decade career in the NFL was suddenly over.

"That's when it becomes, really, kind of scary," he said.

Routines were broken. His brain and body slowed down.

"It all just kind of hit me," he said. "When I was always into the football stuff, I always had that brain part working. Now, you're gone, and then that's when all that stuff started coming out. It was after the fact."

The flushes of anger stemmed from his persistent unemployment, they figured. The long-term memory loss? How could he possibly remember the thousands of teammates and plays and over 400 games he played or coached in?

His once otherworldly balance was off-kilter. Ah, that's due to his deteriorating knees. They also prevented him from working out, so his weight ballooned to 270 pounds—but not the healthy 270 he carried as a player.

As far as he knew he never suffered a concussion—because he was never knocked out. That was the measure then. Was his bell rung? Sure. Ever see stars? Sure, a couple times a game. Whatever.

As they lived through the postcareer years, Cheryl read literature the NFL sent the house about concussions and the potential for long-term brain trauma and its effects. But the dots never quite connected to her, at least initially. She believed his reasons too. And her high school sweetheart wasn't too interested in knowing what real truths lie beneath his truths.

"He was extremely resistant to anything with people saying . . . the NFL will send you all the information," Cheryl began. "You can do this, you can go here, you can do that, and I would read it and look at it and he basically said, 'Why the f— would I want to know if there is anything wrong with me?' That attitude. 'Why the f— would I want to know that?' And I was like 'Okay, maybe you don't.'"

The tipping point came in 2015.

"He just stopped working out," she said, which included no desire to even ride his bicycle. "That was the most dramatic thing. That's when I was like, 'Okay, there's something wrong with him.'"

So Cheryl arranged a "business" meeting with friend and entrepreneur Randall Reed. Reed was on the board of directors of CereScan, a brain scan imaging facility in Littleton, Colorado. The idea was to get Krumrie to acknowledge there might be more to what he was experiencing than surface-level issues like unemployment and knee pain.

In the meeting, Krumrie was told how a simple scan of his brain could point them in the direction of treatments.

The test was called a SPECT scan, which is a type of nuclear imaging that tracks where blood is and isn't flowing from in the brain. Simply, it's a test of how well the brain is functioning.

"The assumption being the more that you use a part of the brain the more blood flow you're going to require," Brent Masel, the national medical director for the Brain Injury Association of America (BIAA) said. "So if you increase blood flow to that part of the brain, the assumption is that that part of your brain is more active."

The SPECT scan is not a tool for detecting chronic traumatic encephalopathy (CTE), and it is different than an MRI or CT scan, which captures the anatomical structure of the brain in both health and disease.

An MRI, which the NFL has used in its testing of former players, had shown Krumrie's brain was normal.

"Badass Tim" Returns

On the three-hour drive back through the mountains to Steamboat Springs from Littleton, Cheryl figured there were two outcomes of her husband's testing.

"One, there's something wrong and you can treat it," she said. "Two, there's nothing wrong and you're just being an a—. And that's the way we approached it."

If members of the military could go through this type of testing, Krumrie felt he could handle it as well. Ready for answers, the Krumries sat with Dr. Gregory Hipskind and director of clinical operations Hilary Morris at CereScan. In the company's conference room, Krumrie's brain was displayed on the wall.

There was heavy damage all over.

Cheryl quickly looked for anything opaque, the one color she knew there was no coming back from. There were none to be found, but the swaths of deep purples, blues, and greens concerned her.

Dr. Hipskind asked if Krumrie had mood swings, if his balance was off, if he lacked the motivation to do physical activity, and if he didn't sleep well. And if he did sleep, if he had vivid, terrible dreams.

"It was the most humbling experience you ever had," Tim Krumrie said.

He then straightened up in his chair. It scared him.

"I was up like this, like, 'What in the Sam-you-know-what is going on here? I'm screwed up.' And all of a sudden, reality hit. Yeah, I have those things. He said, 'Yeah, you have it. We can help you.'"

In that moment, Krumrie woke up.

"Doc, get 'er started up. Let's go."

In that moment, he was familiar again to Cheryl.

"That's part of a professional athlete's demeanor, their psyche, that when they decide to do something, it's just do it and no halfway," she said.

Krumrie had never gone halfway. But to do this his way—all the way—he needed teammates.

"Your wife is the most important part of the whole thing," he said of Cheryl. "They realize that day after day and day in and out. They see what you went through. It's hard on them. Simple things. Short term memory. Go to Starbucks, I don't know."

He paused and shrugged to signify he would forget the order.

"Little things. Things like that. They have to be so patient with people like myself. And if you don't have a good, solid wife, like I have, that understands what is going on and the improvement that went on from remembering things, day-to-day activity . . ."

"She has been terrific."

He noted his adult children, Kelly and Dexter, know he's different than he was. They've come to understand him, though it has been tough.

"Knowing what I have to deal with and now keeping abreast of what's going on, yes, that's very comforting," Cheryl said. "But it's also scary as hell to know where this can lead to."

Committing to the new goal of a better future, armed with family support, information, and a true cause for his problems, Krumrie set about finding a way to fight it. Reed played a role in this too, as a partner for inLight, a Food and Drug Administration–approved Polychromatic Light Therapy (PLT) system that uses infra-red light to stimulate blood flow.

The company outfitted Krumrie with a light-filled cap, which he had to use for 30 minutes a day for three months.

On the first night, he dreamed. There were no fights in the trenches. No violence. Instead, it was of high school coaches and teammates. He woke up recalling names for the first time since . . . well, he couldn't recall.

At the end of that months-long treatment cycle, Krumrie got another scan of his brain.

He taps the screen to wake up his iPad.

He had fiddled with it for over an hour before this moment, flipping open its case, spinning it around on the countertop. He scrolls through the before and after images. It is startling. The purples aren't as intense. Some blues turned to greens, some greens returned to normal gray.

And with each color change, his brain reawakens a little.

Taking Hold of the Future

Heavy on the gas, Krumrie shifts the truck into third gear to climb the roads of the Alpine Mountain and Ranch Club, with an elevation of about 6,800 feet. He does some work up here in the snowfall, clearing and marking snowshoe paths for guests.

Now it's time for the downhill.

"Wanna go faster?" he asks. "I have a big suspension."

He laughs.

Krumrie is still a farm kid from Wisconsin and loves manual labor around the house. He'll clear snow off roofs, detail his cars, clean whatever needs to be cleaned. And the treatments, which serve to wake up the blood cells and increase their flow, have him happily telling you about his high school teammates, teachers, bus drivers, and coaches. There are other tales from college and with the Bengals.

"I couldn't tell those stories," he said. "Couldn't remember 'em. College? Couldn't remember 'em. Pros? Couldn't remember 'em. I lost memory. I'd go to a party and I'd be tapping my wife on the butt."

He laughs. He wasn't flirting. It was a silent signal for her to help remind him who he was speaking to.

He is better at that now, but he isn't cured. The Krumries will be the first to admit that.

"Blood flow does not equate to better brain function—within the normal parameters," National Brain Injury Association director Masel said.

"I can't say that it doesn't help. But it's one patient."

Krumrie needs his sticky notes to remind him of things, a detailed calendar, and pictures of the food he needs to pick up at the grocery store. He says if you asked him to read four paragraphs, he probably won't remember the first one. He wore his AFC Championship ring on November 26 when he was honored at halftime as one of the Bengals' greatest players, and it was still new to him. He knows his manner of speaking—he says he jumps around a bit —takes some getting used to.

"That stuff is still in the works," he says.

To help make it work, though, Krumrie is doing more than just the infrared treatments. He no longer drinks alcohol or his favorite Diet Cokes. He eats healthier. No candy. He's back to a regular workout regimen.

Masel couldn't agree with that game plan more—practicing good physical shape is essential in keeping the brain healthy. He did a study of about a dozen former players involved in the lawsuit against the NFL that was settled for $765 million in 2013 and found only one led a healthy lifestyle. The rest had abused their bodies and minds with poor diet, heavy alcohol use, and lack of activity.

Krumrie, who was not part of the initial filing of the lawsuit but was lumped in with all former players in the class action settlement, knows this, lived it, and wants the league—someone—to map out a course of action once that money is paid out.

"I hope you get millions of dollars," he said. "I hope you do. But God darnit I hope you take care of yourself too."

An unexpected by-product of the physical work Krumrie has put in and his greater understanding of his situation is that a new side of him has emerged.

"There's a definite sensitive side to him that has come out that is really freaky weird," Cheryl said with a smile. "He is extremely sensitive to people and their feelings. He's very empathetic to peo-

ple, where probably as a player most of the guys around him probably said he's an a—. And he probably was."

Her husband is using his rediscovered persona, his coaching
instincts, and this new understanding to convey an important message to former players: Advanced tools are out there. Use them.

"Hey, the reason I say this is because I can," he said. "I'm not
scared. I'm scared of nothin'. I overcome everything."

But Krumrie stresses every football player needs his own scan
and to find his own treatment.

Such tests would include the SPECT scan, but also the more
specific PET scan, which is another form of nuclear medicine that
can track specific harmful proteins in the brain—like the Tau proteins that cause CTE.

"Absolutely," Masel said. "If you know your disease and understand your disease you can manage your disease better. Absolutely
and positively unquestionable."

There's no finality here, even against the starkness of the out-
cropping.

"This is the same ol' Tim that's gonna say, 'Hey, I'm going to
make the team. I'm going to kick your ass every play.' I'm going to
do it. I beat this thing."

Ligaments and muscle shred. Bones break. They can be re-
formed, replaced. This is his brain, though, so he intends to do
what he can to enjoy whatever the future holds.

This is not the end.

Krumrie wheels his truck onto a gravel pull-off, with a clear view
of the mountain range. He gets out and takes it all in, smiling.

It's a long sunrise east of the Rockies, ascending slow and high
over the top of Steamboat Springs. It brings a lot of joy, that view.
Krumrie's not afraid, and he has a big suspension.

STEVE RUSHIN

Rebecca Lobo's Incredible Journey to Basketball Royalty

FROM SPORTS ILLUSTRATED

WHEN RUTHANN LOBO became pregnant with her third child, in 1973, her doctor looked her in the eye and said, "You know, you have a choice now." RuthAnn chose another doctor.

Rebecca was born exactly nine months and two weeks after *Roe v. Wade,* in the first full year of Title IX. When Rebecca was in fifth grade, her teacher sent a note home informing RuthAnn that her youngest child needed to stop playing with the boys at recess and to start dressing like a girl. RuthAnn didn't change her daughter's clothes. She changed her daughter's teacher.

There was a hoop in the driveway in Southwick, Massachusetts, and Rebecca was content to shoot baskets all day, embracing routine like her father, now in his 51st year as a cross-country and track coach at Granby (Connecticut) Memorial High. Nietszche said time is a flat circle, but to Dennis it's a flat oval, parceled out a quarter of a mile at a time.

Rebecca grew up with two siblings—Jason and Rachel—a cat (Froot Loops), a dog (Nike), and a guinea pig (Pinnywig). One evening Nike was sitting impassively in the front yard when a jogger preemptively maced him, at which time the jogger had to run for his life. Not from the German shepherd, mind you—from RuthAnn.

Dennis and RuthAnn sent Rebecca into the world armed with an iron will, a sense of humor, and a medium-range jump shot.

When she chose to attend UConn over Stanford and Notre Dame, RuthAnn—a guidance counselor—said with a sigh, "UConn is a safety school." Even so, in her senior year at UConn, in 1995, the unbeaten Huskies defeated Tennessee in the national championship game, a watershed moment in women's basketball, contested between two future Hall of Fame coaches: Geno Auriemma and Pat Summitt.

A year after that game, on one memorable day in Atlanta, Jason Lobo watched his kid sister's team win Olympic basketball gold and he met a volunteer named Gundi Oberhoessel, to whom he proposed marriage three weeks later. In 2001, at the Dublin House bar in Manhattan, Rebecca confronted an insecure sportswriter who had made a lame joke about women's hoops and invited him to attend a WNBA game. Twenty-three months later, they—which is to say we—were married.

When RuthAnn died of breast cancer on July 19, 2011, the largest of the countless floral arrangements sent by her many admirers was from a kindred spirit named Pat Summitt.

To our kids, Rebecca is now just Mom. She's away 100 nights a year broadcasting basketball on ESPN and makes dinner the other 265—even if it's charred meatballs on a white platter, a meal the kids have memorably dubbed Hate on a Plate. She's the handy one around the house: baller, shot caller, window-treatment installer. She never lets me or the kids win at anything, including H-O-R-S-E, a muscle memory from all those childhood days spent jump-shooting in the driveway just outside Springfield, the birthplace of basketball.

And so there was a localized outbreak of goosebumps last April, when she sent me a text that read: "Tonight you'll be sleeping with a Hall of Famer." From a strip-mall parking lot, I replied: "Yes! Larry Bird?"

Last Friday, Rebecca was officially enshrined in the Naismith Hall of Fame. It's 13 miles from Rebecca's childhood driveway, but she took the scenic route there, through Siberia, the Canary Islands, Rio, and countless other places where she played and now broadcasts the game she loves. The wife of former Oklahoma coach Billy Tubbs once accused him of loving basketball more than he loved her. "Yes," Tubbs replied, "but I love you more than track."

If Rebecca should love basketball more than me, I'll be content because basketball has given us four children, three nephews, endless laughs, and inspiration. "Is LeBron James in the Hall of Fame?" our 11-year-old daughter asked. When I answered no, our 6-year-old daughter said, "So Mom is better than LeBron?"

"Damn right," I told her.

Name of the Father

FROM VICTORY JOURNAL

IT WAS SUPPOSED to be an easy score. Get in, knock the kid unconscious, grab the drugs, and get out. Nothing Jarrod Tillinghast
hadn't done a dozen times. His buddy Donny had been setting this
kid up for weeks. First Donny bought a pound of weed. Then two.
Now Donny wanted 30 pounds. But he had no intention of paying
the $150K. This kid wasn't with the cartel. He was white, a "goof"
from Johnston, a town outside of Providence. This was free money.

Around 6 p.m., Jarrod slid into the passenger seat of his friend
Rodney's Honda Prelude. On this steamy, summer day, Jarrod
wore a white tank top, shorts, and flip-flops. In his waistband he
had a brown paper bag stacked full of newspaper strips, all torn
into the size of $100 bills. He was nervous. Not scared nervous,
but tense and hypervigilant, the same way he felt every time he'd
stepped into the boxing ring. He didn't know exactly how the robbery would go down; no two were ever exactly the same. But one
thing was always certain. He wasn't leaving without what he came
for.

Thirty minutes later Jarrod stepped into the kid's basement
apartment. He didn't like what he saw. Another guy sitting on the
couch—the muscle. This isn't how it's supposed to go down, Jarrod protested. You trying to set me up? Rob me? I'm not comfortable with this shit. I'm going to get my friend Rodney.

With Rodney in the living room with the muscle, Jarrod followed the kid into the bedroom.

"Where's the weed?" asked Jarrod.

"Where's the money?" the kid replied.

Jarrod tossed the paper bag onto the bed. The kid opened the closet door and pointed to three green plastic trash bags. Bingo. But Tillinghast blinked. He looked at the kid's face and his pleasant suburban apartment and couldn't bring himself to knock him out. Instead the 27-year-old threw the kid down between the bed and the wall and turned towards Rodney.

"Grab the bags!" yelled Jarrod.

A second later, the kid grabbed a butcher's knife he'd stashed under the bed and plunged it into Jarrod's skull. A searing pain unlike anything he'd ever felt. Jarrod twisted the kid's arm back and bit his finger until he dropped the knife. With the kid's head wedged between the wall and the bed, Jarrod turned and looked in the mirror. Blood sprayed from his head like a fire hydrant without a cap. An inch either way, thought Tillinghast, and he could have lost an ear or an eye. Furious, he did what he did best. "I hit him with two left hooks," says Tillinghast. "His whole face shattered."

With the deftness of an athlete, he ran into the living room and knocked the other guy out, grabbed the three bags of weed, and bolted for the door. As the two men charged up the stairs a pizza delivery guy was coming down. He screamed, dropped his pizza, and backed against the wall with his hands up. If Jarrod hadn't been drenched in blood, the pizza guy might have recognized him as one of the most promising young Providence boxers in recent memory. If he'd somehow heard Jarrod's last name, he would have definitely known it belonged to one of Rhode Island's most infamous crime families.

I

It's a Friday night in Providence's Federal Hill neighborhood and 43-year-old Jarrod Tillinghast sits at the bar in Costantino's Venda Bar and Ristorante. Built like a bank vault, he is preternaturally tan, owns a halogen smile and scars that dapple his face like cave etchings, each one its own story. The street fight in Silver Lake. The bar brawl in downtown Providence. The butcher's knife incident. "None of 'em ever happened in the ring," he proudly notes. "I didn't like to get hit." Without a word, Frankie, the bartender, refreshes Jarrod's Tito's-and-soda.

A couple across the bar recognizes him. They don't approach, but Jarrod can feel their stares, sees their furtive whispers. Back in the day, depending on how much vodka he'd had, Jarrod might have taken umbrage. Maybe crossed the bar with his left arm locked and loaded. "I always liked to fight," he concedes.

His first bout was at age four in the family home in Cranston. Tired of Jarrod arguing with his eight-year-old brother, Gerry Jr., their old man Jerry Sr. bought them boxing gloves (heavily padded ones for Gerry Jr.) and rearranged the furniture into a makeshift ring. But Gerry Jr. was too tall, too strong, and Jarrod got pushed around. Couldn't get close. To even up the fight, their old man grabbed Gerry Jr.'s arms, allowing Jarrod to unleash his inner animal on his brother. "Jarrod tuned him up," recalls the 71-year-old Jerry. "I couldn't stop him. Gerry Jr.'s yelling, 'That ain't fair!' I told him, 'Life's a bitch, kid.'"

Four years later, the old man wouldn't be at the Coventry boxing gym to see young Jarrod's next two fights. Jerry Sr. and his brother Harold were serving life sentences at MCI-Walpole (Massachusetts Correctional Institution) prison for the 1978 murder of loan shark George Basmajian.

"In the '70s and '80s in Providence you were either the cops or the robbers," explains Seth DeRobbio, Jarrod's cousin. "Our family was the robbers." Since returning from Vietnam, Jerry Sr. had become a legendary enforcer for Raymond Patriarca, the godfather of New England organized crime. Jerry had allegedly been involved in the multimillion-dollar Bonded Vault heist of 1975 (he was acquitted). He'd been a suspect in a plethora of murders. By the early '80s, the Tillinghast name had become as well known in mobbed-up Providence as Gotti in New York and Bulger in Boston.

From maximum security, Jerry Sr. tried to keep his family together. He moved his wife Terry and the kids from Cranston to Walpole so they could visit regularly. He'd call home daily, speak regularly with guidance counselors, teachers, and principals, and had his "spies" on the outside keep a close eye on his children for fear of retribution for the things he'd done to others in his line of work. If any of the kids acted out, Jerry Sr. would dole out the punishment. "He didn't go to prison and disappear," says Jarrod. "His power and control didn't fade. It felt like he was always around."

But the threads holding the family together unraveled. Jerry got transferred to a Florida prison. Jarrod's mother slipped into cycles of abusive boyfriends, alcohol, and drugs. By age 10, Jarrod's home address depended on the day. One week he might stay with his grandmother in Providence, the next with Aunt Sissy in Cranston. His eight siblings boarded with other relatives around the state. Every so often Jarrod would move back in with his mother, but inevitably she'd break down again. "I looked up to normal families, their peace and stability," says Jarrod. "I was always on edge. We weren't the Brady Bunch. We were the Crazy Bunch."

A molten rage began to build in Jarrod's veins. Rage at his father for choosing a life that would take him away from his family forever. Rage at his mother, who didn't have the strength to battle her demons. Rage over brothers and sisters who felt more like strangers than family. "Part of me was so angry," he admits. "Sometimes I'd channel it for good, sometimes for bad."

Good meant tearing it up on the diamond, the hardwood, and the gridiron. Sports were everything Jarrod's life wasn't. There was order, stability. There were reliable teammates and dependable coaches. And that anger served him well whether it was striking out batters or breaking tackles. "He was fantastic," recalls Jerry Sr., who only got to see two games in person throughout Jarrod's childhood. "He was quarterback, running back, and punter for the Edgewood Eagles. Scored a few TDs. He didn't come off the field."

Bad meant running the streets with his crew, Billy, Jamie, Johnny, Tony, Brian, and Jojo. Sometimes there'd be 30 or 40 of them all hanging out at their spot, the park on Daniel Avenue in Silver Lake. They thrived on action, trouble, danger. Jarrod loved the danger; he was the son of a dangerous man and it ran in his DNA. He liked to hurt people because hurting others made him forget about his own pain. If the wrong kid walked past the park, he'd catch a beating. If the fellas were bored, they'd go to The Wall on Plainfield Street or The Flats on Union Avenue and start shit with other kids. By the age of 15, Jarrod—by then a high school dropout—and the Silver Lake crew were boozing on The Hill at wiseguy watering holes like Bobo's and brawling with bouncers and patrons at nightclubs like Confetti's and Mecca.

With a handful of juvenile arrests for mayhem and assault, the Tillinghast name was back on the authorities' radar. "We obviously knew who Jarrod was," says Brian Andrews, a former detective commander for the Rhode Island State Police. "He and his friends were getting involved in low-level crime, smaller-time stuff. A lot of them were sons of mobsters so it wasn't a surprise to see these guys do what they did."

But Jarrod didn't want to follow in his father's footsteps. Find himself doing a 20-year bid. "I wasn't set on breaking the law, being a wiseguy," explains Jarrod. He also didn't want to be known as Jerry Tillinghast's kid. He wanted to make a name for himself, step out of that shadow. But no matter where the old man got transferred—Florida, New Hampshire, Massachusetts—his shadow loomed. "It affected all aspects of Jarrod's life," says DeRobbio. "You got cops looking at you, people in general looking at you. Like his father's name was tattooed on his forehead." He may not have known it at the time, but Jarrod was on a search. A search for an outlet that wouldn't land him in jail. A place where he could combine his passion for sports and fighting. A way to shed the moniker of Jerry's kid and finally be known as Jarrod. On a summer afternoon in 1990, he walked into Manfredo's Gym on Manton Avenue and found precisely what he was looking for.

II

"Street kids are tough," says veteran trainer and gym owner Peter Manfredo Sr. "They're not gonna take a shot and say, 'What am I doing?' They're gonna want to go again. Jarrod had that." Over the next few weeks, the 16-year-old also showed innate talent: fluidity, movement, a tremendous left hook. Yet Manfredo, a longtime fixture on the Rhode Island boxing scene, also knew the significance of his new pupil's last name. "We used to have to go to a lawyer's office every Sunday and talk to Jerry over the phone," says Manfredo. "His father wanted to know how it was going, who's doing what and the next plan."

The immediate plan? The 1991 Golden Gloves. Although Jarrod hadn't ever fought in the ring, Manfredo figured they had nothing to lose. Worst case the kid gets some experience. Learns a little. In his first 156-pound bout, Jarrod squeaked by with a decision. He cruised in the second round, earned a bye in the third, and on February 7, 1991, he found himself at the PAL boxing gym in Fall River, Massachusetts, minutes away from the biggest fight of his life: the Southern New England Golden Gloves novice 156-pound division title bout.

Hundreds of supporters had come; his whole Silver Lake Crew, his father's friends, family, even old football coaches and teachers. This wouldn't be a back alley, one-punch walkover. Jarrod's opponent was a grown man named John Kimbrough. "He was like 30 years old," recalls Tillinghast. "Batman, they called him." To battle the nerves and the doubts that kept creeping up, the 16-year-old stared at the photo of his father he'd taped to the PAL wall. *I am not going to lose,* Jarrod told himself over and over. *This guy is not going to take what I'm there for.*

"Let's roll, Tillinghast!" shouted Manfredo. "It's time!" In black shorts adorned with a skull-and-crossbones emblem, Jarrod walked towards the Fall River PAL ring knowing there was more at stake than a trophy. Those hundreds of fans weren't cheering for Jerry, but for him. To win meant doing something his father had never done. Something that could free Jarrod from that shadow. To lose? Unthinkable.

Local newspapers described it as a war. Back and forth, teenager versus adult. In the final round, Jarrod lost a point for repeatedly spitting out his mouthpiece. The fight was too close to tell until the referee raised Jarrod's arm and the PAL exploded with cheers. The new Golden Gloves champ drove back to Barry's disco in Warwick where he and the Silver Lake boys partied until the sun came up.

For the next five years, Tillinghast tore up the amateurs, winning local and regional Golden Gloves championships. Three times he went to Nationals, only to lose to future pro standout Jose Spearman and world champion Travis Simms. But more important than titles, Jarrod found a calling. "Boxing changed my life," he says. "When I started fighting I wasn't a loose cannon anymore." This isn't to say he became an altar boy. He still went out with the fellas. Still managed to mix it up on the streets. But he'd turned a corner. "I was proud of him," says his father.

By 1996, Jarrod was ready to get serious, take his trade to the next level. "We talked about him going pro," says Jerry Sr. "I was glad he was doing it. I told him if you're gonna fight you might as well get paid for it." The 22-year-old Jarrod didn't have any trouble finding a promoter. Jimmy Burchfield Sr., the man behind Rhode

Island's CES Boxing, saw potential dollars and TV deals. "He was a promoter's dream," says Burchfield Sr. "He had a great left hook, was a good-looking kid, and had a great following." Burchfield Sr. envisioned building up Tillinghast as he'd done with former world champion Vinny Pazienza.

Jarrod didn't disappoint in his pro debut. On a June summer night, fans flocked to the Suffolk Downs racetrack in East Boston. Not all of them well-wishers. "Not everyone loved Jarrod's family history," explains Burchfield Sr. "Like Ali, half of them came to see him win, the other half to see him lose." Jarrod's opponent, Robert Jones, came out swinging. "He threw two punches," explains Jarrod. "But I weaved back, threw a left hook, and *boom*. First punch of the fight. Twelve seconds and he was done. They heard that left hook in the top of the balcony."

Burchfield Sr. hired Donny Denis, a renowned heavyweight from the '70s and '80s (who fought George Foreman and Gerry Cooney) to assist with training. The promoter brought Jarrod along slowly, building his confidence and honing his skills. Like Manfredo, Burchfield Sr. had to deal with some unusual circumstances when it came to his young prospect. "I was worried that we'd get a judge who'd had a problem somewhere down the line involving Jarrod's father," he says. "So we had to do our homework regarding the officials." Jarrod doubled down on his commitment. "I had what it takes," he says. "I knew I could be the best. That I could be champion." By July of 1999, Jarrod was a perfect 7-0 and was on a trajectory to become the most famous Tillinghast in Rhode Island.

III

Sheets of rain swept across Route 37 that June 2000 morning in Cranston. By the time Jarrod noticed the truck barreling down on him, it was too late. It smashed into the back of his black Cherokee. Jarrod's niece in the backseat was unharmed, but the same couldn't be said for his left elbow. Surgery repaired the torn ligament. Doctors also cleaned up bone spurs they discovered. Yet the real damage was the time he'd have to stay out of the ring—and the opportunity to revisit old habits.

Truth is, despite all the sweat and blood he shed while boxing, Jarrod never fully purged the street life. The Silver Lake boys
weren't simply friends; they were the only real family he had. Jarrod's love of danger might have ebbed, but it hadn't disappeared.
Sometimes a man can only change so much. In between fights
as both an amateur and a pro, Jarrod had still been putting back
the Absolut-and-cranberries at Mecca, River Café, and Remy's. Still
getting into the occasional brawl at nightclubs. Still dabbling in
crime. Sidelined with his elbow injury and no fight in the foreseeable future, Jarrod fell right back into his Providence lifestyle.
Only this time the stakes had gotten higher.

"We were criminals," says Jarrod with a smile. What started with
making fake IDs and selling stolen 'scripts evolved into a significant robbery enterprise. "We didn't steal from business owners or
shake down hardworking people," clarifies Tillinghast. "We did
things where the law wouldn't be able to come back on us." Specifically, they ripped off drug dealers and criminals.

"Robbing drug dealers was very common back then," says Andrews. "It started with Raymond Patriarca." While the Silver Lake
crew didn't have the clout or scope of Patriarca's crime family, they
were out "hunting" every night, a territory that included Rhode
Island as well as parts of Massachusetts and Connecticut. "Now we
weren't robbing from Colombian cartels," explains Johnny Angell,
one of Tillinghast's closest friends. "We knew better. We found the
guys who shouldn't be doing it. The wannabe drug dealers."

Some wannabes were kids slinging on the corner. "We'd dress
in jeans and polo shirts like undercover cops," explains Jarrod.
"Then we'd roll up on them and jump out of the car yelling 'Get
on the ground!'" The dealers, thinking they'd been busted, would
fall face first onto the street and give up their stash without a word.

They also found a trove of wannabes in the popular after-hours
and rave scene. "Everyone was so happy-go-lucky in those places,"
laughs Jarrod. "It was like fishing in a pool." Jarrod and a few Silver
Lake boys would show up and ask around about buying some ecstasy. Within minutes a fresh-faced kid with a backpack brimming
with X would appear. Instead of a sale, the kid would find himself
hauled outside and getting arrested. Or so he thought. "I'd sit him
on the curb and get on the phone and pretend I'm calling it in,"
explains Jarrod. "I'd be like, 'Yeah, I don't know what to do with

this kid. What do you think?' I'd pretend to listen to an answer and I'd hang up and turn to the kid and say, 'Today's your lucky day,' as I confiscated the backpack. These kids were so happy not to be going to jail they'd thank me." While he admits he was a criminal, Tillinghast still conducted himself with a code. "Jarrod hated guns," says Angell. "He never used 'em. He'd just beat your fucking skull in."

Sometimes, according to Tillinghast, the dealers would go crying to wiseguys, ask them to help get back their drugs. But the Silver Lake boys never complied. And Jarrod wasn't worried about payback. "I got a pass for my dad, my name," he says. "It gave me leverage. People were gonna think twice about retaliation."

Jarrod shared his father's last name, dabbled in the same line of work, but Jarrod was not Jerry. "Jerry Tillinghast was well known for robbing drug dealers," notes Andrews. But Jarrod's father's MO wasn't a left hook. Jerry was a suspect in the torture and murder of a pair of drug dealers / nightclub owners from Johnston as well as Elliott Bassett, a dealer from Dorchester who was thrown to his death from a New York City hotel window.

You'd think that during their regular phone calls Jarrod might brag about his latest score. Or maybe ask his father for counsel. But Jarrod kept his dad in the dark. "I never told him about robbing," says Jarrod. "He didn't want me in trouble. Didn't want me to go down that path. That I was sure of. So the less he knew the better."

But why risk his boxing career—and potentially his life—at all? For one, money. Jarrod claims to have made upwards of $150,000 one year. Another reason? The rush. "It was fun," admits Jarrod. "The robbing, the cash. We had a lotta of laughs."

Maybe too many laughs. Months running the streets with his Silver Lake crew turned into years. His elbow had long healed but Jarrod didn't walk back into Manfredo's gym. He couldn't bring himself to lace up the gloves. Jarrod points to his arm, claims the pain never went away. But more likely it was his heart and the fire that had gone out. In 1991, fellow Rhode Islander Pazienza also suffered a car accident. Broke his neck. Thirteen months later he returned to the ring and beat future WBC champ Luis Santana. "To get back in that ring by yourself takes a special person," says Burchfield Sr. "You have to have a hunger. When you take a long break, get out of that rhythm, you're making money and not taking punches, why then go back?"

IV

Hunger comes in many forms. At 31, Jarrod no longer had the hunger of a pissed-off teenager trying to outshine his old man. With a union job as a Rhode Island building inspector, he'd never know the desperation to keep a roof over his head or put food on the table. But in 2006 Tillinghast once again found his hunger —through love.

He met Jordana Ruggeri in the spring. She had the looks, the personality, and the pedigree; a monied, upper-middle-class family —the Brady Bunch that Tillinghast had dreamed about since he could walk. That October the pair went to see Peter Manfredo Jr. fight at Providence's Dunkin' Donuts Civic Center. Jordana had gone to school with Manfredo Jr. and she, like the whole crowd, went crazy as he TKO'd undefeated prospect Joe Spina. Jarrod heard the cheering and saw the awe in his girl's eyes and suddenly something clicked.

See, that night Jarrod got stabbed with the butcher's knife changed him. Rodney drove him to Miriam Hospital and somehow he skated out of there with only 40-plus stitches. The cops never found out, the kid he robbed never came back at him, and he didn't have to spend the next few years looking over his shoulder. But in addition to the scar, Jarrod came away with a vision he couldn't shake. The future. A future in a cell like his father. Or worse. So after his wound healed, he began to back away from the street life. Distance himself, just a bit, from the Silver Lake boys. He still wanted something more in life. A chance to remind people of his first name, not his last. There, ringside at the Civic Center, the voice that had been whispering *what if?* in Jarrod's head for the past eight years began screaming. *I got a lot left on the table. I can finish what I started.*

He called his longtime friend Joey Acciardo, a football coach at Johnston High School. Within a week Jarrod was sucking wind every morning at dawn doing wind sprints, steps, and gassers with the team. "Did I ask myself if I was making the right decision?" says Tillinghast. "Yeah. Every time that alarm went off." After three weeks with Acciardo, Jarrod returned to the boxing gym. Working the floor and the treadmill. Sparring, lightly at first, one, two, three rounds. Two months in and Tillinghast had a familiar sensation: he felt, once again, like a fighter.

"A bunch of times he'd talked about coming back but never did it," recalls his cousin DeRobbio. "This time was different. We were excited for him. He got into great shape. Would he be champ? Anything can happen. But he definitely had something left."

Eventually Burchfield Sr. got a call. "I told him get a good physical," says the promoter. "If the doc says okay, I'll get you a fight. No problem." In the first week of May 2007, Tillinghast, in a brown suit and tie, addressed the media about his comeback fight, a card headlined by Manfredo Jr. "I feel like a big brother lost from his family getting reunited again," said Jarrod. "I'm back. I'm gonna put a couple of years in before fighting for a championship myself."

The following Friday, the Tillinghast faithful packed the Twin River Event Center in Lincoln, Rhode Island. Jarrod hoped that one fan in particular would be ringside. Jerry Tillinghast Sr. On January 18, 2007, Jerry walked out of the John J. Moran Security Facility of the Massachusetts Adult Correctional Institution after nearly 30 years in prison. But that seat for the fight would remain empty. "I wanted to go but my parole officer said I couldn't," says Jerry. "I got mad. I asked 'why not?' He said it was the atmosphere. Not good for guys like me."

Around 9 p.m., fans stood up as the lights dimmed. "Wel-come back!" blared out of the arena speakers. "Your dreams are your ticket out." In his skull-and-crossbones shorts, Jarrod entered the ring to the theme of the hit '70s TV sitcom *Welcome Back, Kotter.* The fight, however, would be far from a joke. His opponent, Jeffrey Osbourne Jr. (4-4-1) of Davenport, Iowa, wasn't some hillbilly pushover, but a guy who'd gone to war with five top prospects.

Within the first minute of the bout, Tillinghast's comeback was in jeopardy. An Osbourne overhand right crushed Jarrod's nose, spraying blood across his face. But by the second round, the hometown favorite had settled down. Eight-year layoff? Looked like eight months. Jarrod flashed firepower, danced around the ring, traded bombs with the relentless Osbourne. "This looks like a championship fight!" yelled TV announcer Vinny Pazienza. With the crowd standing for the entire fourth round, Jarrod unleashed a furious barrage of left hooks and right hands. Yet the Iowa middleweight wouldn't go down; and as the final bell rang, the decision was in the hands of the judges. "After four rounds we have your decision," proclaimed ring announcer John Vena. "Your winner, and still undefeated, Jarrod Tillinghast!"

"It's hard to describe how you feel at that moment," says Jarrod, who jumped up and down, then lifted Osbourne in the air out of respect. "Hearing your name again like that? It's electric. A high only a fighter knows."

For Fight of the Night honors, Jarrod earned a $1K bonus. Anxious to maintain the momentum, Burchfield Sr. put Tillinghast on a card the following month at Foxwoods Resort Casino in Connecticut. Again he electrified the fans, knocking Santiago Hillario unconscious in the first round with a brutal left hook.

It would be the last time Jarrod ever stepped in the ring to fight.

V

Mist falls on a Saturday night on The Hill, and Jarrod sits in his regular corner of Costantino's Venda Bar and Ristorante. As the former fighter waits for his boys to show, he sips his Tito's-and-soda and tries to explain his decision to leave boxing for a second time. Pressure from his future father-in-law, he says. Get a degree. Go legit. Civilized adults don't dole out punishment for a living. So a few days before his August 10 bout at Twin River, Jarrod called Burchfield Sr. and said he was taking another break. Over the next few years he got a BA in education online from Ashwood University, married Ruggeri in 2011, and had two sons, Sebastian and Julian. "I've wanted kids all my life," beams Tillinghast. "I'm a great daddy."

As for his own father, Jarrod was thrilled to see him walk free. Happy to have him around. They love each other and both would probably take a bullet for the other, but their relationship is still complicated. "When I came home I said, 'Listen, we're not playing catch-up,'" says Jerry, in regard to lingering resentment. "'I'm sorry. I love you. But either we move on together or we don't. It's your choice.'" Jarrod insists it's not his anger that has caused friction but three decades of institutionalized living. "Was I mad at him for going to jail? There were moments I was pissed," says Jarrod. "But I'm over that. I just figured when he came home we'd spend more time together. I guess everyone's different though. He was programmed different. He's used to being alone."

Even with the recent separation from his wife, Jarrod insists life couldn't be better. For work, he does a bit of private training at Balletto's Gym in Silver Lake and has recently gotten involved in a VIP travel club that he describes as "Netflix for vacations." He can't walk through Providence without friends honking their horn or well-wishers stopping to say hello. He needs an assistant to keep track of his love life.

Despite his laughter and indefatigable optimism, Jarrod can't fully mask tinges of regret. The choices made. The haunting vestiges of what might have been. A deadly puncher. He could have been a franchise. His people didn't care what ticket prices were, they wanted to see him. You don't have that with a lot of fighters. "I left boxing the first time for the wrong reasons," says Jarrod, stirring his drink. "The second time I left for the right reasons. Both sucked."

After a couple more Tito's-and-sodas, Jarrod mentions an idea he's had lately. A comeback. "I'm at a five in terms of shape right now, but I'm coming down from 240." With every sentence his voice grows more animated. "I'd have another fight for all the right reasons. I know at this age the stakes are never higher. My health, my kids. I don't want to get hurt. But at the same time it's one hundred percent on the table. It's why I'm getting down in weight and then I'll make a decision. I'd still sell seats."

"I always say I have a first name before a last. My dad is my dad. I'm Jarrod. A whole other beast. And if you don't respect Jarrod, there's going to be serious trouble. Never mind the dog, beware of the owner."

He smiles and finishes his drink. Then he looks over his shoulder to check if any of his Silver Lake boys are rolling up. But through the restaurant window he sees nothing but the dark, misty night.

Some names and identifying details in this story have been changed to protect the privacy of certain individuals.

MIKE SIELSKI

Michael Brooks and the Son Who Barely Knew Him

FROM THE PHILADELPHIA INQUIRER

MICHAEL JOHNSON-BROOKS STOOD alone at a pale wooden lectern in a La Salle University auditorium in early December, dressed in a man's uniform of mourning: dark suit, white shirt, dark tie. A giant image of his father's mustached face flickered in muted sepia and pewter on a projection screen behind him, blanketing him in shadow. To his left, next to a vase of orange and purple roses, rested a gray, metallic urn. Michael Brooks, 58, the La Salle and West Catholic High School basketball star, had died on August 22 in Switzerland. After a Catholic funeral Mass there, he had been cremated, and his ashes had been shepherded across the Atlantic Ocean during the week of this memorial celebration. It was the first time, alive or dead, he had been in the same room with his son.

Johnson-Brooks pressed a sheet of paper against the lectern's angled top and lowered his head into dull light, leaving in full view only the upper half of his face—the intense eyes, shaped and colored like almonds, and the aquiline nose that so many people told him resembled his father's features. He kept his eyes on the two biblical excerpts printed on that paper, rather than doing what he had done throughout the ceremony's first hour: stealing glances at the urn. Before arriving at La Salle, he had been nervous throughout the morning, setting aside time to pray, asking God to grant him the poise to talk about his father without his voice breaking. Whatever emotions might start simmering inside him, he didn't want to reveal them. He did not know how he was supposed to act in such a moment—what's the proper way to grieve for a man who shared with you so much of his blood and so little of his life?—but he did know that he did not want the moment to overwhelm him.

"That was probably the hardest thing," he said later, "to keep it in."

Sitting among the hundred people in the auditorium, looking up at him and the screen with a proud and melancholy smile, was the woman who called him "Michael Jr.": his aunt Aleta Arthurs Lee, Brooks's youngest sister. More than anyone else, she had provided depth, dimension, and color to Johnson-Brooks's image of his father. For the final 28 years of his life—until, while hospitalized and undergoing treatment for the blood disorder aplastic anemia, he suffered two strokes, the second of which was so massive that he never recovered from it—Brooks had lived in France and Switzerland. He returned to the United States just once, closing himself off for much of that time from the friends he had made in high school and college and the NBA, from the Philadelphia basketball community, from his oldest son. Aleta remained Brooks's strongest connection to his hometown, to the people who had once known him well, to a son who barely knew him at all.

She had attended award ceremonies and Hall of Fame inductions in Brooks's place, happy to stand in for him, honored on his behalf. She had fielded all the questions from those who wondered what he was doing in Europe and why he had been gone for nearly three decades—questions that came with greater frequency after his death. She was the one who had put Michael Jr. in touch with his father, who got them talking once a year or so, who filled the intervals between those phone calls and brief FaceTime sessions by telling Michael Jr. about the big brother she hadn't seen in person since 1998 but still loved so much. She explained her brother, accounted for him, excused him, protected him, devoted herself to the preservation of his good name. She helped Michael Jr. to understand his father and, ultimately, to forgive him. She had given a phantom bone and flesh and hopes and regrets.

Brooks had occupied a unique place in Philadelphia basketball —a national player of the year who had heralded a renaissance in the Big Five and who had been held in such esteem that he was named captain of the 1980 U.S. Olympic team; a native son who was at once famous and forgotten; a once-transcendent figure who had managed, for all practical purposes, to disappear. He had given a brief phone interview, just a half-hour, six weeks before dying, but he had consented to speak publicly only at Aleta's urging, as a response to an article speculating about him and his withdrawal, and in the interview he had shed only so much light about himself. Why had he cocooned himself from the history he had made, from the teammates and coaches and competitors who had witnessed him make it, from a deeper relationship with his eldest child? What, if anything, about his past or his personality led him to that choice? He had left the answers to these inquiries, and others, ambiguous, and his death had renewed interest in and curiosity about the story of his life. Aleta was the one who knew that story best. To tell it as fully as possible, to satisfy that curiosity, you had to begin with her, and with the young man, 28 years old, who was about to speak.

Michael Jr. began without extemporization, in a flat monotone, diving right into Psalm 23, the text so common at funerals and memorials, so recognizable within popular culture. *The Lord is my shepherd. I shall not want* . . . It was better to open with something familiar, with phrases he already knew by heart. *Yea, though I walk through the valley of the shadow of death* . . . It would help him gain, and maintain, his composure. *Surely goodness and mercy shall follow me all the days of my life, and I will dwell in the house of the Lord forever.*

He paused, and his voice acquired volume and texture.

"And I have one that's on behalf of myself," he said. "It's a short, short verse, but it's something special between him and me. It's Proverbs 19:21: 'Many are the plans in a person's heart, but it is the Lord's purpose that prevails.'"

The room silent, he stepped quickly to the front row and sat down, falling in among those who had always assumed they would meet Michael Brooks again, someday.

The Ride to Stardom

Brooks's friends and acquaintances still look for reasons that he cut himself off from his country, from them, and often they home in on his parents' interracial marriage, with his father, Rudolph, who was black, and his mother, Rita, who was Italian. It's a convenient armchair diagnosis to explain that which seems inexplicable—difficult childhood leads to identity crisis, which leads to inner turmoil, which leads to seclusion and comfort on another continent—but it's incomplete. Both he and Aleta said that in the roiling 1960s and '70s, the family's racial and ethnic composition created more tension in their Southwest Philadelphia neighborhood, which was cleaved along the same lines that their household blurred, than it did among the Brookses themselves.

Yes, Aleta heard the stories about what her mother endured while Rita was pregnant with her: blacks skeptically eyeballing her and her belly from a distance, whites egging the Brookses' porch and calling Rita a "n— lover." Yes, on his way home from school, Michael sometimes ran along the underground trolley tracks to avoid the slurs and confrontations. And yes, it wasn't unusual to see Rita emerging from the front door of the Brookses' rowhome, on the 5700 block of Belmar Terrace, to smack Michael's backside with a broom, literally sweeping him back into the house and away from the gangs that patrolled the corners during those charged, anxious times.

This was life for the Brooks children: Michael, the eldest; his sister RiRi, a year and a half younger; and Aleta, eight years younger, the baby of the family. This was normal for them. They didn't like it, Aleta said, but they didn't grapple with it. Who grapples with things that are normal? Any suggestion otherwise practically offended them. After their parents divorced and their father moved out, the three children watched their mother work her way up from teller to assistant manager at a local bank, saving what she could to put them through Catholic school, instilling in them the parallel beliefs that they would always look for the best in people while they lived under her roof and that they could make their own judgments and choices once they were old enough. Besides, if the cruel words of outsiders cut Michael too deeply, there was always that decaying hoop and backboard nailed to a light pole at the corner of 58th and Willows Avenue. There was always a court nearby, where, he said, "I was just Michael Brooks the basketball player, not Michael Brooks the half-breed."

As a freshman at West Catholic, Brooks was the last player on the bench . . . for the freshman team. He was 6-foot-3 but frail and willowy, a kid whose confidence outstripped his ability. Bill McDevitt, one of his classmates and teammates, remembered Brooks arguing in the locker room one day after practice with one of the

team's better players over which of them would make it to the NBA
first. The debate seemed ludicrous to McDevitt at the time, but the
following year, Brooks returned taller, stronger, and more skilled.
It was impossible not to notice his evolution, even if, to his family,
he was the same Michael he'd always been. In the Brooks home,
he was still the prankster big brother, rousing RiRi in the middle
of the night, chasing her around the house as if they were Loo-
ney Tunes characters, then ducking back into his room when Rita
woke up, leaving his sister alone to suffer their mother's wrath. He
had a habit of rocking his head while he slept, and he'd wake up
in the morning with his hair swept up in a cotton-candy-style cone,
then spend several minutes sculpting his Afro and, as Aleta put it,
"practicing his moves" in the mirror to make sure his clothes fit
just so, then ask no one in particular, *I'm a good-looking guy, aren't I?*

The sequence never failed to make his sisters laugh, to keep
them seeing him as a carefree teenager when, on the basketball
court, he was becoming a man before everyone's eyes. In his year-
book graduation photo, he wore a white tuxedo and black bow
tie, and his entry included a nickname that hinted at his physical
maturity: "Feet." By the end of his junior season, local college assistant coaches—Jim Boyle at St. Joseph's, Bill Michuda at La Salle
—had become fixtures at West Catholic practices. During his senior season, 1975–1976, he led the Philadelphia Catholic League
in scoring and rebounding, carried the Burrs to a 28-3 record, and
established one of the city's great individual basketball rivalries,
between him and West Philadelphia High's Gene Banks.

A grade behind Brooks in school, Banks—and his recruitment
—eclipsed every other high school athlete or story in Philadelphia.
The *Daily News* assigned a writer, Gary Smith, to cover Banks and
Banks alone: the man-child as reporting beat. "I benefited from
Gene," Brooks once said. "I could improve without pressure." The
two had competed against each other in ferocious summertime
pickup games at Sherwood Playground and in the Sonny Hill and
Baker Leagues, but they weren't close until Brooks showed up
one afternoon at Banks's house for a visit, an overture to get to
know each other better. Before long, Brooks was charming Banks's
mother, walking her through Rita's spaghetti recipe, helping her
chop peppers and stir the red gravy. "That's where our friendship
grew," Banks said.

Banks eventually chose to play at Duke University, but Brooks picked La Salle, a decision that came with tangible benefits for him, his mother, and his sisters. He received a full athletic scholarship, and Bob Herdelin, a local real estate mogul and himself a former basketball star for the Explorers, bought a 1,700-square-foot twin home on the 5300 block of Chew Avenue, a short walk from campus, for the Brooks family. There is no available evidence that Herdelin was acting on behalf of La Salle and no indication that anyone there knew of the transaction, La Salle athletic director Bill Bradshaw said, and there are no records of Herdelin's making any financial contributions to the university. Property records showed that Herdelin purchased the house for $16,000—he signed both the deed and the mortgage—and both he and Aleta, in separate interviews, confirmed his role in the family's relocation. "We did the Jeffersons thing," Aleta said, "and moved on up."

Regardless of the reasons for his choice, Brooks helped reinvigorate the Philadelphia college basketball scene at a time when its relevance and cachet were in decline. Over the 1974–1975 and 1975–1976 seasons, Villanova, Temple, Penn, St. Joseph's, and La Salle combined for an aggregate winning percentage of .494. Six times in that two-year span, a Big Five team won no more than 11 games. The rivalries had lost their vibrancy; an infamous *Daily News* back-page photo captured Harry "Yo-Yo" Shifren, the endearing vagabond who was the unofficial mascot of the Big Five, sleeping during a sparsely attended doubleheader. But the subsequent four years saw the city's programs ascendant, the Palestra once more a bubbling pot of screams, streamers, sweat. Villanova posted three 23-win seasons and advanced to the 1978 NCAA tournament's regional final. Penn made its astonishing run to the 1979 Final Four. And under two head coaches, Paul Westhead and Dave "Lefty" Ervin, who encouraged breakneck basketball, Brooks became the most dominant player in the city and one of the most thrilling in the country.

Six-foot-seven, with long arms so corded with muscle they resembled giant licorice ropes, Brooks played as if the 40 minutes of competition consumed him, as if nothing else in his life mattered —a melding of abandon and earnestness, freedom and obligation. "When the ball went up, he did not smile," teammate Greg Webster said. "He was almost brooding." At practice, he sprinted throughout every line drill. During games, he dunked the ball at every opportunity, regardless of the situation. The sooner he got out on a fast break, the higher he leaped, the harder he jackhammered the ball through the basket, the better. "If we were playing Hofstra and there were five minutes left in a tight game," said Bradshaw, who in his first stint as La Salle's athletic director at the time, "Michael was going to take a lob and throw it down." In a 108–106 triple-overtime loss to BYU at the Marriott Center in Provo, Utah, in his senior season, Brooks scored 51 points, including all 28 of La Salle's points during one 16-minute stretch. "We tried one, two, and even three men on him," BYU coach Frank Arnold said afterward. "He went over, through, and around them." At the game's conclusion, the 22,791 spectators gave Brooks a standing ovation. Touched by the gesture and exhausted after having played all 55 minutes, he wept.

His ferocity on the court struck a stark contrast with his affability and accessibility off it. "He had a great sense of humor," said Dave Davis, a freshman guard for La Salle when Brooks was a senior. "He was nice to all his teammates, whether you started or sat on the bench. I never remember him getting angry for any reason." Filling out a publicity questionnaire upon entering La Salle, Brooks listed his major as sociology, his hobbies as "listening to music, watching girls," and his postcollege goals as "pro basketball, own[ing] a chain of hotels." He finished his La Salle career with 2,628 points—he remains among the NCAA's top 30 scorers—won the Kodak National Player of the Year award after averaging 24.1 points and 11.5 rebounds as a senior, then played intramural water polo, just for fun. "He was," Bradshaw said, "the most visible and charismatic figure on campus." When Aleta's friends, just beginning their teenage years, happened to encounter her brother on the street, they'd stop to stare and giggle, and Aleta could only shake her head, knowing that all those hours Michael had spent in front of the mirror, practicing his moves, were paying off. "To me," she said, "he was just my goofy big brother. To the girls . . . not so much."

Aleta and her family were just beginning to get a greater, truer sense of Michael's celebrity, of his place in the basketball firmament. In July 1979, he starred for the United States' gold-medal team at the Pan-American Games in San Juan, so impressing coach Bob Knight that Knight reaffirmed in an interview last year what he said of Brooks then: that he was "one of the five best kids I ever coached." In an essay in the August 16, 1979, edition of the

Catholic Standard and Times, RiRi described the family room in the Brookses' Chew Avenue home: "We have a handsome portrait of Michael, surrounded by his many awards. We have named it 'The Shrine.'" But his performance in Puerto Rico and Knight's subsequent praise had elevated his profile well beyond the boundaries of the local press. In January 1980, *Sports Illustrated* profiled him, comparing him to another La Salle legend: Tom Gola. In May —less than three weeks before the San Diego Clippers selected Brooks with the ninth pick in the NBA draft—Dave Gavitt, the head coach of the 1980 U.S. Olympic men's basketball team, announced that Brooks would be the team's captain. The likelihood that President Jimmy Carter would have the U.S. boycott the Moscow Games, to protest the Soviet Union's invasion of Afghanistan, had dissuaded other well-known college players from trying out, but Brooks was enthusiastic about the prospect of representing his country. He felt a sense of relief and happiness upon making the team, he said at the time, and had been honored that Gavitt had thought enough of him to invite him to the Olympic trials. "The least I could do," he said, "was return that respect."

Brooks was one of just two seniors Gavitt kept on the roster; Notre Dame's Bill Hanzlik was the other. Instead of competing in Moscow, the team played a six-game "Gold Medal" series against five NBA all-star teams and the 1976 U.S. Olympic team, a barnstorming-style tour that started in Los Angeles and ended in Greensboro, North Carolina. The Olympians went 5-1, with Brooks leading them in scoring at 13.2 points a game, with Aleta donning a gleaming red-white-and-blue sweat suit for the series' two games at Madison Square Garden and savoring the spectacle almost as much as her brother did. Almost. Hanzlik recalled that the White House, in an attempt to appease the athletes in the wake of boycott, invited them to Washington, D.C., in late July, presenting them with Congressional Gold Medals and putting them up in a posh hotel with an outdoor swimming pool at its center.

"Guys were having a pretty good time, and these female weightlifters and gymnasts and volleyball players were in the pool with the guys," Hanzlik said. "It was pretty crazy. The cops ended up having to come and say, 'You guys have to quiet down.' I was not involved, but I do remember Michael being in the pool."

This was the life that Brooks grew accustomed to, that his family grew accustomed to, as his career advanced into the NBA. He was

3,000 miles away on the West Coast, on the road often, returning to Philadelphia when he could, but it was a life he enjoyed, and as a younger man, he involved his family members in it as much as possible, covering their finances, sharing his newfound wealth.

He would take his mother and sisters out to a late-night dinner at a Morton's, marvel over the lavish spread of his relatives and friends socializing together, and laugh at Rita's objections. *Michael, I am not having ribeye at 11 o'clock at night . . . Aww, come on, Mom! This is when I eat!* He owned a sports coupe, a 280ZX, and when Aleta visited with her daughter Kristin, Brooks frequently took the baby out for an afternoon drive. "She was his chick magnet," Aleta said, "and he just fell in love with her." Once, the Brookses joined one of Michael's teammates and idols, Joe Bryant, for a day with their families at the San Diego Zoo. As Aleta walked the grounds, she pushed a stroller. Strapped into the carriage was the youngest of Joe and Pamela Bryant's three children, a two-year-old toddler named Kobe. Everyone was along for the ride.

"It was like he got shot"

Over his first three seasons with the Clippers, Brooks played in all 246 of the team's games, averaging 14.1 points and 6.5 rebounds, earning his coaches' and peers' respect with his work ethic. "He ran in the streets, ran for conditioning," former Clippers guard and NBA coach Lionel Hollins said. "He was always in the gym, practicing. He *wanted* to be out there." One day after the 1982–1983 season, when the two players were scheduled to become restricted free agents, Hollins called Brooks to recommend a negotiating ploy: both of them had to consider holding out into the following season. If Brooks re-signed for less than market value, Hollins feared that the Clippers would try to lowball him too. But Brooks's consecutive-games streak meant so much to him, according to Hollins, that he refused to go along with the strategy and agreed to a new contract with the Clippers anyway.

"I wasn't going to stop him," Hollins said, "from doing what he wanted to do."

In San Diego, he was not the superstar he had been at La Salle, the higher level of competition exposing weaknesses in his game for which his diligence and natural talent could no longer compensate. At 220 pounds, Brooks wasn't bulky enough, relatively speaking, to be an elite power forward, and he didn't shoot well enough from the outside to excel as a pure small forward. In 1982, the Clippers drafted Terry Cummings, who replaced him in the starting lineup. But there was no doubt that Brooks was a solid professional, reliable, coachable—"He was a delight," said Jim Lynam, a West Catholic alumnus and the Clippers' head coach from 1983 to 1985—and that he was on track for a long NBA career.

Then, on February 4, 1984, in a game at Richfield Coliseum near Cleveland, Brooks stole the ball from the Cavaliers' Paul Thompson, passed it to teammate Billy McKinney, and took a couple of strides before, he said later, he felt the sensation of walking down a flight of stairs and missing one. He fell to the floor and grabbed his right knee. "It was like he got shot," Lynam said. "Absolutely no contact. Boom." He had torn his anterior cruciate ligament—an injury that, without the more-advanced treatment available to athletes today, put his career in jeopardy.

For the next two and a half years, to everyone except his family, it seemed as if Brooks had vanished. Inducted into the Big Five Hall of Fame in 1986, he didn't attend the ceremony. The Clippers relocated to Los Angeles, but he neither used their training facilities nor showed up at any of their games, choosing to carry out his postsurgery rehabilitation near San Diego. "As a young player in the NBA, you think you're invincible," he said last year. "Everything is basically there for you. When you get hurt, if you don't have a good support group, you can really fall into a hole quickly because you feel, 'Where are all these people who were here when everything was going right?' As soon as you get hurt, nobody wants to be around you."

His mother, a devout Catholic, gripped her holy card every morning and prayed that he would walk normally again. The assistance that Aleta lent him was more hands-on; she moved to San Diego to be his caretaker.

"He was trying to get back to where he was with an injury that, at that time, most people didn't even come back from," she said. "Michael was a guy who believed you don't let your slip show. Nobody's going to know he's struggling with something. All they're going to know is, 'I got hurt, and I'll be back.' What happens in that middle is none of anyone else's business."

In early October 1986, he worked out, alone, for the Clippers' coaches and front-office members in the gym at Cal-Poly Pomona, shooting, driving, cutting, shuffling laterally. He began to hyperventilate as he carried out the drills. The Clippers did not sign him. He spent brief stints with the Indiana Pacers and Denver Nuggets, was named the Continental Basketball Association's most valuable player in 1987–1988 while with the Albany Patroons, and returned home in the summer of 1988, joining the Philadelphia Aces of the United States Basketball League.

Brooks played his final basketball game in Philadelphia at St. Joseph's Fieldhouse, scoring 38 points in the Aces' 122–118 loss to the New Haven Skyhawks in the semifinals of the USBL playoffs. Afterward, he met his old West Catholic classmate and teammate Bill McDevitt for beers at a pub near campus; the two had stayed in touch since their freshman year. A month earlier, the Charlotte Hornets had selected Brooks with the 14th overall pick in the NBA expansion draft, but they had angered him by making a more lucrative contract offer to former Lakers forward Kurt Rambis. A professional team in France, Limoges CSP, in turn had offered Brooks a one-year deal worth a reported $170,000. *I'm going to Europe,* Brooks told McDevitt. More, he was leaving the next day.

"I never heard from him again after that night," McDevitt said.

That night was July 27, 1988. Thirty-four days later, on August 30, a baby boy was born at the Hospital of the University of Pennsylvania: 7 pounds, 15 ounces, 22 inches long. His mother's name was Jacklynn Johnson. His first name was his father's.

A Son's Burden

Yo, you're Michael Brooks's son. We're picking you first.

Mount Airy Playground, at the intersection of West Sedgwick Street and Germantown Avenue. A full court and a half-court. Three baskets, three unforgiving double rims. A flock of kids in T-shirts and mesh tank tops and shorts. Michael Johnson-Brooks was 11 years old, in fifth grade, and at his first Jr. NBA camp. Already there was a presumption that he was the chosen one in the crowd, that basketball had been woven into the double helix at the center of every cell in his body. He played that day because he liked the sport, but he was all right, just all right, and he sensed that the kids and the counselors had expectations for him and that he did not meet them, and it hit him like a thunderbolt: *I don't want to do this. I don't want to play basketball.* Only later could he articulate the realization that charged his mind and heart at that moment: *Basketball defined my father. I don't know my father. I will find something else to define me. Screw my father.*

How would you have felt? His parents had met when Brooks was playing in the Sonny Hill and Baker Leagues, and they dated on and off while they were at La Salle together and again after college. But the relationship never could last, and even though Brooks knew he was to be a father before he left to play overseas, he left anyway, his relationship with his firstborn the greatest casualty of his choice.

"That move is what detached them completely," Aleta said. "It really is—Michael not being in the United States and not being accessible to as many people as he should have been."

While Brooks became a legend in France, helping Limoges win two Pro A championships, earning MVP honors each of those years, moving on to play in Levallois and Strasbourg, coaching in France and Switzerland, getting married and divorced and having four more children, his oldest son grew up asking himself that question every son whose father isn't home asks himself: *Is it my fault he's not here?* Jacklynn balanced her parental duties between providing for Michael Jr. and rearing him, opening an accounting practice and insisting that he focus on his studies first. "She's very stern," he said. Though Brooks was not involved in Michael Jr.'s early life, Jacklynn made sure that two male role models were: his grandfather, Jack Johnson, who died when Johnson-Brooks was 12; and his uncle Bill Johnson. Still, Michael Jr. was mindful at all times that neither of them was his father. Neither of them possessed veto power over his actions, the authority to discipline him when he would talk back to his mother or mess up at school or do any of the silly things that a kid does. Neither of them was there every day, as a dad would be, as a dad should be, and his dad wasn't there *any* day. Back then, he said, he never got a concrete explanation for why Brooks wasn't around, why he didn't write, why he didn't pick up the phone. Wouldn't a letter or two, an occasional long-distance call, have let him know that at least his father was thinking of him?

"Yeah," he said, "I probably would have felt better if I knew my dad wanted to hop on a plane and come see me, if my dad was going to bat for his son—you know what I mean? At the end of the day, my mom can have all the control she wants to, but I'm his son. I know he has his own life, but I'm his *son*. He could have put out the effort. He didn't."

Brooks said last year that he had found a new life in Europe with his fiancée, Jacqueline Uberti. His four youngest children— Athena, 27; twins Julien and Jasper, 24; and Sasha, 10—were in France, not far from him. He lived on the western edge of Switzerland in Etoy, a village of lush vineyards and Modern architecture 30 miles north of Geneva, and was coaching Blonay Basket, a men's team in the country's First League. Blonay won the league championship last year, and Brooks—weakened by the aplastic anemia, receiving three blood transfusions a week, pocks dotting his legs and the inside of his mouth—rose out of a hospital bed each morning to drive three hours to coach the team in the semifinals. "He was full of passion for the game," said Yuval Keren, who befriended Brooks while he was coaching Blonay. "He created the motivation for the players and gave them confidence to take chances, to believe in themselves."

His life in the United States? "There are always going to be memories," Brooks said, but he didn't share them often. Keren never heard him talk about the past. He treasured his privacy, the clean start that Europe had afforded him. He considered himself to be on a quest, in search of a culture and an environment that suited him, and he acknowledged that people might resent him for letting them fade from his journey, like jetsam on the sea. "But sometimes," he said, "you have to do that." This was his choice, and he was happy. His achievements, his knee injury, so many friends: amid the seclusion of a Swiss countryside and his contentment there, it was as if they had never happened or no longer existed.

"Regrets are for losers," Brooks said.

What about Michael Jr.? he was asked. Do you have any regrets about your relationship with him? He's your son, after all.

"As far as I know, this is a situation where we never really decided if he was or not," he said. "I would prefer not to speak about that."

Those words stung Michael Jr. He had never had a doubt about his father's identity—no one had—and he knew Brooks had known the truth too. One night while he was a student at Montgomery County Community College, Michael Jr. sat down at his computer and said to himself, *Why the hell not?* Through an online French directory, he found Brooks's home number and dialed, only to hang up when the groggy, slurred male voice on the line made it clear that, forgetting about the difference in time zones, Michael Jr. had probably woken his father from a deep sleep. *Never really decided?* Aleta had kept baby pictures of Michael Jr. for years, then searched for him on Facebook in 2008, found him, and arranged for them to meet at Penn, where Aleta manages meetings and special programs for the university's library system. The two of them embraced on the quad, and Aleta ushered him right up to her office, where she got her brother on the phone, put him on speaker, and let the two Michaels talk to each other for the first time in their lives. And now, Brooks was going to deny that connection? Aleta didn't believe it. Something else had to be at work.

"It was his way of avoiding something that he couldn't talk about because he didn't know enough," she said. "That's the key thing. He didn't know this young man enough to even have a conversation about him. That's not cool, and that's what, I think, he was struggling with.

"He felt like the NBA let him down a little bit, and Europe embraced the heck out of him. I believe his loyalty was to that, because they did that for him. And you have to understand Michael as a person: very laid-back, a don't-bring-me-no-bad-news guy, everything is cool. He liked the fact that European people were just chill like that. Their way of life worked for who he was as a person, and you have to remember he started a family there in addition to his child here. I don't think it's that Michael just didn't want to come back. It's that he didn't really see any need for it at the time. But with age comes wisdom. He was there for 28 years. He started to understand, 'You know, I need to see what I can do, maybe head back.'"

In all those years, though, he returned to the United States just once, to San Diego in 1998 to visit his mother, who lives there still, and Aleta, who was in town on business. He never came east on that trip, never set foot inside West Catholic or the Palestra or on La Salle's campus, never made time to see Michael Jr., and never returned to the United States again. Even after doctors had diagnosed his aplastic anemia, in 2011, Brooks had five years to deepen his relationship with Michael Jr., cognizant that his situation might turn dire, that his body would stop producing blood cells, that he would be vulnerable to infections and other trauma, that he might need a bone marrow transplant. Yet he never really closed the physical or emotional distance between them.

It was just another contradiction that Michael Jr., the more he interacted with Aleta, the more he learned about his father, had come to accept. As he aged, as he gained more perspective, he realized that he couldn't be the reason that Brooks had left and stayed away. Four years ago, he said, he forgave his father for his absenteeism: "I just wanted to release myself of that burden. By forgiving him, that gets rid of the animosity I had toward him. That gets rid of all that kind of stuff. It makes it easier so that when I think about him, it's good thoughts, even though I didn't even know him."

There was an opportunity, then, for a total reconciliation. Aleta talked with Brooks and Uberti about having them fly over to visit, about bringing Michael and Michael Jr. face to face at last. Brooks just needed to get well first. To hear him talk about his condition was to assume his full recovery was a formality, even though he had been undergoing chemotherapy and receiving transfusions and platelets. With each round of treatment, he would tell Aleta, *Well, I knocked out those three,* as if they were nothing more strenuous than a few basketball practices when he was in his prime. In mid-August, there seemed reason to be optimistic: he entered the hospital to receive a bone marrow transplant.

On Friday, August 19, remembering that Aleta's 50th birthday was coming up on the 22nd, he called her after completing four days of chemo and teased her about her age. *Call me Monday,* he said, *so I can wish you a happy birthday.*

On Monday, Aleta's birthday, her husband, Chris, took her to lunch in Chestnut Hill. As they sat outside, she took a photograph because, she said, God had given her such a beautiful day. When they returned to their home in Wissahickon Hills, Aleta phoned Jacqueline Uberti for an update on Brooks. This is how Aleta remembered their conversation:

"Aleta, they say there's no hope."

"What? What are you talking about? They say there's no . . . what? What? What do you mean there's no hope?"

"I don't know. First, let me say happy birthday because he would want me to tell you that."

"Why can't he tell me this?"

"Because he is unconscious. They have him on morphine. They don't think he's going to make it."

Brooks's body had rejected the transplant. Sobbing, Aleta melted to the living room floor. Chris picked her up and put the phone back to her ear. After composing herself, she called Michael Jr. to tell him—"I couldn't believe it," he said—then called Uberti back at 5 p.m. Uberti put her phone to Brooks's ear and told Aleta to talk to him. She did, for 15 minutes.

"I told him I loved him," she said, "and I told him I'm sorry and I don't want to say good-bye to him and this wasn't supposed to happen but he shouldn't be in pain anymore, he shouldn't be suffering, and it's okay."

Regrets are for losers, Michael Brooks had said. But his sister didn't believe he felt that way at the end. She couldn't believe it, because of a conversation they had not long before he died. His doctors were still searching for a bone marrow donor for him, and if they could find one within his family, preferably a male, it would increase the likelihood that the transplant would be successful. Aleta told him that she had discussed this possibility with Michael Jr., and that he was willing to donate his.

No, Brooks told her. *He doesn't owe me that.*

The Only Sound in the Room

One by one that morning in December, from the lectern in that La Salle auditorium, they had shared their remembrances of Michael Brooks—Gene Banks and Bill Bradshaw and Greg Webster and more. They were men Michael Jr. had never met, telling stories he had never heard.

"It gave me a chance to see he was a good man," he said. "He was a good person. People make mistakes in life, and I get that. It was good to hear people reflect on him because it kind of gave me memories of him that I didn't even have."

The urn did not contain all of Brooks's ashes. The rest remain in Europe, with his family there. It took weeks for Aleta to finalize arrangements to have some of them shipped to her on a one-stop flight from Geneva to Philadelphia. Her mother, Rita, having lost her only son, could not bear the responsibility. Her sister, RiRi, suffers from a chronic illness. "I'm my brother's keeper," Aleta said.

Her daughter Alexis accompanied her to the customs area of Philadelphia International Airport on the day the ashes arrived, and when they saw the box, Aleta refused to touch it, because the Michael she knew was 6-foot-7, gentle and powerful, and now there was just this . . . cube . . . that anyone could carry, with HUMAN REMAINS stamped on its side, and she began to cry. She keeps the urn on a table on the second-floor landing of her home. Every day, she descends the stairs, looks at it, and says, *Good morning, Michael.*

She has a video, sent to her by Jacqueline Uberti, of his funeral Mass in Switzerland. She will allow only one other person, Michael Jr., to watch it. He plans to do so on August 22, the one-year anniversary of his father's death. It seems right.

Michael Jr. did not make basketball his life, as his father did. He works full-time in the recording industry, as a marketer and manager, but he has an idea to form a summer basketball league geared toward middle school and high school students who perform well academically. "I love the game," he said. "It's in my blood." Through email and social media, he keeps in contact with his siblings in France. In mid-May, he noticed on Instagram that Jasper would be traveling to New York, and the two of them met for dinner at Gallagher's Steakhouse in Midtown Manhattan. It was the first time he had been in the same room with his brother.

After Michael Jr. had finished speaking at the ceremony, Aleta rose from her seat, hugged him, and went to the front of the lecture hall. "This," she said, "was the true essence of who my brother was." Suddenly, there on the screen behind her was Michael Brooks, sitting at a rich brown table in a white-walled room.

What followed was a two-minute, six-second video that Brooks's friend Yuval Keren had recorded in January 2016. In it, Brooks is bald, skinny as a rope, his face coated by a salt-and-pepper beard, and he is seated at a table, having dinner with several people. One of them holds a pen in front of Brooks's mouth, pretending to interview with him, and asks, "Do you have anything else to say to your family or any of the people watching you over in the States at home, or anybody else?"

Brooks does.

"I miss you. I love you. And God bless you."

He stands up. The lights in the room flicker out, then come back on again, as if he has stepped on stage and a spotlight has found him. He opens his arms with a flourish and recites the narration that begins "Have You Seen Her," the 1971 hit by the Chi-Lites, about a man who has lost the woman he loved.

> *I know I can't hide from a memory*
> *Though day after day I've tried.*

Around the table, the people with Michael Brooks clap in time with the beat as, a cappella, he continues to the next verse. In a flowing black funeral dress, Aleta snapped her fingers and swayed her hips. Michael Jr. leaned forward and listened to the only voice in the room. It was his father's, and it was a song.

ELIZABETH WEIL

Mikaela Shiffrin Does Not Have Time for a Beer

FROM OUTSIDE

MIKAELA SHIFFRIN SLEPT great. She always sleeps great. Then she ate two fried eggs, plus toast, no coffee, as she does every morning. Now it's 9 a.m. on this bright June Thursday, the fourth day of the third week of her six-week early-summer training block. Her schedule prescribes a morning strength session, so off we drive from her parents' house in Avon, Colorado, to the Westin Beaver Creek, where she works out when she's in town.

First: a warm-up on a spin bike. Ten minutes, moving her legs in circles in her Lululemon shorts, much like half the women here are moving their legs in circles in their Lululemon shorts—no big deal. Then we go into a small glass-doored room labeled MIKAE-LA'S CORNER. The Westin didn't know what to do with this space, so the hotel gave it to Mikaela so she could do Olympic lifts. It's an asset for the hotel to have this tanned, blond, 22-year-old ski goddess training here—though she does, let's just say, ruffle some patrons' senses of inner peace. Her body fills out her skin in a way that just looks fuller and better than anybody else. It's like she's a freshly blown-up balloon and the rest of us have been hanging around losing air for a few days or weeks.

But in this private back room, there's no one cowering in self-hatred at the sight of Mikaela's epic, confidence-destroying legs except her father who, of course, feels not self-hatred but pride. Back in their youth, both Jeff Shiffrin and Mikaela's mother, Eileen, raced alpine. When I ask Jeff, who is an anesthesiologist and has come to chat with me on his way to work, how they did it, how they managed to raise this specimen, perhaps the best skier in the world right now, on track to become maybe the best skier of all time, he says it's all very simple. "If you have a kid who is going to a ski race, you go to the lodge beforehand so you can say, 'Here's the nearest bathroom, here's where you put your backpack,' so the kid can be better prepared and have less stress. At age six, you teach her how to juggle, for coordination and focus, and at seven you teach her how to unicycle, for balance." There: now you know.

Mikaela wraps up her set. Papa Shiffrin, who handles the logistics of his daughter's ski racing and refers to himself as "Sure Pa," goes to the hospital to work. So far, so good. Then Mikaela moves out of her corner into the gym proper, and for a while all is still well in the Westin. The other gym-goers, both locals and hotel guests, continue pleasantly about their golden Vail days. Some recognize Mikaela, but whether they do or don't doesn't really matter —this isn't a story about fame, or even winning, exactly. It's a story about being the kind of person who not only knows how to win (that's not really the hard part), but can execute on the never-ending tedium required. Still, to get it out there: Mikaela has won 31 World Cup races, the 2017 World Cup overall title, four World Cup slalom titles, three World Championship slalom races, and an Olympic gold medal in slalom. And she's on track to win more races and more championships than any skier ever. Lindsey Vonn may be only nine races away from catching up to Swedish legend Ingemar Stenmark's record 86 World Cup victories, but Mikaela already has 24 more World Cup wins than Vonn did at her age and three more than Stenmark did when he was 22.

Mikaela tries to keep her success low-key and her mind not on beating others but on being better tomorrow than she is today. After she won gold in Sochi in slalom, she did lose her focus for a few seconds and told a reporter that she wanted to win five medals in the upcoming 2018 Olympic Games in Pyeongchang, South Korea. (Who doesn't?) But then she backpedaled and started talking again about putting in the work and staying strong.

Mikaela's quads look capable of leg-pressing entire alpine villages. Her glutes, halfway up her 5-foot-7 frame, are abrupt, definitive forces of nature, the Rockies rising out of the Midwest. But it's her concentration and discipline, and her ability to turn physical instruction into action, that are the real killers. Today, as almost every day, she isn't working out with a partner or coach. There's no minder, no entourage, no fuss. She does have an esoteric piece of gear called a GymAware PowerTool, which costs $2,200, looks like a small bomb, and measures lifting metrics like bar angle and velocity. But other than that, she's just an extraordinarily fit young woman with an iPhone, a silver watch, a few turquoise anklets, some very cute braids, and a list of reps and sets to get through.

Still, slowly, quietly, all around her, people start flipping out, needing—and failing—to adjust to the fact that here in this gym is this person with these legs and this ass who is flawlessly, unassumingly executing maneuvers that none of them could do with her precision and grace if they made it the focus of their lives. A man goes to pick up a kettlebell from a rack behind Mikaela, who is doing seismic squat jumps, and just melts down, worrying loudly about disrupting her to the point where she has to pause and comfort him. "No, you're fine. You're fine," she says. When she loads a bar with 100 pounds, holds her squat for 45 seconds, and then explodes up into space, another guy bursts out, "That's amazing! I can't believe you can do that! Holy Moses!"

Mikaela does her triple jumps, her agility drills. None of the exercises are that complex. We can all do this stuff, sort of—just like we can all keep ourselves from eating the entire bag of chips.

Eventually, Eileen comes in, after her own workout, wearing Hokas and basketball shorts. Mikaela is on the U.S. Ski Team, but she's also on Team Shiffrin, and her mother serves as her 24/7 unpaid coach. Eileen, it bears noting, does not think Mikaela does everything perfectly. It's her job—not as mother but as coach—to find flaws. She scrutinizes Mikaela's every movement (often repeatedly, forward and backward, in slow motion, on video), searching for imperfections and ways to crush those imperfections out.

Eileen is also here to make sure that I don't intrude too much on Mikaela's two-hour workout and thus keep Mikaela from getting home to her parents' house in time for her nap. In the elevator to the parking garage, I ask Mikaela how she wants our day to go. I could take her out to lunch or dinner. "I need to go on my ride later," she says. Then she adds, with just the slightest hint of an edge, "I don't know what's on your schedule."

The tone is understandable. Given that Mikaela is the U.S.'s designated darling in the run-up to the 2018 Olympics, there have been a lot of nonathletic obligations: photo and video shoots (and attendant hair and makeup) for sponsors Barilla, Bose, Red Bull, and Visa, interviews for other media. But Eileen suggests that, even amid these obligations, there may be room for improvement. "I think you should be nicer," she says.

A word about naps: Mikaela loves to nap. She also loves Bode Miller, and she's seen his movie, *Flying Downhill*, at least 20 times. And she remains so crushed out that even now, when Bode congratulates her on races—for instance, he called her name and hooted at her when she was walking through the crowd on the way to collect her World Cup overall title last March—she says, "I still can't believe he knows who I am."

But the naps: Mikaela not only loves them, she's fiercely committed to them. Recovery is the most important part of training! And sleep is the most important part of recovery! And to be a champion, you need a steadfast loyalty to even the tiniest and most mundane points. Mikaela will nap on the side of the hill. She will nap at the start of the race. She will wake up in the morning, she tells me after the gym, at her house, while eating some pre-nap pasta, "and the first thought I'll have is: I cannot wait for my nap today. I don't care what else happens. I can't wait to get back in bed."

Mikaela also will not stay up late, and sometimes she won't do things in the afternoon, and occasionally this leads to more people flipping out. Most of the time, she trains apart from the rest of the U.S. Ski Team and lives at home with her parents in Vail (during the nine weeks a year she's not traveling). In the summers, she spends a few weeks in Park City, Utah, training with her teammates at the U.S. Ski and Snowboard Center of Excellence. The dynamic there is, uh, complicated. "Some sports," Mikaela says, "you see some athletes just walking around the gym, not really doing anything, eating food. They're first to the lunchroom, never lifting weights."

Last summer, while Mikaela was in Park City, she overheard some of her teammates in the lunchroom talking about what they did for fun the weekend before and what they might do this upcoming one. "You want to go float the river?" Mikaela recalls one saying to another. "Let's get a group of people together."

This mystifies Mikaela. "That takes freaking *five hours* to float the river," she tells me. "And I'm like, honestly . . . Do you forget how wonderful it feels to lie in bed and not be doing something in like the two seconds of spare time you have?"

Her dedication causes some tension, even passive aggression. If you're focused at the expense of being social, and you win all the time, by huge margins, and are blatantly ambitious, you're considered, well, standoffish. And you're going to catch shade.

According to Mikaela, the form this takes in Park City is: teammates will invite her to join them for a movie or a party or whatever and then add, with the faintest whiff of sarcasm, "if that fits in your schedule." Mikaela gets it. That dynamic has dogged her since high school. The day she moved into her dorm room at Burke Mountain Academy, a boarding school in Vermont for elite skiers, her roommate, Brayton "Bug" Pech, remembers saying to her, "You seem like a really nice girl and all, but I just have to hate you when you get in the start gate." Bug, now one of Mikaela's best friends, told me about a morning when the school canceled classes because there was such amazing powder, and while Bug and all the normal (that is, truly excellent) skier-students were out on the hill, freeskiing in the magnificent blower pow, stoked out of their minds, there was Mikaela, on the training hill by herself, working on traverse drills and ankle flexion.

Bug quickly learned that the path to personal happiness around Mikaela is to give yourself a break for being mortal and stand back in awe. "You have to put her in her own category," she says. "She's an anomaly. Most people with Mikaela's talent just rely on their talent. That's why, when the competition gets really serious, they fall apart." Mikaela was different. "I knew she was going to be special, because she was going to make herself into something special."

Skiing is an incredibly complex sport. Unlike, say, swimming or gymnastics, athletes don't just have to learn to control their bodies. The terrain is always changing, the surface is always changing. "The training is very deliberate, and then when the training peaks, the skiing becomes more about feeling," says Kirk Dwyer, who was Mikaela's main coach at Burke and a major influence in her life. "You can think about it like going up a chairlift." What he means is that you're moving along, training, making progress in one mode, and then, to perform, you have to make a 180-degree switch. Mikaela arrived at Burke well suited to the process. "Her mentality is similar to virtuoso musicians like Isaac Stern, always trying to play better," Dwyer says. "She's very intrinsically motivated. She sets the bar high. She focuses."

Mikaela won the national slalom title at 16. Then she started winning in giant slalom. Now she's adding speed events, winning her first alpine combined race—one super-G run, one slalom— earlier this year. She has won events by two or three seconds, in a sport where one-tenth of that is considered a decent margin. This is eminently—and maybe even unavoidably—hateable if you're a female American alpine ski racer not named Julia Mancuso or Lindsey Vonn. Mikaela, like Vonn, has a custom training program in part because she brings money and glory to U.S. skiing and is considered the future of the sport. (None of the American men have a custom program.)

"It's hard to find someone who is really genuinely happy for you if you are having success and they're not," Mikaela says. She knows that's only human. "I just try to be as nice as possible and make fun of myself and laugh at the jokes." But the slacking off, by which Mikaela means floating the river or having a few beers and playing spoons on a Friday night—she has little patience for that. Champions put in the work. Champions prioritize the effort to get better, every day. She makes each decision in her life only after she's weighed whether or not it will help her achieve. She has a new boyfriend, a French ski racer. She's going to meet him in Paris. But she won't visit again if she can't finish her training block strong. "Don't worry about it and you'll be great, said nobody ever," she tells me just before her nap.

Mikaela has a recurring dream. She shows up at the mountain for a race, puts on her boots and helmet, then realizes her clothes are disappearing. So she takes off her boots and helmet, dresses in her thermals and speed suit, then buckles on her boots and helmet again. But by the time she's done this, her speed suit has flown off. This goes on: one piece of gear donned, another vanished. Eventually, she just starts running to the chairlift so she won't miss her start. Every step she takes, the hill gets steeper and steeper until she's falling off a cliff.

To say that Jeff and Eileen Shiffrin are dedicated and passionate skier parents does not even begin to cover it. The Shiffrins did not just click Mikaela's tiny boots into bindings at age three and

drift down the hill with her, snowplowing; they began methodi-
cally coaching her and her elder brother, Taylor. "Mom and Dad
said, 'Let's do this: ski to that tree, in this position, as fast as you
can,'" said Taylor, who just got an MBA at the University of Denver,
where he ski-raced during undergrad, and now works on the business side of tech startups. "There were actually very specific drills
about body position: head in front, knees to skis, pretend you're
holding a tray of hot chocolate and try not to spill it. Let's do it
again, and again, and again."

Eileen started training her daughter on gates when she was six.
The next year, Mikaela began racing. Soon after, she lost control
near the end of a run, spun around in a complete circle, and still
won the race by 10 or 20 seconds. A parent of another skier turned
to Eileen and said, "You've got to be kidding me."

Eileen is casual and friendly, offering me leftovers at a dining
table that has family snapshots hanging above one end and Mikaela's five huge World Cup globes lined up on a credenza nearby.
She's smart and game for anything (including studying German
and chemistry alongside Mikaela while her daughter was finishing
her high school diploma; now the two watch *Madam Secretary* and
Blue Bloods together). She's also a serious athlete. As a girl, Eileen
spent three hours a day hitting a tennis ball against a wall. When
not practicing her ground strokes, she watched as many matches
as she could to study technique. She brings her intense commitment to practice—along with a belief that if you study, you can
master anything—to all parts of her life.

For instance, when Taylor was in sixth grade, he tried out for
the soccer team but didn't make the cut. Eileen bought four soccer nets for the family basement, ordered a complete set of World
Cup soccer DVDs, and spent every evening that winter in the basement with Taylor, running him through drills. At tryouts the following fall, the coach thought Taylor played like Neymar's little
brother. "What on earth have you been doing?" he asked Eileen.

Eileen is not paid by U.S. Ski and Snowboard, but she's recognized by the organization as one of Mikaela's coaches, along
with team coaches Mike Day and Jeff Lackie. She approaches her
job with the sense of purpose and attention to detail of a forensic
scientist at a murder scene. "You have to study the sport like you
would study precalc or physics," she explains. "You have to be willing to think about it that in-depth." Eileen will, say, spend an hour

or so in the evening with Mikaela watching tapes of Marlies Schild, the 2011 slalom world champion, asking questions: Is she keeping her shoulders facing out at this point in the turn? Or is she not really facing her shoulders out but driving her outside shoulder around? How much separation does she have between her upper and lower body? How is she using her ankles and knees?

Few athletes' parents have the time, inclination, or athletic experience to do this, and that has given Mikaela "a pretty big advantage, almost an unfair advantage," Eileen admits. She insists that her parental contribution ends there, that she has not also bequeathed to her daughter a significant competitive streak.

I ask Eileen what I think is a simple question: when did Mikaela become faster than her?

"With skiing?" she says. "I don't know. Mikaela says when she was 11 or 12—which is . . . no. But I don't race against her. I never really compared or had that situation. I still ski pretty fast, faster than a lot of people are comfortable with me skiing. They are always like, 'Why aren't you wearing a helmet?' So, I'm not sure."

"But when did you cross the threshold to saying, 'My kid is a better athlete than me'?" I rephrase.

"Better skier. Well, probably when she was . . ." Her voice trails off.

To be clear, we are talking about 2017 World Cup overall champion Mikaela Shiffrin. "I don't know. I'm not really sure," Eileen says. "That's such a hard question. I never really think about it."

On the slopes, Mikaela steers her body like a Nascar driver classically trained at the Bolshoi Ballet—with such precision, grace, and control that it's hard to comprehend the power required to hold your lower body at a 30-degree angle to the ground while keeping your torso upright, all while moving down iced ruts at 80 miles per hour.

U.S. Ski Team coach Jeff Lackie says, "Mikaela separates herself from the field by using every inch of the turn to extract speed, building momentum whenever possible. You never tire of watching athletic genius."

Right now, Mikaela's focusing on turning before the gate. Pretty much nobody can turn before the gate. If you think about turning before the gate, you've missed turning before the gate and you've probably missed turning before the next gate too. The window of time and the acreage of snow in which to perform the maneuver are just too small. Mikaela recognizes this. She knows the effort to turn before the gate is basically a Zen exercise. You keep working toward it. You keep not getting it. You stay committed to the practice.

Mikaela is a really nice, smart person—I feel compelled to say that. She's thoughtful and grounded, under her beautiful skin and all that muscle, and when I tell her I want to find a way to share the normal 22-year-old side of her life, she gamely takes me through her Instagram feed. We look at a story posted by an actress from *Glee*. Another posted by a cliff-jumping champion also sponsored by Red Bull. A third from a tawny-skinned fashion blogger. "She's #tangoals," Mikaela says. "I would get skin cancer if I was that tan all the time. But still." Later we watch a video of Julia Mancuso training on a beach with her hunky husband. "This is not okay. I would love to be on the beach," Mikaela says. "If I could just dip my toes in an ocean for a second, I would be over the moon." I point out that she could fly to Maui, train on the sand, and dip her entire body in the sea. But as soon as the words are out of my mouth, I regret them. Telling Mikaela now, in the months leading up to the Olympics, that she could fly to Hawaii and train there is really not all that different than her teammates saying, *if that fits in with your schedule.* It's disrespectful—subtly so, perhaps. But still. The remark fails to honor who Mikaela is.

Mikaela is gracious and lets it slide.

Lindsey Vonn has always worked harder than anybody else on the hill. On Instagram, Mikaela finds a post of Vonn doing one of the same core exercises she did this morning—plank position, feet suspended from a rubber band, body stiff in a linear plane. Only Vonn's hands are not anchored to a box, as Mikaela's were; they're clutching rings. Mikaela laughs nervously. "Oh, that's like what I did today, only twice as hard." But she still wants to try it.

Wanting to work the hardest is not just stealth-killer goody-two-shoes behavior. Skiing fast is the result of preparation and flow. This may be the key to success in all sports, maybe all of life. To win you need to work the hardest, because knowing you've worked the hardest is what will allow you to believe in yourself and stay out of your own way in a race. This idea is the core lesson of *The Inner Game of Tennis,* published in 1974 and written by W. Timothy Gallwey, one of the most influential sports training books ever written.

"The player of the inner game comes to value the art of relaxed concentration above all other skills," Gallwey writes. "He discovers a true basis for self-confidence; and he learns that the secret to winning any game lies in not trying too hard."

Eileen loves this book. Kirk Dwyer made all the skiers he coached at Burke read it. Only if you've done enough training, only if you've tried hard beforehand, can you fully relax during a race.

The trouble, for most of us, starts with the fact that we don't always do all the work. We don't do as much as Mikaela, or Lindsey Vonn, and this is not just a technical or physical problem. It undermines our self-confidence. Mikaela makes us see our weaknesses, our lack of full commitment. We want to win, but we don't want to win at all costs. Maybe we're scared to try that hard. Maybe we don't know how. Almost none of us truly give 100 percent. We give 98 percent, or 95 percent, maybe less. Then, even though we may have dedicated our lives to a sport, even though we may be among the best in the world, we go out there and lose. Or we go out there and get hurt. "You don't want to be second-guessing yourself on the way down," Mikaela says. "And you don't want to be skiing at 110 percent." If you stretch yourself too thin, you snap. Mikaela likes to race well within her ability. "One of my theories is that if I just train more than everybody and I'm strong and I watch more video and understand the sport better, my 90 percent will be enough."

Enough so that, come February, she can fly to South Korea, fall asleep on the mountain, and win.

DAVE KINDRED

The Case for Lefty Driesell

FROM THE ATHLETIC

I'M SITTING IN Lefty Driesell's office. It's a room in his fourth-floor condo facing the Chesapeake Bay in Virginia Beach. It's also a Lefty museum filled with portraits, trophies, and memorabilia. There's a picture of Lefty's 1933 Ford convertible and one of Lefty as a high school coach in 1956. The best piece in the museum is Lefty himself.

He played for Duke when Mike Krzyzewski was four years old. He recruited against Dean Smith when Smith was a kid coach being hung in effigy. He breathed thrilling, everlasting life into dead-ass programs at Davidson College and the University of Maryland. Uniquely combative and comic, Lefty Driesell remains one of an unforgettable kind.

I met him 40 years ago at Maryland, where he once called me "that sumbitch." I had last seen him 20 years ago, when he took a job that provided him a tiny, bare, cinderblock office at Georgia State. After he retired, I lost track of him. Then, this fall, I saw a sportswriter's note arguing that Lefty should be in the Naismith Memorial Basketball Hall of Fame. I thought, *He's not in?*

So I went to Virginia Beach. Lefty's 86th birthday comes up Christmas Day. He has a hitch in his gitty-up, which happens if you're old and fall hard on the beach. The good news is he's bright-eyed, alive, laughing, and doing the Lefty thing of telling stories that wander in circles until he lands on a punch line and everybody has had a grand time.

It was a gorgeous day in November 2017 when, without warning, Lefty drops us into 1956. Suddenly, he is in full comic flight. Lefty in comic flight was, is, and forever will be priceless.

We have fallen into another century and Lefty is coaching the Newport News High School basketball team, the mighty Typhoon. It's the last seconds of a big game. A kid on the other team is crying.

"We're one point ahead," Lefty says, "and we fouled the kid and he started cryin'. They could beat us if he made the free throws, but he's cryin'."

Lefty still has that Virginia Tidewater voice, the drawl there but gone raspy. He's a big guy, 6-foot-5, once an athlete shambling along all loosey-goosey. Now he walks so tentatively that he reaches for door frames and leans on a cane. As always, his ears stand away from his bald head. The lobes quiver in tune with his oratory.

Lefty scoots to the edge of his chair. He's leaning forward, about to topple over, and he's rubbing his fists into his eyes, the way a squalling baby might. Lefty is having himself some fun.

"The kid is moanin'. 'Ah cain't shoot, Ah cain't shoot.' He gets down on the floor and he's beatin' on the floor. They want to beat us so bad. They're our big rival from the other side a town. They never beat us. Nobody ever beat us, 25-0 my first year, 57 straight for the school. He's cryin'. 'Ah cain't shoot.' Their coach comes to the official and says he's gotta substitute for the kid. 'He's too emotional, he can't shoot, he's too nervous.'"

That day, in 1956, Lefty was fresh out of Duke. He'd played some there, but no more than you'd expect from a too-small pivot man who couldn't shoot. In that picture on his office wall, Lefty looks about five days older than his Typhoons. No one could have imagined what that guy would do. He would create an era. Not many coaches create eras, and Lefty did it in a good place. He became so famous in Washington, D.C., that he stole newspaper ink and TV time from Nixon, Ford, Carter, and Reagan.

But right now we're back in Newport News, and even if Lefty, the kid coach, was wet behind the ears, he knew what he knew and he knew there was no crying in basketball.

"So the official comes to me about a sub, and I say, 'Absolutely not. You let the boy shoot. I don't care if the boy's cryin' or havin' a nervous breakdown, he's gonna shoot.'"

The kid missed the first one.

"He starts cryin' again and moanin', 'Ah cain't shoot. Ah cain't do it.'"

Lefty was again asked to allow a sub.

"And I say, 'Never.'"

Another miss. Game over.

"Ain't nobody gonna beat me," Lefty says, "with a nervous breakdown."

Charles Grice Driesell coached big-time basketball for 41 seasons. His teams won 786 NCAA Division I games. When he retired in 2003, only Bob Knight, Adolph Rupp, and Dean Smith had a bigger number. A nice number, 786, but only a number, and it doesn't begin to tell you everything Lefty did or even most of what he did. By the power of his personality, he brought in customers eager to see his freewheeling teams and be there for whatever the hell Lefty would think up next.

Maryland's campus is in College Park, a half-hour from the White House. The school's pitch to him for the basketball job included lines Lefty never forgot. It was 1969. Ted Williams managed the Washington Senators. Vince Lombardi coached the Washington Redskins.

"They told me the summers belonged to Ted Williams, the falls belonged to Vince Lombardi and the winters would be Lefty Driesell's," he said. "That sounded pretty darn good."

For $14,000, two courtesy cars (one for his wife, Joyce), a summer camp, and TV-radio pocket change, Maryland hired a man who made no small plans. Driesell intended to make Maryland "the UCLA of the East." That got people's attention, considering that the Terps had been to the NCAA tournament once in 46 years. Lefty started selling. He sold the idea of Lefty, a coach unlike any Maryland had known or would know. He sold players on a school they had never considered. He sold those players on strategies and tactics that let them be improvisational and thus unpredictable. Soon enough, it became apparent that Lefty could sell stoves at a shipwreck.

He brought in seven players who would become NBA draft picks, one of them also a Rhodes Scholar, another headed to Harvard Law School. In his third season, 1971–1972, Maryland went 27-5 and won the National Invitation Tournament when winning it meant you'd done something good. That NIT matched the 16 best teams that didn't make the 25-team NCAA field, then limited to conference champions and a handful of independents.

Once a silent cavern, Cole Field House became bedlam as Driesell upgraded his team and his stagecraft. Almost by accident, he invented Midnight Madness. He put his players through a one-mile run at 12:03 a.m. on October 15, 1971, the first legal day of NCAA practice. Two years later the event morphed into an open practice drawing thousands. Only Lefty would enter a basketball arena to the operatic thunder of *Jesus Christ Superstar.* His finest moment came on nights when Lefty sent his players out of the locker room first. Then, from the darkness of a tunnel, with the school pep band raising the roof, here came Lefty strolling in to an amped-up version of "Hail to the Chief." A January 1972 newspaper story reported the scene: "As the 14,000 madmen in the stands cheer wildly, Driesell parades solemnly to midcourt, bows his head, and raises both arms, his fingers extended in a Churchillian V-for-Victory sign."

At Davidson for 10 seasons and Maryland for 17—places where nobody had won anything—Lefty created programs that won big games at the highest levels. Twice at each school his teams reached the Elite Eight. After Maryland went 46 years with one NCAA appearance, Lefty took eight teams to the tournament. Eight times his Davidson and Maryland teams finished a season in the top 10 in the polls, three times in the top five. From 1960 to 1986, his teams won 524 games and lost 224, a .700 winning percentage.

That body of work across a quarter of a century should get a man elected to the Naismith Hall of Fame, basketball's ultimate honor.

Somehow, Lefty is not in.

We talked long and happily. We talked about a long-ago column in which I explained ACC stereotypes. Dean Smith, I wrote, was beloved in North Carolina but elsewhere considered a blackguard who would burn orphanages for the insurance money. I wrote that Lefty Driesell was a giant among the nation's statesmen, but critics along Tobacco Road believed he couldn't coach a fish to swim.

"You, you're that sumbitch who said I couldn't coach a fish to swim," he said at the time, by way of explaining he wouldn't answer my press-conference question.

Five minutes later, he stopped me in the hallway. My colleague, John Feinstein, had scolded Lefty. "Feinstein says I owe you an apology," he said. As Lefty turned to leave, he said, "Didn't read it, somebody told me. Sorry."

On this day in November, the conversation had moved so lightly that I said, "So, the Hall of Fame doesn't bother you that much?"

"Oh yeah, it bothers me," he said. "It's eatin' at me. Everybody who doesn't get into the Hall of Fame has some demon. I have a demon. It's the Len Bias situation."

Life has been good to the grandson of a German immigrant who opened a mom-and-pop jewelry store in Norfolk 134 years ago. Still married to his high school sweetheart, Lefty has four children and 11 grandchildren, four of them basketball coaches. The Lefty museum has Hall of Fame plaques (15 of them) and Coach of the Year plaques (from each of the four D-I conferences he worked in). There's a file drawer to the left of his chair.

From that drawer he took a folder stuffed with photocopies of dozens of newspaper stories.

"Every one of these stories," he said, handing me the folder, "says it's because of Len Bias."

Actually, the stories don't say that. They suggest it. They guess it because they can think of no other reason.

In those newspaper stories, I noticed one coach on Lefty's side. So I called Mike Krzyzewski and left a number.

Put aside Lefty the salesman and showman. Forget the sport coats of many colors, the foot-stompin' outrage at courtside, the syntactically challenged press conferences. Forget how he picked fights with the biggest names: "Dean Smith's the only coach in history to win more than 800 games and be the underdog in every one of them." Cast it all out of mind, for the important takeaway from those 27 seasons at Davidson and Maryland is that Lefty was a master coach.

The sportswriter Mark Whicker was an astute chronicler of ACC basketball through the 1970s and '80s. "A couple times you could flip a coin as to who was better," he said, "the national champion or Maryland."

With a break here and there, Whicker suggested, Lefty could have won two or three NCAA championships. When I passed along Whicker's line, Lefty did what Lefty does. He began a story, this one about Moses Malone.

"With Moses," he said, "we mighta won four or five."

Malone is a name from the 1970s. He was a great player, a three-time NBA MVP. He loved Lefty. His mother loved Lefty. In 1974 he agreed, mostly to make Lefty happy, to accept a scholarship offer from Maryland. But even as a child Moses had chosen a different path. Lefty had seen what Moses wrote in his Bible. He wanted to be "the first high school player to go pro." So he jumped past Lefty to the pros. Lefty loved Moses even after losing him.

I listened to more Lefty on Moses.

"Pritchett wanted to sleep in the car, at the curb, outside Moses's house," he said.

Dave Pritchett was a basketball zealot, an assistant coach maniacal in his devotion to the game and obsessive in recruiting players. He was called Pit Stop. He earned the nickname with audacious rental-car behavior. Forever speeding toward the next prospect, his habit was to skid his rental to a stop on a sidewalk outside an airport and sprint to a plane. He told me his personal best was seven rental cars in one day.

Of course Pritchett would want to sleep outside Moses's house. It was his job to find players who would make Maryland the UCLA of the East. The zealotry was fired by one unwavering belief. "You can find a wife on any street corner in America," he said, "but it's rare to find a 6-foot-10 man who can play."

Malone was such a rarity. Pritchett had seen him embarrass an NBA star at a summer camp. Everyone wanted Moses, but not everyone was infected with an obsessive recruiter's paranoia.

"We were supposed to be there at 7 a.m., and Pritchett was sure somebody was gonna sneak in ahead of us," Driesell said. "I said no, we're sleeping in a bed."

They arrived at the Malone house at 6:30 a.m. to the sight of VCU coach Chuck Noe walking in the front door.

"I told you," Pritchett said. "I *told* you."

"We'll be okay," Lefty said.

The coach had made friends with Mary Malone. "She was sweet, she was smart, and she liked me," he said. Mary had promised Lefty that if her son played college ball, it would be with Maryland.

Noe came out of the house, defeated.

Lefty and Pit Stop hustled in, smiling.

Lefty remembered the place as a rowhouse "in a terrible neighborhood," one room down, one up. Mary Malone worked for $25 a week as an orderly at a retirement home. "Moses never had a father around," Lefty said. "Mary told me once, 'You know who called me last night? Moses's father! I slammed down the phone so hard I might've broken it.'"

At 7:15 a.m., the coaches went upstairs. Moses was asleep, his bed against a wall with a basketball-size hole to the outside.

"He signed for us that morning," Lefty said, and in the Lefty museum hangs a framed copy of the scholarship offer signed by Moses Eugene Malone on June 20, 1974.

By then, Lefty already had seen what Malone had written in his Bible. It was no surprise, then, that on the first day of classes at Maryland that fall, Malone signed with the Utah Stars of the new American Basketball Association. Nevertheless, the coach and the prospect stayed in touch. Lefty even included Malone on his media guide's page touting "Maryland Players in the Pros." In retirement from the NBA, Malone came to Norfolk for charity golf tournaments and renewed his friendship with Driesell. Then, in September 2015, Malone died in his sleep of heart disease. He was 60 years old.

Malone's family asked Lefty to speak at a memorial in Moses's hometown of Petersburg, Virginia. The old coach doesn't remember what he said that day, "just what a great person he was."

Lefty's stories come with backstories, and the backstories come with digressions and detours, all delightful and some with the added virtue that parts of them may be true. Take a deep breath, there's a long sentence coming. It's a summary of a Lefty tale two days in the telling:

> Lefty was an eight-year-old barefoot waterboy for the high school football team who grew up to be the school's basketball star and might have signed with the University of Tennessee instead of Duke except he couldn't be married at Tennessee and he wanted to marry his high school sweetheart, Joyce Gunter, a cheerleader who liked both him and his 1933 Ford convertible that once was owned by John D. Rockefeller, who gave it to Lefty's uncle, John D's neurosurgeon, who sold it for $300 to Lefty's half-brother, who sold it to Lefty for $900, and Lefty souped it up with a 1950 Ford engine and dressed it up with whitewall tires. It had a rumble seat.

I'll wait while you read that again.
Ready?

Okay, let's go back to John D. Rockefeller's snazzy convertible.

"The '33 Ford," Lefty said, "is the only reason Joyce dated me."

Joyce Driesell has heard this stuff before.

"That car had nothing to do with it," she said. "On our second date, I knew that was the man I would marry. He was just a nice guy."

By the door to his office, Lefty put an arm around his bride.

"They call me a good recruiter," he said. "Best recruiting job I ever did, signing up Joyce."

They went to a justice of the peace on December 14, 1951.

"Lefty kept trying to kiss me before we even got to the *I do* part," Joyce said. "At the end, Lefty asked how much he owed. The justice said, 'Whatever you think it's worth.'"

Here, Joyce laughed.

"So Lefty gave him $2."

I had gone to Virginia Beach to talk with Lefty about basketball. We wound up talking about other important things—such as his marriage to Joyce in its 66th year—and about how a Southerner, born and raised in coastal Virginia, was so good at recruiting athletes that most Southern coaches wouldn't, or couldn't, recruit people like Moses Malone.

The answer begins with a backstory about trolley cars in Norfolk.

Lefty was 12 when he first took a trolley across town. He saw black people, mostly women on their way to work, at the back of the car. He saw no reason for that when there were empty seats up front. Nor did he understand why a black woman had to give up her seat if a white man wanted it. Lefty didn't need fancy sociological, civil-rights-activist language to express the truth.

"Making her get up," he said, "was stupid."

So young Lefty would sit in the back of the trolley. When an African American woman got on, he gave her his seat.

It bothered him in those days to call people black. Negro sounded strange too. Years later, John Lucas Sr., the father of one of Lefty's best players, John Jr., gave the coach a way to talk about race. "John Sr. said, 'We're just more sun-burned,'" Lefty recalled. From that point, he never coached an African American or a black. "But I had a lot of sun-burned players."

In 1965, long before he walked into the Malones' house, Lefty wanted a sun-burned player named Charlie Scott. A 6-foot-5 guard who could do anything any guard ever did, Scott would be a two-time All-America. He would be a pro basketball star for a decade.

I count Scott as one of Lefty's players because he counts himself as one of Lefty's players despite never playing for Lefty.

"Lefty's vivacious and infectious," Scott said. "If you don't like Lefty, there's something wrong with you. He was my friend from the start. Lefty believed in me when nobody else did. Lefty's still my coach. Lefty and Coach Smith."

Coach Smith was Dean Smith, the North Carolina coach, elected to the Naismith Hall of Fame in 1983. Some people think of Smith as a civil rights advocate who integrated the ACC by bringing Scott to Carolina in 1966. Some people forget that Scott was the ACC's fourth black player, arriving after Billy Jones and Julius Johnson at Maryland and Claudius Claiborne at Duke.

People also forget, or never knew, that Lefty had Charlie Scott before Dean had him. "There'd be no Charlie Scott," Scott told me, "if there'd been no Lefty Driesell."

Lefty said, "Dean didn't even know who Charlie Scott was until I got him."

Lefty was coaching at Davidson College, a small, private liberal arts school a couple of hours southwest of Chapel Hill. He had moved directly from Newport News High to the Division I job in 1960. He quickly turned Davidson into one of the nation's best programs. Lefty said he had a $500 recruiting budget. He said he spent the occasional night sleeping in the school station wagon with a pistol under his head.

By the spring of 1965, Lefty's Davidson teams had won 67 of their last 80 games, and the Wildcats were No. 6 in the final AP poll. Then he went after Scott, a New York City kid living in Laurinburg, North Carolina, 120 miles southeast of the Davidson campus.

"Lefty told me I could choose the other four players I wanted to come to Davidson with me," Scott said.

Scott and his high school coach, an African American named Frank McDuffie, liked everything about Davidson. And then they met Lefty at a restaurant.

"Lefty was eating black-eyed peas and rice." Scott said. The coach asked the player and the coach to sit down and order. "After a while," Scott said, "the owner of the restaurant came to our table and said, 'My wife and I don't serve (n-word, plural) on this side of the restaurant.' It didn't bother me as much as it did Coach McDuffie."

Not much later, on a recruiting visit to Chapel Hill, Scott was treated to a fancy dinner (without insult), given concert tickets (The Temptations, Smokey Robinson), and shown around campus (by VIPs).

Today, a half-century later, Scott's decision would seem clear-cut. Not so much in 1966. Davidson and Lefty had become something big, while Carolina with Dean was an ACC also-ran. (This wasn't long after Smith, replacing the legendary Frank McGuire, had been hung in effigy in Chapel Hill.) Lefty's last two teams had gone 45-9, Dean's 31-20.

But McDuffie lobbied for North Carolina. In the end, Scott said, "I decided the importance of being the first black athlete at the University of North Carolina was greater than the significance of being the first black at Davidson."

Lefty's summary: "Dean stole him from me."

Bad enough for Lefty, it got worse. Scott led North Carolina to NCAA East Regional final victories over Davidson in 1968 (with 18 points) and 1969 (with 32, the last two points a dagger from 30 feet at the buzzer to make it 87–85).

Twice, then, Scott took Smith to the Final Four at Lefty's expense. Twice he denied Lefty Driesell a distinction that would elude him the rest of his career.

Scott is 68. He says he owes Driesell so much that he will do whatever he can to get the coach into the Naismith.

"He deserves to be there," Scott said. "I played for Hall of Fame coaches. I played for Coach Smith, Hank Iba, John McClendon, Ray Meyer, Larry Brown, Red Auerbach. Lefty belongs with them."

I was listening to a story when Krzyzewski called.

"Hi, Mike," I said. "So tell me about Lefty."

Driesell sat still, listening.

"I love Lefty," Krzyzewski said.

He waited a beat. "I *love* Lefty."

And: "Look what he's done for basketball. Besides the number of wins, which are astronomical, his personality brought people into the college game."

And: "The year he lost to North Carolina State and only the

winner could go to the NCAA—that was one of the epic games ever."

In January 1974, North Carolina State was ranked No. 1, Maryland No. 4. Each team used seven players, and eight of the 14 would be NBA draft picks. State's stars were David Thompson and Tom Burleson; Maryland's were Len Elmore, John Lucas, and Tom McMillen. The game is a landmark in ACC history for its breathtaking pace of high-quality play and its effect on college basketball. A year later, a conference could send two teams to the NCAA tournament; two years later, there was no limit.

"Lefty's team that year," Krzyzewski said, "was probably as good as 20 national champions."

After North Carolina State won 103–100 in overtime, Driesell made his way onto the winners' team bus to congratulate them. A week later, Maryland's proud, dejected players turned down an invitation to the NIT that they'd won two years earlier. North Carolina State went on to win the national championship.

I asked Krzyzewski about the theory that Bias's 1986 death is a reason why Lefty is not in the Hall.

"If that had not happened, or if it happened and Lefty was not made a scapegoat . . ."

Hold that thought. Scapegoat.

". . . and if he was around for the 20 years after that, imagine what he could have done at Maryland. Imagine the total number of wins. Imagine what could have happened for him and Maryland. What *should* have happened."

Krzyzewski's take: "For everything he did in college basketball, Lefty is definitely worthy of being in the Naismith Hall of Fame."

Driesell has made it to the final round of Naismith voting four times, most recently in 2016. As to why he has fallen short, or by how many votes he has missed, we are left to guess.

The Naismith process is secretive. Nominations go to screening committees that recommend names to an Honors Committee of 24, with 18 votes necessary for election. The electors are not named publicly; the idea is to prevent lobbying, but the effect is to sow suspicions of political machinations by people who cannot be held accountable.

Most guesses come down to two things. First, Lefty never made the Final Four. Second, he is stained by the fallout following Bias's cocaine-intoxication death, 48 hours after he was selected by the Boston Celtics with the second pick in the '86 NBA draft.

The first guess is simple fact. That argument is lame. Of the 63 NCAA Division I men's coaches in the Hall, 23 never got to the Final Four.

The second guess is simply unfair. Driesell was Bias's coach, not his 365/24/7 guardian.

A grand jury investigation into the Bias tragedy revealed campus-wide drug use virtually uncontrolled by school authorities. When the investigation moved into the basketball program, some of Driesell's players were shown to be players first and students only when they felt like it. (As if all other athletes at all other institutions were models of academic perseverance.)

In the fall of 1985, Maryland had so admired Lefty's long record of success and promise of more to come that it rewarded him with a 10-year contract. Then Bias died. The school chancellor, John Slaughter, kept his job despite the grand jury's scathing report detailing the university's failures. Meanwhile, the chancellor moved on Driesell. Rather than try to fire a coach to whom he had just given a new contract, Slaughter reassigned Driesell to athletic department duties. Lefty said he was paid in full for 10 years, even after he left College Park in 1988 to coach at James Madison University.

Bottom line: To blame Lefty for his players' brain-fades makes no more sense than giving him credit for developing two Rhodes Scholars at Davidson and Maryland. The job of a big-time basketball coach is to win games. Otherwise, in its infinite complexity, the world spins beyond his reach.

One of Maryland's most distinguished alums, a man who played for Driesell's best teams, stands up for his coach. Tom McMillen was an All-America in the early 1970s who became a Rhodes Scholar, played 11 years in the NBA, was elected four times to the U.S. Congress, and served from 2007 to 2015 as a regent of the university.

"If they were looking for an excuse to remove Lefty," McMillen said, "that was the Len Bias situation. I think it's specious."

McMillen means, to borrow an idea we heard from Krzyzewski, that Driesell was made a scapegoat for the mistakes of others.

Some famous coaches—John Wooden, Dean Smith, Bob Knight, Adolph Rupp—are in the Hall despite good reasons to raise an eyebrow. Wooden forever ignored a sugar-daddy booster buying recruits. Bogus classes helped North Carolina players stay eligible in Smith's time. Knight was fired for belligerent boorishness. Rupp's teams had two All-Americas taking gamblers' money to fix games.

And how about today's coaching stars? John Calipari is in after leaving two programs on NCAA probation. As with Smith, some of Roy Williams's North Carolina players didn't go to class because the class didn't exist. Once upon a simpler time, it was the NCAA sniffing around Rick Pitino; now, it's the FBI.

"There was never innuendo about Lefty doing anything wrong," McMillen said.

Beyond those two guesses—missing the Final Four, the Bias fallout—there is a more complicated, nuanced explanation for Lefty's failure to be elected. A perfect storm of forces has worked against him.

The Naismith has financial difficulties. To increase attendance at its site in Springfield, Massachusetts, it has leaned toward electing a diverse class of coaches—high school, women, NBA, international—along with active college coaches familiar to today's television audiences.

One former Honors Committee member told me, "I've never heard anyone say the Bias death had anything to do with Lefty. He has fallen through the cracks, like a lot of older coaches."

The Naismith is now debating whether a coach should be retired three years before becoming eligible for consideration. Nine still-active coaches have been elected since 2000.

"A rule like that would thin out the nominees," the former elector said, "and that would help Lefty."

Joyce Driesell had prepared an elegant breakfast. We sat in a small kitchen nook with a long, broad view of Chesapeake Bay. A stiff wind shoved whitecaps toward the beach. We had scrambled eggs, bacon, toast, jam, coffee. The silverware was shining, napkins folded perfectly, everything beautiful.

Big binoculars sat on a windowsill.

"We see everything out there," Lefty said. Norfolk is home to a major U.S. Navy base. "Battleships, aircraft carriers, cruise ships."

"Lefty uses the binoculars to watch girls in bikinis," his bride said.

They have come a distance, Lefty and Joyce. Married as teenagers, they were "broke but didn't know it," to quote her. Together they figured out life. They moved from Durham and set out on a coaching journey that began in Norfolk and took them from Newport News to Davidson to Maryland to James Madison to Georgia State. Lefty won more than 100 games at all four of the D-I schools, and he's still the only coach who has done that. Lefty brought home the money; Joyce raised the couple's four children.

We finished breakfast. Lefty looked across the table. "You're so pretty," he told Joyce.

She turned to me. "He's always saying that."

"I'm always right," he said.

Lefty called me the other day. He said the Naismith thing still bothers him.

"But y'know," he said, "I woke up Thanksgiving morning and I told Joyce, 'If I die tomorrow, I've had a wonderful life.' I've got a beautiful wife, and we've had a bunch of kids and a bunch of grandkids. I loved coaching, and I won a lot of games and I was pretty good at it. I'm thankful for everything."

I'm thinking the Naismith needs Lefty more than Lefty needs the Naismith, and I'm also thinking the old coach needs to find that justice of the peace and add a few bucks to the $2 he paid 66 years ago.

Contributors' Notes

LARS ANDERSON is the *New York Times* best-selling author of nine books, including, most recently, *The Truth About Aaron*. He is currently a contributing writer at *The Athletic*, after three years as a senior writer at *Bleacher Report* and 20 years at *Sports Illustrated*. A native of Lincoln, Nebraska, Anderson lives outside Birmingham, Alabama, where he has served as an instructor of journalism at the University of Alabama, with his wife and their three children.

KENT BABB is a sports features writer for the *Washington Post*, where he frequently writes about the intersection of sports and cultural, societal, and political issues. *Not a Game*, his 2015 biography of Basketball Hall of Fame member Allen Iverson, was a finalist for the PEN/ESPN Award for Literary Sports Writing, and his work was previously included in the 2013 edition of *The Best American Sports Writing*. A proud graduate of the University of South Carolina, Babb lives in northern Virginia with his wife and daughter.

CHRIS BALLARD is a senior writer for *Sports Illustrated* and the author of four books. He lives in the San Francisco Bay Area and is a lecturer at the UC Berkeley Graduate School of Journalism. "'You Can't Give In': Monty Williams on Life After Tragedy" is his sixth story to be included in *The Best American Sports Writing*.

JANE BERNSTEIN is the author of five books, including the memoirs *Bereft: A Sister's Story* and *Rachel in the World*. Her essays have been published in the *New York Times Magazine, Broadly,* and *Creative Nonfiction*. She lives in Pittsburgh, Pennsylvania, where she teaches at Carnegie Mellon University.

SAM BORDEN is a global sports contributor for ESPN. A graduate of Emory University, Borden began his career with the *New York Daily News* and later worked at the *Florida Times-Union,* the *Journal News,* and the *New York Times.*

JOHN BRANCH has been a sports reporter for the *New York Times* since 2005. In 2013, he was awarded the Pulitzer Prize in feature writing for his tale of a deadly avalanche, "Snow Fall," and was a finalist the previous year for his story about the late NHL enforcer Derek Boogaard, who died of a painkiller overdose and was found to have CTE, the degenerative brain disease. He is the author of two books, including 2018's *The Last Cowboys,* about a family of saddle-bronc rodeo champions. He lives near San Francisco.

TIM BROWN has covered baseball for more than 25 years, the past 10 for *Yahoo Sports.* He has coauthored two *New York Times* best-sellers — *The Phenomenon,* with Rick Ankiel, and *Imperfect,* with Jim Abbott. In 2016, he was awarded first place in beat writing by the Associated Press Sports Editors.

HOWARD BRYANT is the author of eight books, including *The Heritage: Black Athletes, a Divided America, and the Politics of Patriotism* and *The Last Hero: A Life of Henry Aaron.* He is a senior writer for ESPN.com and *ESPN: The Magazine* and has served as the sports correspondent for NPR's *Weekend Edition Saturday* since 2006. He was guest editor of *The Best American Sports Writing 2017* and also appeared in the 2011 edition. He has been a finalist for the National Magazine Award for commentary in 2016 and 2018 and earned the 2016 Salute to Excellence Award from the National Association of Black Journalists.

REID FORGRAVE'S journalism career has led him from home and garden writer to national sportswriter, reporting on everything from presidential politics to a former NBA prospect in jail for attempted murder. He currently writes for CBSSports.com and freelances for publications such as *GQ,* the *New York Times Magazine,* and *Mother Jones.* He previously wrote for FOXSports.com, the *Des Moines Register,* the *Cincinnati Enquirer,* and the *Arkansas Democrat-Gazette.* He lives in Minneapolis with his wife and their two sons.

STEVE FRIEDMAN is the author of four books, the coauthor of two, and a two-time National Magazine Award finalist for feature writing. He grew up in St. Louis, graduated from Stanford University, and lives in New York City. This is his 10th appearance in *The Best American Sports Writing.*

LEE JENKINS left the *New York Times* and joined *Sports Illustrated* and SI.com as a senior writer in September 2007. He had previously worked at the *Orange County Register* and the *Colorado Springs Gazette.* A San Diego native, Jenkins graduated in 1999 from Vanderbilt University, which he attended on the Grantland Rice–Fred Russell Thoroughbred Racing Association Sportswriting Scholarship.

SALLY JENKINS is a columnist for the *Washington Post* and the author of twelve books, four of which have been *New York Times* best-sellers. The most recent is *Sum It Up,* written with legendary basketball coach Pat Summitt. She is also the author of *The Real All Americans,* a historical account of how the Carlisle Indian School took on the Ivy League powers in college football at the turn of the century and won. Her work has been featured in *Smithsonian, GQ,* and *Sports Illustrated.* A native of Texas, she graduated from Stanford and lives in Sag Harbor, New York.

CHANTEL JENNINGS is a national college football writer for *The Athletic.* She previously worked for ESPN.com after graduating from the University of Michigan in 2011.

TOM JUNOD has twice been awarded the National Magazine Award and has been a finalist a total of ten times. Before joining ESPN as a senior writer, he wrote for *Atlanta, Life, Sports Illustrated, GQ,* and *Esquire,* where he spent eleven years as writer at large.

DAVE KINDRED is the 2018 winner of the PEN America / ESPN Lifetime Achievement Award for Literary Sports Writing. He lives in Carlock, Illinois.

MICHAEL LANANNA is a national writer for *Baseball America* who specializes in features and long-form pieces. He has covered sports at every level, including a season reporting on the Los Angeles Dodgers for MLB.com and coverage of Atlantic Coast Conference basketball, football, and baseball. He is a graduate of the University of North Carolina's School of Media and Journalism and resides in Durham, North Carolina.

JIM OWCZARSKI is a staff writer at the *Cincinnati Enquirer,* covering the Cincinnati Bengals. A graduate of North Central College with degrees in journalism and sociology, he is from Tinley Park, Illinois, and calls Milwaukee and Cincinnati home with his wife, Michelle Rutkowski.

DAVID ROTH is a cofounder of *The Classical* and an editor at *Deadspin.* He is from New Jersey and lives in New York.

STEVE RUSHIN of *Sports Illustrated* is the author of *The Caddie Was a Reindeer, Pint Man, Road Swing,* and *The Baseball Grenade.* His work has been anthologized in *The Best American Sports Writing, The Best American Travel Writing,* and *The Best American Magazine Writing* collections, and he has contributed to *Time* magazine and the *New York Times.* He and his wife, Rebecca Lobo, have four children and live in Connecticut.

MIKE SIELSKI has been a sports columnist for the *Philadelphia Inquirer,* the *Philadelphia Daily News,* and Philly.com since 2013. The author of two books, he previously spent three years as a reporter with the *Wall Street*

Journal, and in 2015 the Associated Press Sports Editors voted him the top sports columnist in the country. He lives in Bucks County, Pennsylvania, with his wife and two sons. This is his second appearance in *The Best American Sports Writing.*

BRYAN SMITH is the senior writer at *Chicago* magazine and also a contributing editor for *Men's Health.* The recipient of many writing honors, he has twice been named Writer of the Year by the City and Regional Magazine Association, an award for which he has been a finalist six times. His work has previously appeared in *The Best American Sports Writing* and *The Best American Newspaper Writing.*

TIM STRUBY is a longtime writer whose work has appeared in *ESPN: The Magazine, Victory Journal, Playboy,* and *The New Yorker.* He lives in New York City.

WRIGHT THOMPSON is a senior writer for *ESPN: The Magazine.*

TYLER TYNES is a staff writer for *SB Nation,* based in Washington, D.C. Previously, he worked for *Huffington Post, The Press of Atlantic City,* and the *Philadelphia Daily News.*

ELIZABETH WEIL is a contributing writer to the *New York Times Magazine* and *Outside,* as well as coauthor of *The Girl Who Smiled Beads: A Story of War and What Comes After.* She lives in San Francisco with her husband and their two daughters.

Notable Sports Writing of 2017

SELECTED BY GLENN STOUT

THE BEST AMERICAN SERIES®

FIRST, BEST, AND BEST-SELLING

The Best American Comics

The Best American Essays

The Best American Food Writing

The Best American Mystery Stories

The Best American Nonrequired Reading

The Best American Science and Nature Writing

The Best American Science Fiction and Fantasy

The Best American Short Stories

The Best American Sports Writing

The Best American Travel Writing

Available in print and e-book wherever books are sold.

hmhco.com/bestamerican